Philosophical Arguments

Philosophical Arguments

CHARLES TAYLOR

HARVARD UNIVERSITY PRESS
Cambridge, Massachusetts
London, England

First Harvard University Press paperback edition, 1997

LIBRARY OF CONGRESS CATALOGING-IN-PUBLICATION DATA

Taylor, Charles, 1931–
Philosophical arguments / Charles Taylor.
p. cm.
Includes bibliographical references (p.   ) and index.
ISBN 0-674-66476-0 (cloth)
ISBN 0-674-66477-9 (pbk.)
1. Philosophy, Canadian—20th century.   2. Philosophical
anthropology.   3. Language and languages—Philosophy.   4. Philosophy
and social sciences.   I. Title.
B995.T3P47 1995   94-36548
191—dc20   CIP

Contents

Preface

This collection of essays may appear rather disparate. In some ways it is, since the principle of selection was partly temporal: most of what appears here was written in the last ten years. But there are nevertheless some basic themes that recur—not surprisingly, because they raise issues that go on worrying me, where I never feel I have said, fully and satisfactorily, what I want to say.

These themes have been bothering me for decades, but some appeared earlier then others in my published writing. The oldest theme in this sense is the one I deal with head on in the very first essay, "Overcoming Epistemology." I say "head on" because I attempt a direct attack on the Hydra whose serpentine heads wreak havoc throughout the intellectual culture of modernity—in science, in criticism, in ethics, in political thinking, almost anywhere you look.

I call the Hydra "epistemology," which sounds rather unfair, because that's the name of a problem area, and what I have in my sights must be something in the nature of a doctrine. But the name is deserved, in the sense that the philosophical assumptions it designates give epistemology pride of place. These are the assumptions Descartes gave articulation to; central is the view that we can somehow come to grips with the problem of knowledge, and then later proceed to determine what we can legitimately say about other things: about God, or the world, or human life. From Descartes's standpoint, this seems not only a *possible* way to proceed, but the only *defensible* way. Because, after all, whatever we say about God or the world represents a knowledge claim. So first we ought to be clear about the nature of knowledge, and about what it is to make a defensible claim. To deny this would be irresponsible.

I believe this to be a terrible and fateful illusion. It assumes wrongly that we can get to the bottom of what knowledge is, without drawing on our never-fully-articulable understanding of human life and experience. There is a temptation here to a kind of self-possessing clarity, to which our modern culture has been almost endlessly susceptible. So much so that most of the enemies of Descartes, who think they are overcoming his standpoint, are still giving primacy of place to epistemology. Their *doctrine* about knowledge is different, even radically critical of Descartes, but they are still practicing the structural idealism of the epistemological age, defining their ontology, their view of what is, on the basis of a prior doctrine of what we can know. Figures as different, and as mutually hostile, as Quine and Derrida continue to function in this post-Cartesian universe, which in my view is a kind of "upside-down world," to borrow Hegel's famous expression.

If I am right about this, then loud denunciations of Descartes are not of themselves a sign of a writer's having escaped Descartes's baleful influence. Contemporary doctrines, sometimes called "postmodern," are a good example of this. I mentioned Derrida above. In his view the fundamental error, in which Descartes participates, is even more deeply rooted. It is the whole western metaphysical tradition which accords illusory privilege to "Presence," to a kind of unmediated epistemic contract with reality. Derrida's response to this is a high-level, abstract, a priori argument to the impossibility of Presence, so defined; on which he then draws to make all sorts of affirmations about thought, language, history, power relations, ethics, politics, and so on. But this is only to repeat the epistemological démarche in the negative mode.

There is a challenge that this kind of philosophical argument has yet to meet. Can you establish the possibility or impossibility of Presence? Can you even satisfy yourself that it's a useful term, without a more careful examination of how we actually think, judge, or feel? I believe that epistemological thinking is unable to meet this test.

This raises a number of questions about the nature and scope of a priori argument, and in particular about what have been called since Kant "transcendental arguments." This is an issue I tackle in the second chapter. I give an account of transcendental arguments which tries to do justice both to their compelling nature and to their revisability. In virtue of the latter, they are not really a priori in the full Leibniz-Kant sense. But, then, no interesting philosophical argument is. The belief that this could be so was another product of the epistemological illusion.

Various other papers in the volume follow out of ramifications of this debate with epistemology, such as Chapters 4, 6, 8, and 9. But here we come to the point of overlap with a second theme that has concerned me over the years: the nature of language.

There has always been a tendency, at least in the western tradition, to define human beings as language animals. That, in any case, can be a permissible translation of Aristotle's expression in *Ethics* 1.7, *zoion ekhon logon,* which was usually rendered "rational animal." But since the Renaissance, the understanding of human beings through the crucial trait of language has taken on a new meaning—in fact, two new meanings, in two stages. There is the seventeenth-century preoccupation, visible in Locke, with language as the prime instrument for the construction of our picture of the world, the concern with its proper use and, very anxiously, with its potential abuse. Then there is the expressivist understanding of language and art in the Romantic period, which sharply criticizes the Lockean view and proposes a quite different notion of creativity. Herder is in some ways the key figure in this.

It is not hard to see how someone obsessed with the epistemological issue would become concerned with this one too. They are closely interwoven. The place of language for Hobbes, Locke, and Condillac was circumscribed by their theory of knowledge. Language was the crucial instrument of knowledge. And it is just this instrumentality of language which the Romantic generation criticized. The proponents and developers of the Romantic theory have been among the most passionate critics of the epistemological tradition, from Hamann's review of Kant's *Critique of Pure Reason* to the writings in our century of Heidegger, of the later Wittgenstein, and of certain postmodernists.

This is, indeed, one of the ways in which the epistemological issue colors and shapes our philosophical anthropology: perhaps the most fateful of all, considering the importance of language for a definition of what human beings are. The language debate itself reverberates through a number of hotly debated questions in aesthetics, poetics, literary criticism, philosophy, human sciences.

The debate itself has become more than two-sided. It is crucial to the Romantic theory that it stresses the constitutive nature of language. This is not seen primarily as an instrument whereby we order the things in our world, but as what allows us to have the world that we have. Language makes possible the disclosure of the human world. There is a combination here of creation and discovery, which is not easy to define. Quite naturally, descendants of the Hamann-Herder revolution have differed on this definition, and in particular on how to relate the element of creation to that of discovery. Some have come close to giving exclusive stress on the first. The human world becomes something constructed, something we have made and can remake at will. Others (such as the later Heidegger) have protested against this "subjectivism." Those who remain within the Lockean perspective, even as renewed and transformed by Frege, find these intramural debates incomprehensible and perplexing.

I am interested in both debates, both that which opposes the two main traditions and that which is taking place within the second. I am very much a proponent of the "Romantic" view. I try to state something of what I think is at stake here in Chapter 5. But the main language debate between the two traditions also echoes through Chapters 6, 7, and 9. On the intramural debate there is not much in this collection; it is evoked in Chapter 6 but not extensively explored anywhere. This is something I am now working on.

My third main theme is explored in the last four chapters. It can perhaps be summed up as an attempt to define the political culture of modernity. The intuition behind this is that modern society is different from those of preceding ages not just in the novel institutions and practices of representative democracy, the market economy, institutionalized scientific discovery, and steady technological advance; it is different not just in moral and political principles, in authenticity, rights, democratic legitimacy, equality, nondiscrimination. The notion is that alongside these changes, connected with them and in a relationship of mutual support, is a set of changes in the way we have come to *imagine* society. That is, the repertory of means available to understand how we relate to others in society has altered in a fundamental way. We see ourselves as linked, for instance, in an "economy," global or national, which is at least notionally distinct from the ties that bind us into nation-states. We see ourselves participating in public spheres, exchanging and (sometimes) reaching consensus with people we have never met and will most likely never meet. We think there is something called "society" distinct from and sometimes in opposition to the state. And we have this peculiar modern understanding of the state, which we tend falsely to attribute to our ancestors and to other civilizations. But the most powerful mode of solidarity that people in our age have felt is independent of the state; it is that of the "nation," an imagined community which is peculiarly modern.

How to understand these new forms? What, if anything, links them together? What had to change in our culture, in our understanding of society, time, religion, or the cosmos, to make them possible? These are the questions I am trying to answer, and have explored in a fragmentary and rudimentary way in the last chapters. I am partly drawn to this by the desire, widely shared, to understand just what makes up this new age we are living in. So these explorations of our public culture are like additional chapters to my *Sources of the Self*. But these questions press themselves in on us for another reason: it is impossible to deal sensibly with the issues of contemporary politics without some understanding of the modern forms.

Recently the press and the public in the North Atlantic world have turned their attention again to nationalism—as though some ugly ghost of the past, thought to be long laid to rest, had reemerged from its grave. The events that triggered this change of focus are obvious and distressing enough. But what is also evident was the confusion and lack of understanding of what nationalism is, of its various forms and what drives them. What you think of this makes a big difference for the policies you are tempted to adopt. Of course living where I do, in Montreal, I haven't been allowed to forget that nationalism exists. But this has advantages when you come to think about it. And thinking about it brings you to the whole range of issues I gather under the name of the political culture of modernity. Some of the same issues are relevant to the politics of multiculturalism, which I discuss in Chapter 12.

There is still another reason. Like most people today, I am struggling to find a language to understand and mediate cultural difference. The theoretical problems and puzzlements in this domain turn out to be of more and more urgent practical importance. But here's where our view of modernity can lead us astray. According to a widespread understanding, modernization is transforming "traditional" cultures, making societies everywhere more alike. This is the understanding behind such fashionable notions as "the end of history."

Now on a superficial level this may seem right: societies are converging on such structural features as the bureaucratic state and the market economy, for instance. On a deeper level, however, it's dead wrong. Traditional cultures are being transformed, but it doesn't follow that they will converge. No society can develop a modern state and a market economy without some important change. And what comes out depends partly on what went into the change. From this point of view, we should speak instead of "alternative modernities," different ways of living the political and economic structures that the contemporary age makes mandatory. How these are worked out in India will not be the same as in Japan, which is in turn different from the North Atlantic region—which in its turn again has much inner diversity.

An important factor in the modern world is cultural borrowing. Although this has always been a feature of human life, today its rate and scale are unprecedented. Still it doesn't follow that what is borrowed will be a carbon copy of the original. In most cases it plainly is not.

This means that finding a language for cultural diversity is partly finding a language for alternative modernities; or finding a way of understanding modernity which makes room for these alternatives. It is to this end that I find the study of the political culture of (what I must now call western) modernity indispensable. And in general, one might say, the finer-grained the understanding of our own path to modernity in the West, the better equipped we become to understand the differences with other cultures.

We find a link here with the other two main themes of this book. The instrumental theory of language made different languages look relatively easy to translate between. It was the Romantic theory which brought out the deep-lying differences. And behind this homogenizing effect of Lockean language theory is the culturally unindexed Cartesian theory of knowledge. The converging view of modernity draws on some of the same philosophical sources to present a picture of cultural difference as not all that intractable, and narrowing in any case with the march of time. I have been drawing on the rival tradition to present my somewhat different picture, which emerges in Chapter 8 and in the last three chapters.

I have been greatly helped in writing these chapters by discussions at and under the aegis of the Center for Transcultural Studies in Chicago, which has provided a kind of interdisciplinary exchange that I among others have found extremely fruitful. These essays are a kind of interim progress report on a continuing study of modernity, its interchanges and differences. But then an analogous point could be made about the tentative nature of each chapter in this volume. They are all on themes I have not yet managed to capture in full.

Philosophical Arguments

— 1 —

Overcoming Epistemology

Epistemology, once the pride of modern philosophy, seems in a bad way these days. Fifty years ago, during the heyday of logical empiricism, which was not only a powerful movement in philosophy but also immensely influential in social science, it seemed as though the very center of philosophy was its theory of knowledge. That was clearly philosophy's main contribution to a scientific culture. Science went ahead and gathered knowledge; philosophical reflection concerned the validity of claims to knowledge. The preeminence of epistemology explains a phenomenon like Karl Popper. On the strength of his reputation as a theorist of scientific knowledge, he could obtain a hearing for his intemperate views about famous philosophers of the tradition, which bore a rather distant relation to the truth.[1] It is reminiscent of a parallel phenomenon in the arts, whereby the political opinions of a great performer or writer are often listened to with an attention and respect that their intrinsic worth hardly commands.

Of course, all this was only true of the Anglo-Saxon world. On the Continent the challenge to the epistemological tradition was already in full swing. Heidegger and Merleau-Ponty had a wide influence. It would be too simple to say that this skeptical stance has now spread to the English-speaking world. Rather it seems true to say that epistemology has come under more intensive critical scrutiny in both cultures. In France, the generation of structuralists and poststructuralists was if anything even more alienated from this whole manner of thinking than Merleau-Ponty had been. In

England and America, the arguments of both generations of continental thinkers have begun to have an impact. The publication of Richard Rorty's influential *Philosophy and the Mirror of Nature* (1979) helped both to crystallize and to accelerate a trend toward the repudiation of the whole epistemological enterprise.

In some circles it is becoming a new orthodoxy that the whole enterprise from Descartes, through Locke and Kant, and pursued by various nineteenth- and twentieth-century succession movements, was a mistake. What is becoming less and less clear, however, is what exactly it means to overcome the epistemological standpoint or to repudiate the enterprise. Just what is one trying to deny?

Rorty's book seems to offer a clear and plausible answer. The heart of the old epistemology was the belief in a *foundational* enterprise.[2] What the positive sciences needed to complete them, on this view, was a rigorous discipline that could check the credentials of all truth claims. An alleged science could be valid only if its findings met this test; otherwise it rested on sand. Epistemology would ultimately make clear just what made knowledge claims valid, and what ultimate degree of validity they could lay claim to. (One could, of course, come up with a rather pessimistic, skeptical answer to the latter question. Epistemology was not necessarily a rationalist enterprise. Indeed, its last great defenders were and are empiricists.)

In practice, epistemologists took their cue from what they identified as the successful sciences of their day, all the way from Descartes's infatuation with mathematics to the contemporary vogue for reduction to physics. But the actual foundational science was not itself supposed to be dependent on any of the empirical sciences, and this obviously on pain of a circularity that would sacrifice its foundational character. Arguments about the source of valid knowledge claims were not supposed to be empirical.

If we follow this description, then it is clear what overcoming epistemology has to mean. It will mean abandoning foundationalism. On this view, Quine would figure among the prominent leaders of this new philosophical turn, since he proposes to "naturalize" epistemology, that is, deprive it of its a priori status and consider it as one science among others, one of many mutually interacting departments of our picture of the world.[3] And so Rorty does seem to consider him, albeit with some reservations.[4]

But there is a wider conception of the epistemological tradition, from whose viewpoint this last would be a rather grotesque judgment. This is the interpretation that focuses not so much on foundationalism as on the understanding of knowledge that made it possible. If I had to sum up this understanding in a single formula, it would be that knowledge is to be seen as correct representation of an independent reality. In its original form, it saw knowledge as the inner depiction of an outer reality.[5]

The reason why some thinkers prefer to focus on this interpretation, rather than merely on the foundationalist ambitions that are ultimately (as Quine has shown) detachable from it, is that it is bound up with very influential and often not fully articulated notions about science and about the nature of human agency. Through these it connects with certain central moral and spiritual ideas of the modern age. If one's aim is, in challenging the primacy of epistemology, to challenge these ideas as well, then one has to take it up in this wider—or deeper—focus, and not simply show the vanity of the foundational enterprise.

I would like now to trace some of these connections. One of them is evident: the link between the representational conception and the new, mechanistic science of the seventeenth century. This is, in fact, twofold. On one side, the mechanization of the world picture undermined the previously dominant understanding of knowledge and thus paved the way for the modern view. The most important traditional view was Aristotle's, according to which when we come to know something, the mind *(nous)* becomes one with the object of thought.[6] Of course this is not to say that they become materially the same thing; rather, mind and object are informed by the same *eidos*.[7] Here was a conception quite different from the representational model, even though some of the things Aristotle said could be construed as supporting the latter. The basic bent of Aristotle's model could much better be described as participational: being informed by the same *eidos,* the mind participates in the being of the known object, rather than simply depicting it.

But this theory totally depends on the philosophy of Forms. Once we no longer explain the way things are in terms of the species that inform them, this conception of knowledge is untenable and rapidly becomes almost unintelligible. We have great difficulty in understanding it today. The representational view can then appear as the only available alternative.

This is the negative connection between mechanism and modern epistemology. The positive one obtrudes as soon as we attempt to explain our knowing activity itself in mechanistic terms. The key to this is obviously perception, and if we see it as another process in a mechanistic universe, we have to construe it as involving as a crucial component the passive reception of impressions from the external world. Knowledge then hangs on a certain relation holding between what is "out there" and certain inner states that this external reality causes in us. This construal, valid for Locke, applies just as much to the latest artificial-intelligence models of thinking. It is one of the mainsprings of the epistemological tradition.

The epistemological construal is, then, an understanding of knowledge that fits well with modern mechanistic science. This is one of its great strengths, and certainly it contributes to the present vogue of computer-based models of the mind. But that's not all this construal has going for it. It is in fact heavily overdetermined. For the representational view was also powered by the new ideals of science, and new conceptions of the excellence of thought, that arose at the same time.

This connection was central to Descartes's philosophy. It was one of his leading ideas that science, or real knowledge, does not simply consist of a congruence between ideas in the mind and the reality outside. If the object of my musings happens to coincide with real events in the world, this doesn't give me *knowledge* of them. The congruence has to come about through a reliable method, generating well-founded confidence. Science requires certainty, and this can only be based on that undeniable clarity Descartes called *évidence*. "Toute science est une connaissance certaine et évidente," runs the opening sentence of the second rule in *Rules for the Direction of the Mind*.

Now certainty is something the mind has to generate for itself. It requires a reflexive turn, where instead of simply trusting the opinions you have acquired through your upbringing, you examine their foundation, which is ultimately to be found in your own mind. Of course, the theme that the sage has to turn away from merely current opinion, and make a more rigorous examination that leads him to science, is a very old one, going back at least to Socrates and Plato. But what is different with Descartes is the reflexive nature of this turn. The seeker after science is not directed away from shifting and uncertain opinion toward the order of the unchanging, as with Plato, but rather within, to the contents of his own mind. These have to be carefully distinguished both from external reality and from their illusory localizations in the body, so that then the correct issue of science, that is, of certainty, can be posed—the issue of the correspondence of idea to reality, which Descartes raises and then disposes of through the supposition of the *malin génie* and the proof of his negation, the veracious God.

The confidence that underlies this whole operation is that certainty is something we can generate for ourselves, by ordering our thoughts correctly—according to clear and distinct connections. This confidence is in a sense independent of the positive outcome of Descartes's argument to the existence of a veracious God, the guarantor of our science. The very fact of reflexive clarity is bound to improve our epistemic position, as long as knowledge is understood representationally. Even if we couldn't prove that the *malin génie* doesn't exist, Descartes would still be in a better position than the rest of us unreflecting minds, because he would have measured the full degree of uncertainty that hangs over all our beliefs about the world, and clearly separated out our undeniable belief in ourselves.

Descartes is thus the originator of the modern notion that certainty is the child of reflexive clarity, or the examination of our own ideas in abstraction from what they "represent," which has exercised such a powerful influence on western culture, way beyond those who share his confidence in the power of argument to prove strong theses about external reality. Locke and Hume follow in the same path, although Hume goes about as far in the direction of skepticism as any modern has. Still, it remains true for Hume that we purge ourselves of our false confidence in our too-hasty extrapolations by focusing attention on their origin in our ideas. It is *there* that we see, for instance, that our beliefs in causation are based on nothing more than constant conjunction, that the self is nothing but a bundle of impressions, and so on.

This reflexive turn, which first took form in the seventeenth- and eighteenth-century "way of ideas," is indissolubly linked to modern representational epistemology. One might say it presupposes this construal of knowledge. If Plato or Aristotle were right, the road to certainty couldn't be inward—indeed, the very notion of certainty would be different: defined more in terms of the kinds of being that admit of it, rather than by the ordering of our thoughts. But I believe there is also a motivational connection in the other direction: the ideal of self-given certainty is a strong incentive to construe knowledge in such a way that our thought about the real can be distinguished from its objects and examined on its own. And this incentive has long outlived the original way of ideas. Even in an age when we no longer want to talk of Lockean "ideas" or of "sense data," where the representational view is reconstrued in terms of linguistic representations or bodily states (and these are perhaps not genuine alternatives), there is still a strong draw toward distinguishing and mapping the *formal* operations of our thinking. In certain circles it would seem that an almost boundless confidence is placed in the defining of formal relations as a way of achieving clarity and certainty about our thinking, be it in the (mis)application of rational choice theory to ethical problems or in the great popularity of computer models of the mind.

The latter is an excellent example of what I called the "overdetermination" of the epistemological construal. The plausibility of the computer as a model of thinking comes partly from the fact that it is a machine, hence living "proof" that materialism can accommodate explanations in terms of intelligent performance; but partly too it comes from the widespread faith that our intelligent performances are ultimately to be understood in terms of formal operations. The computer, it has been said, is a "syntactic engine."[8] A controversy rages over precisely this point. The most perspicuous critics of the runaway enthusiasm with the computer model, such as Hubert Dreyfus,[9] tirelessly point out how implausible it is to understand certain of our intelligent performances in terms of a formal calculus, including our most common everyday actions, such as making our way around rooms, streets, and gardens or picking up and manipulating the objects we use. But the great difficulties that computer simulations have encountered in this area don't seem to have dimmed the enthusiasm of real believers in the model. It is as though they had been vouchsafed some revelation a priori that it *must* all be done by formal calculi. Now this revelation, I submit, comes from the depths of our modern culture and the epistemological model anchored in it, whose strength is based not just on its affinity to mechanistic science but also on its congruence to the powerful ideal of reflexive, self-given certainty.

For this has to be understood as something like a moral ideal. The power of this ideal can be sensed in the following passage from Husserl's *Cartesian Meditations* (1929), all the more significant in that Husserl had already broken with some of the main theses of the epistemological tradition. He asks in the first meditation whether the "hopelessness" of the current philosophical predicament doesn't spring from our having abandoned Descartes's original emphasis on self-responsibility:

> Sollte die vermeintlich überspannte Forderung einer auf letzte erdenkliche Vorurteilslosigkeit abgestellten Philosophie, einer in wirklicher Autonomie aus letzten selbst erzeugten Evidenzen sich gestaltenden und sich von daher absolut selbstverantwortenden Philosophie nicht vielmehr zum Grundsinn echter Philosophie gehören?[10]

The ideal of self-responsibility is foundational to modern culture. It emerges not only in our picture of the growth of modern science through the heroism of the great scientist, standing against the opinion of his age on the basis of his own self-responsible certainty—Copernicus, Galileo (he wobbled a bit before the Holy Office, but who can blame him?), Darwin, Freud. It is also closely linked to the modern ideal of freedom as self-autonomy, as the passage from Husserl implies. To be free in the modern sense is to be self-responsible, to rely on your own judgment, to find your purpose in yourself.

And so the epistemological tradition is also intricated in a certain notion of freedom, and the dignity attaching to us in virtue of this. The theory of knowledge partly draws its strength from this connection. But, reciprocally, the ideal of freedom has also drawn strength from its sensed connection with the construal of knowledge seemingly favored by modern science. From this point of view it is fateful that this notion of freedom has been interpreted as involving certain key theses about the nature of the human agent; we might call them anthropological beliefs. Whether these are in fact inseparable from the modern aspiration to autonomy is an open question, and a very important one, to which I will return briefly later. But the three connected notions I want to mention here are closely connected historically with the epistemological construal.

The first is the picture of the subject as ideally disengaged, that is, as free and rational to the extent that he has fully distinguished himself from the natural and social worlds, so that his identity is no longer to be defined in terms of what lies outside him in these worlds. The second, which flows from this, is a punctual view of the self, ideally ready as free and rational to treat these worlds—and even some of the features of his own character—instrumentally, as subject to change and reorganizing in order the better to secure the welfare of himself and others. The third is the social consequence of the first two: an atomistic construal of society as constituted by, or ultimately to be explained in terms of, individual purposes.

The first notion emerges originally in classical dualism, where the subject withdraws even from his own body, which he is able to look on as an object; but it continues beyond the demise of dualism in the contemporary demand for a neutral, objectifying science of human life and action. The second originates in the ideals of the government and reform of the self that have such an important place in the seventeenth century and of which Locke develops an influential version;[11] it continues today in the tremendous force that instrumental reason and engineering models have in our social policy, medicine, psychiatry, politics, and so on. The third notion takes shape in social-contract theories of the seventeenth century, but continues not only in their contemporary successors but also in many of the assumptions of contemporary liberalism and mainstream social science.

We don't need to unpack these ideas any further to see that the epistemological tradition is connected with some of the most important moral and spiritual ideas of our civilization—and also with some of the most controversial and questionable. To challenge them is sooner or later to run up against the force of this tradition, which stands with them in a complex relation of mutual support. Overcoming or criticizing these ideas involves coming to grips with epistemology. But this means taking it in what I identified as its broad focus, the whole representational construal of knowledge, not just as the faith in foundationalism.

When we turn to the classic critiques of epistemology, we find that they have, in fact, mostly been attuned to this interpenetration of the scientific and the moral. Hegel, in his celebrated attack on this tradition in the introduction to the *Phenomenology of Spirit,* speaks of a "fear of error" that "reveals itself rather as fear of the truth."[12] He goes on to show how this stance is bound up with a certain aspiration to individuality and separatedness, refusing what he sees as the "truth" of subject-object identity. Heidegger notoriously treats the rise of the modern epistemological standpoint as a stage in the development of a stance of domination to the world, which culminates in contemporary technological society. Merleau-Ponty draws more explicitly political connections and clarifies the alternative notion of freedom that arises from the critique of empiricism and intellectualism.[13] The moral consequences of the devastating critique of epistemology in the later Wittgenstein are less evident, since he was strongly averse to making this kind of thing explicit. But those who followed him have shown a certain affinity for the critique of disengagement, instrumental reason, and atomism.

It is safe to say that all these critics were largely motivated by a dislike of the moral and spiritual consequences of epistemology and by a strong affinity for some alternative. Indeed, the connection between the scientific and the moral is generally made more evident in their work than in that of mainstream supporters of the epistemological standpoint. But an important feature of all these critiques is that they establish a new moral outlook *through* overturning the modern conception of knowledge. They don't simply register their dissidence from the anthropological beliefs associated with this conception, but show the foundations of these beliefs to be unsound, based as they are in an untenable construal of knowledge.

All four of the men I have mentioned—whom I take to be the most important critics of epistemology, the authors of the most influential forms of critique—offer new construals of knowledge. Moreover, in spite of the great differences, all four share a basic form of argument, which finds its origins in Kant and which one might call "the argument from transcendental conditions."

By this I mean something like the following. We argue the inadequacy of the epistemological construal, and the necessity of a new conception, from what we show to be the indispensable conditions of there being anything like experience or awareness of the world in the first place. Just how to characterize this reality, whose conditions we are defining, can itself be a problem, of course. Kant speaks of it simply as "experience"; but Heidegger, with his concern to get beyond subjectivistic formulations, ends up talking about the "clearing" *(Lichtung)*. Where the Kantian expression focuses on the mind of the subject and the conditions of having what we can call experience, the Heideggerian formulation points us toward another facet of the same phenomenon, the fact that anything can *appear* or come to light at all. This requires that there be a being *to* whom it appears, *for* whom it is an object; it requires a knower, in some sense. But the *Lichtung* formulation focuses us on the fact (which we are meant to come to perceive as astonishing) that the knower-known complex *is* at all, rather than taking the knower for granted as "subject" and examining what makes it possible to have any knowledge or experience of a world.[14]

For all this extremely important shift in the center of gravity of what we take as the starting point, there is a continuity between Kant and Heidegger, Wittgenstein, or Merleau-Ponty. They all start from the intuition that this central phenomenon of experience, or the clearing, is not made intelligible on the epistemological construal, in either its empiricist or rationalist variants. That construal offers an account of stages of the knower consisting of an ultimately incoherent amalgam of two features: (a) these states (the ideas) are self-enclosed, in the sense that they can be accurately identified and described in abstraction from the "outside" world (this is, of course, essential to the whole rationalist thrust of reflexive testing of the grounds of knowledge); and (b) they nevertheless point toward and represent things in that outside world.

The incoherence of this combination may be hidden from us by the existence of things that seem to have feature (a), such as certain sensations, and even of states that seem to combine (a) and (b), such as stable illusions. But what clearly emerges from the whole argument of the last two centuries is that the condition of states of ourselves having (b) is that they cannot satisfy (a). This already began to be evident with classical empiricism in its uncertain shuffling between two definitions of the "idea" or "impression": on one reading, it was simply a content of the mind, an inner quasi-object, and it called for an object-description; on another, it had to be a claim about how things stood, and it could only be captured in a *that*-clause.

Feature (b) is what later came to be called in the Brentano-Husserl tradition "intentionality": our ideas are essentially *of* or *about* something. Here is another way of characterizing the central condition of experience or the clearing. What Kant calls transcendental conditions are conditions of intentionality, and the lines of argument that descend from Kant can be seen as exploring what these have to be.[15]

Kant already showed that the atomistic understanding of knowledge that Hume espoused was untenable in the light of these conditions. If our states were to count as experience of an objective reality, they had to be bound together to form a coherent whole, or bound together by rules, as Kant conceived it. However much this formulation may be challenged, the incoherence of the Humean picture, which made the basis of all knowledge the reception of raw, atomic, uninterpreted data, was brilliantly demonstrated. How did Kant show this? He established in fact an argument form that has been used by his successors ever since. It can be seen as a kind of appeal to intuition. In the case of this particular refutation of Hume (which is, I believe, the main theme of the transcendental deduction in the first edition of the *Critique of Pure Reason*), he makes us aware, first, that we wouldn't have what we recognize as experience at all unless it were construable as of an object (I take this as a kind of proto-thesis of intentionality), and second, that their being of an object entails a certain relatedness among our "representations." Without this, Kant says, "it would be possible for appearances to crowd in upon the soul and yet to be such as would never allow of experience." Our perceptions "would not then belong to any experience, consequently would be without an object, merely a blind play of representations, less even than a dream."[16]

I think this kind of appeal to intuition is better understood as an appeal to what I want to call our "agent's knowledge." As subjects effectively engaged in the activities of getting to perceive and know the world, we are capable of identifying certain conditions without which our activity would fall apart into incoherence. The philosophical achievement is to define the issues properly. Once this is done, as Kant does so brilliantly in relation to Humean empiricism, we find there is only one rational answer. Plainly we couldn't have experience of the world at all if we had to start with a swirl of uninterpreted data. Indeed, there would be no "data," because even this minimal description depends on our distinguishing what is given by some objective source from what we merely supply ourselves.[17]

Now the four authors I mention push this argument form further, and explore conditions of intentionality that require a more fundamental break with the epistemological tradition. In particular, they push it far enough to undermine the anthropological beliefs I described earlier: beliefs in the disengaged subject, the punctual self, and atomism.

The arguments of Heidegger and Merleau-Ponty put paid to the first view. Heidegger, for instance, shows—especially in his celebrated analysis of being-in-the-world—that the condition of our forming disengaged representations of reality is that we must be already engaged in coping with our world, dealing with the things in it, at grips with them.[18] Disengaged description is a special possibility, realizable only intermittently, of a being *(Dasein)* who is always "in" the world in another way, as an agent engaged in realizing a certain form of life. That is what we are about "first and mostly" *(zunächst und zumeist).*

The tremendous contribution of Heidegger, like that of Kant, consists in having focused the issue properly. Once this is done, we can't deny the picture that emerges. Even in our theoretical stance to the world, we are agents. Even to find out about the world and formulate disinterested pictures, we have to come to grips with it, experiment, set ourselves to observe, control conditions. But in all this, which forms the indispensable basis of theory, we are engaged as agents coping with things. It is clear that we couldn't form disinterested representations any other way.

But once we take this point, then the entire epistemological position is undermined. Obviously foundationalism goes, since our representations of things—the kinds of objects we pick out as whole, enduring entities—are grounded in the way we deal with those things. These dealings are largely inarticulate, and the project of articulating them fully is an essentially incoherent one, just because any articulative project would itself rely on a background or horizon of nonexplicit engagement with the world.

But the argument here cuts deeper. Foundationalism is undermined because you can't go on digging under our ordinary representations to uncover further, more basic representations. What you get underlying our representations of the world—the kinds of things we formulate, for instance, in declarative sentences—is not further representation but rather a certain grasp of the world that we have as agents in it. This shows the whole epistemological construal of knowledge to be mistaken. It doesn't just consist of inner pictures of outer reality, but grounds in something quite other. And in this "foundation," the crucial move of the epistemological construal—distinguishing states of the subject (our "ideas") from features of the external world—can't be effected. We can draw a neat line between my *picture* of an object and that object, but not between my *dealing* with the object and that object. It may make sense to ask us to focus on what we *believe* about something, say a football, even in the absence of that thing; but when it comes to *playing* football, the corresponding suggestion would be absurd. The actions involved in the game can't be done without the object; they include the object. Take it away and we have something quite different—people miming a game on the stage, perhaps. The notion that our understanding of the world is grounded in our dealings with it is equivalent to the thesis that this understanding is not ultimately based on representations at all, in the sense of depictions that are separately identifiable from what they are of.[19]

Heidegger's reflections take us entirely outside the epistemological construal. Our reflections on the conditions of intentionality show that these include our being "first and mostly" agents in the world. But this also ruins the conception of the agent as one whose ideal could be total disengagement. This turns out to be an impossibility, one that it would be destructive to attempt. We can't turn the background against which we think into an object for us. The task of reason has to be conceived quite differently: as that of articulating the background, "disclosing" what it involves. This may open the way to detaching ourselves from or altering part of what has constituted it—may, indeed, make such alteration irresistible; but only through our unquestioning reliance on the rest.

And just as the notion of the agent underpinning the ideal of disengagement is rendered impossible, so is the punctual notion of the self. Heidegger and Merleau-Ponty both show how the inescapability of the background involves an understanding of the depth of the agent, but they do so by exploring the conditions of intentionality in complementary directions. Heidegger shows how *Dasein's* world is defined by the related purposes of a certain way of life shared with others. Merleau-Ponty shows how our agency is essentially embodied and how this lived body is the locus of directions of action and desire that we never fully grasp or control by personal decision.

This critique also puts in question the third anthropological belief I singled out above, atomism. I have just mentioned how Heidegger's notion of *Dasein*'s way of life is essentially that of a collectivity. A general feature of paradigm-setting critiques is that they strongly reject this third view and show instead the priority of society as the locus of the individual's identity. But crucially this point is made through an exploration of the role of language. The new theory of language that arises at the end of the eighteenth century, most notably in the work of Herder and Humboldt, not only gives a new account of how language is essential to human thought, but also places the capacity to speak not simply in the individual but primarily in the speech community.[20] This totally upsets the outlook of the mainstream epistemological tradition. Now arguments to this effect have formed part of the refutation of the atomism that has proceeded through an overturning of standard modern epistemology.

Important examples of arguments of this kind are Hegel's in the first chapter of the *Phenomenology of Spirit,* against the position he defines as "sensible certainty," where he shows both the indispensability of language and its holistic character; and Wittgenstein's famous demonstrations of the uselessness of "ostensive definitions," where he makes plain the crucial role played by language in identifying the object and the impossibility of a purely private language.[21] Both are, I believe, excellent examples of arguments that explore the conditions of intentionality and show their conclusions to be inescapable.

It is evident that these arguments give us a quite different notion of what it is to overcome epistemology from those that merely eschèw foundationalism. We can measure the full gulf by comparing any of the four—Heidegger, perhaps, or Merleau-Ponty—with the Quine of "Epistemology Naturalized." It is plain that the essential elements of the epistemological construal have remained standing in Quine, and not surprisingly therefore the central anthropological beliefs of the tradition. Disengagement emerges in his "taste for desert landscapes"; the punctual self in his behaviorism; and atomism in his particular brand of political conservatism.[22] In face of differences of this magnitude, a question arises concerning what it means to "overcome epistemology."

A picture has been emerging here of what this ought to be—a tendentious one, I freely admit. It accepts the wider or deeper definition of the task:

overcoming the distorted anthropological beliefs through a critique and correction of the construal of knowledge that is interwoven with them and has done so much to give them undeserved credit. Otherwise put: through a clarification of the conditions of intentionality, we come to a better understanding of what we are as knowing agents—and hence also as language beings—and thereby gain insight into some of the crucial anthropological questions that underpin our moral and spiritual beliefs.

For all its radical break with the tradition, this kind of philosophy would in one respect be in continuity with it. It would be carrying further the demand for self-clarity about our nature as knowing agents, by adopting a better and more critically defensible notion of what this entails. Instead of searching for an impossible foundational justification of knowledge or hoping to achieve total reflexive clarity about the bases of our beliefs, we would now conceive this self-understanding as awareness about the limits and conditions of our knowing, an awareness that would help us to overcome the illusions of disengagement and atomic individuality that are constantly being generated by a civilization founded on mobility and instrumental reason.

We could understand this as carrying the project of modern reason, even of "self-responsible" reason, further by giving it a new meaning. This is how Husserl conceived the critical project in his last great lectures on the "crisis of European science," given in Vienna in 1935. Husserl thinks of us as struggling to realize a fundamental task, that of the "europäischen Geist," whose goal is to achieve the fullness of reflexive clarity. We should see ourselves as philosopher-functionaries ("Funktionäre der neuzeitlichen philosophischen Menschheit"). The first foundation *(Urstiftung)* of the European tradition points to a final foundation *(Endstiftung)*, and only in the latter is the former fully revealed:

> nur von ihr [Endstiftung] aus kann sich die einheitliche Ausgerichtetheit aller Philosophen und Philosophien eröffnen, und von ihr aus kann eine Erhellung gewonnen werden, in welcher man die vergangene Denker versteht, wie sie selbst sich nie hätten verstehen können.[23]

Husserl's hope here sounds ridiculously overstated, which may have something to do with his having failed to push through his critique of foundationalism to the end. Overstatement has played an important role, as we will see, in casting discredit on the task as I have outlined it. But if we purge Husserl's formulation of the prospect of a "final foundation" where absolute apodicticity would at last be won, if we concentrate merely on the gain for reason in coming to understand what is illusory in the modern epistemological project and in articulating the insights about us that flow from this, then the claim to have taken the modern project of reason a little farther, and to have understood our forbears a little better than they understood themselves, is not so unbelievable.

What reflection in this direction would entail is already fairly well known. It involves, first, conceiving reason differently, as including—alongside the familiar forms of the Enlightenment—a new department, whose excellence consists in our being able to articulate the background of our lives perspicuously. We can use the word "disclosure" for this, following Heidegger. And along with this goes a conception of critical reasoning, of especial relevance for moral thinking, that focuses on the nature of transitions in our thought, of which "immanent critique" is only the best-known example.[24]

In moral thought, what emerges from this critique is a rejection of moralities based purely on instrumental reason, such as utilitarianism; and also critical distance from those based on a punctual notion of the self, such as the various derivations of Kant. The critique of John Rawls's theory by Michael Sandel, in the name of a less "thin" theory of the agent, is an excellent example of this.[25] In social theory, the result is a rejection of atomist theories, of reductive causal theories (such as "vulgar" Marxism or sociobiology), and of theories that cannot accommodate intersubjective meaning.[26] Social science is seen as being closer to historiography of a certain kind. In politics, the antiatomist thrust of the critique makes it hostile to certain forms of contemporary conservatism, but also to radical doctrines of nonsituated freedom.[27] I believe there is a natural affinity between this critique, with its stress on situated freedom and the roots of our identity in community, on the one hand, and the civic humanist tradition on the other, as the works of a number of writers, from Humboldt to Arendt, testify.[28]

It might seem now as though everything should run on smoothly, toward a set of anthropological conclusions with a certain moral-political hue. But in fact all this is hotly contested, not just by those who wish to defend the epistemological tradition, which would be understandable, but by those who consider themselves its critics. Foremost among these are a range of thinkers who have defined themselves in relation to a certain reading of Nietzsche. The most interesting and considerable of them, in my opinion, is Foucault. In keeping with the themes of this chapter, we can perhaps get most directly to the basis of their dissent if we go to the moral or spiritual outlook they wish to defend. In the case of Foucault this became relatively clear at the end of his life. He rejected the concept of the punctual self, which could take an instrumental stance toward its life and character—this is indeed what arises out of the practices and "truths" of the disciplinary society he painted in such repellent colors (whatever protestations of neutrality accompanied the depiction). But he couldn't accept the rival notion of a deep or authentic self that arises out of the critical traditions of Hegel and, in another way, Heidegger or Merleau-Ponty. This seemed to him another prison. He rejected both in favor of a Nietzschean notion of the self as potentially self-making, the self as a work of art, a central conception of an "aesthetics of existence."[29]

Something analogous, but on a much more frivolous level, seems to animate some of the poststructuralist thinkers—Derrida, for instance. Paradoxically, for all the talk of the "end of subjectivity," one of the strong attractions of this kind of position is precisely the license it offers to subjectivity, unfettered by anything in the nature of a correct interpretation or an irrecusable meaning of either life or text, to effect its own transformations, to invent meaning. Self-making is again primary.

Nietzsche's insights into the way in which language imposes order on our world, into theory as a kind of violence, were crucial to all views of this kind. It offers an alternative to the kind of possible critique of epistemology in which we discover something deeper and more valid about ourselves in carrying it through—the kind I have been describing. Instead it attacks the very aspiration to truth, as this is usually understood. All epistemic orders are imposed, and the epistemological construal is just another one of those orders. It has no claim to ultimate correctness, not because it has been shown inadequate by an exploration of the conditions of intentionality, but because all such claims are bogus. They mistake an act of power for a revelation of truth. Husserl's *Urstiftung* takes on a quite different and more sinister air.

Clearly this is the critique of epistemology that is most compatible with the spiritual stance of self-making. It makes the will primary in a radical way, whereas the critique through conditions of intentionality purports to show us more of what we really are like—to show us, as it were, something of our deep or authentic nature as selves. So those who take the Nietzschean road are naturally very reluctant to understand the critique as a *gain* in reason. They would rather deny that reason can have anything to do with our choices of what to be.

This is not to say that they propose the end of epistemology as a radical break. Just as the critique through conditions of intentionality represents a kind of continuity-through-transformation in the tradition of self-critical reason, so the Nietzschean refusal represents a continuity-through-transformation of another facet of the modern identity—the primacy of the will. This played an important role in the rise of modern science and its associated epistemological standpoint; in a sense, a voluntaristic anthropology, with its roots in a voluntaristic theology, prepared the ground over centuries for the seventeenth-century revolution, most notably in the form of nominalism. It is a crucial point of division among moderns, what we think of primacy of the will. This is one of the issues at stake between these two conceptions of what it means to overcome the epistemological tradition.

Although this represents perhaps the most dramatic opposition among critics of epistemology, it is far from exhausting the field. Habermas, for instance, has staked out a position equivalent to neither. Against the neo-Nietzscheans, he would strongly defend the tradition of critical reason, but he has his own grounds for distrusting Heideggerian disclosure and wants instead to hold on to a formal understanding of reason and, in consequence, a procedural ethic, although purged of the monological errors of earlier variants. He has drawn heavily on the critique of epistemology in the four authors mentioned above, but fears for the fate of a truly universal and critical ethic if one were to go all the way with this critique.[30]

How do we adjudicate this kind of dispute? How do we decide what it really means to overcome epistemology? I can't hope to decide the issue here, only to make a claim as to how it should be settled. In order to define this better, I want to return to the most dramatic dispute, that between the neo-Nietzscheans and the defenders of critical reason.

It seems to me that, whoever is ultimately right, the dispute has to be fought on the terrain of the latter. The Nietzschean position also stands and falls with a certain construal of knowledge: that it is relative to various ultimately imposed "regimes of truth," to use Foucault's expression. This has to show itself to be a superior construal to that which emerges from the exploration of the conditions of intentionality. Does it?

Certainly the Nietzschean conception has brought important insights: no construal is quite innocent, something is always suppressed; and what is more, some interlocutors are always advantaged relative to others, for any language.[31] But the issue is whether this settles the matter of truth between construals. Does it mean that there can be no talk of epistemic gain in passing from one construal to another? That there is such a gain is the claim of those exploring the conditions of intentionality. This claim doesn't stand and fall with a naive, angelic conception of philosophical construals as utterly uninvolved with power. Where is the argument that will show the more radical Nietzschean claim to be true and the thesis of critical reason untenable?

I regret to say that one hears very little serious argument in this domain. Neo-Nietzscheans seem to think that they are dispensed from it since it is already evident or, alternatively, that they are debarred from engaging in it on pain of compromising their position. Derrida and his followers seem to belong to the first category. The main weight of argument is carried here by an utterly caricatural view of the alternative as involving a belief in a kind of total self-transparent clarity, which would make even Hegel blush. The rhetoric deployed around this has the effect of obscuring the possibility that there might be a third alternative to the two rather dotty ones on offer; and as long as you go along with this, the Derridian view seems to win as the least mad, albeit by a hair.

Others try to argue on behalf of Foucault that he couldn't enter the argument concerning construals of knowledge without abandoning his Nietzschean position, that there is nothing to *argue* between them. True enough, but then the issue whether there is something to argue itself demands some kind of support. Something can surely be said about that. Indeed, much *has* been said, by Nietzsche for one, and some also by Foucault—in talking for instance of "regimes of truth"; the question is whether it is really persuasive or involves a lot of slippery slides and evasion.

In short, the arguments for not arguing seriously are uniformly bad. And in fact Foucault did on one occasion make a serious attempt to engage with the exploration of the conditions of intentionality, and that was in the latter part (chapter 9) of *The Order of Things,* where he talks about the invention of Man and the "transcendental-empirical double." This was admittedly prior to his last, much more centrally Nietzschean phase, but it can be seen as preparing the ground for this, as indeed Dreyfus and Rabinow see it.[32]

The arguments here seem to me much more to build on the Heideggerian and Merleau-Pontyan critique against Kant rather than to challenge this critique. And the arguments, if valid, would have the consequence that nothing coherent could be said at all about the conditions of intentionality. I can't see how this could fail to undercut the Nietzschean view as well. In *The Order of Things* Foucault takes refuge in a species of structuralism, which is meant to avoid this question altogether. But he abandons it soon afterwards, and we are left uncertain where the argument is meant to take us. In general among neo-Nietzscheans, however, an atmosphere reigns in which this issue is felt as already settled. We are exhorted by Lyotard not to take metanarratives seriously any more, but the argument for this seems to rely on caricature.[33]

If I am right, the issue is far from settled. And yet at stake in this struggle over the corpse of epistemology are some of the most important spiritual issues of our time. The question, what it is to overcome epistemology, turns out to be of more than just historical interest.

2

The Validity of
Transcendental Arguments

Whrnen and why are transcendental
arguments valid? This sums up (rather tendentiously) the question I want
to discuss here. What I meant by "transcendental argument" is a certain
mode of argument that comes down to us from Kant, of which the first and
paradigmatic instances are to be found in the "Transcendental Analytic," but
which has been tried in other forms by contemporaries.

The arguments I want to call "transcendental" start from some feature of
our experience which they claim to be indubitable and beyond cavil. They
then move to a stronger conclusion, one concerning the nature of the subject or the subject's position in the world. They make this move by a regressive argument, to the effect that the stronger conclusion must be so if the
indubitable fact about experience is to be possible (and being so, it must
be possible).

Thus we can see Kant in the transcendental deduction starting from the
insight that we must be able to distinguish within experience an objective
order of things from a merely subjective order. For otherwise we would
have experience which was not experienced as being *of* anything; it would
be an experience without an object, and this we can see to be an impossibility. We wouldn't have the minimum awareness and grasp of what is going
on necessary for what passes in us to constitute *experience,* if it really were
of nothing in this sense.

This, I believe, is one of the starting points we can identify in the arguments which are gathered together in the transcendental deduction in both

editions of the first *Critique*. From it, Kant moves pretty quickly to the need for some coherent unity of the representations which make up experience as a necessary condition of its being experience of an object. We could consider this a first step in a transcendental argument, a regression from an unquestionable feature of experience to a stronger thesis as the condition of its possibility. Or we could take the need for a coherent unity as so obvious that it constitutes the starting point itself.

Kant does something like this when he takes what I believe ultimately amounts to a somewhat different route in the second edition. Here he gets us to accept the indubitable necessity that our experiences have a unity so that for each one of us all our experiences belong to us as subjects. I must be able to recognize of all my experiences that they are mine; otherwise put, the "I think" must be able to accompany all my representations. If anything were beyond the reach of this potential recognition of ownership, it couldn't be an experience; it would lack that minimum degree of awareness, of a grasp on things, which an experience must have.

Kant's argument in both editions relates these two kinds of necessary coherence to each other and to a common ground in the application of the categories to experience by the understanding. The latter is taken to be what alone makes the coherences possible. And since the coherences can't be questioned—for we do in fact have experience—this stronger condition, which incorporates the necessary applicability of certain categories to the world of experience, must also hold. A somewhat similar argument, only applied in detail, is deployed in the different "Analogies of Experience": for instance, the condition of there being a distinction between objective and subjective succession of experiences—which we can all recognize as essential if experience is to be *of* anything, hence to be experience at all—is the applicability of the category of causation to the world we experience. Hence we can be a priori certain that this category applies.

I don't want to discuss the validity of these arguments, only to illustrate the type of argument. This type is worth identifying because, I believe, it still plays an important role in twentieth-century philosophy. I think that some of the arguments adumbrated by the later Wittgenstein, and which have been taken up by others from him, can most illuminatingly be spelled out as arguments of this mold. I haven't got the space to spell this out convincingly here. But, less controversially, I believe that the conception of the subject as embodied agency, which has developed out of modern phenomenology, as in the works of Heidegger and Merleau-Ponty, has been deployed and argued for in a way which is ultimately derived from the paradigm arguments of the first *Critique*. This is the more evident in that this conception has been worked out in a consciously critical stance toward Kant and neo-Kantianism.

It is this conception of embodied agency which interests me as a living attempt to deploy an argument of the transcendental type and hence as a continuation, at least in one sense, of the enterprise Kant started. I want to focus on this, to examine just what it proves and how it proves it, if indeed it proves anything at all.

This is a conception of the subject as essentially an embodied agent, engaged with the world. In saying that the subject is essentially embodied, we are not just saying that our being a subject is causally dependent on certain bodily features: for instance, that you couldn't see if the eyes were covered, or think if you were under severe bodily stress, or be conscious at all if the brain were damaged. The thesis is not concerned with such empirically obvious truisms.

Rather the claim is that our manner of being as subjects is in essential respects that of embodied agents. It is a claim about the *nature* of our experience and thought, and of all those functions which are ours qua subject, rather than about the empirically necessary conditions of these functions. To say we are essentially embodied agents is to say that it is essential to our experience and thought that they be those of embodied beings.

This kind of claim needs to be shown, not just so as to be believed, but also so that we can understand more fully what is being shown. I can best explicate what this thesis amounts to by deploying some of the argument for it, which I reconstruct largely from Maurice Merleau-Ponty. I also hope that this will enable me to show later on how this kind of argument descends from Kant's.

Merleau-Ponty argues the thesis of embodied agency from the nature of perception. This should be valid, because perception is basic to us as subjects. To be a subject is to be aware of a world. I can be aware of the world in many ways. I can be pondering the situation in Namibia or last year at Marienbad, considering the second law of thermodynamics, and so on. But the one way of having a world which is basic to all this is my perceiving it from where I am, with my senses, as we say. This is basic, first because it is always there, as long as I am aware at all; and second because it is the foundation of other ways of having a world. We can ponder distant events, or theoretical perspectives on things, because we are first of all open to a world which can be explored, learned, theorized about, and so on. And our primary opening to this world, the inescapable background to all others, is through perception.

Now our perception of the world is essentially that of an embodied agent, engaged with or at grips with the world. And once again the term "essentially" carries the force discussed above; the claim is not just that perception depends causally on certain states of our bodies—that I couldn't see if my eyes were not in good condition, or the like. The claim is rather that our perception as an experience is such that it could only be that of an embodied agent engaged with the world. Let's consider.

Our perceptual field has an orientational structure, a foreground and a background, an up and down. And it must have; that is, it can't lose this structure without ceasing to be a perceptual field in the full sense, our opening onto a world. In those rare moments where we lose orientation, we don't know where we are; and we don't know where or what things are either; we lose the thread of the world, and our perceptual field is no longer our access to the world, but rather the confused debris into which our normal grasp on things crumbles.

Now this orientational structure marks our field as essentially that of an embodied agent. It is not just that the field's perspective centers on where I am bodily—this by itself doesn't show that I am essentially agent. But take the up-down directionality of the field. What is it based on? Up and down are not simply related to my body; up is not just where my head is and down where my feet are. For I can be lying down, or bending over, or upside down; and in all these cases "up" in my field is not the direction of my head. Nor are up and down defined by certain paradigm objects in the field, such as earth or sky: the earth can slope, for instance.

Rather, up and down are related to how one would move and act in the field. For it is of course as a bodily agent functioning in a gravitational field that "up" and "down" have meaning for me. I have to maintain myself upright to act, or in some way align my posture with gravity. Without a sense of "which way is up," I falter into confusion. My field has an up and a down because it is the field of an agent of this kind. It is structured as a field of potential action.

It may seem a little quick to deny that up and down are related to paradigm objects, or features of the world. How do I ever know what is up, unless by seeing where the ground is? or the water? or the floor? or whatever. But there is a potential confusion here. We certainly need to perceive the world to know which end is up; and we can be fooled if our perception is restricted in some way, e.g., if we have to look through a narrow aperture or through oblique mirrors. To speak psychological language, we need adequate cues. But what we grasp through the cues is the up-down directionality of the field, and this is not defined by relation to any paradigm objects. What up and down *are*, rather, are orienting directions of our action and stance.

Perceiving up-down is not perceiving the gravitational field of the earth. This may be what underlies our perceptual structure of up-down, but it is not the perceptual structure, as we can see in a space capsule. It is an interesting correlation that we discover that on earth the up-down directionality goes with the gravitational field of the earth.

But up-down directionality *is* the line of possible upright stance and action; that is, it is a perception of the field as a locus of our activity. This is because there is no sense to imagining that we *discover* that up-down is the most appropriate, feasible, or convenient orientation in which to stand, act, and so on.

Thus although we may grasp this orientation from cues—lay of land, ground, sky—*what* we perceive is not the lay of the land or the sky. We grasp a directionality of the field which is, however, essentially related to how we act and stand.

What this example suggests is that our perceptual field has the structure it has because it is experienced as a field of potential action. We perceive the world, in other words, or take it in, through our capacities to act in it. What I mean by this will be clearer if we look more closely at this example. The up-down directionality of my field is a feature which only makes sense in relation to my action. It is a correlative of my capacity to stand and act in equilibrium. Because my field is structured in a way which only makes sense in relation to this capacity, I can say that the world as I perceive it is structured by it; or that I see the world through this capacity.

But a field of this structure can only be experienced by an embodied agent. It is essentially the perceptual field of such an embodied agent.

Similar arguments could be deployed starting from other features of our perception: for instance, we could show that our perception required a sense of orientation, that if this were totally to fail, our grasp on things would fall apart in a confusion that would no longer amount to perception. This orientation, in turn, could be shown to depend on our sense of where we are and how we stand, as embodied agents; hence to be essentially the sense of orientation of such an agent.

It is in arguments of this kind that Merleau-Ponty builds up his conception of the human subject as *être-au-monde:* our primary access to the world is through perception, and this is essentially that of an embodied agent, who is engaged with the world. We are essentially living beings, and as such we act in and on the world; our activity is directed to the things we need and use and the other subjects we engage with. We are thus inescapably open to the world; and our manner of being open to the world, our perception, is essentially that of an agent at grips with the world. We perceive the world through our activity, in the sense described above.

On this view, our perception of the world as that of an embodied agent is not a contingent fact we might discover empirically; rather our sense of ourselves as embodied agents is constitutive of our experience. I borrow the term here from the sense it has in the distinction between constitutive and regulative rules. It has been pointed out that the rule about the queen's movement in chess is a constitutive rule and not a rule for regulating an independently existing activity, because the game of chess wouldn't exist without such rules as that the queen moves sideways and diagonally. Similarly here, the connection is constitutive and not a mere correlation, because we couldn't have a subject with a field articulated like ours who as a matter of contingent fact might not be an embodied agent. His being an embodied agent helps to constitute his field.

I believe this view has some affinities with that adumbrated in late Wittgenstein; but I can't argue this now. What I want to claim is that the arguments by which this view is deployed are of the type I called "transcendental" above. They attempt to convince us by pointing to what appear undeniable essential features of experience, e.g., the up-down structure of the field, or our orientation in a wider environment. We are meant to concur that unquestionably without these there would be nothing that we could call perception. Then the argument goes on to show that our having a sense of ourselves as embodied agents is a necessary condition of our experience having these features. The stronger thesis, that our experience is essentially that of embodied agents, thus seems established by regressive argument.

What do these arguments establish? And how do they establish it?

To the first question, we might be tempted to reply simply that, if valid, they establish that we are in fact embodied subjects. But things aren't so simple. If we took this as an ontological thesis concerning the nature of man, from which we ought to be able to derive conclusions, for instance, about how human action, thought, or perception should be explained, then we would be exceeding the potential scope of the argument. If we really are embodied agents in this sense, then no dualistic account of our thoughts or action will be valid; nor will a reductive mechanistic thesis be valid, since it takes no account of the categories of embodied agency, but treats us as bodily beings essentially on the same footing as inanimate nature.

But no conclusion this strong can be drawn from such an argument. What is shown is that our thought, our experience, and in general our function as subjects must be described as essentially the thought or experience of embodied agents. This says something about the nature of our life as subjects. It says, for instance, that our experience is constituted by our sense of ourselves as embodied agents. So we are inescapably to ourselves embodied subjects. Put in other terms, we can't effectively exercise subjectivity, and be aware of a world, without a sense of ourselves as embodied subjects; for this sense is constitutive of our awareness.

But this doesn't assure us that we can't give an account of what underlies this experience and thought in, say, reductive neurophysiological terms. Some philosophers have thought that the fact that we can't be mechanistic systems in our self-understanding forecloses the question whether we are such systems in fact; that we cannot give a deterministic account of our own behavior entitles us to infer that no such account can be valid. But this doesn't follow. For the possibility remains open that what we are in our own self-awareness may be in important ways misleading; a deeper level explanation of the functioning of human beings might be based on quite other principles.

In this connection, it is clear that there are certain ontological questions which lie beyond the scope of transcendental arguments. Kant recognized this in allowing that his arguments established nothing about things as they are in themselves, but only about the world as we experience it. And Barry Stroud has cautioned against trying to use transcendental arguments as an instrument to refute skepticism.[1]

But if they don't decide what we are, then what do these arguments decide? What does it amount to, to show that we are inescapably embodied agents to ourselves? Is this really a stronger thesis than the starting points of these arguments, the particular features identified as essential to experience?

Don't both simply deal with the nature of experience? And if it is no stronger, then what becomes of the claim that transcendental arguments can establish something stronger than their starting points by the regressive argument of necessary conditions?

My claim is that the conclusion of these arguments is highly significant, and goes well beyond their points of departure. For while it may not show that a reductive mechanistic account is impossible, a proof that we are inescapably embodied agents to ourselves does show the form that any account must take which invokes our own self-understanding. And this is decisive for the greater part of anthropology, politics, sociology, linguistics, psychoanalysis, developmental psychology, in short, virtually the entire range of the human sciences as we know them. A proper following through of Merleau-Ponty's arguments would, if they were valid, show a wide range of approaches in these sciences to be mistaken—those which involved applying mechanistic or dualistic categories to thought or experience, as Merleau-Ponty himself clearly saw. The results may not be valid, but the issue is clearly significant.

I want to turn now to the second question and discuss it at greater length: how do these arguments prove whatever they prove?

There are three important features of these arguments that require explanation. First, they consist of a string of what one could call indispensability claims. They move from their starting points to their conclusions by showing that the condition stated in the conclusion is indispensable to the feature identified at the start. Thus the applicability of the categories is alleged to be indispensable to the kind of coherence necessary for experience; or the sense of ourselves as embodied agents is indispensable to our perceptual field's having an up-down orientation.

But the starting points themselves consist of indispensability claims. The point of departure is that experience must be coherent to be experience, that perception is impossible without the up-down orientation. Hence we can see these arguments as chains of indispensability claims. The first such claim defines the point of departure, and the argument builds further ones onto that. The argument has a minimum of two steps, but may have more. Thus we could spell out Kant's transcendental deduction in the first edition in three stages: experience must have an object, that is, be *of* something; for this it must be coherent; and to be coherent it must be shaped by the understanding through the categories.

The second point is that these indispensability claims are not meant to be empirically grounded, but a priori. They are not merely probable, but apodictic. I would suggest further that they are supposed to be self-evident. Certainly the first claim, which starts off the chain of argument, is thought so to be. We just *see* that experience must be *of* something to be experience, or that the "I think" must be able to accompany all my representations. But the latter phases are supposed to be equally certain, and grounded in the same kind of certainty. We are meant to see with equal clarity that there can't be experience *of* something unless it is coherent; or that there can't be coherence if the categories don't apply. It is just that it takes a little more explaining for us to appreciate this point.

And so we have a chain of apodictic indispensability claims. The third point is that these claims concern experience. This gives the chain an anchor without which it wouldn't have the significance it does. For an argument that D is indispensable for C, which is indispensable for B, which is in-dispensable for A, tells us nothing definitive about the status of D, unless we already know the status of A. If the existence of A can be doubted, then so can that of D. The significance of the fact that transcendental arguments deploy indispensability claims about experience is that it gives us an unchallengeable starting point. For how can we formulate coherently the doubt that we have experience?

So transcendental arguments are chains of apodictic indispensability claims which concern experience and thus have an unchallengeable anchoring. What they show things to be indispensable *to* can't be shrugged off.

But then what grounds the apodictic certainty or the self-evidence that these claims are supposed to enjoy? And if they are self-evident, why do we have to work so hard to demonstrate them? And why is there any argument afterwards, as there always seems to be?

I think that these questions can be answered and the three features ex-plained, if we see these arguments as based on articulating an insight we have into our own activity. This kind of insight does entitle us to make some apodictic indispensability claims. An activity has a point. Qua having a point, certain things are essential to it, that is, their absence would void the point of the activity. What constitutes the point of an activity is not a merely verbal matter. It may, of course, be an arbitrary question of classifi-cation where we draw the boundaries between activities, but for any activity once circumscribed and distinguished from others, what constitutes its point is not just a verbal question.

Now the agent must have some insight into the point of his activity. The insight will not be total; some things will be hidden from him. But he must have some grasp of what he is doing, that grasp which is involved in doing it. What this amounts to will vary with different actions. But for some which involve a degree of consciousness and understanding, self-awareness is itself part of their point. For these, the point of the activity—the absence of which would void the point—must itself include the agent's awareness of the point.

Take a game like chess. To move the pieces around at will, without regard to the rules of the game, would void the point of the activity. But so would your moving the pieces around in a way which in fact coincides with a legal set of moves, although you have no grasp of why this is right. You can't be playing chess without some grasp of the rules.

Thus it is that we can be certain of a judgment, say that the queen rule is a constitutive rule of chess. It is clearly integral to the point of the activity that we abide by rules like this. And this requires that we understand the significance of the rules, that we grasp how integral they are to the activity. Thus, once we are playing chess, we know with unquestionable certainty that this rule is a constitutive rule. Or otherwise put, we couldn't doubt this without doubting that we are playing chess. You can't play chess and not know *this*.

The only question, then, is how seriously we can doubt that we play chess. Who could ask the question? A child, pushing around the pieces as she saw her parents doing, could say: "Mummy, am I playing chess?" Her asking would show that the answer ought to be no. Or we could imagine asking whether we play the game that they played in Persia a thousand years ago, or in India even earlier. We think of this as true chess, and want to know if our game is still the same.

But in the ordinary sense of the word, where "chess" is the name of the game we all play, it is hard to see how one could make sense of the doubt that we know how to play chess and are now playing it. Perhaps a doubt about our playing chess at the moment may arise in this form: am I dreaming? But a doubt about whether we know how to play chess can't be given any sense. It is like doubting whether I speak English. Of course, if you mean by "English" what the plays of Shakespeare and the King James Bible are written in, then we don't speak *that;* but in the ordinary sense, English is just what we all speak.

Thus my grasp of the rules of chess as a player among others is in an important sense indubitable. And this is what justifies my certainty in judgments such as that the queen rule is a constitutive rule. You couldn't formulate a doubt that made sense here, that is, conceive a way I could be wrong.

Earlier I made a parallel between the judgment about the queen rule and the thesis that our perception is essentially that of an embodied agent, because both of these make claims that something is constitutive. Now I should like to draw the parallel closer and assert that they are both established in the same way. They are both articulations of our insight into the point of our activity.

What is the activity insight into which licenses our transcendental arguments? It is the activity of our being aware of our world, grasping the reality in which we are set. Of course, this way of putting it begs the questions that transcendental arguments are meant to resolve, such as: is there a reality of which we are aware? But the activity can be given a more minimal description, say that of being aware of whatever there is that we can be aware of, whether impressions, appearances, real physical objects, or whatever.

Now anyone engaged in this activity must be able to recognize certain conditions of failure which amount to breakdown of the activity even under the minimal description. For instance, my awareness may have no object, is not of anything; or it may totally lack coherence; or my perception may totally lack orientation as to up and down, far and near; in all these cases, my awareness falls apart into such confusion as not to constitute awareness in any proper sense. Anyone capable of awareness is capable of recognizing this.

So far, there is a parallel with the queen-rule case. But there is an important difference. In the case of chess, we can expect players already to know the status of the queen rule, in the sense that we have already accepted some formulation of it. This is because chess as played in our civilization is a game that cannot be played without formulating a great deal in words: "you're in check," or "I'm threatening your queen," and so on. And people are always taught by *explaining* them the rules. Perception by contrast is an inarticulate activity; it starts off entirely so, and remains largely so. And even when we learn to articulate what we see, we never (except when doing philosophy) try to articulate what it is to see.

Thus we can't just say: whoever is aware must *know* the basic conditions of failure, in the sense of having already accepted some formulation of them. But we can say that we must be able to recognize these as conditions of failure. For the activity of being aware is one of those, like chess in this respect, where understanding their point is itself part of their point. That is, if I couldn't recognize that, when all broke down into confusion, awareness had failed, then you couldn't think of me as aware in the first place. We aren't aware at all unless we can recognize this difference.

And so here too there are things of which we can be certain in virtue of what we are engaged in. It is clear to us that a total lack of coherence in our perception would be a breakdown of awareness. And it is hard to see how we could even raise the question that we might be wrong about this. I can be unable to recognize whether I'm meeting the criteria of success for writing a fugue or solving a problem, even though I'm engaged in these activities. But we can't be aware without being able to recognize a breakdown as a breakdown. So the question whether I may not be wrong to identify coherence as one of the conditions of awareness comes down to a question: am I aware? And what could I possibly be asking here? Awareness is just that condition of grasp on things which enables me, inter alia, to formulate questions.

The chain of indispensability claims anchors here in something unchallengeable. I may hyperbolically doubt whether my memory of chessplaying is not a confused dream, which will turn out incoherent if I dwell on it, as so many dreams do. I may doubt whether I am "truly" aware, of ultimate reality, that is. But I cannot formulate a coherent doubt whether I'm aware in the sense of conscious, awake, and grasping something. Transcendental arguments articulate indispensability claims concerning experience as such.

My submission is that these claims can be certain because they are grounded in our grasp of the point of our activity, that grasp we must have to carry on the activity. They articulate the point, or certain conditions of success and failure; and we can be certain that they do so rightly, because to doubt this is to doubt that we are engaged in the activity, and in this case such a doubt is senseless.

But transcendental arguments are *arguments:* we need a lot of discourse to establish them because, unlike the queen-rule-in-chess case, we have to *articulate* the boundary conditions of awareness. In the normal course of life we are focused on the things we are observing and dealing with (our way of being is *être-au-monde,* in Merleau-Ponty's phrase); we are unconcerned with what it is to perceive, to be aware. The exigencies of the philosophical debate require that we *formulate* the limiting success conditions which we cannot but recognize once we grasp the formulation.

A transcendental argument will usually have more than one stage, because richer descriptions of the boundary conditions will be harder to formulate, and the formulations will be harder to grasp. So we start off with a sketchy characterization which can be seen right off as a formulation of a limiting condition: say that experience must be *of* something. Then we go on to show that this involves experience having coherence; and then we try to show that this coherence must consist in the applicability of the categories. But there is nothing sacred about the number of steps. We might try to formulate the requirement of a coherent objectivity in one stage.

Indeed, the first stage is different in nothing from the later stages, except in being easier to grasp. It appears self-evident; but the later steps must also be made to appear self-evident. They constitute indispensability claims, but so does the first stage. The big change is that the argument moves us from weaker to stronger thesis, from experience being *of* something to the applicability of the categories. It is this I want to explain as the move from sketchier to richer descriptions. As the argument goes on, we spell out further what is involved in the limiting conditions we captured in our first, sketchy formulation. We try to show that the richer description's holding is indispensable to the sketchier one's holding, because the former simply spells out what the latter adumbrated.

Transcendental arguments thus have to formulate boundary conditions we can all recognize. Once they are formulated properly, we can see at once that they are valid. The thing is self-evident. But it may be very hard to get to this point, and there may still be dispute. We can now resolve this paradox, that the conclusions of transcendental arguments are apodictic and yet open to endless debate.

For although a correct formulation will be self-evidently valid, the question may arise whether we have formulated things correctly. This is all the more so since we are moving into an area that the ordinary practice of life has left unarticulated, an area we look through rather than at. It is an area where there are no formulations available in ordinary speech, and where it is hard to make things clear. Our language has to be inventive to do so. We have to speak of things like the "I think" which can accompany all my representations, or the up-down orientation of the perceptual field. We have to innovate in language, and bring the limits of experience to clarity in formulations that open up a zone normally outside our range of thought and attention.

And these formulations can distort. The deeper we go, that is, and the richer the description, the more a cavil can be raised. Thus we may find it too easy to accept the first stages of Kant's transcendental deduction as formulated here. It may seem clear that experience must have an object and must be coherent. But it is not at all clear that this coherence must be that of the applicability of the categories, and even less clear that the particular categories as Kant formulates them are the ones indispensably applicable. We can easily feel that Kant's attempt to formulate the boundary conditions of experience was infected by certain philosophical doctrines of his time, and that the nature of this necessary coherence should be characterized quite differently.

Transcendental arguments thus turn out to be quite paradoxical things. I have been asking here what arguments of this kind prove, and how they prove it. They appear to be rather strange in both dimensions.

They prove something quite strong about the subject of experience and the subject's place in the world; and yet since they are grounded in the nature of experience, there remains an ultimate, ontological question they can't foreclose—for Kant, that of the things in themselves; for the thesis of embodied agency, the basic explanatory language of human behavior.

When we ask how they prove what they prove, we see another paradoxical mixture. They articulate a grasp of the point of our activity which we cannot but have, and their formulations aspire to self-evidence; and yet they must articulate what is most difficult for us to articulate, and so are open to endless debate. A valid transcendental argument is indubitable; yet it is hard to know when you have one, at least one with an interesting conclusion. But then that seems true of most arguments in philosophy.

— 3 —

Explanation and Practical Reason

Our modern conceptions of practical reason are shaped—I might say distorted—by the weight of moral skepticism. Even conceptions that intend to give no ground to skepticism have frequently taken form in order best to resist it, or to offer the least possible purchase to it. In this, practical reason falls into line with a pervasive feature of modern intellectual culture, which one could call the primacy of the epistemological: the tendency to think out the question of what something *is* in terms of the question of how it is *known*.

The place of what I call skepticism in our culture is evident. By this I don't mean just a disbelief in morality or a global challenge to its claims—though the seriousness with which a thinker like Nietzsche is regarded shows that this is no marginal position. I'm also thinking of the widespread belief that moral positions can't be argued, that moral differences can't be arbitrated by reason, that when it comes to moral values, we all just ultimately have to plump for the ones which feel best to us. This is the climate of thought which Alasdair MacIntyre calls (perhaps a bit harshly) "emotivist,"[1] which at least ought to be called in some sense "subjectivist." Ask any undergraduate class of beginners in philosophy, and the majority will claim to adhere to some form of subjectivism. This may not correspond to deeply felt convictions. It does seem to reflect, however, what these students think the intellectually respectable option to be.

What underpins this climate? Some rather deep metaphysical assumptions when one gets down to it. But certainly, on the immediate level, it is fostered by the actual experience of moral diversity. On an issue like abortion, for instance, it doesn't seem to be possible for either side to convince the other. Protagonists of each tend to think that their position is grounded on something self-evident. For some it just seems clear that the fetus is not a person, and it is absurd to ruin the life of some being who undeniably has this status in order to preserve it. For others, it is absolutely clear that the fetus is both life and human, and so terminating it can't be right unless murder is. Neither side can be budged from these initial intuitions, and once you accept either one the corresponding moral injunctions seem to follow.

If the seeming helplessness of reason tells us something about its real limits, then a worrying thought arises: what if some people came along who just failed to share our most basic and crucial moral intuitions? Suppose some people thought that innocent human beings could be killed in order to achieve some advantage for the others, or make the world more aesthetically pleasing, or something of the sort? And haven't we actually experienced people who stepped way outside the bounds of our core morality: the Nazis for instance? Is reason as powerless before such people as it seems to be to arbitrate the dispute about abortion? Is there no way to show them wrong?

Here's where our implicit model of practical reason begins to play an important role. If "showing them" means presenting facts or principles which they cannot but accept and which are sufficient to disprove their position, then we are indeed incapable of doing this. But one could argue that that is a totally wrong view of practical reason. Faced with an opponent who is *unconfusedly* and *undividedly* convinced of his position, one can indeed only hope to move him rationally by arguing from the ground up, digging down to the basic premises we differ on, and showing him to be wrong there. But is this really our predicament? Do we really face people who quite lucidly reject the very principle of the inviolability of human life?

In fact, this doesn't seem to be the case. Intellectual positions put forward to justify behavior like the Nazis'—to the extent that any of their ravings justify this appellation at all—never attack the ban on murder of conspecifics frontally. They are always full of special pleading: for instance, that their targets are not really of the same species, or that they have committed truly terrible crimes which call for retaliation, or that they represent a mortal danger to others. This kind of stuff is usually so absurd and irrational that it comes closer to mania than to reason. And, of course, with people on this kind of trip, reason is in fact ineffective as a defense. But this is not to say that reason is powerless to show them wrong. Quite the contrary. The fact that these terrible negations of civilized morality depend so much on special pleading, and of a particularly mad and irrational sort, suggests that there are limits beyond which *rational* challenges to morality have great trouble going.

This might indicate a quite different predicament of, and hence task for, practical reasoning. Its predicament would be defined by the fact that there are limits to what people can unconfusedly and undividedly espouse; so that, for instance, in order to embrace large-scale murder and mayhem, they have to talk themselves into some special plea of the sort mentioned above, which purports to square their policies with some recognized version of the prohibition against killing. But these pleas are vulnerable to reason, and in fact barely stand up to the cold light of untroubled thought.

The task of reasoning, then, is not to disprove some radically opposed first premise (say killing people is no problem), but rather to show how the policy is unconscionable on premises which both sides accept, and cannot but accept. In this case, its job is to show up the special pleas.

On this model—to offer at any rate a first approximation—practical argument starts off on the basis that my opponent already shares at least some of the fundamental dispositions toward good and right which guide me. The error comes from confusion, unclarity, or an unwillingness to face some of what he can't lucidly repudiate; and reasoning aims to show up this error. Changing someone's moral view by reasoning is always at the same time increasing his self-clarity and self-understanding.

Here are two quite different models of practical reason: let's call them the apodictic and the ad hominem respectively. I think that John Stuart Mill was making use of a distinction of this kind, and opting for the second, in his famous (perhaps notorious) remarks in *Utilitarianism.* "Questions of ultimate ends are not amenable to direct proof," he avers, and yet "considerations may be presented capable of determining the intellect either to give or to withhold its assent to the doctrine (sc. of utility); and this is the equivalent to proof."[2] This may sound like someone trying to squirm his way out of a contradiction, but the distinction is quite clear and sound. You can't argue people into accepting an ultimate end, utility or any other, if they in fact reject it. But in fact the whole case of utilitarians is that people *don't* reject it, that they all do operate by it, albeit in a confused and self-defeating fashion. And this is why there may be considerations "capable of determining the intellect." And in fact Mill shows us what he thinks these are in chapter 4, where he goes on to argue that what people really desire is happiness. The appeal is to what the opponent already seeks, a clear view of which has to be rescued from the confusions of intuitionism.

But, it might be thought, this invocation of Mill is enough to discredit the ad hominem model irremediably. Isn't this exactly where Mill commits the notorious "naturalistic fallacy," arguing from the fact that men desire happiness to its desirability, on a glaringly false analogy with the inference from the fact that men see an object to its visibility?[3] Derisive hoots echo through philosophy classes since G. E. Moore, as beginning students cut their teeth on this textbook example of a primitive logical error.

There is no doubt that this argument is not convincing as it stands. But the mistake is not quite so simple as Moore claimed. The central point that the Moorean objection indicates is the special nature of moral goals. This is a phenomenon I have tried to describe with the term "strong evaluation."[4] Something is a moral goal of ours not just in virtue of the fact that we are de facto committed to it. It must have a stronger status, that we see it as demanding, requiring, or calling for this commitment. While some goals would have no more claim on us if we ceased desiring them, such as my present aim to have a strawberry ice cream cone after lunch, a strongly evaluated goal is one such that, were we to cease desiring it, *we* would be shown up as insensitive or brutish or morally perverse.

That's the root of our dissatisfaction with Mill's argument here. We feel that just showing that we always desire something, even that we can't help desiring it, by itself does nothing to show that we *ought* to desire it, that it is a moral goal. Suppose I were irremediably addicted to smoking. Would that prove that I ought to smoke? Clearly not. We understand smoking from the beginning as a weakly evaluated end. We have to distinguish between showing of some end that we can't help desiring it and showing that all our strong evaluations presuppose it, or involve it, once we overcome our confusions about them. In the second case, we would have demonstrated that we can't be lucid about ourselves without acknowledging that we value this end. This is the sense in which it is inescapable, not after the fashion of some de facto addiction. Whereas addictions are rightly declared irrelevant to moral argument, except perhaps negatively, the proof of inescapable commitment is of the very essence of the second, ad hominem mode of practical reasoning, and is central to the whole enterprise of moral clarification.

Mill is plainly on to some intuition like this in deploying the argument in *Utilitarianism*. One of the things he is trying to show is that everyone else's commitments collapse into his. But the argument is botched because of a crucial weakness in the doctrine of utility itself, which is based on the muddled and self-defeating attempt to do away with the whole distinction between strong and weak evaluation. The incoherence of Mill's defense of the "higher" pleasures on the grounds of mere de facto preference by the "only competent judges"[5] is also a testimony to the contradictions this basically confused theory gives rise to.

But this does point to one of the most important roots of modern skepticism. We can already see that people will tend to despair of practical reason to the extent that they identify its mode of argument as apodictic. This clearly sets an impossible task for it. But this model will be accepted to the degree that the alternative, ad hominem model appears inadequate or irrelevant. And this it is bound to do, as long as the distinction between strong and weak evaluation is muddled over or lost from sight. The confusion can only breed bad arguments à la Bentham and Mill, and these, once denounced, discredit the whole enterprise.

But utilitarianism doesn't come from nowhere. The whole naturalist bent of modern intellectual culture tends to discredit the idea of strong evaluation. The model for all explanation and understanding is the natural science that emerges out of the seventeenth-century revolution. But this offers us a neutral universe; it has no place for intrinsic worth or goals that make a claim on us. Utilitarianism was partly motivated by the aspiration to build an ethic that would be compatible with this scientific vision. But to the extent that this outlook has a hold on the modern imagination, even beyond the ranks of utilitarianism, it militates in favor of accepting the apodictic model, and hence of a quasi-despairing acquiescence in subjectivism.

The link between naturalism and subjectivism is even clearer from another angle. The seventeenth-century scientific revolution destroyed the Platonic-Aristotelian conception of the universe as the instantiation of Forms, which defined the standards by which things were to be judged. The only plausible alternative construal of such standards in naturalist thought was as projections of subjects. They were not part of the fabric of things, but rather reflected the way subjects react to things, the pro-or-con attitudes they adopt. Now perhaps it's a fact that people's attitudes tend to coincide—a happy fact, if true; but it does nothing to show that this point of coincidence is righter than any other possible one.[6]

The opposition to this naturalist reduction has come from a philosophical stance that might in a broad sense be called "phenomenological." By this I mean a focus on our actual practices of moral deliberation, debate, understanding. The attempt is to show, in one way or another, that the vocabularies we need to explain human thought, action, feeling, or to explicate, analyze, justify ourselves or each other, or to deliberate on what to do, all inescapably rely on strong evaluation. Or put negatively, that the attempt to separate out a language of neutral description, which combined with commitments or pro/con attitudes might recapture and make sense of our actual explanations, analyses, or deliberations leads to failure and will always lead to failure. It seems to me that this case has been convincingly made out, in a host of places.[7]

This kind of argument is, of course, not only a justification of the very foundation of the ad hominem mode of reasoning, but an example of it. It tries to show us that in all lucidity we cannot understand ourselves, or each other, cannot make sense of our lives or determine what to do, without accepting a richer ontology than naturalism allows, without thinking in terms of strong evaluation. This might be thought to beg the question, establishing the validity of a mode of argument through a use of it. But the presumption behind this objection ought to be challenged: what in fact ought to trump the ontology implicit in our best attempts to understand/explain ourselves? Should the epistemology derived from natural science be allowed to do so, so that its metaphysical bias in favor of a neutral universe overrules our most lucid self-understandings in strongly evaluative terms? But doesn't this rather beg the crucial question—whether and to what extent human life is to be explained in terms modeled on natural science? And what better way to answer this question than by seeing what explanations actually wash?

Enough has been said above, I hope, to show that one of the strongest roots of modern skepticism and subjectivism in regard to ethics is the naturalist temper of modern thought. This tends to discredit in advance the ad hominem mode of argument, which actually might hold out the hope of settling certain moral issues by reason, and leaves only the apodictic model in the field, which clearly sets an impossible standard. Within a human situation inescapably characterized in strongly evaluative terms, we can see how argument aimed at self-clarification might in principle at least bring agreement. In a neutral universe, what agreement there is between attitudes seems merely a brute fact, irrelevant to morals, and disagreement seems utterly inarbitrable by reason, bridgeable only by propaganda, arm twisting, or emotional manipulation.

But this analysis brings to mind another source of modern skepticism, constituted by the independent attractions of the apodictic model itself. Here's where we really measure the tremendous hold of epistemology over modern culture.

This model emerges pari passu with and in response to the rise of modern physical science. As we see it coming to be in Descartes and then Locke, it is a foundationalist model. Our knowledge claims are to be checked, to be assessed as fully and responsibly as they can be, by breaking them down and identifying their ultimate foundations, as distinct from the chain of inferences which build from these toward our original unreflecting beliefs. This foundationalist model can easily come to be identified with reason itself. Modern reason tends to be understood no longer substantively but procedurally, and the procedures of foundationalism can easily be portrayed as central to it. But from the foundationalist perspective, only the apodictic mode of reasoning is really satisfactory; the appeal to shared fundamental commitment seems simply a recourse to common prejudices. The very Enlightenment notion of prejudice encapsulates this negative judgment.

This brings us to another aspect. Foundationalist reasoning is meant to shake us loose from our parochial perspective. In the context of seventeenth-century natural science, this involved in particular detaching us from the peculiarly human perspective on things. The condemnation of secondary qualities is the most striking example of this move to describe reality no longer in anthropocentric but in "absolute" terms.[8]

But if the canonical model of reasoning involves maximally breaking us free from our perspective, then the ad hominem mode cannot but appear inferior, since by definition it starts from what the interlocutor is already committed to. And here a particularly important consideration comes into play. Starting from where your interlocutor is not only seems an inferior mode of reason in general, but it can be presented as a peculiarly bad and, indeed, vicious form of practical reason. For all those whose instinct tells them that the true demands of morality require radical change in the way things are, and the way people have been trained to react to them, starting from the interlocutor's standpoint seems a formula for conservatism, for stifling at the start all radical criticism, and foreclosing all the really important ethical issues.

This has always been one of the strongest appeals of utilitarianism, and one of the greatest sources of self-congratulation by partisans of utility. It is not only that their theory has seemed to them the only one consonant with science and reason, but also that they alone permit of reform. Mill argues against views based on mere "intuition" that they freeze our axiomata media forever, as it were, and make it impossible to revise them, as mankind progresses and our lights increase. "The corollaries from the principle of utility . . . admit of indefinite improvement, and, in a progressive state of the human mind, their improvement is perpetually going on."[9]

Here is a source of modern skepticism and subjectivism which is as powerful as naturalism, and tends to operate closely in tandem with it: the belief that a critical morality, by its very nature, rules out the ad hominem mode of practical reasoning. Naturalism and the critical temper together tend to force us to recognize the apodictic mode as the only game in town. The obvious severe limitations of this mode in face of ethical disagreement then push us toward a half-despairing, half-complacent embracing of an equivocal ethical subjectivism.

This identification of the demands of critical morality with a procedural understanding of reason and the apodictic mode is deeply mistaken. But erroneous or not, it has been immensely influential in our intellectual culture. One can see this in the way people unreflectingly argue in terms of this model.

Discuss the question of arbitrating moral disputes with students, graduate or undergraduate, and very soon someone will ask for "criteria." What is aimed at by this term is a set of considerations such that, for two explicitly defined, rival positions X and Y, (a) people who unconfusedly and undividedly espouse both X and Y have to acknowledge them, and (b) they are sufficient to show that Y is right and X is wrong, or vice versa. It is then driven home, against those who take an upbeat view of practical reason, that for any important moral dispute, no considerations have both (a) and (b). If the rift is deep enough, things that are (b) must fail of (a), and vice versa.

The problem lies with the whole unreflecting assumption that "criteria" in this sense are what the argument needs. We shall see, as we explore it further, that this assumption, as it is usually understood in the context of foundationalism, amounts to ruling out the most important and fruitful forms of the ad hominem mode.

But this whole assumption that rational arbitration of differences needs "criteria" has become very problematic, not only for practical reason. It is a notorious source of puzzlement and skeptical challenge in the history of science as well. It is some underlying assumption of this kind which has driven so many people to draw skeptical conclusions from the brilliant work of Thomas Kuhn (conclusions to which Kuhn himself has sometimes been drawn, without ever succumbing to them). For what Kuhn persuasively argued was the "incommensurability" of different scientific outlooks which have succeeded each other in history. That is, their concepts are not inter-translatable, and—what is even more unsettling—they differ as to what features or considerations provide the test of their truth. The considerations each recognizes as having (b) are diverse. There are no criteria. And so the radical inference of a Feyerabend has seemed widely plausible: "anything goes."

But as MacIntyre has also argued,[10] it is clear that what needs revision is our metatheory of scientific reasoning, rather than, say, our firmly established conviction that Galileo made an important step forward relative to Aristotelian physics. The blind acceptance of a foundationalist, apodictic model of reasoning is perhaps just as damaging here as in ethics. Calling to mind how inadequate the model is can both help to weaken its hold on us in general and allow us to see more exactly what is truly peculiar to practical reason.

MacIntyre argues very convincingly that the superiority of one scientific conception over another can be rationally demonstrated, even in the absence of what are normally understood as criteria. These are usually seen as providing some externally defined standard, against which each theory is to be weighed independently. But what may be decisive is that we be able to show that the *passage* from one to the other represents a gain in understanding. In other words, we can give a convincing narrative account of the passage from the first to the second as an advance in knowledge, a step from a less good to a better understanding of the phenomena in question. This establishes an asymmetrical relation between them: a similarly plausible narrative of a possible transition from the second to the first couldn't be constructed. Or to put it in terms of a real historical transition, portraying it as a *loss* in understanding is not on.[11]

 What I want to take from this is the notion that we can sometimes arbitrate between positions by portraying *transitions* as gains or losses, even where what we normally understand as decision through criteria—qua externally defined standards—is impossible. I will sketch here three argument forms, in ascending order of radical departure from the canonical, foundationalist mode.

1. The first takes advantage of the fact that we are concerned with transitions, that the issue here is a comparative judgment. On the standard, unreflecting assumptions of foundationalism, comparative judgments are usually secondary to absolute ones. Rival positions X and Y are checked against the facts, and one is shown superior to the other because it predicts or explains certain facts which the other does not. The comparative judgment between the two is based on absolute judgments concerning their respective performance in face of reality. The role of criteria here is taken by facts, observations, protocols, or perhaps by standards to be applied to explanations of facts—such as elegance, simplicity. Just as in a football game, the comparative verdict, team X won, is founded on two absolute assessments: team X scored 3 goals, and team Y scored 2 goals. The most popular theory of scientific reasoning with this traditional structure, Karl Popper's, resembles indeed the elimination rounds in a championship match. Each theory plays the facts, until it suffers defeat, and then is relegated.

But as MacIntyre shows, comparative reasoning can draw on more resources than this. What may convince us that a given transition from X to Y is a gain is not only or even so much how X and Y deal with the facts, but how they deal with each other. It may be that from the standpoint of Y, not just the phenomena in dispute, but also the history of X and its particular pattern of anomalies, difficulties, makeshifts, and breakdowns can be greatly illuminated. In adopting Y, we make better sense not just of the world, but of our history of trying to explain the world, part of which has been played out in terms of X.

The striking example, which MacIntyre alludes to, is the move from Renaissance sub-Aristotelian to Galilean theories of motion. The Aristotelian conception of motion, which entrenched the principle of no motion without a mover, ran into tremendous difficulty in accounting for "violent" motion, as in the motion of a projectile after it leaves the hand or cannon mouth. The Paduan philosophers and others looked in vain for factors which could play the continuing role of movers in pushing the projectile forward. What we now see as the solution doesn't come until theories based on inertia alter the entire presumption of what needs explaining: continued rectilinear (or for Galileo circular) motion is not an explanandum.

What convinces us still that Galileo was right can perhaps be put in terms of the higher "score" of inertial theories over Aristotelian ones in dealing with the phenomena of motion. After all this time, the successes of Galileo are only too evident. But what was and is also an important factor—and which obviously bulked relatively larger at the time—is the ability of inertial theories to make sense of the whole pattern of difficulties that beset the Aristotelians. The superiority is registered here not simply in terms of their respective scores in playing "the facts," but also by the ability of each to make sense of itself and the other in explaining these facts. Something more emerges in their stories about each other than was evident in a mere comparison of their several performances. This shows an asymmetrical relation between them: you can move from Aristotle to Galileo realizing a gain in understanding, but not vice versa.

2. This is still not a radical departure from the foundational model. True, decisive criteria are not drawn from the realm of facts or universally accepted principles of explanation. But the crucial considerations are accessible to both sides. Thus the pre-Galileans were not unaware of the fact that they had a problem with violent motion. In Kuhnian language, this was an "anomaly" for them, as their intellectual perplexity and the desperate expedients they resorted to testify. The decisive arguments are transitional, concerning what each theory has to say about the other and about the passage from its rival to itself, and this takes us beyond the traditional way of conceiving validation, both positivist and Popperian. But in the strict sense of the definition above, there are still criteria here, for the decisive considerations are such that both sides must recognize their validity.

But, it can be argued, if we look at the seventeenth-century revolution from a broader perspective, this ceases to be so. Thus if we stand back and compare the dominant models of science before and after the break, we can see that different demands were made on explanation. The notion of a science of nature, as it came down from Plato and especially from Aristotle, made explanation in terms of Forms (*eide* or species) central, and beyond that posited an order of forms, whose structure could be understood teleologically, in terms of some notion of the good or of what ought to be. Principles like that of plenitude, which Lovejoy identifies and traces, make sense on that understanding: we can know beforehand, as it were, that the universe will be so ordered as to realize the maximum richness.[12] Similarly, explanations in terms of correspondences are possible, since it follows from the basic conception that the same constellation of ideas will be manifested in every domain.

Now if science consists of a grasp of order of this kind, then the activity of explaining why things are as they are (what we think of as science) is intrinsically linked to the activity of determining what the good is, and in particular how human beings should live through attuning themselves to this order. The notion that explanation can be distinct from practical reason, that the attempt to grasp what the world is like can be made independent of the determination of how we should stand in it, that the goal of understanding the cosmos can be uncoupled from our attunement to it, this makes no sense on the premodern understanding.

But notoriously the seventeenth-century revolution brought about an uncoupling of just this kind. The turn to mechanism offers a view of the universe as neutral; within it, cause-effect relations can be exploited to serve more than one purpose. Galileo and his successors, we might say, turn toward an utterly different paradigm of explanation. If scientific explanation can always be roughly understood as in some sense rendering the puzzling comprehensible by showing how the phenomenon to be explained flows from mechanisms or modes of operation we understand, then the seventeenth century sees a massive shift in the kind of understanding that serves as the basic reference point.

There is certainly one readily available mode of human understanding which the Platonic-Aristotelian tradition drew on. We are all capable of understanding things in terms of their place in a meaningful order. These are the terms in which we explain the at-first puzzling behavior of others, or social practices which seemed at first strange, or some of the at-first odd details of a new work of art, and the like. In another quite different sense of "understanding" we understand an environment when we can make our way about in it, get things done, effect our purposes. This is the kind of understanding a garage mechanic has, and I unfortunately lack, of the environment under the hood of my car.

One of the ways of describing the scientific revolution is to say that one of these paradigms of understanding comes to take the place of the other as the basic reference point for the scientific explanation of nature.[13] But this has as an ineluctable consequence the diremption of explanation from practical reason I mentioned above. Only the first type of understanding lends itself to a marriage of the two.

But once we describe it this way, the scientific revolution can be made to appear as not fully rationally motivated. Of course, we all accept today that Galileo was right. But can we *justify* that preference in reason? Was the earlier outlook shown to be inferior, or did its protagonists just die off? If you ask the ordinary person today for a quick statement why modern science is superior to the premodern, he or she will probably point to the spectacular technological payoff that has accrued to Galilean science. But here's where the skeptic can enter. Technological payoff, or the greater ability to predict and manipulate things, is certainly a good criterion of scientific success on the post-Galilean paradigm of understanding. If understanding is knowing your way about, then modern technological success is a sure sign of progress in knowledge. But how is this meant to convince a pre-Galilean? For in fact he is operating with a different paradigm of understanding, to which manipulative capacity is irrelevant, which instead proves itself through a different ability, that of discovering our proper place in the cosmos and finding attunement with it. And, it could be argued, modern technological civilization is a spectacular failure at *this,* as ecological critics and green parties never tire of reminding us.

Is the argument then to be considered a standoff between the two, judged at the bar of reason? Here the skeptical spinoff from Kuhn's work makes itself felt. Once you overcome anachronism and come to appreciate how different earlier theories were, how great the breaks are in the history of knowledge—and this has been one of the great contributions of Kuhn's work—then it can appear that no *rational* justification of the transitions is possible. For the considerations of each side diverge. Each theory carries with it its own built-in criteria of success—moral vision and attunement in one case, manipulative power in the other—and is therefore invulnerable to the other's attack. In the end, we all seem to have gone for manipulative power, but this has to be for some extra-epistemic consideration, not because this mode of science has been shown superior as *knowledge.* Presumably, we just like that payoff better. In terms of my earlier discussion, what we lack here are criteria; there are no decisive considerations that *both* sides must accept.

Some people are driven by their epistemological position to accept an account of this kind.[14] But this seems to me preposterous. Once more, it can appear plausible only because it fails to think of the transition between the two views. It sees each as assessing a theory's performance in face of reality by its own canons. It doesn't go further and demand of each that it give an account of the existence of the other; that is, not just explain the world, but explain also how this rival (and presumably erroneous) way of explaining the world could arise.

Once you make this demand, you can appreciate the weakness of pre-

Galilean science. There is a mode of understanding which consists of knowing your way about. This is universally recognized. In making another mode the paradigm for scientific explanation, pre-Galilean science drew on a set of assumptions which entailed that this manipulative understanding would never have a very big place in human life. It always allowed for a lower form of inquiry, the domain of "empirics" who scramble around to discover how to achieve certain effects. But the very nature of the material embodiment of Forms, as varying, approximate, never integral, ensured that no important discoveries could be made here, and certainly not an exact and universal body of findings. So the very existence of such a body of truths, and the consequent spectacular manipulative success, represents a critical challenge for premodern science. Indeed, it is difficult to see how it could meet this challenge. On its basic assumptions, modern science shouldn't have got off the empiric's bench, emerged from the dark and smelly alchemist's study to the steel-and-glass research institutes that design our lives.

The problem then is not some explanatory failure on its own terms, not some nagging, continuing anomaly, as in the narrower issue of theories of motion; it is not that pre-Galilean science didn't perform well enough by its own standards, or that it doesn't have grounds within itself to downgrade the standards of its rivals. If we imagine the debate between the two theories being carried on timelessly on Olympus, before any actual results are obtained by one or the other, then it is indeed a standoff. But what the earlier science can't explain is the very success of the later *on the later's own terms.* Beyond a certain point, you just can't pretend any longer that manipulation and control are not relevant criteria of scientific success. Pre-Galilean science died of its inability to explain/assimilate the actual success of post-Galilean science, where there was no corresponding symmetrical problem. And this death was rationally motivated. On Olympus the grounds would have been insufficient; but faced with the actual transition, you are ultimately forced to read it as a gain. Once again, what looks like a standoff when two independent, closed theories are confronted with the facts turns out to be conclusively arbitrable in reason when you consider the transition.[15]

I have been arguing that the canonical, foundationalist notion of arbitrating disputes through criteria generates skepticism about reason, which disappears once we see that we are often arguing about transitions. And we have seen that this skepticism affects some of the more important transitions of science just as much as it does the disputes of morality, and for the same reason—the seeming lack of common criteria. In particular, it tends to make the history of science seem less rational than it has in fact been.

Now the second case is in a sense a more radical departure from the canonical model than the first. For the defeat doesn't come from any self-recognized anomaly in the vanquished theory. Nevertheless, there was *something* which the losing theory had to recognize outside the scope of its original standards—that the very success of mechanistic science posed a problem. If we ask why this is so, we are led to recognize a human constant: a mode of understanding of a given domain D, which consists in our ability to make our way about and effect our purposes in D. We might borrow a term from Heidegger, and call this understanding as we originally have it prior to explicitation or scientific discovery "pre-understanding." One of the directions of increasing knowledge of which we are capable consists in making this pre-understanding explicit, and then in extending our grasp of the connections which underlie our ability to deal with the world as we do. Knowledge of this kind is intrinsically linked with increased ability to effect our purposes, with the acquisition of potential recipes for more effective practice. In some cases, it is virtually impossible to extend such knowledge without making new recipes available; and an extension of our practical capacities is therefore a reliable criterion of increasing knowledge.

Because of these links between understanding and practical ability, we cannot deny whatever increases our capacities its title as a gain in knowledge in some sense. We can seek to belittle its significance, or deem it to be by nature limited, disjointed, and lacunary, as Plato does. But then we have to sit up and take notice when it manages to burst the bounds we set for it; and this is what has rendered the transition to Galilean science a rational one.

The mediating element is something deeply embedded in the human life form, of which we are all implicitly aware and which we have to recognize when made explicit: the link between understanding (of a certain kind) and practical capacity. But then isn't the predicament of reason here coming to look analogous to the description I offered above of moral disputes? The task is not to convince those who are undividedly and unconfusedly attached to one first principle that they ought to shift to an entirely different one. So described, it is impossible. Rather, we are always trying to show that, granted what our interlocutors already accept, they cannot but attribute to the acts or policies in dispute the significance we are urging.

Now here it has been a question of altering the first principles of science—the paradigms of understanding underlying it and the standards of success. And we can see a rational path from one to the other, but only because in virtue of what pre-Galileans already accept they cannot but recognize the significance of Galilean science's massive leap forward. No more in one case than in the other, it is a question of radical conversion from one ultimate premise to the other. That would indeed be irrational. Rather we show that the pre-Galileans could not undividedly and unconfusedly repudiate the deliverances of post-Galilean science as irrelevant to the issue that divides them.

Perhaps, then, those ultimate breakpoints we speak of as scientific revolutions share some logical features with moral disputes. They both are rendered irrational and seemingly inarbitrable by an influential but erroneous model of foundationalist reasoning. To understand what reason can do in both contexts, we have to see the argument as being about transitions. And as the second case makes plain, we have to see it as making appeal to our implicit understanding of our form of life.

This brings to the fore one of the preconceptions that has bedeviled our understanding here and fostered skepticism. On the standard foundationalist view, the protagonists are seen as closed explicit systems. Once one has articulated their major premises, it is assumed that all possible routes of appeal to them have been defined. So the pre-Galilean model, with its fixed standards of success, is seen as impervious to the new standards of prediction and control. But the real positions held in history don't correspond to these watertight deductive systems, and that is why rational transitions are in fact possible.

We could argue that there are also moral transitions which could be defended in a way very analogous to the scientific one just described. When we read the opening pages of Michel Foucault's *Surveiller et punir,* with its riveting description of the torture and execution of a parricide in the mideighteenth century, we are struck by the cultural change we have gone through since the Enlightenment. We are much more concerned about pain and suffering than our forebears; we shrink from the infliction of gratuitous suffering. It would be hard to imagine people taking their children to such a spectacle today, at least openly and without some sense of unease and shame.

What has changed? It is not that we have embraced an entirely new principle, or that our ancestors would have thought the level of pain irrelevant, providing no reason at all to desist from some course of action involving torture or wounds. It is rather that this negative significance of pain was subordinated to other, weightier considerations. If it is important that punishment in a sense undo the evil of the crime, restore the balance—what is implicit in the whole notion of the criminal making *amende honorable*—then the very horror of parricide calls for a particularly gruesome punishment. It calls for a kind of theater of the horrible as the medium in which the undoing can take place. In this context, pain takes on a different significance; there has to be lots of it to do the trick. The principle of minimizing pain is trumped.

But then it is possible to see how the transition might be assessed rationally. If the whole outlook that justifies trumping the principle of minimizing suffering—which involves seeing the cosmos as a meaningful order in which human society is embedded as a microcosm or mirror—comes to be set aside, then it is rational to want above all to reduce suffering. Of course, our ultimate judgment will depend on whether we see the change in cosmology as rational; and that is the issue I have just been arguing in connection with the scientific revolution. If I'm right there, then here too the transition can perhaps be justified.

Of course, I'm not claiming that all that has been involved in this important change has been the decline of the earlier cosmology. There are other, independent grounds in modern culture which have made us more reluctant to inflict pain. Some of them may have sinister aspects, if we believe Foucault himself. I haven't got space to go into this here.[16] But surely we must recognize the decline of the older notion of cosmic-social order as *one* consideration which lends a rational grounding to modern humanitarianism. This change would not only be linked to that in scientific theory, it would also be analogous to it in rational structure; to something which has always been recognized, although formerly in a subordinate place (the link between understanding and practice, the good of reducing pain), we are now constrained to give a more central significance because of changes which have taken place.

But the analogy I have been trying to draw between the justification of some scientific and moral revolutions can't hide the fact that a great many moral disputes are much more difficult to arbitrate. To the extent that one can call on human constants, these are much more difficult to establish. And the suspicion dawns that in many cases such constants are of no avail. The differences between some cultures may be too great to make any ad hominem form of argument valid between them. Disputes of this kind would be inarbitrable.

3.   But this form of argument, from the constants implicitly accepted by

the interlocutor, doesn't exhaust the repertoire of practical reason. There is one more form, which is also an argument about transitions, but is an even more striking departure from the canonical model. In both forms above, the winner has appealed to some consideration that the loser had to acknowledge—his own anomalies or some implicit constant. In the light of this consideration, it was possible to show that the transition from X to Y could be shown as a gain, but not the reverse. So there is still something like a criterion operating here.

But we can imagine a form of argument in which no such consideration is invoked. The transition from X to Y is not shown to be a gain because this is the only way to make sense of the key consideration; rather it is shown to be a gain directly, because it can plausibly be described as mediated by some error-reducing move. This third mode of argument can be said to reverse the direction of argument. The canonical foundationalist form can only show that the transition from X to Y is a gain in knowledge by showing that, say, X is false and Y true, or X has probability n and Y has $2n$. The two forms we have been considering focus on the transition, but they too only show that the move from X to Y is a gain, because we can make sense of this transition from Y's perspective but not of the reverse move from X's perspective. We still ground our ultimate judgment in the differential performance of X and Y.

But consider the possibility that we might identify the transition directly as the overcoming of an error. Say we knew that it consisted in the removing of a contradiction, or the overcoming of a confusion, or the recognition of a hitherto ignored relevant factor. In this case, the order of justifying argument would be reversed. Instead of concluding that Y was a gain over X because of the superior performance of Y, we would be confident of the superior performance of Y because we knew that Y was a gain over X.

But are we ever in a position to argue in this direction? In fact, examples abound in everyday life. First take a simple case of perception. I walk into a room and see, or seem to see, something very surprising. I pause, shake my head, rub my eyes, and place myself to observe carefully. Yes, there really is a pink elephant with yellow polka dots in the class. I guess someone must be playing a practical joke.

What has gone on here? In fact, I'm confident that my second perception is more trustworthy, not because it scores better than the first on some measure of likelihood. On the contrary, if what I got from the first look was something like "maybe a pink elephant, maybe not," and from the second "definitely a pink elephant with yellow polka dots," there's no doubt that the first must be given greater antecedent probability. It is after all a disjunction, one of whose arms is overwhelmingly likely in these circumstances. But in fact I trust my second percept, because I have gone through an ameliorating transition. This is something I know how to bring off; it is part of my know-how as a perceiver. And that is what I in fact bring off by shaking my head (to clear the dreams), rubbing my eyes (to get the rheum out of them), and setting myself to observe with attention. It is my direct sense of the transition as an error-reducing one which grounds my confidence that my perceptual performance will improve.

Something similar exists in more serious biographical transitions. Joe was previously uncertain whether he loved Anne, because he also resents her, and in a confused way he was assuming that love is incompatible with resentment. But now he sees that these two are distinct and compatible emotions, and the latter is no longer getting in the way of his recognizing the strength of the former. Joe is confident that his present self-reading (I certainly love Anne) is superior to his former self-reading (I'm not sure whether I love Anne), because he knows that he passed from one to the other via the clarification of a confusion—a move that in its very nature is error-reducing.

Some of our gains in moral insight prove themselves to us in just this way. Pete was behaving impossibly at home, screaming at his parents, acting arrogantly with his younger siblings, and he felt resentment all the time and was very unhappy. He felt a constant sense of being cheated of his rights, or at least that's how it was formulated by his parents to the social worker. Now things are much better. Pete applies this description himself to his former feelings. In a confused way, he felt that something more was owed to him as the eldest, and he resented not getting it. But he never would have subscribed to any such principle, and he clearly wants to repudiate it now. He thinks his previous behavior was unjustified, and that one shouldn't behave that way toward people. In other words, he's gone through a moral change; his views of what people owe each other in the family have altered. He's confident that this change represents moral growth, because it came about through dissipating a confused, largely unconsciously held belief, one that couldn't survive his recognizing its real nature.

These three cases are all examples of my third form of argument. They are, of course, all biographical. They deal with transitions in a single subject, whereas the standard disputes I have been discussing fall between people.

And they are often (in the first case, always) cases of inarticulate, intuitive confidence; and hence arguably have nothing to do with practical *reason* at all, if this is understood as a matter of forms of *argument*.

These two points are well taken. I have chosen the biographical context because this is where this order of justification occurs at its clearest. But the same form can be and is adapted to the situation of interpersonal argument. Imagine I am a parent, or the social worker, reasoning with Pete before the change. Or say I am a friend of Joe's talking out his confused and painful feelings about Anne. In either case, I shall be trying to offer them an interpretation of themselves which identifies these confused feelings as confused and which thus, if accepted, will bring about the self-justifying transition.

This is, I believe, the commonest form of practical reasoning in our lives, where we propose to our interlocutors transitions mediated by such error-reducing moves, by the identification of contradiction, the dissipation of confusion, or by rescuing from (usually motivated) neglect a consideration whose significance they cannot contest. But this is a form of argument where the appeal to criteria, or even to the differential performance of the rival views in relation to some decisive consideration, is quite beside the point. The transition is justified by the very nature of the move that effects it. Here the ad hominem mode of argument is at its most intense, and most fruitful.

In conclusion I would like to draw together the threads of this perhaps rambling discussion. I argued at the outset that practical arguments are in an important sense ad hominem. As a first approximation, I described these as arguments that appeal to what the opponent is already committed to, or at the least cannot lucidly repudiate. The notion that we might have to convince people of an ultimate value premise they undividedly and unconfusedly reject is, indeed, a ground for despair. Such radical gaps may exist, particularly between people from very different cultures; in this case, practical reason is certainly powerless.

But the discussion in the second section allows us to extend our notion of this kind of argument. It is not just cases where we can explicitly identify the common premise from the outset that allow of rational debate. This was in fact the case with my opening example. Both Nazi and myself accept some version of the principle "thou shalt not kill," together with a different set of exclusions. Rational argument can turn on why he can permit himself the exclusions he does; and in fact this historic position doesn't stand up very long to rational scrutiny. It was really mob hysteria masquerading as thought.

But our discussion of transitions shows how debate can be rationally conducted even where there is no such explicit common ground at the outset. Now these arguments, to the effect that some transition from X to Y is a gain, are also ad hominem, in two related ways. First, they are specifically directed to the holders of X, in a way that apodictic arguments never are. A foundational argument to the effect that Y is the correct thesis shows its superiority over the incompatible thesis X only incidentally. That proof also shows Y's superiority over all rivals. It establishes an absolute, not just a comparative claim. If I establish that the correct value for the law of attraction is the inverse square and not the inverse cube of the distance, this also rules out the simple inverse, the inverse of the fourth power, and so on.

It is crucial to transition arguments that they make a more modest claim. They are inherently comparative. The claim is not that Y is correct *simpliciter* but just that whatever is "ultimately true," Y is better than X. It is, one might say, less false. The argument is thus specifically addressed to the holders of X. Its message is: whatever else turns out to be true, you can improve your epistemic position by moving from X to Y; this step is a gain. But nothing need follow from this for the holders of third, independent positions. Above all, there is no claim to the effect that Y is the ultimate resting point of inquiry. The transition claim here is perfectly compatible with a further one which might one day be established, identifying a new position Z, which in turn supersedes Y. As MacIntyre puts it,

> we are never in a position to claim that now we possess the truth or now we are fully rational. The most that we can claim is that this is the best account which anyone has been able to give so far, and that our beliefs about what the marks of "a best account so far" are will themselves change in what are at present unpredictable ways.[17]

Now these arguments all make their case by bringing to light something the interlocutor cannot repudiate. Either they make better sense of inner difficulties than the interlocutor can (case 1); or they present a development which cannot be explained on the interlocutor's own terms (case 2); or they show the transition to Y to come about through a move that is intrinsically described as error-reducing (case 3). But in relation to the original example of arguing with a Nazi, these greatly extend the range of rational debate. For what they appeal to in the interlocutor's own commitments is not there, explicit at the outset, but has to be brought to light. The pattern of anomalies and contradiction only comes clear, and stands out as such, from the new position (case 1); the full significance of a hitherto marginalized form of understanding only becomes evident when the new position develops it (case 2); that my present stance reposes on contradiction, confusion, or screening out the relevant only emerges as I make the transition—indeed, in this case, making the transition is just coming to recognize this error (case 3).

The range of rational argument is greatly extended, in other words, once we see that not all disputes are between fully explicit positions. Here the canonical foundationalist model is likely to lead us astray. As we saw above with the second case, pre-Galilean science is indeed impregnable if we just think of its explicit standards of success: it has no cause to give any heed to technological payoff. But in fact this payoff constitutes a devastating argument, which we can only do justice to by articulating implicit understandings that have hitherto been given marginal importance. Now I would argue that a great deal of moral argument involves the articulation of the implicit, and this extends the range of the ad hominem far beyond the easy cases where the opponent offers us purchase in one explicit premise.

Naturally none of the above shows that all practical disputes are arbitrable in reason. Above all, it doesn't show that the most worrying cases, those dividing people of very different cultures, can be so arbitrated. Relativism still has something going for it, in the very diversity and mutual incomprehensibility of human moralities. Except in a dim way, which does more to disturb than enlighten us, we have almost no understanding at all of the place of human sacrifice, for instance, in the life of the Aztecs. Cortés simply thought that these people worshipped the devil, and only our commitment to a sophisticated pluralism stops us from making a similar lapidary judgment.

And yet I want to argue that these considerations on practical argument show that we shouldn't give up on reason too early. We don't need to be so intimidated by distance and incomprehensibility that we take them as sufficient grounds to adopt relativism. There are resources in argument. These have to be tried in each case, because nothing assures us either that relativism is false. We have to try and see.

Two such resources are relevant to this kind of difference. First, there is the effect of working out and developing an insight which is marginally present in all cultures. In its developed form, this will make new demands, ones which upset the moral codes of previous cultures. Yet the insight in its developed form may carry conviction; that is, once articulated it may be hard to gainsay. This is analogous to case 2 above, where the spectacular development of technology makes post-Galilean science hard to reject.

Second, the practices of previous cultures so challenged often make sense against the background of a certain cosmology, or of semiarticulate beliefs about the way things have to be. These can be successfully challenged and shown to be inadequate. Something of the kind was at stake in the discussion of our changed attitude to suffering. Indeed, that case seems to show both factors at work: we have developed new intuitions about the value and importance of ordinary life,[18] and, at the same time, we have fatally wounded the cosmology that made sense of the gruesome punishments. These together work to feed our convictions about the evil of unnecessary suffering.

Perhaps something similar can make sense of and justify our rejection of human sacrifice or—to take a less exotic example—of certain practices of subordinating women. In the latter case, the positive factor—the developed moral insight—is that of the worth of each human being, the injunction that humans must be treated as ends, which we often formulate in a doctrine of universal rights. There is something very powerful in this insight just because it builds on a basic human reaction, which seems to be present in some form everywhere: that humans are especially important and demand special treatment. (I apologize for the vagueness in this formulation, but I'm gesturing at something that occurs in a vast variety of different cultural forms.)

In many cultures, this sense of the special importance of the human being is encapsulated in religious and cosmological outlooks, and connected views of human social life, which turn it in directions antithetical to modern rights doctrine. Part of what is special about humans can be that they are proper food for the gods; or that they embody cosmic principles differentially between men and women, which imposes certain roles on each sex.

The rights doctrine presents human importance in a radical form, one that is hard to gainsay. This affirmation can be taken on several levels. Just empirically there seems to be something to it, although establishing this is not just a matter of counting heads, but of making a plausible interpretation of human history. One that seems plausible to me goes something like this: recurrently in history, new doctrines have been propounded which called on their adherents to move toward a relatively greater respect for human beings, one by one, at the expense of previously recognized forms of social encapsulation. This has been generally true of what people refer to as the higher religion. And, of course, it has been the case with modern secular ideologies like liberalism and socialism. Where these appeared, they exercised a powerful attraction for human beings. Sometimes their spread can be explained by conquest (Islam in the Middle East, liberalism in the colonial world) but frequently not (Buddhism in India, Christianity in the Mediterranean world, Islam in Indonesia). Disencapsulated respect for the human seems to say something to us humans.

But of course this is a remark from the "external" perspective, and doesn't by itself say anything about the place of reason. Can we perspicuously reconstruct these transitions in terms of *arguments?* This is hazardous, and what follows can only be a crude approximation. But I think it might be seen this way. Disencapsulated respect draws us because it articulates in a striking and far-reaching form what we already acknowledge in that vague term "human importance." Once you can grasp this possibility, it can't but seem prima facie right. A demand is "prima facie right" when it is such as to command our moral allegiance, if only some other, weightier considerations don't stand in our way. Probably most of us feel like this about the ideal anarchic communist society: we'd certainly go for it, if only . . .

But of course the condition I mentioned, "if one can grasp the possibility," is not pro forma. For many societies and cultures, a disencapsulated view is literally unimaginable. The prescriptions of general respect just seem like perverse violations of the order of things.

Once you get over this hump, however, and can imagine disencapsulation, a field of potential argument is established. Universal respect now seems a conceivable goal, and one that is prima facie right, if only . . . The argument now turns on whatever fits into this latter clause. Yes, women are human beings, and there is a case for giving them the same status as men, but unfortunately . . . the order of things requires that they adopt roles incompatible with this equality, or . . . they are crucially weaker or less endowed, and so can't hack it at men's level, or . . . and so on.

Here reason can get a purchase. These special pleadings can be addressed, and many of them found wanting, by rational argument. Considerations about the order of things can be undermined by the advance of our cosmological understanding. Arguments from unequal endowment are proven wrong by trying out equality. Inequalities in capacity that seem utterly solid in one cultural setting just dissolve when one leaves this context. No one would claim that argument alone has produced the revolution in the status of women over the last centuries and decades in the West. But it all had something to do with the fact that the opponents of these changes were thrown onto a kind of strategic defensive; that they had to argue about the "if onlys" and "but unfortunatelys." They had a position that was harder and harder to defend in reason.

But, one might argue, this is exactly where we are in danger of falling into ethnocentrism. The plight of, say, nineteenth-century opponents of women's franchise is utterly different from that of, say, certain Berber tribesmen today. On one account, the Berbers see the chastity of their womenfolk as central to the family honor, to the point where there can be a recognized obligation even to kill a kinswoman who has "lost" her virtue. Try telling them about Kant's second *Critique* or the works of John Stuart Mill, and you'll get a different reaction from that of mainstream western politicos of the nineteenth century.

The gap can seem unbridgeable: there is this claim about honor, and what can you say to that? Honor has to do with avoiding shame, and can you *argue* with people about what they find shameful? Well, yes and no. If honor and shame are taken as ultimates, and if the fact that they are differently defined in different societies is ignored or discounted as only showing the depravity of the foreigner, then no argument is possible. But if one takes seriously the variety of definitions and, alongside this, if one acknowledges that there are other moral or religious demands with which honor must be squared, then questions can arise about what really should be a matter of honor, what is true honor, what price honor, and the like. The thought can arise: maybe some other people have a better conception of honor, because theirs can be squared with the demands of God, say, or those of greater military efficacy, or control over fate.

The watershed between these two attitudes is more or less the one I mentioned above, whereby we become capable of conceiving a disencapsulated condition, or at least of seeing our society as one among many possible societies. This is undoubtedly among the most difficult and painful intellectual transitions for human beings. In fact, it may be virtually impossible, and certainly hazardous, to try to *argue* people over it. But what does this say about the limitations of reason? Nothing, I would argue. The fact that this stance is hard to get to doesn't show in any way that it isn't a more rational stance. In fact, each of our cultures is one possibility among many. People can and do live human lives in all of them. To be able sympathetically to understand this—or at least to understand some small subset of the range of cultures, and realize that we ought ideally to understand more—is to have a truer grasp of the human condition than those for whom alternative ways are utterly inconceivable. Getting people over this hump may require more than argument, but there is no doubt that this step is an epistemic gain. People may be unhappier as a result, and may lose something valuable that only unreflecting encapsulation gives you, but all that wouldn't make this encapsulation any less blind.

Even the most exotic differences, then, don't put paid to a role for reason. Of course, no one can show in advance that the "if onlys" or "but unfortunatelys" which stand in the way of universal rights can be rationally answered. It is just conceivable that some will arise which will themselves prove superior; more likely that there will be some where reason cannot arbitrate; and almost certain that we pay a price for our universalism in the loss of some goods bound up with earlier, more encapsulated forms of life. But none of this gives us cause a priori to take refuge in an agnostic relativism.

Unless, that is, we have already bought the faulty metaethic I've been attacking here. I want to end with the basic claim with which I started, since it underlies this whole exploration: that modern philosophy, and to some extent modern culture, has lost its grip on the proper patterns of practical reason. Moral argument is understood according to inappropriate models, and this naturally leads to skepticism and despair, which in turn has an effect on our conception of morality, gives it a new shape (or misshapes it). We are now in a better position to see some of the motivations of this misunderstanding.

I believe that we can identify in this discussion three orders of motivation which combine to blind us. First, the naturalist temper, with its hostility to the very notion of strong evaluation, tends to make the ad hominem argument seem irrelevant to ethical dispute. To show that your interlocutor is really committed to some good proves nothing about what he ought to do. To think it does is to commit the naturalistic fallacy.

Second, naturalism together with the critical temper have tended to brand ad hominem arguments as illegitimate. Reason should be as disengaged as possible from our implicit commitments and understandings, as it is in natural science, and as it must be if we are not to be victims of the status quo with all its imperfections and injustices. But once we neutralize our implicit understandings, by far the most important field of moral argument becomes closed and opaque to us. We lose sight altogether of the articulating function of reason.

This distorts our picture not only of practical reason, but also of much scientific argument. And this brings us to the third motive: the ascendancy of the foundationalist model of reasoning which comes to us from the epistemological tradition. This understands rational justification as (a) effected on the basis of criteria, (b) judging between fully explicit positions, and (c) yielding in the first instance absolute judgments of adequacy/inadequacy and comparative assessments only mediately from these. But we have just been seeing what an important role in our reasoning is played by irreducibly comparative judgments—judgments about transitions—by articulating the implicit, and by the direct characterization of transitional moves that make no appeal to criteria at all. To block all this from view through an apodictic model of reasoning is to make most moral discussion incomprehensible. But it also does not leave unimpaired our understanding of science and its history, as we have amply seen. The connections are in fact close between scientific explanation and practical reason: to lose sight of one is to fall into confusion about the other.

— 4 —

Lichtung or Lebensform: Parallels between Heidegger and Wittgenstein

When people mention Heidegger and Wittgenstein in the same breath, it is often to cite them both as thinkers who have helped us emerge, painfully and with difficulty, from the grip of modern rationalism. The emergence has also been only partial, and is still contested; indeed, it is always menaced with being rolled back. Hence the continuing relevance of the works of these philosophers, some of which appeared more than a half a century ago.

I use the term "rationalism" here, and this could be criticized even by people basically sympathetic to the current of thought I'm trying to articulate. There are a number of different ways of articulating the outlook, more a set of semiarticulate assumptions, that these two major thinkers "deconstructed." It has a number of different features, and we can argue about which are more fundamental. In speaking of rationalism, I suppose that a certain conception of reason played a determining role. My view is, in short, that the dominant conception of the thinking agent that both Heidegger and Wittgenstein had to overcome was shaped by a kind of ontologizing of rational procedure. That is, what were seen as the proper procedures of rational thought were read into the very constitution of the mind, made part of its very structure.

The result was a picture of the human thinking agent as disengaged, as occupying a sort of proto-variant of "the view from nowhere," to use Thomas Nagel's suggestive phrase.[1] Both Heidegger and Wittgenstein had to struggle to recover an understanding of the agent as engaged, as embedded in a culture, a form of life, a "world" of involvements, ultimately to understand the agent as embodied.[2]

I'd like to say a few things about this issue of engaged agency, because it is still difficult and controversial. What does "engagement" mean here? It is to say something like: the world of the agent is shaped by one's form of life, or history, or bodily existence. But what does it mean to have your "world shaped" by something? This is a relation subtly different from the ordinary causal link it is sometimes confused with.

Let's take a particular aspect of engagement: being embodied. That is, let's focus on the way our world is shaped by our being bodily agents of the kind that we are. This is something different from the way some of our functions as agents are determined by physical causes. For instance, as a perceiving agent I can't see the wall behind me. This can be explained by certain causal relations in physical terms: the light refracted off the surface of the wall behind me can't reach my retina. The behavior of light and my physical constitution are so disposed as to make this impossible. In this sense, my embodiment undoubtedly shapes my perception, and hence in a sense my world.

But this is a rather different relation from the following example. As I sit here and take in the scene before me, I see a complex structure. It is oriented vertically, some things are "up," others are "down"; and in depth, some are "near," others "far." Some objects "lie to hand," others are "out of reach"; some constitute "unsurmountable obstacles" to movement, others are "easily displaced." My present position doesn't give me a really good purchase on the scene—for that I would have to shift farther to the left. And so on.

Here is a "world shaped" by embodiment in the sense that the way of experiencing or living the world is essentially that of an agent with this particular kind of body. It is an agent who acts to maintain equilibrium upright, who can deal with things close up immediately, and has to move to get to things farther away, who can grasp certain kinds of things easily and others not, can remove certain obstacles and not others, can move to make a scene more perspicuous; and so on. To say that this world is essentially that of this agent is to say that the terms in which we describe this experience—say those in quotes in the previous paragraph—make sense only against the background of this kind of embodiment. To understand what it is to "lie to hand" you have to understand what it is to be an agent with the particular bodily capacities that humans have. Some creature from another planet might be unable to grasp this as a projectible term. Of course, it might work out some descriptions that were roughly extensionally equivalent, but to project this term the way we do, you have to understand what it is to be human.

Thus there are two quite different kinds of relationship which might be expressed by saying that our experience is shaped by our bodily constitution. In the first—the case of the wall behind me—we note some consequences of this constitution for our experience, however characterized. In the second, we point out how the nature of this experience is formed by this constitution, and how the terms in which this experience is described are given their sense only in relation to this form of embodiment. The first kind of relation is asserted in an ordinary statement of contingent causality. The second concerns by contrast the conditions of intelligibility of certain terms. It is this second relation I want to invoke in speaking of our "world being shaped" by body, culture, form of life. The ways in which our world is so shaped define the contours of what I am calling engaged agency—what Heidegger sometimes referred to as the "finitude" of the knowing agent.[3]

Now the other half of my claim is that the dominant rationalist view has screened out this engagement, has given us a model of ourselves as disengaged thinkers. In speaking of the "dominant" view I am not only thinking of the theories which have been preeminent in modern philosophy, but also of an outlook which has to some extent colonized the common sense of our civilization. This offers us the picture of agents who in perceiving the world take in "bits" of information from their surroundings, and then "process" them in some fashion, in order to emerge with the "picture" of the world they have; who then act on the basis of this picture to fulfill their goals, through a "calculus" of means and ends.

The popularity of this view is part of what makes computer models of the mind so plausible to laypeople in our day. These models fitted neatly into already established categories. The "information-processing" construal builds on a long-supported earlier conception, whereby atomic "ideas" were combined in the mind and made the basis of a calculation underlying action. Classical Cartesian and empiricist epistemologies provided earlier variants of this conception, which combine an atomism of input with a computational picture of mental function. These two together dictated a third feature: "factual" information is distinguished from its "value," its relevance for our purposes. This separation is dictated by atomism, since the merely factual features can be distinguished from their having some role to play in our goals. But it is also encouraged by another underlying motivation, which I will come to in a minute. In any case, the composite traditional conception has a third feature, which we might call "neutrality," whereby the original input of information is shorn of its evaluative relevance, is merely the registering of "fact."

Now in some respects this view has roots in the common sense of (in any case) our civilization, going back before the modern era. But in other important respects, this conception was shaped and entrenched in modern times. And one of the factors it was shaped by was modern reason—or so I want to suggest in my perhaps tendentious term "rationalism."

There are two facets of modern reason which are relevant here. The first is that the modern conception, starting with Descartes, focuses on procedure. Reason is not that faculty in us which connects us to an order of things in the universe which itself can be called rational. Rather reason is that faculty whereby we think properly. In its theoretical employment, reason serves to build a picture of the world. Rationality requires that we scrutinize this building closely, and not let our view of things just form itself distractedly, or self-indulgently, or following the prejudices of our day. Rationality involves a careful scrutiny by thinking of its own processes. This determines the reflexive turn of modern rationalism. Careful construction of our picture of things requires that we identify and follow a trustworthy procedure. Modern thinkers differ on what this is, and there is a crucial and hotly contested difference in the seventeenth century between, for instance, that defined by the clear and distinct perception of Descartes and that organized around the rules of believable evidence of Locke. But both views call for reflexive self-policing in the name of a canonical procedure.

More to the point, both procedures require that we break down our too hastily acquired beliefs into their components, and scrutinize their composition to see if they are properly to be trusted. They both require that we treat candidate beliefs in this sense atomistically. Now a "method" of this sort is, in certain domains, an uncontestable advance over earlier ways of proceeding. The fateful step was not so much its formulation, but rather what I called its ontologizing, that is, the reading of the ideal method into the very constitution of the mind. It was one thing to call on us to break down our beliefs into their possibly separable components, another to think that the primitive information which enters the mind must do so in atomic bits. The "simple ideas" of Locke are a classical example of such a reification of procedure, pouring it as it were in theoretical concrete and building it into the constitution of the mind itself.

But this reification has been immensely influential, conferring on the resulting model of the mind all the prestige and unchallengeable force that the procedures of reason have acquired in our civilization. The more we learn to treat things rationalistically, the more we are inclined to accept the corresponding view of how we "really" operate. The atomist-computational view owes part of its powerful hold on common sense to this.

"Simple ideas" result from reifying the procedure of challenging too-hasty interpretations and inferences in order to get back to the basic data. But there was another important feature of correct, scientific thought as conceived in the seventeenth-century revolution, which has also strongly influenced our ontology of the subject. This is the feature that Nagel calls "objectivity." Our thinking is objective when it escapes the distortions and parochial perspectives of our kind of subjectivity, and grasps the world as it is. Seventeenth-century thinkers were impressed with the way our embodied experience, and our ordinary way of being in the world (to use contemporary language), could mislead us. Descartes pointed out how the way we take our everyday experience leads us to attribute, say, the color to the object or to situate the pain in the tooth. These localizations were fine for Aristotelian theory, but the new mechanism showed that they were illusory. Only "primary" properties were really "in" the objects; "secondary" properties, such as color, were effects produced in the mind by concatenations of primary properties in things. Seeing things as really colored was one of those distorting effects of our peculiar constitution as a substantial union of soul and body. What comes to be called objectivity requires an escape from this.

Again, because of our situation in the world, we tend to "see" the sun "rising" and "setting," we "feel" directly that objects stop when they are no longer being pushed, and the like. One of the recurrent themes of seventeenth-century scientific discovery was the gap it showed between the real underlying constitution of things and the way things appeared to common sense. Sometimes the common appearance "regestalted" under the impact of the discovery: before Galileo people "saw" that cannonballs shot straight forward and then dropped to the ground. After, it was "obvious" that their trajectory was curved. But in very many cases, we still can't help seeing things in the old way. The development of science since then has only entrenched this sense of strangeness, of the distance between underlying truth and our ordinary ways of seeing. An experience of everyday space which remains Euclidean coexists with our settled convictions about the curvature of space.

All this has nourished the aspiration to objectivity as Nagel defines it:

"The attempt is made to view the world not from a place within it, or from the vantage point of a special kind of life or awareness, but from nowhere in particular and no form of life in particular at all. The object is to discount for the features of our pre-reflective outlook that make things appear as they do, and thereby to reach an understanding of things as they really are."[4]

There is nothing wrong with this aspiration as it stands—except perhaps the hyperbolic form in which it is stated here. If we stated it slightly more modestly, as the goal of disengaging from those features of our pre-reflective outlook which we come to discover are distortive of reality, then it is not only unexceptionable but an indispensable condition of pursuing, say, modern physics. The fateful move was, once again, the ontologizing of this disengaged perspective, reading it into the constitution of the mind itself, and relegating the distortions to the periphery, as the result of error, inattention, mere lapse; or as a feature only of the brute pre-processed input, not touching the procedures of processing themselves.

Thus the authors of the *Port Royal Logic* describe it as a culpable weakness in us that we tend to attribute color or heat to the things we experience.[5] They and the other foundational thinkers of seventeenth-century epistemology could agree that the input to our minds was extremely limited and lacunary, but the constitution of the mind as a thinking agency was unaffected by these limitations, which offered no real excuse for, even if they helped to explain the prevalence of, the distortions we typically fall prey to. The disengaged perspective, which might better have been conceived as a rare and regional achievement of a knowing agent whose normal stance was engaged, was read into the very nature of mind. This was the major motivation I alluded to as underpinning the third major feature in the modern common-sense view of the mind, the "neutrality" of the original input.

This ontologizing of the disengaged perspective took two major forms. One was dualism, as with Descartes. Disengagement can be seen as getting free of the perspective of embodied experience. It is this perspective which is responsible for our attributing the color to the object; it is this which makes us give disproportionate importance to the senses and imagination in our account of knowing. That the thinking activity of the mind is really in its essential character free from these distorting media shows that the mind is essentially nonbodily. So argues Descartes in the celebrated passage about the piece of wax which closes the second *Meditation*.

But what looks like a totally antithetical ontology could do just as well, that of monistic mechanism: thinking is an event realized in a body, mechanistically understood. This idea is given its modern form in Hobbes, and thus has just as long a pedigree as the Cartesian alternative. Mechanism can do as well as dualism to underpin the disengaged perspective, because the underlying belief was that we need to attain this perspective in order to do justice to a mechanistic universe. The assumption is common ground to Descartes and to his empiricist or mechanist critics. But to the extent that we understand our thinking mechanistically, we have to understand it outside any context of engagement. The very relationship to something that defines a "world shaping," and hence identifies a form of agency as engaged, can't be stated in a mechanistic perspective. The other relationship, of the causal dependency of experience on some physical conditions, can of course figure in such an account. It is, indeed, of the essence of this kind of explanation. But nothing can be said about the conditions of intelligibility. That's why mechanists constantly misunderstand descriptions of experience as engaged as statements of causal dependency, and are puzzled when they are described as denying such engagement. But in fact their denial is of the most effective sort, that of leaving a rival thesis no ontological room for coherent formulation.

To the extent that we explain thinking mechanistically, as with the present wave of computer-based theories of mind, what it means to say that the agent finds the input intelligible can only be described in terms of the operations he can put this input through. The unintelligible is what can't be processed. But these operations are themselves mechanistically explained. So any statement of something like "conditions of intelligibility" for some input would have to take the form of some statement about how the mechanism is hard-wired or contingently programmed, that is, about the causal relations of the input to the series of steps it can trigger off. The world-shaping relation as defined above can't be stated.[6]

Both dualism and mechanism are thus ontologies of disengagement. With the decline over the centuries in the credibility of dualism, mechanism has gained ground. But what has helped to underpin the credibility of both, or rather of the view that sees them as the only two viable alternatives, is the power of the disengaged model of the mind, which draws on the prestige of the procedures of disengagement, channeling its authority into a picture of the mind and its constitution which has the three features mentioned above. What I have called the ontologizing move brings about this (dubiously legitimate) transfer. The disengaged picture of mind then adds strength to mechanism; and since mechanistic explanations themselves have great prestige because of their association with the spectacular successes of natural science, support can flow the other way as well. A picture of mind and an underlying theory of its explanation are thus locked into a posture of mutual support, and this complex has sunk deep into the common sense of our age. When one runs into trouble, the other comes to its support. If the picture can be made to seem implausible on the phenomenological level (and this is not hard to do), we can be reassured by the reflection that it all has to be explained mechanistically on a more basic level anyway, and at that level the picture *must* be right. Reciprocally, the force of otherwise powerful arguments against mechanism is neutralized by the thought that in some sense we "know" that thinking is all information processing anyway, so surely some computer-based explanation must hold in the last analysis.

When I say that this rationalist model has entered common sense, I mean partly that the first reaction of most people when asked to theorize about thinking takes the form of this model, but also that it benefits from the onus of argument. That is, it stands as the default position. Powerful philosophical arguments have to be marshaled to convince people to think differently about these matters, to shake them out of what seems obvious. But in the absence of such a challenge, the model itself seems to need no defense.

Now as I said at the outset, Heidegger and Wittgenstein are grouped because they marshaled such powerful arguments, in each case in favor of a view of human agency as finite or engaged. The parallel can be taken farther, before we allow them to diverge. Both have helped to prize us loose from rationalism by making us appreciate the role of the background, in one sense of this widely used term.

The sense I'm pointing to here is that which arises inevitably in connection with any view of engaged agency. Engaged agency as I described it is an agency whose experience is only made intelligible by being placed in the context of the kind of agency it is. Thus our embodiment makes our experience of space as oriented up-down understandable. In this relation the first term, the form of agency (embodiment), stands to the second (our experience), as a context conferring intelligibility. When we find a certain experience intelligible, what we are attending to, explicitly and expressly, is this experience. The context stands as the unexplicited horizon within which—or to vary the image, as the vantage point out of which—this experience can be understood. To use Michael Polanyi's language, it is subsidiary to the focal object of awareness; it is what we are "attending from" as we attend to the experience.[7]

Now this is the sense in which I want to use the term "background." It is that of which I am not simply unaware, as I am unaware of what is now happening on the other side of the moon, because it makes intelligible what I am uncontestably aware of; at the same time, I am not explicitly or focally aware of it, because that status is already occupied by what it is making intelligible. Another way of stating the first condition, that I am not simply unaware of it, is to say that the background is what I am capable of articulating, that is, what I can bring out of the condition of implicit, unsaid contextual facilitator—what I can make articulate, in other words. In this activity of articulating, I trade on my familiarity with this background. What I bring out to articulacy is what I "always knew," as we might say, or what I had a "sense" of, even if I didn't "know" it. We are at a loss exactly what to say here, where we are trying to do justice to our not having been simply unaware.

But if the background is brought to articulacy, doesn't it then lose the second feature, that of not being the focal, explicit object? This seemingly plausible inference is based on a misunderstanding. The background is what makes certain experiences intelligible to us. It makes us capable of grasping them, makes them understandable. So it can be represented as a kind of explicit understanding, or "pre-understanding" in Heidegger's term. To bring it to articulacy is to take (some of) this and make it explicit. But the reason for the two words in parentheses in my preceding sentence is that the idea of making the background completely explicit, of undoing its status as background, is incoherent in principle.

Remember that the background is what arises with engaged agency. It is the context of intelligibility of experience for this kind of agent. If a given kind of agency is engaged in this sense, then its experience is not intelligible outside this context. But this goes just as much for bits of articulation of what was formerly pre-understanding as it does for the experience this made intelligible. There must always be a context from which we are attending if we are to understand the experience of a being like this. So bringing to articulation still supposes a background. In this regard the two words in parentheses in the preceding paragraph are misleading. They might make us think of articulating the background in qualitative terms. We do some of it now, so why not, bit by bit, do all of it eventually? But if we treat it as a standing condition of intelligibility, from which we have to attend (in Polanyi's terminology), then the incoherence of this notion becomes clear.

The paradoxical status of the background can then be appreciated. It can be made explicit, because we aren't completely unaware of it. But the expliciting itself supposes a background. The very fashion in which we operate as engaged agents within such a background makes the prospect of total expliciting incoherent. The background can't in this sense be thought of quantitatively at all.

One of the features that distinguishes a view of human agency as engaged from the disengaged view is that the former has some place for this kind of background. On the disengaged view, and in particular the mechanist theory that often underpins it, there is of course no explicit rejection of this notion, but the entire issue to which it provides some answer doesn't arise. Intelligibility is assumed from the start and doesn't need a context to provide it. It is understood that the bits of input information are taken as such from the beginning, and that the operations that follow amount to a processing of the information. In the case of computer-based theories of the mind, this reading of input and process is built into the very definition of what occurs as the realization of a program. Its being describable as such is a sufficient condition of its counting as such.[8]

So it is not surprising that the philosophies which have challenged the disengaged picture have all had some place for a notion of background. I have referred to Heidegger's notion of pre-understanding, or a pre-thematized understanding of our world. Wittgenstein makes use of a similar notion, as when he shows what has to be supposed as already understood when we try to define something ostensively or to name something.

But the background doesn't figure in these philosophies only as a doctrine. It also plays a crucial role in their argumentative strategy. They overturn the disengaged picture through an articulation of the background that it too has to suppose. In doing this, they can be seen as answering a potential challenge that a defender of the disengaged view might throw back at critics: if you're right, and we are always drawing on a background understanding that gives intelligibility to our experience, then even my account of the knowing agent in terms of the disengaged picture must draw on such a background to be intelligible to me. For according to you, what I'm really describing is the disengaged stance, which you see as a special and regional achievement by an agent whose experience as a whole is made intelligible only by a background of the kind you invoke. As a special stance, one among the many possibilities of this agent, having a determinate place in the world, this must as well be made intelligible by some background understanding. So articulate for me the implicit understanding I'm allegedly drawing on; show me the pre-understanding I couldn't be doing without. Then I'll have to believe you. Otherwise, stop prattling about my being held captive by a picture, caught in a fly-bottle, or suffering from *Seinsvergessenheit*.

The line of argument of the major deconstructors of the disengaged picture could serve as an answer to this challenge. It undermines the picture by bringing out the background we need for the operations described in the picture to make sense, whereby it becomes clear that this background can't fit within the limits that the disengaged view prescribes. Once understood against its background, the account shows itself to be untenable.

The pioneer in this kind of argument, in whose steps all deconstructors find themselves treading, is Kant. Not that he intended to refute the disengaged view as such. But he did manage to upset one of its crucial features, at least in an earlier variant. The arguments of the transcendental deduction can be seen in a number of different lights. But one way to take them is as a final laying to rest of a certain atomism of the input that had been espoused by empiricism. As this came to Kant through Hume, it seemed to be suggesting that the original level of knowledge of reality (whatever that turned out to be) came in particulate bits, individual "impressions." This level of information could be isolated from a later stage in which these bits were put together, such as in cause-effect beliefs. We find ourselves forming these beliefs, but we can by taking a stance of reflective scrutiny (which we have seen is fundamental to modern epistemology) separate the basic level from the too-hasty conclusions we leap to. This analysis allegedly reveals, for instance, that nothing in the phenomenal field corresponds to the necessary connection we so easily interpolate between cause and effect.[9]

Kant undercuts this whole way of thinking by showing that it supposes that each particulate impression is being taken as a bit of potential information. It purports to be *about* something. The primitive distinction recognized by empiricists between impressions of sensation and those of reflection amounts to an acknowledgment of this. The buzzing in my head is discriminated from the noise I hear in the neighboring woods, in that the first is a component of how I feel, and the second tells me something about what's happening out there. So even a particulate "sensation," really to be sensation (in the empiricist sense, as opposed to reflection), has to have this dimension

of "aboutness." This will later be called "intentionality," but Kant speaks of
the necessary relation between knowledge and its object (A104).

With this point secured, Kant argues that this relationship to an object
would be impossible if we really were to take the impression as an utterly
isolated content, without any link to others. To see it as about something is
to place it somewhere, at the least out in the world as against in me, to give
it a location in a world that, while it is in many respects indeterminate and
unknown to me, can't be wholly so. The unity of this world is presupposed
by anything that could present itself as a particulate bit of *information,* and
so whatever we mean by such a bit, it couldn't be utterly without relation to
others. The background condition for this favorite supposition of empiricist
philosophy, the simple impression, forbids our giving it the radical sense
that Hume seemed to propose for it. To attempt to violate this background
condition is to fall into incoherence. Really to succeed in breaking all links
between individual impressions would be to lose all sense of awareness of
anything.

The transcendental deduction, and related arguments in the *Critique of
Pure Reason,* can be seen as a turning point in modern philosophy. With
hindsight, we can see it as the first attempt to articulate the background that
the modern disengaged picture itself requires for the operations it describes
to be intelligible, and to use this articulation to undermine the picture.
Once you go through this transition, the whole philosophical landscape
changes, because the issue of background understanding is out in the open.
A crucial feature of the reified views which arise from ontologizing the
canonical procedures of modern epistemology is that they make this issue
invisible. The conditions of intelligibility are built into the elements and
processes of the mind as internal properties. The isolated impression *is* intelligibly information on its own, just as the house is red or the table is square.
It has all the particulate, separable existence of an external object. Locke
treats simple ideas as analogous to the materials we use for building.[10] This
outlook forgets that for something to be intelligibly X is for it to *count as*
intelligibly X, and that there are always contextual conditions for anything
to count as something.

In its original Kantian form, this revolutionary notion sweeps away the
atomism of modern epistemology. In this sense Kant is followed by all those
who have come after. The very move that de-reifies our account of the
knowing agent has an inherently holistic bent. What was formerly built into
the elements is now attributed to the background they all share.

Heidegger and Wittgenstein follow this pioneering Kantian form of argument. In *Sein und Zeit* (Being and Time) Heidegger argues that things are disclosed first as part of a world, that is, as the correlates of concerned involvement, and within a totality of such involvements. This undercuts the first and the third feature of the disengaged picture, and hence makes the second feature inoperative. The first feature, the atomism of input, is denied by the notion of a totality of involvements. The third feature, neutrality, is undercut by the basic thesis that things are first disclosed in a world ready to hand *(zuhanden)*. To think of this character as something we project onto things which are first perceived neutrally is to make a fundamental mistake.[11]

Heidegger's discussion in *Sein und Zeit* is sometimes taken by unsympathetic readers to be an interesting discussion of everyday existence which has no relevance to the philosophical issues of ontology he claims to be discussing. So we usually treat things as tools or obstacles, in their relevance to our activities—what does this show about the priority of neutral information? Of course we aren't *aware* of things most of the time as neutral objects, but this doesn't show that the disengaged account is wrong. Our ordinary everyday consciousness must itself be seen as a construct. We should not make the pre-Galilean mistake of thinking that things are as they appear, even in matters of the mind. So runs a common complaint by supporters of the disengaged view against "phenomonology."

But Heidegger's intention is plainly other than just reminding us of what it's like to live in the world at an everyday level. The purport of his argument is the same as Kant's and could also be invoked as an answer to the challenge I voiced above. The aim is to show that grasping things as neutral objects is one of our possibilities only against the background of a way of being in the world in which things are disclosed as ready to hand. Grasping things neutrally requires modifying our stance to them, which primitively has to be one of involvement. Heidegger is arguing, like Kant, that the comportment to things described in the disengaged view requires for its intelligibility to be situated within an enframing and continuing stance to the world that is antithetical to it—hence this comportment couldn't be original and fundamental. The very condition of its possibility forbids us to give this neutralizing stance the paradigmatic place in our lives that the disengaged picture supposes.

This argument about the conditions of possibility, the conditions of intelligibly realizing the stance, is carried in Heidegger's use of the term *ursprünglich*. It doesn't just mean "prior in time," but something stronger. Our *ursprünglich* stance comes before but also as a condition of what follows and modifies it. It is carried in his repeated use of the phrase *zunächst und zumeist* (first and mostly). Once again this sounds deceptively weak. It is applied to a way of being that is not just there earlier and more frequently, but also provides the background for what is not it.

Wittgenstein's line of argument in the *Philosophical Investigations* is even more obviously parallel with Kant's. In a sense, he does for an atomism of meaning what Kant did for an atomism of information input. His target is a theory of language and meaning which, although he finds its paradigm in Augustine, was also espoused and developed by thinkers of the disengaged view. The atomism of meaning consisted in the view that a word was given meaning by being linked to an object in a relation of "naming" or "signifying." There is not only a parallel here to the atomism of post-Cartesian epistemology, but the two were interwoven in the classical statements of this theory of mind. Locke argues that a word gets its meaning not by signifying the object directly, but rather the idea in the mind that represents this object.[12] This amendment to the Augustinian theory is what opens the way to the supposition that each person might speak a different language, since different inner ideas might correspond in each person's mind to some public object being named. A quite private language, in which words mean things for me that no one else can know, now seems a distinct possibility, a skeptical threat not to be easily conjured. It is against this "modernized" form of the theory that Wittgenstein's array of arguments is largely deployed.

The atomism of meaning turns out to be untenable for exactly the same reason that Kant demonstrated for the atomism of input. Its proponents suppose that a word can be given meaning in some ceremony of naming, or that its meaning can be imparted by pointing to the object it names. A good part of Wittgenstein's argument in the *Investigations* consists in showing that this kind of ostensive definition works only if the learner understands a great deal about the workings of language, and the place of this particular word in it. The "grammar" of the relevant part of the language is presupposed, because "it shows the post where the new word is stationed." Naming something seems like a primitive, self-sufficient operation, but when one takes it as such, "one forgets that a great deal of stage-setting in the language is presupposed if the mere act of naming is to make sense."[13]

Wittgenstein is explicit in this last remark about the conditions of intelligibility. The idea that the meaning of a word consists only in its relation to the object it names, a conception by its nature atomistic, comes to grief on the realization that each such relation draws on a background understanding and doesn't make sense without it. But this understanding concerns not individual words, but the language games in which they figure, and eventually the whole form of life in which these games have sense. The Augustinian theory does come close to modeling bits of our understanding of language. But when we see the conditions of intelligibility of these bits, we are forced to abandon it as a model for understanding language in general. The theory was born of a reifying move. It built this background understanding into individual word-thing relations and made them self-sufficient. The liberating step comes when we see that they need a background and can explore this in all its richness and variety.

The theory supposes this whole background understanding, which we only acquire when we learn language, as already built into the first word-thing relation we learn. This is the kind of position we're in when we learn a *second* language. We already know what it is for a word to have a place in the whole, and usually have a sense of what the place is of the word they're now trying to teach us. The error is to read this condition back into the acquisition of our original language. "Augustine describes the learning of human language as if the child came into a strange country and did not understand the language of the country; that is, as if it already had a language, only not this one" (32).

I have been drawing Wittgenstein and Heidegger together in these pages, seeing their philosophies as parallel attacks on the disengaged picture of the mind. Both put forward against this an account of engaged agency. Heidegger speaks of "finitude" in his account of human being *(Dasein)*. Wittgenstein places the meanings of our words in the context of our form of life *(Lebensform)*. Both are therefore concerned with the context of intelligibility of knowledge, thought, and meaning. Both propose some notion of background; and, more, both articulate some part of this background whose neglect has allowed the disengaged view to seem plausible. Articulation plays a crucial part in their argumentative strategy; it is central to the innovating force of their philosophy.

There are therefore good reasons for mentioning them in the same breath, as there are for going back again and again to their arguments. What makes the latter so necessary is the hold of the disengaged view on our thought and culture, which has a lot to do, of course, with the hegemony of institutions and practices that require and entrench a disengaged stance:

science, technology, rationalized forms of production, bureaucratic administration, a civilization committed to growth, and the like. The kind of thinking of which both are variants has a certain counter-cultural significance,
an inherent thrust against the hegemonic forms of our time. This emerges,
for instance, in their both being critics of modern technological civilization:
Heidegger explicitly, in some of his best-known writings, such as the essay
on technology ("Die Frage nach der Technik"); Wittgenstein in taking his
distance from the chauvinism of modern instrumental-rational culture, as in
his "Reflections on Frazer's *Golden Bough.*"

But this anti-hegemonic thrust can be worked out in a wide variety of
ways. And here perhaps our two authors part company. We can't be dogmatic here, because each of them is rather enigmatic when it comes to
the ultimate ethical-political direction of his work. Heidegger notoriously
thought he discerned a definite political direction in Nazism. But not only
did he retreat from this (in a shamelessly unforthright manner, it is true),
but it is not very clear just how this particular political commitment flowed
from his early insights, as articulated, say, in *Sein und Zeit.* If it can be connected to the passages on resoluteness and authenticity, the close connection
between these and the pathbreaking existential analytic of being-in-the-
world is yet to be convincingly established, to say the least.

Perhaps we can get at the divergence by taking up a further feature of
the disengaged picture from which they both depart. I mentioned three
features above: atomism, processing, neutrality. But there is a fourth, which
has been of enormous significance, not least ethically and politically. This
view is what one might call monological. It situates thought and knowledge
within the mind of the individual. Of course we share things, such as bodies
of knowledge and language, but these are seen as matters we converge on.
It means, for instance, that my language is close to yours and to hers and to
his. If I am to be a speaker, then there must be such a thing as my language,
my idiolect; and if there is to be common knowledge, then it must be first
of all my knowledge, and yours, and hers and his.

The disengaged view is irresistibly monological, because the explicit
knowledge it focuses on must consist of input and processing, which can
only take place in individuals. Once we underpin it with a mechanistic
account, monologicality is reinforced by the thought that all this must be
going on within individual organisms. But once we see the crucial role of
the background, we are liberated from this perspective. The background
understanding we share, interwoven with our practices and ways of relating,

isn't necessarily something we partake in as individuals. That is, it can be part of the background understanding of a certain practice or meaning that it is not mine but ours; and it can indeed be "ours" in a number of ways: as something intensely shared, which binds a community; or as something quite impersonal, where we act just as "anyone" does. Bringing in the background allows us to articulate the ways in which our form of agency is nonmonological, in which the seat of certain practices and understandings is precisely *not* the individual but one of the common spaces between.

Both Heidegger and Wittgenstein bring out nonmonological facets of human agency. Heidegger does so, for instance, in according primacy to *das Man* (the crowd); Wittgenstein, for instance, in valorizing the way in which a word like "pain" gets its sense in transactions between people rather than in a contemplative grasp of inner experience; both in their understanding of language as that first and foremost of a community.

But at this point there seems to be a divergence. Heidegger connects the anti-monological thrust to a general attack on "subjectivism" or "humanism," doctrines that try to understand awareness and thought as powers or properties of the human subject. Heidegger's desire to avoid these is of a piece with his central concern for *Lichtung* (clearing). What Heidegger is trying to get at in this term, and in some of his uses of "being," is the fact that there is any disclosure at all, that things can appear and be experienced and known. The central account of this reality in the ancient tradition descending from Plato turns on the notion of the Idea. When that became incredible, an account arose which sees disclosure as depending on a capacity of the subject to mirror things in inner representation. Heidegger wants to argue that this account is distortive in an equal and opposite way to the Platonic one, and he wants to use the anti-monological thrust of an analysis of finitude to take us out of the subject again. *Lichtung* comes about through being-in-the-world—which the Platonic view failed to acknowledge; but it is not simply an inner capacity of humans. Coming to recognize this is part of a transformed stance toward the world in which the will to power would no longer be central. The principal failing in the human-centered accounts of *Lichtung* is that they cannot do justice to the ways in which, in articulating the world, we are responding to something that is not us. Objectivity is something we recognize only in the disengaged stance; when our articulation is not in the service of a description of the neutral universe, we tend to think of it as dedicated to self-expression. Another possibility is systematically blocked out: an articulation of things which would lay out their meanings for us (and hence where the discourse would not be that of science) but where the meanings would not be merely human-centered (and hence the discourse would not be one of self-expression).

One might be able to argue that something analogous could be found in the deeply puzzling and enigmatic religious dimension of Wittgenstein's thought. But on the surface, a work like the *Philosophical Investigations* points in a quite different direction. The ultimate term to which the account of meaning refers us is that of *Lebensform*. And this seems to offer the prospect of an account of the human way of life which would overcome the illusions of the disengaged perspective and help us to see more clearly the distortions that our hegemonic practices and institutions have imposed on us. Wittgenstein's philosophy has been seen as the basis of a kind of liberating naturalism.[14] It could, in other words, be seen as the basis for a new humanism.

"Humanism" versus "anti-humanism": the two philosophies can easily be portrayed as antithetical. But I'm not sure that's accurate. Quite apart from the uncertainties of my interpretation, and the enigmatic character of both philosophers, it is far from established that Heidegger's anti-humanism must be taken as a rejection of the aspirations we associate with the term humanism. It has been so considered by Derrida and other French "Heideggerians." It might in a rather different form be part of an attack on the central aspirations of modernity itself, say freedom and reason—although those who want to make such a frontal attack are often suspicious of Heidegger as well. But the thesis that we have to go beyond subjectivism in our articulation of meanings—a stance that we can perhaps see expressed in some of our best modern artists and writers—is not itself tied to either position.

Reciprocally, a Wittgensteinian humanism would have an important place for a critique of "subjectivism." Perhaps these two important twentieth-century philosophers, for all their difference of language and the divergent paths they explored, can both serve as sources for the kind of humanism that would raise an adequate challenge to the hegemony of bureaucratic-technical reason in our lives.

─ 5 ─

The Importance of Herder

Isaiah Berlin helped to rescue Herder from his relative neglect by philosophers.[1] His seminal role in the creation of post-Romantic thought and culture has gone largely unnoticed, at least in the English-speaking world. The fact that Herder is not the most rigorous of thinkers probably makes it easier to ignore him. But deeply innovative thinkers don't have to be rigorous in order to originate important ideas. The insights they capture in striking images can inspire other, more philosophically exigent minds to more exact formulation. This was exemplified, I believe, in the relation of Herder to Hegel. The consequence has been that the earlier thinker drops out of sight, and the later becomes the canonical reference point for certain ideas, such as what I call, following Berlin, the "expressivist" understanding of the human person.[2]

This losing sight of origins can be of more than historiographical significance. It may also be that we still have something important to learn from the original statement of certain foundational ideas that has yet to be captured in recognized "philosophical" formulations. I think this is true of another one of Herder's crucial contributions, his expressivist theory of language. My (perhaps overdramatic) claim is that Herder is the hinge figure who originates a fundamentally different way of thinking about language and meaning. This way has had a tremendous impact on modern culture. It has not quite swept all before it, since there are important segments of contemporary thought which resist these insights, but even they have been transformed in ways that can be traced to the Herder revolution.

79

I can't make good this claim across its whole extent here. My strategy will be rather to focus on a key passage in Herder, his rejection of Condillac's theory of the origin of language and the related invocation of *réflexion* as essential to language. I hope to make visible in this microcosm certain basic themes and assumptions of our contemporary understanding of language.

I call Herder a hinge figure: he swings our thought about language into a quite different angle. And as so often happens, the resulting change of perspective makes it hard to grasp just what has happened. People in the old and new perspectives tend to talk past each other, constantly translating the interlocutor's claims into their own terms and thus distorting them.

The old perspective, which has a venerable pedigree, is the one Wittgenstein attacks in the form of an influential statement by Augustine.[3] It can be defined in terms of its "designative" approach to the question of meaning.[4] Words get their meaning from being used to designate objects. What they designate is their meaning. This ancient view gets a new lease on life in the seventeenth century with the theories of Hobbes and Locke, where it is interwoven with the new "way of ideas." From the amalgam emerges a powerful picture of the role of language in human thought.

In the following century a new question arises. In keeping with the eighteenth-century preoccupation with origins, which we can also see reflected in theories of social evolution by Smith and Ferguson, there is a growing interest in explaining how language first arose. Condillac's answer, one of the most influential, draws on Locke's designative theory. In his book he offers a fable, a "just so" story, to illustrate how language might have arisen.[5] Two children in a desert utter certain cries and gestures as natural expressions of feeling. These are what Condillac calls "natural signs." By contrast, language uses "instituted signs." The story is meant to explain how the second emerged out of the first. He argues that each child, seeing the other, say, cry out in distress, would come to see the cry as a sign of something (what caused the distress). Then the child would be able to take the step of using the sign to refer to the cause of distress. The first sign would have been instituted. The children have their first word, and language is born. The lexicon would then increase slowly, term by term.

Herder in his *Abhandlung über den Ursprung der Sprache* (Essay on the Origins of Language; 1772) zeroes in on this story and declares it utterly inadequate.[6] As an account of origins, it presupposes just what we want explained. It takes the relation of signifying for granted, as something that the children already grasp instinctively or that will unproblematically occur to them upon reflection: "ils parvinrent insensiblement à faire," says Condillac, "avec réflexion, ce qu' ils n'avoient fait que par instinct."[7] Condillac, says Herder, has answered the question before his book even begins: "hat das ganze Ding Sprache schon vor der ersten Seite seines Buches erfunden vorausgesetzt." His explanation amounts to saying that words arose because words were already there.

The problem is that Condillac endows his children from the beginning with the capacity to understand what it means for a word to stand for something, what it means therefore to talk about something with a word. But *that* is the mysterious thing. Anyone can be taught the meaning of a word, or even guess at it, or even invent one, once they have language. But what is this capacity, which we have and animals don't, to endow sounds with meaning, to grasp them as referring to, and used to talk about, things?

Here is where the two perspectives come apart. What is hard is to define just what Herder thinks Condillac presupposes and fails to explain. To get this clear would bring us to the animating center of Herder's new outlook. It's not easy to do because the rival perspective has a residual hold on us. To grasp Herder's outlook, we have to take two steps, against which there is still some resistance in our intellectual culture.

First you have to place yourself in the standpoint of the speaker, and ask yourself what he or she has to understand in order to learn a new word. In other words, you have to go beyond the standpoint of the external observer, from which it might seem sufficient to account for the learning as the setting up of a connection between word and thing, such that the subject's use of the word can be correlated to the appearance of the thing. You can remain in this external standpoint, even while developing a very sophisticated theory linking words to things or descriptions to truth conditions, which invokes the subject's other meanings and his beliefs and desires.

These last phrases are meant to evoke the influential theories of Donald Davidson, whom I consider to be a prominent contemporary representative of the camp Herder was attacking. He belongs in a sense to the Locke-Condillac tradition. This tradition has, of course, gone through a profound transformation since the eighteenth century. It has become much more sophisticated, and in some respects has taken on board certain discoveries of Herder.

Nevertheless, there is an important continuity in this sense: Davidson insists that when I understand you, I can be seen to be applying a theory of the meaning of your utterances, which maps these onto features of the objective world. The descriptive kernel of your utterances maps onto their truth conditions. Davidson is quite clear that once I have a theory that enables me with tolerable accuracy to make sense of you, and within limits to predict your behavior, there can be no further question whether you and I understand these utterances in the same way. A subjective understanding of meaning (which Davidson, unlike behaviorists, doesn't want to deny) must be exhaustively grasped in terms of truth conditions, along with illocutionary forces and the apparatus of speech-act theory. Questions about it can be answered *only* in these terms.[8]

This is not the relatively uncontroversial thesis that where there is a difference between our subjective understandings of a term, this is almost bound to come out somewhere in a difference between the extensionally defined truth conditions we acknowledge for expressions employing this term. It is the much stronger claim that agreement about truth conditions is criterial for agreement in understanding. Put in terms of a popular science-fiction scenario, the possibility that some sophisticated robot might be built out of transistors, which matched us in the correlations of utterance to world and yet might not *understand* anything, makes no sense on Davidson's view. And the same must be said of the scenario of exile: we might meet up with a people to whom we could attribute truth conditions to parts of their utterances, and in this way coordinate our actions with theirs and predict them, whereas on a deeper level there remains a profound gap between our conceptual schemes.[9]

To understand Herder's objection to Condillac, we have to take the inner standpoint, that of the agent: we can't accept an account of how a creature possesses language exclusively in terms of the correlations an observer might identify between its utterances, behavior, and surroundings. Beyond this we have to define conditions of subjective understanding, because Herder's whole argument turns on a particular definition of these conditions.

But this isn't enough to get Herder's point. We can focus on understanding and still take it as something obvious, unproblematical. This is in fact what Condillac and other designative theorists did. That words can stand for things is taken as something immediately comprehensible. It's just a clever idea that can occur to someone, and after a while a predicament like that of the desert children is pretty well bound to occur. What Herder did was to make us appreciate that this understanding doesn't go without saying;

that other kinds of creatures would respond quite differently to the correlations between cry and danger; that acquiring this kind of understanding is precisely the step from not having to having language. So it is just this step that a theory of origins would have to explain.

Ironically, Herder does no better in explaining this. The objection has often been made,[10] but it doesn't dispose of his criticism. In respect of their common failure, Herder and Condillac are in good company. No one has come even close to explaining the origin of language. But by focusing on the framework understanding which language requires, Herder opened a new domain of insights into its nature. These have enabled us to get a better grasp of the essential conditions of language, which have in turn shown that theories like those of Locke and Condillac are untenable.

What Herder is doing, I want to claim, anticipates (and perhaps distantly influences, through many intermediaries) what Wittgenstein does when he lays out the background understanding we need to grasp an "ostensive definition." What Wittgenstein's opponent takes as quite unproblematic and simple turns out to be complex and not necessarily present. Appreciating this blows the opponent's theory of meaning out of the water.

What then is Herder's point? What is the framework understanding necessary for language? I want to define this in my own terms, departing at first from Herder's terminology. I think it can best be defined in terms of a contrast. What Condillac's children have to grasp in order to learn a new word is different from what animals grasp when they learn to respond to signals. For instance, rats can be trained to respond differentially to different shapes and colors. And chimpanzees, as is well known, can learn not only to respond to much more elaborate signals but also to emit them.

This capacity to operate with signals was not always clearly distinguished from human language by eighteenth-century writers; and it is even more clearly assimilated to our language by contemporaries who are in the grip of the external perspective, as the debate about chimp language attests. Central to Herder's point, if I understand him, is that a crucial distinction has to be made here.

Both responding to signals and speaking are achievements. Some mastery is acquired. We can speak in either case of the animal or human getting it right or wrong. But in the first case, getting it right is responding to or making the signal appropriate to carry out some task or get some result. It's right to go through the door with the triangle, not the square, because that gets the cheese. Signaling "want banana" has been made right because it gets the banana, or perhaps attention. To learn to use the signal is to learn to apply it appropriately in the furtherance of some non-linguistically-defined purpose or task.

The complex hyphenated adjective here is crucial. The rightness of the signal is defined by success in a task, where this success is not in turn defined in terms of the rightness of the signal. The relation is unidirectional.

But this is clearly not the case with some of the uses of human language. Consider a gamut of activities, including disinterested scientific description, articulating one's feelings, the evocation of a scene in verse, a novelist's description of character. A metaphor someone coins is right, profound. There is a kind of "getting it right" here. But in contrast to animal signaling, this can't be explained in terms of success in a task not itself linguistically defined.

Otherwise put, if we want to think of a task or goal which would help to clarify the rightness of words that occur in the human activities just mentioned, it would itself have to be defined in terms like truth, descriptive adequacy, richness of evocation, or something of the sort. We can't define the rightness of word by the task without defining the task in terms of the rightness of the words. There is no unidirectional account that can translate out rightness of word in terms of some independently defined form of success. Rightness can't be reductively explained.

These activities define what I will call the "linguistic dimension." To attribute these activities to some creature is to hold that it is sensitive to irreducible forms of rightness in the signs it deploys. A creature is operating in the linguistic dimension when it can use and respond to signs in terms of their truth, or descriptive rightness, or power to evoke some mood, or re-create a scene, or express some emotion, or carry some nuance of feeling, or in some such way to be *le mot juste*. To be a linguistic creature is to be sensitive to irreducible issues of rightness. This is not to say that they are always or even usually raised. We just talk and understand. But it means that we can raise them, understand them when raised, and frequently defend our unreflecting practice ex post by articulating reasons relevant to this issue ("of course I used the right word because I meant . . ."). Whether a creature is in the linguistic dimension in this sense isn't a matter of what correlations hold between the signals it emits, its behavior, and the surroundings—the kind of things the proponents of chimp language focus on. It is a question of subjective understanding, of what rightness consists in for it, qua what word is right.

From this point of view, a creature acquires language in the human sense when it enters the linguistic dimension. The rat who learns to get the cheese by going through the door with the red triangle is not yet in this dimension, because the rightness of response is defined by what gets the cheese. The same is true when one bird in a flock emits a characteristic cry of danger on perceiving a predator: if we want to speak of rightness in connection with this unlearned behavior, it is because cry and response together get the flock out of danger.

The gap between these cases and human language is perhaps clear enough. People are more tempted to believe that the chimps who learn to signal in American Sign Language possess something much like human language. It would be a mistake to be prematurely dogmatic, but does the evidence force us to suppose that some sense of irreducible rightness is playing a role here? Or could we just explain the performance as a very elaborate and impressive case of signal learning, where the rightness is to be understood in terms of the trainer's responses?

The question at least needs to be asked. And to this end, we have to distinguish the issue of irreducible rightness from other features of human language, which chimps undoubtedly do exhibit but which seem to be separable from it.

Combinatorial relations. What's impressive about the chimps as against lower animals is that they can learn the sign for "want" and the sign for "banana," and then combine them appropriately. Building phrases out of components is a crucial feature of human language, remarked on by Humboldt and Chomsky, and central to theories like Davidson's. Along with the possibility of endless recursion, it allows us to use finite means to infinite ends, in Humboldt's famous phrase. Impressive as this is, it is not the same thing as operating in the linguistic dimension.

Play. Chimps are sometimes said to play with their repertory. They emit the signals they have been taught even outside a context of communication with the trainer. This kind of activity, running through bits of one's repertory when not using it with serious intent, is common among higher mammals and involves all sorts of other capacities besides signaling. Once again, it is clearly distinct from the issue of linguistic rightness.

Signaling. Chimps not only respond to signals but also learn to produce them, unlike other higher mammals we train. But this achievement also has no necessary connection with the linguistic dimension. It signifies only that, whatever signals mean for chimps, they can give them as well as respond to them.

Bonding. Curiously, there is another feature of human language on which chimps seem further away from us than more fully domesticable animals like dogs and horses. It is the way that language creates a kind of bond, a common understanding between those who share it. As Vicki Hearne has pointed out, something similar gets set up between a dog and its trainer, a rapport we don't seem to be able to establish with chimps: the adult Washoe was no friend of her human caretakers, as Hearne so tellingly describes.[11]

One of the reasons for doubting that the linguistic dimension plays a role in chimp signing is the absence of any of its other candidate manifestations, beyond pointing to and calling for an object. For a human language, it is pervasive, a constitutive part of all sorts of activities and purposes beyond the merely designative. Take a ritual, say a rain dance. If we thought of it just as a tool which has proved handy in bringing on rain (or thought to be so proved), then we could construe it as an elaborate signal. But plainly the very sense of its efficacy is bound up with its felt rightness as evocative of, or akin to, the forces producing rain. This kind of "sympathetic magic" can only be practiced by creatures that are already in the linguistic dimension.

Or, again, think of the expressive dimension of human speech. As we converse, even about the most severely factual matters, we establish our stance, and our footing with the interlocutor, by the way we stand and speak. We take up an "objective" stance, for instance, coldly examining the objects under review, and this emerges in our style of speech and the words we use, while at the same time we hold our interlocutor at a distance with our aloof air; or else perhaps we invite him warmly into the brotherhood of initiates, distinct from the surrounding unscientific world. We both take up and broadcast these stances through our expressive behavior, which means that another species of properly linguistic rightness is in play. For we have to distinguish the way in which my severe mien and choice of neutral words express my aloofness toward you, from the way in which my facial twitches or trembling may show you my agitation. The first is genuinely expression, and it is a condition for this that, even if at an entirely unarticulated level, these behaviors carry the meaning of aloofness for me; whereas nothing of the sort need hold for the second. In other words, however "unconscious" I may be of what I'm doing, I must be sensitive to the rightness of this mien as expressing aloofness—my stance must be reflecting this sensitivity—if we are to speak of expression. But this expressive dimension, inseparable from any human conversation, seems utterly absent from the signing of chimps.

We can bring out the main distinction in still another way. For full language users, even when they are using words just to signal, a question can arise about the intentional description of the thing signaled. I make you aware of mortal danger just in time by calling "Watch out for the bull!" or perhaps, on another occasion, just "Tiger!" There is an answer to the question of what the first locution commands you to do, or what the second single-word exclamation describes. That is why Quine can raise the issue he does about the sense of my informant's utterance "Gavagai."[12] But there is no sense to the question whether the red triangle for the rat means "run here," or "cheese," or "run here for cheese," or "forward" or whatever; any more than we can ask whether the bird cry means "danger" rather than "skedaddle." If we want to talk of "meaning" here, we will be tempted to describe the meaning in terms of the response aroused, as Mead does.[13] But this assimilation just ignores the whole issue of the linguistic dimension (and, incidentally, causes trouble for Mead, but that would take us too far afield).

It's a consequence of this that we can speak of human language users as having a gamut of illocutionary forces in their repertory. For this requires that we distinguish linguistic meaning from action undertaken, and distinguish these in turn from the result encompassed (the "perlocutionary effect," in Austin's terminology[14]), distinctions that get no purchase on the bird's cry.

I have taken this excursus from my discussion of Herder in order to explain the basis for his objection to Condillac. The connection is this: Herder sees that what is essential, if the children are to learn to take their cries as words, is that they come to function in the linguistic dimension. That is, of course, my way of putting it. What I am trying to gloss in these terms is Herder's notion of *Besonnenheit* (reflection). It is reflection that enables us to be language users: "Der Mensch in den Zustand von Besonnenheit gesetzt, der ihm eigen ist, und diese Besonnenheit zum ersten Mal frei wirkend, hat Sprache erfunden."[15]

Herder then glosses this notion of reflection in his own just-so story about the invention of the first word. And he does it in a fashion I have imitated, by contrasting the language user's response to a target object from that of prelinguistic creatures. A particular thing, say a lamb, figures in the world of various animals in characteristic ways: as prey for the "hungry wolf on its scent" or the "bloodlicking lion"; as a sexual partner for the "ram in heat." For other animals, who have no need for sheep, the lamb passes by barely noticed. For all these creatures, the lamb can figure only as relevant to some (nonlinguistic) purpose.

Herder's reflection is the capacity to focus on the lamb in a way which is no longer tributary to any such purpose. This is its negative characterization. Positively, what is it? How does the lamb figure as object of the reflective stance? It is recognized as a being of a certain type through a distinguishing mark *(Merkmal)*. This mark in Herder's story is its bleating. Indeed, some onomatopoeic imitation of bleating could well have been the first word for *lamb,* he thinks. In other words, in the reflective stance the lamb is first recognised *as* a lamb; it is first recognized as an object rightly classed as "the bleating one." An issue of rightness arises, which cannot be reduced to success in some life task. This for Herder is inseparable from language. It is defined by the capacity to focus on objects by recognizing them, and this creates, as it were, a new space around us. Instead of being overcome by the ocean of sensations as they rush by us, we are able to distinguish one wave, and hold it in clear, calm attention. It is this new space of attention, of distance from the immediate instinctual significance of things, which Herder wants to call reflection.[16]

This is what he finds missing in Condillac's account. Condillac does have a more sophisticated idea of the move from animal to human signs than Locke does. Animals respond to natural and accidental signs (smoke is an accidental sign of fire, clouds portend rain). Humans also have instituted signs. The difference lies in the fact that by means of the latter humans can control the flow of their own imagination, whereas animals passively follow the connections triggered off in them by the chain of events.[17] There is obviously some link between Herder's description of our interrupting the "ocean of sensations" and Condillac's idea of taking control. But what is missing in the French thinker is any sense that the link between sign and object might be fundamentally different when one crosses the divide. It is still conceived in a reified way, typical of the followers of Locke, a thing-like connection whereby the only issue allowed is whether it drives us or we drive it. Condillac belongs to the mode of thought that conceives language as an instrument, a set of connections we can use to construct or control things. The point of language is to give us "empire sur notre imagination."[18] The wholly different issue about rightness escapes him.

To raise this issue is to swing our perspective on language into a new angle. But it's easy to miss. Condillac was unaware that he had left anything out. He wouldn't have known where Herder was "coming from," just as his heirs today, the proponents of chimp language, talking computers, and truth-conditional theories of meaning, find the analogous objections to their views gratuitous and puzzling. That is why Herder stands at such an important divide in our understanding of language.

To appreciate this better, let's examine further what Locke and Condillac were missing, from Herder's standpoint. Their reified view of the sign didn't come from their taking the external observer's standpoint on language, as the people I've just mentioned as their heirs do in our day. On the contrary, they wanted to explain it very much from the inside, in terms of the agent's experience of self. They weren't trying out a behaviorist theory, in which linguistic rightness plays no role. Rather they assumed this kind of rightness as unproblematically present. People introduced signs to "stand for" or "signify" objects (or ideas of objects), and once instituted these plainly could be rightly or wrongly applied. Their error from a Herderian perspective was that they never got this constitutive feature into focus.

Such failure is easy, one might almost say natural, because when we speak, and especially when we coin new terms, all this is in the background. It is what we take for granted when we coin expressions, that words can stand for things, that there is for us such a thing as irreducible linguistic rightness. The failure is so natural that it goes all the way back to Augustine, as Wittgenstein said.

What is being lost from sight here is the background of our action, something we usually lean on without noticing. More particularly, what the background provides is treated as though it were built into each particular sign, as though we could start right off coining our first word and have this understanding of linguistic rightness already incorporated in it. Incorporating the background understanding about linguistic rightness into the individual signs has the effect of occluding it very effectively. Background is easy to overlook anyway; once we build it into particular signs, we bar the way to recognizing it altogether.

This is a fault in any designative theory of meaning. But the reification wrought by modern epistemology since Descartes and Locke, that is, the drive to objectify our thoughts and mental contents, made it worse. The furniture of the mind was accorded a thing-like existence, something objects can have independent of any background. The occluding of background prepared the way for its elision altogether in those modern behaviorist theories that try to explain thought and language strictly from the standpoint of the external observer. The associations of thing-like ideas were easily transposed into the stimulus-response connections of classical behaviorism. An obvious line of filiation runs from Locke through Helvétius to Watson and Skinner.

In this context, we can see that any effort to retrieve the background had to run against the grain of an important component of modern culture, the epistemology so readily associated with the scientific revolution. In fact, some of what we now recognize as the most important developments in philosophy in the last two centuries have been tending toward this retrieval, culminating in different ways in the work of Heidegger and Wittgenstein, to name the most celebrated variants. When I called Herder a hinge figure, I meant that he had an important place as one of the originators of this counter-thrust. This is not to say that he went all the way to this retrieval. On the contrary, he often failed to draw the conclusions implicit in the new perspective he adopted—but he did play a crucial role in opening up this perspective.

There have been two common and related directions of argument in this counter-thrust, both of which can be illustrated in Herder's views on language. The first consists in articulating a part of the background, in such a form that our reliance on it in our thought, or perception, or experience, or understanding language, becomes clear and undeniable. The background so articulated is then shown to be incompatible with crucial features of the received doctrine in the epistemological tradition. We can find this type of argument in Heidegger, Wittgenstein, and Merleau-Ponty. But the pioneer, in whose steps all the others have followed, is Kant.

The arguments of the transcendental deduction can be seen in many different ways. But one way to take them is as an overturning of that atomism of input espoused by the empiricists. Coming through Hume, it held that the original knowledge of reality came in particulates, individual impressions. At a later stage the bits were connected together, as in beliefs about cause and effect. We may form such beliefs, but we can upon scrutiny separate the basic level from any quick conclusions. This analysis reveals, for instance, that nothing in the phenomenal field corresponds to the connection we assume between cause and effect.

Kant overturns empiricism by showing that each individual impression is taken as a piece of potential information; this is the background understanding that lies under all of our perceptual discriminations. The empiricists themselves acknowledge a distinction between sensation and reflection: the sensation has to be about something. It will later be called intentionality, but Kant speaks of the necessary relation to an object of knowledge: "Wir finden aber, dass unser Gedanke von der Beziehung aller Erkenntnis auf ihren Gegenstand etwas von Notwendigkeit bei sich führe" (A104).[19]

Kant goes on to argue that this relation between knowledge and object would be impossible if we really were to take the impression as utterly isolated, with no link to others. To see it as about something is to place it somewhere, to give it a location in a world that has to be familiar to us in some respects. To succeed in breaking every link between individual impressions would be to fall into incoherence, to lose all sense of anything: "Diese [Wahrnehmungen] würden aber alsdann auch zu keiner Erfahrung gehören, folglich ohne Objekt und nichts als ein blindes Spiel der Vorstellungen, d.i. weniger als ein Traum sein" (A112).

So Kant, by articulating the background understanding of aboutness, sweeps away the empiricist atomism of experience. I would suggest that Herder does something analogous. By articulating the background understanding of the linguistic dimension, he also undercuts and transforms the designative theory of language dominant in his day. And to make the parallel closer, one of the features swept away is precisely its atomism, the view that language is a collection of independently introduced words.

The second main direction of argument in the counter-thrust to Cartesianism-empiricism has been the attempt to place our thinking in the context of our form of life. The early modern epistemologies gave a notoriously disengaged picture of thinking. This was no accident. The foundationalist drive, the attempt to lay bare a clear structure of inference on the basis of already interpreted bits of evidence, pushed toward a disengagement from embodied thinking and the assumptions buried in everyday custom.[20] The move toward a more situated understanding of thinking is evident enough in the work of Wittgenstein and Heidegger—but Herder is one of its pioneers. He constantly stresses that we have to understand human reason and language as an integral part of our life form. They cannot be seen as forming a separate faculty which is simply added on to our animal nature, "like the fourth rung of a ladder on top of the three lower ones." We think like the kind of animal we are, and our animal functions (desire, fear, etc.) are those of rational beings: "überall . . . wirkt die ganze unabgeteilte Seele."[21]

These two directions, retrieving the background and situating our think-ing, are obviously interwoven. In fact, it is the firm belief in situated think-ing which leads Herder to his articulation of the linguistic dimension. Just because he cannot see language/reason as a mere addition to our animal nature, he is led to ask what kind of transformation of our psychic life attends the rise of language. It is this question to which "reflection" is an answer. To see our thinking as situated makes us see it as one mode among other possible forms of psychic life. And this makes us aware of its distinc-tive background.

It is by embarking on these two related directions of argument that Herder brings about a rotation of our thought about language. The fact that Herder himself failed on many occasions to liberate his thinking from the older forms, to draw the full conclusions, shouldn't hide from us how many of our contemporary modes of thought are implicit in the steps he took.

1.   Herder's first important insight was to see that expression constitutes the linguistic dimension. This emerged from his understanding of linguistic thought as situated. Reflection arises in an animal form that is already deal-ing with the world around it. Language comes about as a new, reflective stance toward things. It arises among our earlier stances toward objects of desire or fear, to things figuring as obstacles, supports, and the like. Our stances are literally bodily attitudes or actions on or toward objects. The new stance can't be in its origins entirely unconnected with bodily posture or action. But it can't be an action just like the others, since those are defin-able outside the linguistic dimension. It has to be seen rather as an expressive action, one that both actualizes this stance of reflection and also presents it to others in public space. It brings about the stance whereby we relate to things in the linguistic dimension.

The action that expresses and actualizes this new stance is speech. Speech is the expression of thought. But it isn't simply outer clothing for what could exist independently. It is constitutive of reflective (linguistic) thought, of thought which deals with its objects in the linguistic dimension. In its origins it is close to and interwoven with gesture.[22] Later we can detach some of our thinking from public expression, and even from natural lan-guage. But our power to function in the linguistic dimension is tied for its everyday uses, as well as its origins, to expressive speech, as the range of actions in which it is not only communicated but realized.

This doctrine is obviously contested, first by those who have remained tied to the "intellectualism" of the old disengaged epistemology, but also surprisingly enough by some thinkers who have explicitly built on post-Herderian themes, for instance, Derrida.[23] It has, however, been central to those who have tried to give a picture of human agency as embodied.[24] But can we attribute it to Herder? One can contest this because Herder himself doesn't seem to take the point in the very passage about the birth of language quoted above. Instead of stressing the crucial role of overt expression, he speaks of the recognition of the animal through a distinguishing mark as the discovery of a "Wort der Seele."[25] The new mark is indeed a sound, the bleating, but it can become the name of the sheep, "even though [the human's] tongue may never have tried to stammer it."

Still, I want to see the origin of this idea in Herder, not just because it so obviously flows from his concern to situate thought in a life form, but because he himself stresses elsewhere (including elsewhere in this same work) the importance of speech and vocal expression for the human life form.[26]

2. One of the most important and universally recognized consequences of Herder's discovery was a certain holism of meaning. A word has meaning only within a lexicon and a context of language practices, which are ultimately embedded in a form of life. In our day Wittgenstein's is the most celebrated formulation of a thesis of this kind.

This insight flows from the recognition of the linguistic dimension as Herder formulated it. Once you articulate this bit of our background understanding, an atomism of meaning becomes as untenable as the parallel atomism of perceptions does after Kant. The connection can be put in the following way.

To possess a word of human language is to have some sense that it's the right word, to be sensitive, I said above, to this issue of its irreducible rightness. Unlike the rat who learns to run through the door with the red triangle, I can use the word "triangle." This means that I can not only respond to the corresponding shape, but can recognize it as a triangle. But to be able to recognize something as a triangle is to be able to recognize other things as nontriangles. For the description "triangle" to have any sense for me, there must be something with which it contrasts; I must have some notion of other kinds of figures. "Triangle" has to contrast in my lexicon with other figure terms. But, in addition, to recognize something as a triangle is to focus on a certain property dimension; it is to pick the thing out by its shape, and not by its size, color, composition, smell, aesthetic properties. Here again some kind of contrast is necessary.

Now at least some of these contrasts and connections we have to be able to *articulate*. Someone can't be recognizing "triangle" as the right word and have absolutely no sense whatever of what makes it the right word, doesn't even grasp that something is a triangle by virtue of its shape, not its size or color. But we can't have any sense of this if we can't say anything at all, even under probing and prompting. There are cases, of course, where we can't articulate the particular features peculiar to something we recognize, say a certain emotional reaction or an unusual hue. But we know to say that it is a feeling or a color. And we can state its ineffability. The zone where our descriptions give out is situated in a context of words. If we couldn't say any of this, even that it was a feeling or that it was indescribable, we couldn't be credited with linguistic consciousness at all; and if we did utter some sound, it couldn't be described as a word. We would be out of the linguistic dimension altogether.

In other words, a being who emitted a sound when faced with a given object but was incapable of saying why—showed no sign of having any sense that this is the (irreducibly) right word, other than emitting the sound—would have to be deemed to be merely responding to signals, like the animals described earlier. Like a parrot, it has learned to respond to that thing appropriately, but it has no recognition of the word's rightness.

What flows from this is that a descriptive word, like "triangle," couldn't figure in our lexicon alone. It has to be surrounded by a skein of terms, some that contrast with it and some that situate it, place it in its property dimension, not to speak of the wider matrix of language in which the various activities are situated where our talk of triangles applies (measurement, geometry, design), and where description itself figures as one kind of speech act among others.

This is what the holism of meaning amounts to: individual words can be words only within the context of an articulated language. Language is not something that can be built up one word at a time. Mature linguistic capacity just doesn't come like this, and couldn't, because each word supposes a whole of language to give it full force as a word, as an expressive gesture that places us in the linguistic dimension. When infants start to say their "first word," they are certainly on the road to full human speech, but this first word is quite different from a single word within developed speech. The games the infant plays with this word express and realize a quite different stance to the object than the adult descriptive term does. It's not a building block out of which adult language is gradually built.

But this was exactly the error of the traditional designative view. For Condillac, a one-word lexicon was quite conceivable. His children acquire first one word, then others; they build language up, term by term. He ignores the background understanding necessary for language, and builds it unremarked into the individual words. But Herder's articulation of the real nature of linguistic understanding shows this to be impossible. Herder rightly says in the passage quoted earlier that Condillac presupposes "das ganze Ding Sprache."

This expression seems happily to capture the holistic nature of the phenomenon. And yet here too Herder disappoints us in the conclusions he actually draws in his passage on the birth of language. The just-so story, after all, tells of the birth of a single word. And at the end of it, he unfortunately throws in a rhetorical question: "Was ist die ganze menschliche Sprache als eine Sammlung solcher Worte?" (What is the whole of human language if not a collection of such words?). And yet I'd like to credit him, again, with putting us on the track to holism—not only because it is clearly implicit in what he did articulate, but also because he himself made it part of the mediating argument.

He sees that the recognition of something as something, the recognition that allows us to coin a descriptive term for it, requires that we single out a distinguishing mark. The word for X is the right word in virtue of something. Without a sense of what makes it the right word, there is no sense of a word as right: "Deutlich unmittelbar, ohne Merkmal, so kann kein sinliches Geschöpf ausser sich empfinden, da es immer andere Gefühle unterdrücken, gleichsam vernichten und immer den Unterschied von zweien durch ein drittes erkennen muss."[27]

So Herder's articulation of the linguistic dimension, properly understood and as he began to work it out, shows the classical designative story of the acquisition of language to be in principle impossible. This story involves a deep confusion between the mere signal and the word. For there *can* be one-signal repertoires. You can train a dog to respond to a single command, and then add another one, and later another one. In your first phase, whatever isn't your one signal isn't a signal at all. But there can't be one-word lexica. That's because getting it right for a signal is merely responding appropriately. Getting it right for a word requires more, a kind of recognition: we are in the linguistic dimension.

The holism of meaning has been one of the most important ideas to emerge from Herder's new perspective. Humboldt took it up in his image of language as a web. And it takes its most influential form early in this century in the celebrated principle of Saussure: "dans la langue il n'y a que des différences sans termes positifs" (in language a term gets its meaning only in the field of its contrasts).[28] In this form, the principle has achieved virtually universal acceptance. It is an axiom of linguistics.

But perhaps its most powerful application in philosophy is in the later work of Wittgenstein. His devastating refutation of "Augustine's" designative theory of meaning constantly recurs to the background understanding we need to draw on to speak and understand. Where the traditional theory sees a word acquiring meaning by being used to name some object or idea, and its meaning is then communicated through ostensive definition, Wittgenstein points out the background that these simple acts of naming and pointing presuppose.[29] Our words have the meaning they have only within the "language games" we play with them, and these in turn find their context in a whole form of life.

3. These two insights combined, the constitutive role of expression and the holism of meaning, lead to a series of further transformations in our understanding of language. I want to mention four of them here.

(A) On the classical designative view, language is an assemblage of separable words, instruments of thought that lie, as it were, transparently to hand and can be used to marshal ideas. This was the principal function of language for Hobbes, Locke, and Condillac. Ideally we should aspire fully to control and oversee its use, taking care of our definitions, and not losing them from sight in inconsiderate speech, whereby we become "entangled in words, as a bird in lime twigs."[30]

But on the new perspective, language is rather something in the nature of a web, which, to complicate the image, is present as a whole in any one of its parts. To speak is to touch part of the web, and this makes the whole resonate. Because the words we use have sense only through their place in the whole web, we can never in principle have a clear oversight of the implications of what we say at any moment. Our language is always more than we can encompass; it is in a sense inexhaustible. The aspiration to be in no degree whatever a prisoner of language, so dear to Hobbes and Locke, is unrealizable. So much seems to follow from holism.

But this difference has to be seen in the context of expression. Language can't be seen as a set of instruments, ready to hand, of words to which meanings have been attached. The crucial feature of language is now that it is a form of activity in which, through expression, reflection is realized. Language, as Humboldt put it, has to be seen as speech activity, not as work already done; as *energeia*, not *ergon*.[31]

Language as a finished product, a set of tools forged for future use, is in fact a precipitate of the ongoing activity. It is created in speech, and is in fact being continuously recreated, extended, altered, reshaped. This Humboldtian notion is the basis for another famous contribution of Saussure, his distinction between *langue* and *parole*.

If we combine these two insights, then we will come to see language as a pattern of activity by which we express/realize a certain way of being in the world, that which defines the linguistic dimension; but the pattern can be deployed only against a background we can never fully dominate. It is also a background we are never fully dominated by, since we are constantly reshaping it. Reshaping it without dominating it, or being able to oversee it, means that we never fully know what we are doing to it. In relation to language, we are both makers and made.

(B) The classical picture of language as a set of designative terms can also be upset from another direction. Early modern theories of language focused on its functions of recording and communicating thought. The emphasis was on the descriptive dimension. Later, in the eighteenth century, interest also turned to the expressive uses of language, but these were conceived after the same model. Certain feelings become linked with certain cries and gestures (or perhaps are so linked by nature), and this allows them to be communicated to others, in both senses: that is, the cry can both impart information to you about what I feel and evoke the same feeling in you. The basis was laid for the later distinction between "descriptive" and "emotive" meanings, both conceived in the same fashion as independent contents of thought or emotion associated with a signal.[32]

Herder's discovery adds a new dimension. If language serves to express a new kind of awareness, then it may not only make possible a new awareness of things, an ability to describe them; it may also open new ways of responding to things, of feeling. If in expressing our thoughts about things we can come to have new thoughts, then in expressing our feelings we can come to have transformed feelings.

This quite overturns the eighteenth-century view of the expressive function of language. Condillac and others conjectured that at the origin of language was the expressive cry, the expression of anger or fear. This later acquired designative meaning and could serve as a word. But the underlying assumption was that expression was of already existing feelings, which were unaltered in being expressed.

The revolutionary idea implicit in Herder was that the development of new modes of expression enables us to have new feelings, more powerful or more refined, and certainly more self-aware. In being able to express our feelings, we give them a reflective dimension that transforms them. The language animal can feel not only anger but indignation, not only love but admiration.

Seen from this angle, language can't be confined to the activity of talking about things. We experience our essentially human emotions not primarily in describing but in expressing them. Language also serves to express/realize ways of feeling without identifying them in descriptions. We often give expression to our feelings in talking about something else: we give vent to indignation in condemnation of unjust actions, and voice our admiration through praise of some person's remarkable traits. And much of what we feel is conveyed not in words at all, but in the way we stand and move, in our closeness and distance from others, and the like.

(C) From this perspective, we can't draw a boundary around the language of prose in the narrow sense, and divide it off from those other symbolic-expressive human creations: poetry, music, art, dance. If we think of language as essentially used to say something *about* something, then prose is indeed in a category of its own. But in light of the constitutive nature of speech, then talking *about* is only one of the provinces it constitutes. Human emotion is another, and in this some uses of prose are akin to some uses of poetry, music, and art. The idea that we can get a good grasp of the phenomena by drawing a boundary around descriptive prose comes to seem less probable, and the surmise gains ground that any adequate theory of language must be able to give some account of the whole range of "symbolic forms," in Ernst Cassirer's term.

(D) But the post-Herderian view has not only transformed and extended our conception of the uses of language. It has also transformed our conception of the subject of language. If language must be seen primarily as activity, if it is what is constantly created and recreated in speech, then it becomes relevant to note that the primary locus of speech is conversation. We speak together, to each other. Language is fashioned and grows not principally in monologue but in dialogue or, better, in the life of the speech community.

Hence Herder's notion that the primary locus of a language was the *Volk* who carried it. Humboldt takes up the same insight. Language is shaped by speech, and so can grow up only in a speech community. The language I speak, the web I can never fully dominate and oversee, can never be just *my* language; it is always *our* language.

This opens up another field of the constitutive functions of language. Speech also serves to express different relations in which we stand to each other: intimate, formal, official, casual, joking, serious. In naming them, we shape our social relations, as husbands and wives, parents and children, as equal citizens in a republic, subjects of the same monarch, or followers of a war leader. From this point of view, we can see that it is not only the speech community that shapes and creates language, but language that constitutes and sustains the speech community.

I have just enumerated four ideas that have had a major impact on our thought about language in this century. Not that they are uncontested. On the contrary, they are not only contested by those who resist the whole drift away from designative theories, but they are also a source of division among those who embrace them. We are not clear yet, certainly not agreed, on what to make of them. A and D together helped to inspire the sort of structuralist theories for which Lévi-Strauss's work was paradigmatic, and through them issued in poststructuralism. The confusions, willed and involuntary, of the latter have temporarily obscured some of the important implications of Herder's seminal insights. In particular, the significance of D, the dialogical nature of language, is still being articulated in fundamentally different ways: by Habermas and other followers of G. H. Mead, in one way; thinkers inspired by Heidegger in another; by those working in the wake of Vygotsky or Bakhtin in a third and fourth. The debate will rage for some time.

Herder first articulated the insights that have given point to these multifaceted debates. For better or for worse. We may regret this turn in our thought about language. I for one welcome it, but I can understand others feeling dismay, particularly when we survey the nonsense that has been generated along the way. My aim here has not been to justify the turn, but to show Herder's irreducible role in it.

— 6 —

Heidegger, Language, and Ecology

Heidegger's philosophy is anti-subjectivist, even as he puts it, polemically, "anti-humanist." There are certainly dark and worrying aspects to his attack on humanism, but one consequence which seems clear and perhaps benign is that it aligns him with the ecological protest against the unreflecting growth of technological society. This is a drift we can discern in Heidegger's later work, well before we have come to grips with the philosophical insights it contains.

But there are many kinds of protest against technological society, which differ both in what they condemn and in the grounds of their condemnation. On the first issue, some people condemn technology as such; others complain of its misuse. On the second, some point to the disastrous long-term consequences for human beings of runaway technology; others argue that we have reason to set limits to our domination of nature which go beyond our own flourishing, that nature or the world can be seen as making demands on us. This last is the path of so-called deep ecology.

Here are two issues, with two major positions on each. One of the interesting things about Heidegger is that, on closer examination, he seems to fit into neither of the established positions on either issue. Heidegger's philosophy of ecology is sui generis.

I can't explore all of this here. I want rather to concentrate on working out Heidegger's position on the second issue. In this, he does come close to a deep ecological position. Indeed, one might want simply to attribute the second answer to him, that something beyond the human makes demands on us, or calls us. But this source can't be identified with nature or with the universe. Defining what the source is would bring us to the heart of one of the most puzzling features of his later philosophy. I want to start approaching it here.

I believe this question can be best approached through Heidegger's philosophy of language, and so most of this chapter will be devoted to that. Only at the end will I indicate in what way our status as language beings can be thought to lay us open to ecologically relevant demands. I'll only be able to sketch this, but I hope that by then such a line of thought will have begun to appear convincing and potentially fruitful.

Heidegger's later doctrine of language is so anti-subjectivist that he even inverts the usual relation in which language is seen as our tool, and talks of *language speaking* rather than human beings speaking.[1] This formulation is hardly transparent on first reading. But I think we can understand it if we first set Heidegger against the background of an important tradition of thought about language which has flourished in the last two centuries; and then define his originality in relation to this tradition.

I call this line of thinking "expressive-constitutive." It arose in the late eighteenth century in reaction to the prevailing doctrine about language which had developed within the confines of modern epistemology, the philosophy articulated in different ways by Hobbes, Locke, and Condillac. On that classical view, language is conceived as an instrument. The constitutive theory, on the other hand, reacts against this, and Heidegger's conception of language speaking can be seen as a development of this early counter-response.

The contention between the two views can perhaps be understood in this way. The instrumental view is an "enframing" theory.[2] I shall use this term to describe attempts to understand language within the framework of a picture of human life, behavior, purposes, or mental functioning, which is itself described and defined without reference to language. Language can be seen as arising within this framework, and fulfilling a certain function within it, but the framework itself precedes or at least can be characterized independently of language. By contrast, a "constitutive" theory gives us a picture of language as making possible new purposes, new levels of behavior, new meanings, and hence is not explicable within a framework of human life conceived without language.

The classical case, and the most influential first form of enframing theory, was the set of ideas developed from Locke through Hobbes to Condillac.[3] Briefly, the Hobbes-Locke-Condillac (HLC) theory seeks to understand language within the confines of the modern representational epistemology made dominant by Descartes. In the mind there are "ideas." These are bits of putative representation of reality, much of it "external." Knowledge consists in having representation actually square with the reality. But we can only hope to achieve this if we assemble our ideas according to a responsible procedure. Our beliefs about things are constructed; they result from a synthesis. The issue is whether the construction will be reliable and responsible, or indulgent, slapdash, and delusory.

Language plays an important role in this construction. Words are given meaning by being attached to the things represented via the ideas that represent them. The introduction of words greatly facilitates the combination of ideas into a coherent picture. This facilitation is understood in different ways. For Hobbes and Locke, words allow us to grasp things in classes, and hence make possible synthesis wholesale, whereas nonlinguistic intuition would be confined to the painstaking association of particulars. Condillac thinks that the introduction of language gives us for the first time control over the whole process of association; it affords us "empire sur notre imagination."[4]

The constitutive theory finds its most robust early expression in Herder, in a critical response to Condillac. In a famous passage from the *Ursprung der Sprache* (Essay on the Origin of Language), Herder repeats Condillac's fable of how language might have arisen between two children in a desert.[5] But he finds something lacking in that account. It seems to him to presuppose what it is meant to explain. What it is meant to explain is language, the passage from a condition in which the children emit nothing but animal cries to the stage where they use words meaningfully. The association between sign and some mental content is already there with the animal cry (what Condillac calls the "natural sign"). What is new with the "instituted sign" is that the children can now use it to focus on and manipulate the associated idea, and hence direct the whole play of their imagination. The transition amounts to their stumbling onto the notion that association can be used in this way.

This is the classic case of an enframing theory. Language is understood in terms of certain elements: ideas, signs, and their association, which precede its arising. Before and after, the imagination is at work and association takes place. What is new is that now the mind is in control. This itself is, of course, something that did not previously exist. But the theory establishes the maximal possible continuity between before and after. The elements are the same, combination continues, only the direction changes. We can surmise that it is precisely this continuity which gives the theory its seeming clarity and explanatory power: language is robbed of its mysterious character, is related to elements that seem unproblematic.

But Herder starts from the intuition that language makes possible a different kind of consciousness, which he calls reflective *(besonnen)*. That is why he finds a continuity explanation like Condillac's so frustrating and unsatisfactory. The issue of what this new consciousness consists in and how it arises is not addressed, as far as Herder is concerned, by an account in terms of preexisting elements. So he accuses Condillac of begging the question: "The Abbot Condillac . . . had already revealed the entire essence of language before the first page of this book."[6]

What did Herder mean by "reflection"? This is harder to explain. We might try to formulate it this way: prelinguistic beings can react to the things that surround them. But language enables us to grasp something *as* what it is. This explanation is hardly transparent, but it puts us on the right track. Herder's basic idea seems to be that while a prelinguistic animal can learn to respond to some object appropriately in the light of its purposes, only the being with language can identify the object as of a certain kind, can, as we might put it, attribute such and such a property to it. An animal, in other terms, can learn to give the right response to an object—fleeing a predator, say, or going after food—where "right" means "appropriate to its (nonlinguistic) purposes." But language use involves another kind of rightness. Using the right word involves identifying an object as having the properties that justify using that word. We cannot give an account of this rightness in terms of extralinguistic purposes. Rightness here is irreducible to success in some extralinguistic task.[7]

Now to be sensitive to the issue of nonreductive rightness is to be operating, as it were, in another dimension. Let's call this the "semantic dimension." Then we can say that properly linguistic beings are functioning in the semantic dimension. And that can be our way of formulating Herder's point about reflection. To be reflective is to operate in this dimension, which means acting out of sensitivity to issues of irreducible rightness.

But we need to extend somewhat our notion of the semantic dimension. My remarks above seemed to concern purely descriptive rightness. But we do more things with language than describe. There are other ways in which a word can be *le mot juste*. For instance, I come up with a word to articulate my feelings, and thus at the same time shape them in a certain manner. This is a function of language which cannot be reduced to simple description, at least not description of an independent object. Or else I say something which reestablishes the contact between us, puts us once again on a close and intimate footing. We need a broader concept of irreducible rightness than just that involved in aligning words with objects.

Thus when I hit on the right word to articulate my feelings and acknowledge that I am motivated by envy, say, the term does its work because it is the right term. In other words, we can't explain the rightness of the word "envy" simply in terms of the condition that using it produces; rather, we have to account for its producing this condition—here, a successful articulation—in terms of its being the right word. A contrasting case should make this clearer. Imagine that every time I feel stressed, tense, or cross-pressured, I take a deep breath, then exhale explosively out of my mouth, producing "How!" I immediately feel calmer and more composed. This is plainly the right *sound* (not a word) to make, as defined by this desirable goal of restored equilibrium. The rightness of "How!" admits of a simple task account. That is because we can explain the rightness simply in terms of its bringing about calm, and don't need to explain its bringing about calm terms of rightness.

This last clause points up the contrast with "envy" as the term that both articulates and clarifies my feelings. It brings about this clarification, to be sure, and that is essential to its being the right word here. But central to its clarifying is its being the right word. So we can't simply explain its rightness by its de facto clarifying. You can't define its rightness by the de facto causal consequence of clarifying; in other words, you can't make this outcome criterial for its rightness, because you don't know whether it is clarifying unless you know that it is the right term. Whereas in the case of "How!" all there was to its rightness was its having the desired outcome; the bare de facto consequence is criterial. That is why normally we wouldn't be tempted to treat this expletive as if it had a meaning.

Something similar can be said about my restoring the intimacy between us by saying "I'm sorry." This was "the right thing to say" because it restored contact. But at the same time, we can say that these words are efficacious in restoring contact because of what they mean. Irreducible rightness enters into the account here, because what the words mean can't be defined by what they bring about. Again, we might imagine that I could also set off a loud explosion in the neighborhood, which would so alarm you that you'd forget about our tiff and welcome my presence. This would then be, from a rather cold-blooded, strategic point of view, the "right move." But the explosion itself "means" nothing.

What this discussion is moving us toward is a definition of the semantic dimension in terms of the possibility of a reductive account of rightness. A simple task account of rightness for some sign reduces it to a matter of efficacy for some nonsemantic purpose. We are in the semantic dimension when this kind of reduction can't work, when a kind of rightness is at issue which can't be cashed out. That is why the image of a new dimension seems to me apposite. To move from nonlinguistic to linguistic agency is to move to a world in which a new kind of issue is at play, a right use of signs which is not reducible to task-rightness. The world of the agent has a new axis on which to respond; its behavior can no longer be understood just as the purposive seeking of ends on the old plane. It is now responding to a new set of demands. Hence the image of a new dimension.

If we interpret Herder in this way, we can understand his impatience with Condillac. The latter's "natural signs" were things like cries of pain or distress. Their right use in communication could only be construed on the simple task model. Language supposedly arose when people learned to use the connection already established by the natural sign, between the cry and what caused the distress, in a controlled way. The "instituted sign" is born, an element of language properly speaking. Herder can't accept that the transition from prelanguage to language consists simply in taking control of an existing process. What this leaves out is precisely that a new dimension of issues becomes relevant, that the agent is operating on a new plane. Hence in the same passage in which he declares Condillac's account circular, Herder reaches for a definition of this new dimension, with his term "reflection."

On my reconstruction, Herder's reflection is to be glossed as the semantic dimension, and his importance is that he made it central to any account of language. Moreover, Herder's conception of the semantic dimension was multifaceted, along the lines of the broad conception of rightness. It did not just involve description. Herder saw that opening this dimension has to transform all aspects of the agent's life. It will also be the seat of new emotions. Linguistic beings are capable of new feelings which affectively reflect their richer sense of their world: not just anger, but indignation; not just desire, but love and admiration.

The semantic dimension also made the agent capable of new kinds of relations, new sorts of footing that agents can stand on with each other, of intimacy and distance, hierarchy and equality. Gregarious apes may have what we call a "dominant male," but only language beings can distinguish between leader, king, president, and the like. Animals mate and have offspring, but only language beings define kinship.

Underlying both emotions and relations is another crucial feature of the linguistic dimension: it makes possible value in the strong sense. Prelinguistic animals treat something as desirable or repugnant, by going after it or avoiding it. But only language beings can identify things as *worthy* of desire or aversion. For such identifications raise issues of intrinsic rightness. They involve a characterization of things which is not reducible simply to the way we treat them as objects of desire or aversion. They involve a recognition beyond that: they *ought* to be treated in one or another way.

Now this theory of language which gives a privileged place to the semantic dimension deserves the appellation "constitutive" in an obvious sense, in that language enters into or makes possible a whole range of crucially human feelings, activities, and relations. It bursts the framework of prelinguistic life forms, and therefore renders any enframing account inadequate. But the constitutive theory that Herder's critique inaugurates has another central feature: it gives a creative role to expression.

Views of the HLC type related linguistic expression to some preexisting content. For Locke, a word is introduced by being linked with an idea, and henceforth becomes capable of expressing it.[8] The content precedes its external means of expression. Condillac develops a more sophisticated conception. He argues that introducing words ("instituted signs"), because it gives us greater control over the train of thoughts, allows us to discriminate more finely the nuances of our ideas. This means that we identify finer distinctions, which we in turn can name, which will again allow us to make still more subtle discriminations, and so on. In this way, language makes possible science and enlightenment. But at each stage of this process, the idea precedes its naming, albeit its discriminability results from a previous act of naming.

Condillac also gave emotional expression an important role in the genesis of language. His view was that the first instituted signs were framed from natural ones. But natural signs were just the inbuilt expressions of our emotional states—animal cries of joy or fear. That language originated from the expressive cry became the consensus in the learned world of the eighteenth century. Yet the conception of expression here was inert. What the expression conveyed was thought to exist independently of its utterance. Cries made fear or joy evident to others, but they did not help to constitute these feelings themselves.

Herder develops a quite different notion of expression. This is in the logic of a constitutive theory, as I have just described it. This tells us that language constitutes the semantic dimension, that is, possessing language enables us to relate to things in new ways, say as loci of features, and to have new emotions, goals, or relationships, as well as being responsive to issues of strong value. We might say: language transforms our world, using this last word in a clearly Heidegger-derived sense. We are talking not about the cosmos out there, which preceded us and is indifferent to us, but about the world of our involvements, including all the things they incorporate in their meaning for us.

So we can rephrase the constitutive view by saying that language introduces new meanings in our world: the things that surround us become potential bearers of properties; they can have new emotional significance for us, as objects of admiration or indignation; our links with others can count for us in new ways, as lovers, spouses, or fellow citizens; and they can have strong value.

This involves, then, attributing a creative role to expression. Bringing things to speech can't mean just making externally available what is already there. There are many banal speech acts where this seems to be all that's involved. But language as a whole must involve more than this, because it is also opening possibilities for us which would not be there in its absence.

The constitutive theory turns our attention toward the creative dimension of expression, in which, to speak paradoxically, it makes possible its own content. We can actually see this in familiar, everyday realities, but it tends to be screened out from the enframing perspective, and it took the development of constitutive theories to bring it to light.

A good example is the body language of personal style. We see the leather-jacketed motorcycle rider step away from his machine and swagger toward us with an exaggeratedly leisurely pace. This person is "saying something" in his way of moving, acting, speaking. He may have no words for it, though we might want to apply "macho" as at least a partial description. Here is an elaborate way of being in the world, of feeling and desiring and reacting, which involves sensitivity to certain things (such as slights to one's honor: we are now the object of his attention because we unwittingly cut him off at the last intersection) and cultivated but supposedly spontaneous insensitivity to others (such as the feelings of yuppies or females), which involves certain prized pleasures (riding around at high speed with the gang) and others that are despised (listening to sentimental songs); and this way of being is coded as strongly valuable—that is, being this way is admired, and failing to be earns contempt.

But how coded? Not, presumably, in descriptive terms, or at least not adequately. The person may not have a term like "macho" to articulate the value involved. What terms he does have may be woefully inadequate to capture what is specific to this way of being; the epithets of praise or opprobrium may only be revelatory in the whole context of this style of action; by themselves they may be too general. Knowing that X is one of the boys and Y is an outsider may tell us little. The crucial coding is in the body's expressive language.

The biker's world incorporates the strong value of this way of being. Let's call it (somewhat inadequately, but we need a word) "machismo." But how does this meaning exist for him? Only through the expressive gesture and stance. It is not just that an outside observer would have no call to attribute machismo to him without this behavior. It is more radically that a strong value like this can exist for him only when it is articulated in some form. It is this expressive style that enables machismo to exist for him, and more widely this domain of expressive body language is the locus of a whole host of different value-coded ways of being for humans in general. The expression makes possible its content; the language opens us out to the domain of meaning it encodes. Expression is no longer simply inert.

But when we turn back from this rather obvious case to the original case, which was central to HLC theories, we see it in a new light. Here too expression must be seen as creative, where language opens us to the domain it encodes. What descriptive speech encodes is our attribution of properties to things. But possessing this descriptive language is the condition of our being sensitive to the issues of irreducible rightness which must be guiding us if we are really to be attributing properties, as we saw above. So seeing expression as creative generates Herder's constitutive theory as applied to descriptive language.

This illustrates the inner connections, both historical and logical, between the constitutive theory and a strong view of expression. Either the espousal of the first can lead us to look for places where expression obviously opens us to its own content, which we will find in this domain of body language and with emotional expression generally. Or else the sense that expression is creative, which will likely strike us if we are attending closely to the life of the emotions, will lead us to revise our understanding of the much-discussed case of description. For Herder, the connections probably go in both directions, but if anything the second is more important than the first. The major proponents of the HLC theories were all rationalists in some sense; one of their central goals was to establish reason on a sound basis, and their scrutiny of language had largely this end in view. The proto-Romantic move to dethrone reason, and to locate the specifically human capacities in feeling, naturally led to a richer concept of expression than was allowed for in Condillac's natural cries, which were inert modes of utterance. From the standpoint of this richer notion, even the landscape of descriptive speech begins to look very different. But whatever the route, a road links the constitutive insight with the strong view of expression, so that the alternative to the enframing theory might with equal justice be called the constitutive-expressive.[9]

There are three more features of this view as it developed into its mature form. The first is that attributing the central role to expression leads to a redefinition of what it is to acquire language. The crucial step is no longer seen as taking on board a *mental capacity* to link sign and idea, but as coming to engage in the *activity* of overt *speech*. In Humboldt's famous formulation, we have to think of language primarily as *energeia*, not just as *ergon*.[10]

This speech activity has an inescapable expressive-projective dimension; even when we are engaged in disinterested description, we are as speakers projecting a certain stance to our interlocutors and to the matter at hand. But it has a second feature as well: conversation. The first and inescapable locus of language is in exchange between interlocutors. Language involves certain kinds of links with others. In particular, it involves the link of being a conversational partner with somebody, an "interlocutor." Standing to someone as an interlocutor is fundamentally different from standing to him or her as an object of observation or manipulative interaction. Language marks this most fundamental distinction in the difference of persons. I address someone as "you," speak of them as "him" or "her."

What this corresponds to is the way in which we create a common space by opening a conversation. A conversation has the status of a common action. When I open up about the weather to you over the back fence, what this does is make the weather an object for *us*. It is no longer just for you or for me, with perhaps the addition that I know it is for you and you know it is for me. Conversation transposes the weather into an object we are considering together. The considering is common, in that the background understanding established is that the agency which is doing the considering is us together, rather than each of us on our own managing to dovetail our action with the other.[11]

Third, implicit in this Herder-Humboldt understanding of language is the recognition that the constitutive forms of expression, those that open us to a new range of meanings, go beyond descriptive language, and even beyond speech of any form, to such things as gesture and stance.

This suggests that the phenomenon which needs to be carved out for explanation is the whole range of expressive-constitutive forms; we are unlikely to understand descriptive language unless we can place it in a broader theory of such forms, which must hence be our prior target. This view is strengthened when we reflect how closely connected the different forms are. Our projections are carried at once in linguistic form (speech style and rhetoric) and in extralinguistic form (gesture, stance). Description is always embedded in acts which also projectively express. The idea that these could be treated as a single range was already delineated in the definition I gave earlier of the semantic dimension. For even the projections of body language fit within its scope, as having their own kind of intrinsic rightness. The swagger of our biker is right in relation to the way of being he values, in a way that cannot be accounted for in terms of a simple task.

So constitutive theories go for the full range of expressive forms (what Cassirer called "symbolic forms").[12] Now within these falls another subrange not mentioned so far, the work of art, something that is neither expressive projection nor description. In a sense, the work of art played an even more important role in the development of expressivism than what I've been calling projection. We can see this in the conception of the symbol, as opposed to the allegory, which played an important role in the aesthetics of the Romantic period and, indeed, since. As described, for instance, by Goethe, the symbol was a paradigm of what I call constitutive expression.

A work of art that is "allegorical" presents us with some insight or truth which we could also have access to more directly. An allegory of virtue and vice as two animals, say, will tell us something which could also be formulated in propositions about virtue and vice. By contrast, a work of art has the value of a symbol[13] when it manifested something which could not be thus "translated." It opens access to meanings which cannot be made available any other way. Each truly great work is in this way sui generis. It is untranslatable.

This notion, which has its roots in Kant's third *Critique*, was immensely influential. It was taken up by Schopenhauer and all those he influenced, in their understanding of the work of art as manifesting what cannot be said in the assertions of ordinary speech. Its importance for Heidegger in his own variant needs no stressing.

The work of art as symbol was perhaps the paradigm on which the early constitutive theories of language were built. In its very definition, there is an assertion of the plurality of expressive forms, in the notion that it is untranslatable into prose. From this standpoint, the human expressive-constitutive power—alternatively, the semantic dimension—has to be seen as a complex and multilayered thing, in which the higher modes are embedded in the lower ones.

Beyond the attribution of properties, I mentioned three other ranges of meanings which are opened to us by language: the properly human emotions, certain relations, and strong value. But each of these is also carried on the three levels of expressive form: the projective, the symbolic (in works of art), and the descriptive. We express our emotions, establish our relations, and articulate our values in our body language, style, and rhetoric; but we can also articulate all of that in poetry, novels, dance, music; and we can also bring all of that to descriptive articulation, where we name the feelings, relations, values, and describe and argue about them.

I have developed this portrait of the constitutive-expressive theory at length because I think Heidegger's views on language stand squarely within this tradition. Heidegger is a constitutive theorist. By this I mean not just that he happens to have such a theory of language, but that it plays an essential role in his thinking.

There may be some question about this in relation to Heidegger's early writings, but his thinking after "Die Kehre" (The Turning; 1949) seems to be articulating the central notions of the constitutive view. To describe language as the "house of being," for instance, is to give it more than instrumental status. Indeed, Heidegger repeatedly inveighs against those views of language which reduce it to a mere instrument of thought or communication. Language is essential to *Lichtung,* the clearing.

Heidegger stands in the Herder tradition. But he transposes this mode of thinking in his own characteristic fashion. While Herder in inaugurating the constitutive view still speaks in terms of "reflection," which sounds like a form of consciousness, Heidegger clearly turns the issue around, and sees language as what opens access to meanings. Language discloses. The deeper and darker, more difficult and problematic thesis, that language speaks, is something I will go into shortly. But at least here it is clear that language is seen as the condition of the human world being disclosed. The disclosure is not intrapsychic, but occurs in the space between humans; indeed, it helps to define the space that humans share.

This is already clear in "Der Ursprung des Kunstwerkes" (The Origin of the Work of Art)[14] as is, incidentally, Heidegger's debt to the whole expressivist topos of the symbol. The work of art brings about the crucial constituting disclosure of a way of life, in a way that no set of mere descriptive propositions could. These could as descriptions be "correct"; that is, they could correctly represent reality. But the work of art is not a representation, at least not primarily: "Ein Bauwerk, ein griechischer Tempel, bildet nichts ab" (A building, a Greek temple, does not represent; 30). It defines the objects of strong value: "Das Tempelwerk fügt erst und sammelt zugleich um sich die Einheit jener Bahnen und Bezüge, in denen Geburt und Tod, Unheil und Segen, Sieg und Schmach, Ausharren und Verfall die Gestalt und den Lauf des Menschenwesens in seinem Geschick gewinnen" (It is the templework that first fits together and at the same time gathers around itself the unity of those paths and relations in which birth and death, disaster and blessing, victory and disgrace, endurance and decline, acquire the shape of destiny for the human being; 31). It does this not for individuals, but for a people: "Die waltende Weite dieser offenen Bezüge ist die Welt dieses geschichtlichen Volkes" (The all-governing expanse of this open relational context is the world of this historical people).

These crucial theses of the expressive-constitutive view are clearly recaptured by Heidegger in his own fashion, no longer as truths about "consciousness," but as crucial conditions of Being, or the clearing.[15]

But Heidegger is more than just a constitutive theorist. He also has his own original position within this camp, particularly in his later philosophy. Here we find those dark sayings I mentioned above, that it is not humans who speak, but language. I don't claim to understand these fully, but I think they can be made partly intelligible if we develop certain potentialities, implicit in any constitutive theory, which were not fully explored by his predecessors.

This theory rests on the central intuition that it is through language that disclosure to humans takes place. Animals may have their own kind of clearing,[16] but ours is constituted by language. In particular, ours is a world in which things have worth, in which there are goods in the strong sense: things *worth* pursuing.

Goods show up through finding expression, paradigmatically "symbolic," in terms of Goethe's distinction—as the goods of the Greeks showed up in the temple. Human beings build the temple. So constitutive theory puts a new question on the agenda: what is the nature of this (in one obvious sense) human power of expression, with all its fateful consequences?

This is the basis for a massive parting of the ways. Different answers to the question are central to most traditions of continental philosophy, from the followers of Schopenhauer, through Heidegger and those he has influenced, to the deconstructionists and postmodernists. The issue has also been central to modernist poetics. Enframing theories, either in mainstream semantics or in post-Fregean theories of language like Donald Davidson's, are on a completely different wavelength, because for them the question doesn't even exist. How could it? Only a constitutive theory can put it on the agenda. This, I think, is one of the most important sources of that "talking past each other" we see when these two modes of philosophizing meet.

This issue connects in a certain way with the very beginnings of our philosophical tradition. Aristotle defined the human being as *zoion ekhon logon*. This was usually translated as "rational animal." But Heidegger suggested that we go beyond the traditional interpretation this rendering enshrines, and simply say "animal possessing logos," with all the polysemy of that latter term, which nevertheless centers on language. Humans are language animals. They are beings that somehow possess, or are the locus of, this constitutive power of expression. In order to know the essence of human beings, you have to understand language in the broad sense in which constitutivists use the term. This will give you the *areté* of human beings, what life is proper for them. Aristotle can be read as proceeding in this way,[17] and so can Heidegger, even with all the massive differences between them.

So the task is: explain the constitutive dimension of language; explain the power of expression. One immediate temptation is to see it as *our* power, something we exercise; disclosure is what we bring about. For Heidegger this is a deeply erroneous view—not just a trivial mistake, but one generated out of the whole thrust of our culture and tradition. This reading can be called subjectivist. But in fact it can take a number of forms, and in order to understand them, we should examine what is at stake.

Language is essential to what we could argue is the central focus of Heidegger's philosophy, the fact or event that things show up at all. This is his concept of the clearing. Heidegger teaches us to reorder the history of philosophy and culture in the light of how the clearing has been understood.

One crucial point for Heidegger is that the clearing should not be identified with any of the entities that show up in it. It is not to be explained by them as something they cause, or as one of their properties, or as grounded in them. Later Heidegger thought that some pre-Socratics had a vision which avoided this identification. But with Plato, western culture starts on a fatal course. Plato's notion of the Idea places the clearing among beings. An Idea is not just another entity waiting to be discovered. It is not like the things that participate in it. It can be understood as self-manifesting. It gives itself to be understood. That is what underlies the image of light in which Plato frequently expounds the Idea, particularly that of the Good. The Good is likened to the sun; turning from the changing things of this world to the Ideas is likened to leaving the dark cave. He speaks of the soul turning to the illuminated side. And so on.

Plato, it can be said, had an ontic account of the clearing. It is still in an obvious sense a nonsubjectivist one. But Heidegger thinks that it put us on a slide toward subjectivism. Perhaps because the very act of ontically placing the clearing reflects a drive toward grasping it, exercising intellectual control over it; and this, fully worked out, will emerge in the will to power. But in any case, the Platonic understanding is transformed after Aristotle through a series of intermediate steps, each one more subjectivist, into a modern mode of thinking which explains the clearing through a power of the subject, that of representation. The understanding of reality as disposed through the power of a subject is greatly furthered by the medieval view of the world as the creation of an omnipotent God. This at first coexists with Platonic and Aristotelian theories of the Idea; it is the high noon of what Heidegger calls "onto-theology." But its inherent thrust pushes toward a definition of being as what it is through the disposition of subjective power.

In the modern age, this takes form at first in the idealism which emerges out of the central tradition of modern epistemology, and which Heidegger thinks is already implicit in its founding figures, Descartes and Locke. The real is what can be represented by a subject. This view culminates in various forms of nonrealism. But for Heidegger the same thrust leads to our conceiving reality itself as emanating from will. It is not to be understood only in relation to the knowing subject, but to a subjectivity of striving and purpose. Leibniz is obviously one of the key figures in this development. It reaches its culmination in the Nietzschean claim that everything is Will to Power.

Modern subjectivism onticizes the clearing in the opposite way from Platonism. Now things appear because there are subjects who represent them and take a stand on them. The clearing is the fact of representation; and this only takes place in minds, or in the striving of subjects, or in their use of various forms of depiction, including language.

But the real nature of the clearing is neither of the above. Both views can be seen as making equal and opposite mistakes. Each misses something important about it. The Platonic mode can't acknowledge the human role. The clearing in fact comes to be only around *Dasein*. It is our being-in-the-world which allows it to happen. At least the representational theory grasps that. But it for its part can't appreciate that the clearing doesn't just happen within us, and/or is not simply our doing. Any doing of ours, any play with representations, supposes as already there the disclosure of things in language. We can't see this as something that we control or that simply happens within our ambit. The notion that it is in our heads already supposes, in order to make sense, that we understand our heads and ourselves as placed in a world, and this understanding doesn't happen only in our heads. This would be Heidegger's recreation of Hegel's disproof of the Kantian thing-in-itself. The idea that the clearing is our doing collapses into incoherence as well; it is only through the clearing that we have any idea of doing at all, that action is in our repertory.

So the clearing is Dasein-related, yet not Dasein-controlled. It is not our doing. Here we can see how for Heidegger enframing theories of language are redolent of modern subjectivism. They purport to understand language, that whereby the clearing comes to be, as a mode of representation which functions within a human life whose purposes are not themselves set by language. Language is enframed, and can be seen as performing a set of functions which can, except for representation itself, be defined non-linguistically. Language is something we can use; it is an instrument. This instrumentalization of the clearing is one of the furthest expressions of the will to power.

Heidegger's position can be seen from one point of view as utterly different from both Platonism and subjectivism because it avoids onticizing altogether; from another point of view, it can be seen as passing between them to a third position which neither can imagine, Dasein-related but not Dasein-centered.[18]

Now it seems obvious that Heidegger found some of the background he needed to develop this position out of the constitutive-expressive tradition. Its understanding of expression, in particular of the symbol, begins to explore this middle ground. The symbol is both manifestation and creation, partakes of both finding and making. The philosophies that arose out of the Romantic phase (which can't necessarily be called "Romantic," as in Schelling and Hegel), begin to stake out a middle position. In a sense, they have something in common with Plato, and with the whole ancient and medieval conception of a cosmic order that embodies Ideas. For Hegel reality conforms to the Idea. But at the same time, they see the cosmos as crucially incomplete until brought to its adequate expression in human-sustained media—say Hegel's Art, Religion, and Philosophy. The Idea isn't a reality independent of the Being which can bring it to manifestation, that is, human being. But this way of differing from the ancients does not take the standard modern form of locating the clearing in representation. The expression-articulation of the Idea is not mere representation, but a kind of completing; at the same time, the completing is not itself only a human achievement. The human agent here is an emanation of cosmic spirit.

So we can see that the idea of expression itself can nudge us toward a third way of locating the clearing. It gives us a notion of the clearing which is essentially Dasein-related; in this it is at one with the standard modern view. But it doesn't place the clearing simply inside us as a representation; it puts it in a new space constituted by expression. And in some versions it can acknowledge that the constituting of this space is not simply our doing. Can acknowledge, but doesn't necessarily do so. There are two issues here. The first concerns the ontic status of the clearing. The second is more a clutch of issues, and touches the nature of the expressive power itself.

1.   As to the first: the space of expression is not the same as, that is, can't be reduced to, either ordinary physical space or inner psychic space, the domain of the "mind" on the classic epistemological construal. It is not the same as the first because it only gets set up between speakers. (It is Dasein-related.) It is not the same as the second because it cannot be placed "within" minds, but rather is out there between interlocutors. In conversa-

tion, a public or common space gets set up, in which the interlocutors are together.

If we see the clearing as the space opened by expression, then the basis is there for a de-onticizing move, relative to the categories of our modern ontology: matter and mind. For this space is neither. The move is made possible, but it isn't taken right away. Hegel still draws heavily on the old onto-theology, and the great chain of being, to ground the manifestations of spirit. Later, with Schopenhauer, a strange twist is introduced. The ontic basis of expression is will. But this is no longer seen as the benign source of being and goodness, but as the source of endless, disordered striving and suffering. This reversal undoubtedly helped to prepare the way for the move which Heidegger is the first to make explicitly, though one can perhaps see forerunners among those who prepared the way for modernist poetics, Mallarmé for one. In declaring the ontological difference, Heidegger is realizing a potentiality opened by expressivism.

2. When we turn to the second gamut of issues, we can see that the expressivist turn did not put an end to subjectivism. On the contrary, it opened up a whole new range of forms, some of them among the most virulent. Here again there is a potentiality, which may remain unrealized. What expressivism does is to open the issue of the nature of expressive power. The options are many. We can perhaps single out three subissues, which open up a three-dimensional problem space in which different thinkers and writers have located themselves.

A. If like the earlier theorists, such as Hegel, you see expression as bringing something to manifestation, then you can think of this reality as the self; and the essential activity is self-expression. Or you can identify it as something beyond the self; in Hegel's case, with a cosmic spirit or process. This is one dimension in which you can move toward either subjective or objective poles.

B. But then, more radically, you can challenge the whole idea that expression manifests something; you can see it not as a bringing-to-light, but as a bringing-about. The space is something we make. The potentiality for this more radical subjectivisim is already there in the canonical notion of the symbol current in the Romantic era. The symbol manifests something; but this does not mean that it simply copies some model already in view. Instead it creates the medium in which some hitherto hidden reality can be manifest. Prior to expression, this reality is not something which *can* be in view, and hence there can be no question of copying. Manifesting through the symbol therefore involves an element of creation, the making of a medium in which the reality can for the first time *appear*. If we add, as did Hegel and others, that appearance is part of the potentiality of what comes to light, then this creation also counts as bringing this reality to completion.

Expression partakes of both finding and making. In the original variant, there is a balance between the two, but the second basically is in the service of the first. The radical step is to overturn this balance, and to see the clearing as something projected. Through the power of expression we make this space, and what appears in it should not be seen as a manifestation of anything. What appears is a function of the space itself. Once again, Mallarmé might be seen as a pioneer of this view, with his image of *le néant*. Nietzsche can be read as poised on a knife edge between the two views, and a term like "transfiguration" remains ambivalent between them. But the major proponents of the radical, "creationist" view today are deconstructionists, particularly Derrida, with slogans like "il n'y a pas de hors-texte."

C.   There is a third issue on which we can be more or less subjectivist, and that is the question of the "who" of expression. Is it the work of the individual agent? Or is it rather something which arises out of conversation, so that its locus is the speech community? Or should we think of the interlocutors themselves purely as artifacts of the space of expression, so that there is no "who" of expression at all? The first answer has been more or less discredited in the constitutivist tradition, for reasons touched on earlier. The second, Humboldtian one has been the most widespread. All speakers, as they enter the conversation from infancy, find their identity shaped by their relations within a preexisting space of expression. In this sense, they are the creatures of this space. But as they become full members of the conversation, they can in turn contribute to shape it, and so no simple, one-sided relation of dependence can capture the reality of speakers and language, as the third theory supposes.

The third theory is exemplified by Derrida: *différance* is the nonagent setting up the space of expression. This might be thought to be on the far anti-subjectivist end of the spectrum of this third question. But I believe that one should rather see the second, Humboldtian solution as the truly non-subjectivist one. The Derridean theory is in fact the mirror image of subjectivism. It gets its plausibility from the implausibility of this outlook, which Derrida parades before us in its more extreme forms as the only alternative. But I have no space to argue this here.

These two main questions, the latter divided into three subissues, set up a problem space with many possible positions, combining different options on the various dimensions. The Derridean philosophy combines a radical creationist position on subissue B (hence question A, which asks what is manifested, does not arise), with a relegation of the speaker to purely derivative status when it comes to C. This is what gives Derridean philosophy its strongly anti-subjectivist appearance, which I suggested is mere appearance. The rhetoric of the end of the subject masks the option in favor of a highly subjectivist stance on B. In fact, one might argue that the relegation of the speaker on C is just another consequence of the radical creationism on B. It is a corollary of the idealist thesis that there is nothing outside the text.

Heidegger stands quite differently in this space, I want to argue, so that Derridean readings gravely misperceive him. He is a "manifestationist" on subissue B; his strong anti-subjectivist stance is taken on subissue A. Expression is not self-expression; creative language is a response to a call. On subissue C, he comes quite close to the Humboldtian view. Statements like the famous "spricht die Sprache" I understand as conveying his anti-subjectivist stand on A, rather than a proto-Derridean invocation of a super-(non)agent.

This makes Heidegger come pretty close to a commonly held position in the constitutivist tradition on the second complex of issues, about the nature of the expressive power. Where he departs radically is rather on the first main issue, in his thoroughgoing insistence that the clearing is not to be ontically grounded. This might be confused with the creationist view of the expressive power of subissue B. But these are quite different questions. To see the clearing as not ontically grounded, or locatable, is not to see it as self-enclosed, as related to nothing outside it. A self-enclosed picture of the clearing would run clean against Heidegger's brand of anti-subjectivism.

What emerges with Heidegger is thus a novel position, one that was hard to imagine before he began to pose the questions of philosophy in his own peculiar way. The confusion between a de-onticized view of the clearing and a creationist one is easy to make if we operate in familiar categories. For most manifestationist readings of the space of expression were based on some firm ontic posits, which were thought to be the essential underpinnings of this reading, like Hegel's spirit or Schopenhauer's will or Nietzsche's will to power, for that matter. Denying these seemed to mean opting for a view of the space of expression as purely made.

But Heidegger alters the whole philosophical landscape by introducing the issue of the clearing and its ontic placing. Once we separate out this question from that of the nature of the expressive power, we can combine a manifestationist view on the latter with a rejection of all ontic grounding. But on what, then, do we base this manifestationist view, if we can no longer recur to ontic underpinnings of the familiar kind? On a reading of the space of expression itself. Otherwise put, the clearing itself, or language itself, properly brought to light, will show us how to take it. Heidegger as always moves to retrieve what is hidden, not in some distant point, but in the event of disclosure itself.

This is why I believe that articulating the themes of the constitutive view of language can help in explaining Heidegger. He draws on them because he formulates the clearing through describing the action or event which makes it possible, and these are crucially linguistic.

Let me try to reconstruct Heidegger's *démarche* drawing on what has been said about language in the broad sense of the constitutivist tradition, that is, about the expressive power. We can follow the Aristotle-derived thread I mentioned earlier: read the expressive power to glean the excellence, the *areté,* implicit in it.

Through language, a world is disclosed; a world in which features are located, which is also a locus of strong goods, of objects of the specifically human emotions, and of human relations. So plainly one telos, or range of *tele,* which we find in language prescribes that this disclosure be properly done: that the features be correctly located, that the goods be fully acknowledged, that our emotions and relations be undistortedly discerned. Some of this range of goals is carried out in what we define as science; other parts require other types of discourse, including literature and philosophy and the other arts.

This range of goals gives a manifestationist cast to the clearing. In the case of natural science, one might define the end as more like depiction, the representation of an independent object, but in, say, clarifying emotions, language also helps to constitute or complete; the model of the symbol is the appropriate one. Attributing this approach to language to Heidegger makes of him an uncompromising realist, and that's what I think he was.

But beyond these goals of first-order disclosure, there is a telos in the clearing to disclose itself, to bring itself undistortedly to light. If its goal is undistorted uncovering, then how can this uncovering itself be an exception? Showing up should itself show up. But this raises a problem, because Heidegger argues that there is a tendency precisely to distort our understanding of the clearing. At least in the tradition determined by our western "destining," we come to see language as our instrument, and the clearing as something that happens in us, reflecting our goals and purposes. At the end of this road is the reduction of everything to standing reserve in the service of a triumphant will to will. In the attempt to impose our light, we cover the sources of the clearing in darkness. We close ourselves off to them.

That this second-order disclosure is part of the telos of language becomes clear in Heidegger's notion that the total mobilization of everything as standing reserve threatens the human essence.[19] For this is just the next stage in a basically Aristotelian line of argument. "The human is indeed in its nature given to speech."[20] So what goes against the telos of language goes against human essence.

But I can sense that some readers may be uneasy at this Aristotelizing of Heidegger. So let me hasten to point out the difference. The human essence is not here derived from the ontic examination of a particular species of hairless ape, which happens to use language. We don't derive this from the nature of the "rational animal." It is, on the contrary, purely derived from the way of being of the clearing, by being attentive to the way that language opens a clearing. When we can bring this undistortedly to light, we see that it is not something we accomplish. It is not an artifact of ours, our *Gemächte*. It must be there as the necessary context for all our acting and making. We can only act insofar as we are already in the midst of it. It couldn't happen without us, but it is not our doing. It is the basis for all the sense that our lives make—or that anything makes. Hence the sense of our lives must at least include as a central element the part we play in the clearing's coming to be. This is not the major role that a creator would have, but a secondary one, helping it to happen, protecting and maintaining it. We have to take care of *(pflegen)* being, spare *(schonen)* it.[21] The human agent is "the shepherd of Being."[22]

Denying this role, trying to transform it into something else, acting as though we were in control, is going against our essence and can only be destructive. The parallel with Aristotle's line of reasoning is unmistakable. It has been transposed, however, into a new key. Our essence is not derived from any ontic description, but from our role in relation to the clearing.

That is why Heidegger sees his philosophy as anti-humanist, aligning "humanism" as he does with an anthropocentric doctrine of human control.

But how do you acknowledge the way of being of the clearing? How do you make showing up undistortively show up? Disclosure is not some extra entity over and above the ones which show up. So meta-disclosure occurs in the way that first-order entities show up. And for Heidegger this means that they, or an important subset of them, have to show up as "things," not simply as objects or, even worse, as standing reserve.

The thing about a "thing" is that in being disclosed it co-discloses its place in the clearing. Later Heidegger introduces the notion of the "fourfold" to explain this: mortal and divine beings, earth and sky. Take a humble entity like a jug. As it shows up in the world of a peasant, still unmobilized by modern technology, it is redolent of the human activities in which it plays a part, of the pouring of wine at the common table, for instance. The jug is a point at which this rich web of practices can be sensed, made visible in the very shape of the jug and its handle, which offers itself for this use. So much for the human life that co-shows up in this thing.

At the same time, this form of life is based on and interwoven with strong goods, matters of intrinsic worth. These are matters which make a claim on us. They can be called "divine." So these too are co-disclosed. Heidegger imagines this connection as arising from an actual ritual of pouring a libation from the jug. But I doubt if the Christian, Black Forest peasantry of Swabia (as against ancient Greeks) actually did this kind of thing; and it is sufficient to point out that the human modes of conviviality that the jug co-discloses are shot through with religious and moral meaning. Perhaps the pastor said grace, but even if he didn't, this life together has central meaning in the participants' lives.

The jug is something shaped and fashioned for human use. It is one of those objects which is already clearly identified as a locus of features. As such it stands on and emerges out of a vast domain of still unformed and unidentified reality. This is a field of potential future forming, but it is limitless, inexhaustible. All forming is surrounded by and draws on this unformed. If we are not closed to it, the jug will also speak of its history as a formed entity, of its emergence from unformed matter, of its continuing dependency on the unformed, since it can only exist as an entity as long as it is supported by the whole surrounding reality. It rests ultimately on the earth, and that is the word Heidegger uses for this dimension of co-disclosure.

Finally, the jug and the whole round of activities it speaks of, and the earth, are open to greater cosmic forces which are beyond the domain of the formable, and which can either permit them to flourish or sweep them away. The alternation of day and night, storms, floods, earthquakes, or their benign absence—these are the things that Heidegger gathers under the title "sky." They provide the frame within which the earth can be partly shaped as our world.

All these are co-disclosed in the thing. Heidegger says that it assembles (*versammelt*) them, and they sojourn *(verweilen)* in it.[23] When this happens, then the clearing itself can be said to be undistortively disclosed. The undistorted meta-disclosure occurs through this manner of first-order showing up. Being among things in such a way that they show up is what Heidegger calls "dwelling" *(wohnen)*. It involves our "taking care" of them.

> Staying with things is the only way in which the fourfold stay within the fourfold is accomplished at any time in simple unity. Dwelling preserves the fourfold by bringing the presencing of the fourfold into things. But things themselves secure the fourfold *only when* they themselves *as* things are let be in their presencing. How is this done? In this way, that mortals nurse and nurture the things that grow, and specially construct things that do not grow.[24]

As is evident from this passage, things include more than made objects. They include living things. And they go beyond that: "But tree and pond, too, brook and hill, are things, each in its own way."[25] So part of what is involved in preserving the fourfold is "saving the earth."[26]

Living among things in this way allows the fourfold to be manifest in their everyday presence. This is already an effect of language, because the fourfold can be co-disclosed only to us, who have already identified the thing itself and marked out the four dimensions in language. But there is a more concentrated mode of language, where we try to bring to its own proper expression what is co-disclosed in the thing. We try to capture this in a deliberate formulation through an expressive form. Heidegger's own form of philosophizing (properly, "thinking") is an attempt to do this. But it can also be done in works of art. So the peasant woman, as she puts on her shoes, experiences her life in the fields and the seasons and ripening corn. She "knows all this without observation or consideration." But in van Gogh's painting of the peasant's shoes, their thingly nature is shown as something we can contemplate, in an express formulation we can consider and observe.[27]

But we close ourselves to all this when we turn away from living among things, and formulating what they co-disclose in art, and identify them as context-free objects, susceptible of scientific study; and even more so when we are swept up in the technological way of life and treat them as standing reserve. If we make this our dominant stance to the world, then we abolish things, in a more fundamental sense than just smashing them to pieces, though that may follow. "Science's knowledge, which is compelling within its own sphere, the sphere of objects, already had annihilated things as things long before the atom bomb exploded."[28]

So what does this tell us about language? It has a telos, which requires that entities show up in a certain way. This is already made possible through language. But more, when it is lost, an essential role in its retrieval devolves on certain uses of language in philosophy and art or, in Heideggerese, "Denken" and "Dichten." And when we understand the potential role these can have, we understand that the original way of dwelling we have lost flowed itself from some founding acts of one or the other.

So language, through its telos, dictates a certain mode of expression, a way of formulating matters which can help restore thingness. It tells us what to say, dictates the poetic or thinkerly word, as we might put it. We can go on talking, mindful only of our purposes, unaware that there is anything else to take notice of. But if we stop to attend to language, it will dictate a certain way of talking. Or, otherwise put, the entities will demand that we use the language which can disclose them as things. In other words, our use of language is no longer arbitrary, up for grabs, a matter of our own feelings and purposes. Even, indeed especially, in what subjectivism thinks is the domain of the most unbounded personal freedom and self-expression, that of art, it is not we but language that ought to be calling the shots.

This is how I think we have to understand Heidegger's conception of language speaking. It is why Heidegger speaks of our relation to language in terms of a call (Ruf) we are attentive to. "Die Sterblichen sprechen insofern sie hören." And he can speak of the call as emanating from a silence (Stille).[29] The silence is where there are not yet (the right) words, but where we are interpellated by entities to disclose them as things. Of course this does not happen before language; it can only happen in its midst. But within language and because of its telos, we are pushed to find unprecedented words, which we draw out of silence. This stillness contrasts with the noisy Gerede in which we fill the world with expressions of our selves and our purposes.

These unprecedented words ("sayings" is better but "word" is pithier) are words of power; we might call them words of retrieval. They constitute authentic thinking and poetry.[30] They are on a different level from everyday speech—not because they are "heightened" speech, but because everyday speech is a kind of dulling, a falling off, a forgetfulness of the more full-blooded disclosure that words bring.[31] That is why I want to speak of retrieval.

Heidegger is on to something very important, a power of words that enframing theories can make no sense of. It has tremendously positive uses, but terrifyingly dangerous ones as well. Heidegger characteristically is only aware of the former. The danger comes from the fact that so much can be retrieved from the gray zone of repression and forgetfulness. There are also resentments and hatreds and dreams of omnipotence and revenge, and they can be released by their own appropriate words of power. Hitler was a world-historical genius in only one respect, but that was in finding dark words of power, sayings that could capture and elevate the fears, longings, and hatreds of a people into something demonic. Heidegger has no place for the retrieval of evil in his system, and that is part of the reason why Hitler could blindside him, and why he could never get a moral grasp on the significance of what happened between 1933 and 1945.[32]

But there is also a positive relevance of Heidegger's philosophy to modern politics, which is especially important today. I return here to the issue raised at the outset. Heidegger's understanding of language, its telos, and the human essence can be the basis of an ecological politics, founded on something deeper than an instrumental calculation of the conditions of our survival (though that itself ought to be enough to alarm us). It can be the basis of a "deep" ecology.

As I put it above, we can think of the demands of language also as a demand that things put on us to disclose them in a certain way. This amounts to saying that they demand that we acknowledge them as having certain meanings. But this manner of disclosure can in crucial cases be incompatible with a stance of pure instrumentality toward them. Take wilderness, for instance. It demands to be disclosed as "earth," as the other to "world." This is compatible with a stance of exploration, whereby we identify species and geological forms, for instance, as long as we retain a sense of the necessary inexhaustibility of the wilderness surroundings. But a purely technological stance, whereby we see the rain forests as only a standing reserve for timber production, leaves no room for this meaning. Taking this stance is "annihilating" wilderness in its very meaning, even before we step in and fell all the trees, to parallel Heidegger's remark about things and the atom bomb.

This stance does violence to our essence as language beings. It is a destruction of us as well, even if we could substitute for oxygen and compensate for the greenhouse effect. This way of putting it might make it sound as if Heidegger's ecological philosophy were after all a shallow one, grounded ultimately on human purposes. But we have already seen how this misconstrues his view. For the purposes in question are not simply human. Our goals here are fixed by something we should properly see ourselves as serving. So a proper understanding of our purposes has to take us beyond ourselves. Heidegger has perhaps in that sense bridged the difference between shallow and deep ecology, and come up with a genuine third position. As I indicated at the outset, his position is unclassifiable in the terms the issue is generally debated in. It breaks genuinely new ground.

Properly understood, the "shepherd of Being" can't be an adept of triumphalist instrumental reason. That is why learning to dwell among things may also amount to "rescuing the earth." At this moment, when we need all the insight we can muster into our relation to the cosmos in order to deflect our disastrous course, Heidegger may have opened a vitally important new line of thinking.

— 7 —

Irreducibly Social Goods

Are there any irreducibly social goods? For some political strands of thinking in our culture, it is obvious that there are. For another influential tradition of academic thought, it is obvious that there are not. Common sense is divided on the issue, and confused.

The line of thought that takes the negative side is dominant, among other places, in economics. It is often taken as self-evident truth in that congeries of thoughts, calculations, and reflections called "welfare economics." And it is the bedrock of an influential strand of philosophical thought which has been taking up a lot of the intellectual space in our civilization over the last three centuries, which we can roughly call "utilitarian."

Amartya Sen in his celebrated essay "Utilitarianism and Welfarism" offers a definition:

> Welfarism: The judgement of the relative goodness of alternative states of affairs must be based exclusively on, and taken as an increasing function of, the respective collections of individual utilities in these states.[1]

There are three crucial philosophical assumptions built into this definition. The first is consequentialism: the idea that our value judgments ought to weigh outcomes, states of affairs. They should not concern themselves, as some other modes of ethical thinking do, with the intrinsic moral quality of acts. On a traditional theory which makes the notion of virtue central, such as Aristotle's, a crucial consideration can be whether an action is one of, say, courage or cowardice, loyalty or treachery. But for the consequentialist what counts is the outcome, what results. Hence judgments of value can be made by weighing states of affairs. This is the rational way to evaluate.

The second assumption is utilitarian. The philosophy of utility can be seen as a species of consequentialism, adding one further step to what a rational evaluation procedure ought to be like. The states of affairs are to be assessed for their utility, that is, the happiness or satisfaction they give to agents. This "happiness" is to be understood in its raw form. That is, there must be no metaphysical winnowing, whereby some kinds or sources of satisfaction are considered depraved or lower and hence not sources of real or true happiness. Whatever people find satisfying is satisfying. What they rank as more satisfying must be judged as quantitatively superior, and so on. There is to be no second guessing of the agent in terms of a doctrine of human nature or the good life. Here again there is a sharp contrast with much traditional ethical theory, including Aristotle, for whom happiness was closely tied to a conception of the good life.

The utilitarian theory is, of course, not committed to the view that every person will always understand their own interests best; an agent may be mistaken about what will bring about states he finds satisfying. He may be ignorant enough to think that drinking methyl alcohol has precisely the same consequences as drinking wine, and he knows that the state induced by wine is highly satisfying. So he may have to be protected from the results of his own ignorance. But it is clear that the warrant for saying he needs protection—the harmful consequences of drinking raw alcohol—come from his own tastes and reactions. He himself would not find blindness satisfying.

The third assumption comes almost as an anticlimax. It is atomism: the utilities to be weighed in states of affairs are those of individuals. This seems truistic because the modern philosophy of utilitarianism is from its very foundations committed to atomism. From within this philosophy it just seems self-evident that all goods are in the last analysis the goods of individuals. By the time you get this far along in the outlook of welfarism, the third assumption almost disappears from sight as an assumption. It looks like the most banal common sense.

Sen deals a solid blow to welfarism by showing the fragility of its utilitarian assumption. I want to tackle the atomist part. But just because this is so well embedded in the philosophical underpinnings of the other two, I have

to dig somewhat deeper to get at it. As my spade cuts into the marshy soil
under the welfarist construction, I come across two more struts that should
be laid bare. They both contribute to making it seem self-evident that goods
must be in the last resort individual.

Of course the expression "in the last resort" involves an important quali-
fication. Naturally every school of thought recognizes public goods. There
clearly are measures or institutions or states of affairs which offer satisfactions
to more than one individual. And in some cases these can't in the nature of
things be brought about in such a way as to benefit a single individual, but
must benefit many or none. National defense is often cited as an example.
Or we might think of a dam on a stream designed to stop flooding in
springtime. This saves my cottage, but can't be so designed as to save mine
without also saving yours. Bentham offered the concept of a good which
would be public not in the sense of benefitting all members of a collectivity,
but of conducing to the good of a number of individuals who could not be
identified beforehand. If the municipality builds a handrail on steps that are
likely to be covered with ice in winter, this will help whoever happens to
be using those stairs after a bout of freezing rain. Similarly, erecting a street-
light will make passage easier and safer for whoever happens to be passing
along at night.

But in all these cases, it can be argued, the good is a good only because
it benefits individuals. In some cases, there may be many such, indeed, the
benefits may encompass all the individuals of a given collectivity (say all
citizens who are defended from the enemy, or all dwellers beside the stream
that is dammed). In other cases it may not be possible to say exactly who
benefits. But in the end, the measure or state of affairs is only good because
it delivers satisfaction to individuals.

This last sentence catches the crucial thesis, that public and social goods
are necessarily "decomposable." It seems evident because of the two underpinnings I mentioned above. The first is a philosophical atomism that lies
very deep in the modern tradition of social science. It draws on the atomism
that was foundational to the modern revolution in natural science, and its
originating figure is probably Hobbes. All wholes have to be understood in
terms of the parts that compose them—but societies are made up of individuals. The events and states which are the subject of study in society are
ultimately made up of the events and states of component individuals. In
the end, only individuals choose and act. To think that society consists of
something else, over and above these individual choices and actions, is to

invoke some strange, mystical entity, a ghostly spirit of the collectivity, which no sober or respectable science can have any truck with. It is to wander into the Hegelian mists where all travelers must end up lost forever to reason and science.

This atomism comes to the fore frequently in the plea for what is called "methodological individualism," which enjoins us to treat all collectivities as composed of individuals. To those whose sentiments are expressed by the above paragraph, this just seems elementary common sense, advice you ignore at your peril. But then the thesis that social goods are necessarily decomposable falls out as an obvious application of a much more general principle, and one that seems unchallengeable. This is one supporting strut that my spade has laid bare, and soon I'll have to try to saw it through.

But before lifting the saw (or as aggression mounts, the ax), I want to expose the second strut. Let's call it "subjectivism." This is implicit in the utilitarian conception of happiness, which as we saw is deliberately noncritical. Happiness, and thus the good, is measured in terms of what makes people feel happy. We are ultimately referred to subjective feelings, or satisfactions; in terms of a more up-to-date version of utilitarianism, to preferences. The good, or the objects of value, is ultimately determined by what goes on in people's minds or feelings. But then the atomist understanding seems all the more appropriate, since no one supposes that there is a locus of thought or feeling other than the minds of individuals. Unless one takes refuge in a group mind of some strange sort, it simply appears evident that the good so understood must be ultimately decomposable into states of individuals. Subjectivism adds force to atomism in contributing to the unshakable force of this thesis.

Now I want to go to work on the first strut, on atomism. What is it that makes methodological individualism seem so self-evident to so many people? Plainly it is the consideration that in some obvious sense societies consist of nothing other than human beings. Of course, once you're living in a society, or even studying how it works, you have to take account of all sorts of things which are not simply people or concatenations of people: roles, offices, statuses, rules, laws, customs. These can easily bemuse you. But if you stand back and reflect for a minute, you have to realize that all there actually is here is a bunch of human organisms interacting. Take them away and you have nothing left. Their interaction may involve their having certain thoughts, and the contents of these involve roles, offices, etc. But these are ultimately the predicates of the component individuals.

Some reflections of this kind underlie methodological individualism. We can recognize the influence of a no-nonsense brand of naturalism in our scientific culture. But plausible as this reasoning is, it is dead wrong. It is of course true in some sense that there being things like roles, offices, laws, statuses, and the like is dependent on humans being capable of thought; in the sense that, to beings incapable of thinking, we could never attribute any of these features, which are essential to understanding our social life. It is even dubious whether it makes sense to speak as we tend to do of "hierarchy" for a group of baboons. Certainly one strong male may keep the others at bay and cowed, while he controls the females. But if we reflect on the conditions of using a term like "rank," it becomes evident that applying it involves reading something into baboon life we have no reason to think is there. Someone of a certain rank is *owed* acknowledgment; some infraction is committed when this is withheld or denied. Using this term implies that the subjects it is applied to make these distinctions, and that means they have these thoughts or some of this range: "That's unconscionable" or "That's an insult" or "At last he's behaving properly."

So roles, and the like, require thoughts. And thoughts occur as events in the minds of individuals. So much is true. But this still doesn't add up to a justification of atomism. That's because of the peculiar nature of thoughts (and hence of all the things that require thought in order to exist). Thoughts exist as it were in the dimension of meaning and require a background of available meanings in order to be the thoughts that they are.

Bad historical novels remind us of this all the time. If a character in a novel set in the middle ages rejects a course of action because it is not "fulfilling," or a man who figures in a story about a neolithic village thinks of his lover as "sophisticated," our sensibility is jarred by the incongruity. It is similar, but also importantly different, to the incongruity of their using twentieth-century technology. In both cases we know they "couldn't" be saying/thinking/doing what is described. But in the case of the incongruous thought or speech, it's not just the absence of certain artifacts in their environment. It's not something which could be remedied by a time warp which allowed certain devices to be delivered to them. The impossibility rather consists in that this whole gamut of meanings didn't exist for them; the whole way of classifying things as "fulfilling" or "sophisticated," and their various opposites and alternatives, wasn't part of the background of possible descriptions for them. Their language lacked these resources.

This illustrates what is in some respects a truism of human existence, the way in which thoughts presuppose and require a background of meanings to be the particular kind of thoughts they are. But the terms "presuppose" and "require" in the previous sentence point to a peculiarly strong relation. It is not a contingently causal one, which we could imagine a way around—the kind we invoke when we say that neolithic villages couldn't have built pyramids because this requires and presupposes a larger labor force. We can always imagine here a constellation of circumstances, perhaps very far from the actual course of things, but nevertheless not absurd as a supposition in which this requirement might be circumvented: say that a race of people with much greater physical strength inhabited these villages. But in the case of thoughts and words, a supposition of this kind would make no sense. Nothing that these people could say could ever *count as* describing something as "fulfilling" or "sophisticated," as long as they had their particular linguistic background.

The impossibility is stronger here because we're in the domain of meaning, the domain in which "counting as" and "validity" play an essential role. To have the descriptive thought "That's a fulfilling life" or "There's a sophisticated girl" is to be making a claim about these objects. The general form of the claim in this kind of case can be summed up as the claim that these are the right terms to be applied here. In this respect, there are analogies between thinking and making a move in some rule-governed human activity in which questions of validity and invalidity arise—such as, for instance, a game. This was of course the basis for Wittgenstein's celebrated use of the game image in his discussions of language and thinking. Whatever the weaknesses that may arise when this image is overapplied, it has this kernel of justification: we are in the domain of validity.

But then we can readily see why in a strong sense certain thoughts are impossible in certain circumstances. Nothing could count as making the claim "she's sophisticated" among neolithic farmers in upper Syria (if our surmises are right about their culture), in somewhat the same way as nothing could count as making the queen's gambit in a checkers game. The move presupposes a background of rules or, in the case of language, conditions of possible validity; and in both these cases the background is missing.

I invoked the name of Wittgenstein, and he is undoubtedly the most celebrated among those who have forced on contemporary philosophy this crucial feature of thought and language. A given linguistic item only has the meaning it has against the background of a whole language. The use of a single term, separated from that background, is unthinkable. The supposition that one might, through the invention of learning, think of such a single term makes no sense. Wittgenstein uses this point to great effect in arguing against the possibility of a private language, as when he asks us to imagine the case of someone who wants to give a name to an inner sensation without reference to the rest of language.[2] In order to know what I myself am saying, I would have to place this entity somewhere, would have to say at least that what I'm naming is a *sensation*. Wittgenstein relies on the same point to show up the limitations of ostensive definition. In order for others to understand what I mean when I explain the meaning of a word by pointing to something, they have to grasp what kind of thing is being alluded to. I point to an object and say "brown." But do I mean the kind of object, the distance from me, the shape, or the color? Only if you know it's the color do you read me right.

Once we have Wittgenstein's point, we look back in amazement at the unsophisticated (*we* can use this term) theories of meaning that dominated early modern philosophy, those of Hobbes, Locke, and Condillac.[3] The last gives an account of the origin of language in which he sees his originators learning to use first one word, then two, then three, then more. The implication was that there could be such a thing as a one-word lexicon, something that doesn't seem to have been challenged in the classical period, but whose full absurdity Wittgenstein exposes.[4]

What underlay this naive view? It was that thought and the use of language were assimilated to ordinary kinds of events, which don't require a background of meaning. What emerged from my discussion about the two kinds of impossibility, instanced respectively in the neolithic village by the inability to think "sophisticated" and the inability to build a pyramid, was a distinction between two kinds of events, those that do and those that do not presuppose a background of meaning which lays down validity conditions. Let's call them "plain events" and "meaning events." The early theories of language took thinking a thought and introducing a word as plain events. There was an idea in the mind, a sound in the vicinity, and the individual thinker simply set up a connection between the two. These theories ignored altogether the existence of meaning events, and imagined they could deal with everything as a plain event. Now exactly this error is what underlies modern atomism and its offshoot, methodological individualism.

Once the point is made that all thoughts occur in individual minds, we might think that the case for methodological individualism is sufficiently made. But this suffices only if we are treating them as plain events. In a parallel way, Locke argues that the connection between idea and word has to be set up in someone's mind, so that lexica are always of individuals.[5] Once we see that we are dealing with meaning events, the story becomes more complicated. We can't just focus on the event that occurs; we have also to take account of the background that gives it its meaning. But this background is not an event, nor can it be located in individuals. It is a language, and locating it is no simple matter. From one standpoint, it can't be located at all; it can be seen as an ideal entity, like Pythagoras' theorem or the rule of *modus ponens*. But if we want to see how it is embedded in human life, then we have to say something like this: a language is created and sustained in the continuing interchanges that take place in a certain linguistic community. The latter is its locus; and that is what ultimately rules out methodological individualism.

Meaning events exist in a kind of two-dimensional space. They are particular events, but only in relation to a background of meaning. This is the basis of the Saussurian distinction between *langue* and *parole*.[6] Language can't be understood, Saussure claimed, unless we make this distinction. There is a code (langue), and this code is drawn on in each particular act of speech (parole). These are in a characteristic circular relation. The acts of parole all presuppose the existence of langue, but the latter is constantly recreated in the acts of parole. At any one moment, synchronically, language can be considered as an ideal system, but over time or diachronically it changes and evolves, and does so under the impact of parole, as people misspeak or deliberately innovate, and deviant usage gradually becomes standard.

Now let us say that each act of parole can be attributed to an individual or (decomposably) to individuals (I'm not sure I want to concede this at the end of the day, but it certainly seems a commonsense assumption). It still doesn't follow that we can give an atomist account of language. To do so is to collapse the other dimension, that of langue, which is not an individual matter but the normative practice of a community. Nor does it help to point to the fact that over time langue is given the shape it has through acts of parole. This doesn't make it decomposable, because the acts which so shape it are only such acts against the background of the langue of their day. The two dimensions can't be collapsed into one.

But methodological individualism involves attempting just such a collapse. It is based on the belief that the background can either be ignored (treating the acts of parole as plain events) or can somehow be reduced and decomposed into these acts. On either variant, it's a fundamental mistake.

What emerges, then, is the very deep intrication in our intellectual and cultural history of two issues: atomism versus the social perspective, on one hand, and denying versus acknowledging the dimension of meaning on the other. Once you collapse the dimension of meaning, ignore the independent role of langue, once there are no more meaning events but all are plain, then it just seems unproblematic on generally agreed naturalist grounds to conclude to atomism in politics, as was once the norm in physics. In this theory of language, since everything is now accounted for in terms of parole, and all acts of parole are those of individuals, it seems that language too must be ultimately an individual affair, that the hookup between sound and idea must occur in individuals, just as the classical theorists thought. What upsets this line of thought is not some mysterious collective consciousness but the nature of meaning events. Acknowledging the independent place of the dimension of langue means accepting something into one's social ontology which can't be decomposed into individual occurrences. This is the crucial step out of atomism.[7]

In the last paragraphs I've been speaking about language. But the discussion started with such crucial features of social life as roles, laws, offices, statuses. We got on to language because these are clearly connected with our having certain thoughts, and our thoughts are conditioned by our language. But it should be clear now that, in virtue of these connections, these features partake of the two-dimensional nature described in Saussurian terms. I am now filling a certain role, say that of father or teacher. This is evidently not a plain state, but a meaning state.[8] I can only fill that role because there are conditions of validity defined in the set of practices and institutions which shape the life of my society. The way in which I and others fill these roles, or fall short of doing so, may bring about diachronic change in this background set of conditions; finally, the practices and institutions are sustained in the particular form they have only through the ongoing interchanges of our social life. Each individual filling of a role is an act of parole which presupposes a background langue; and this in turn is sustained through constantly renewed acts. The Saussurian circle applies here too, and we can't reduce it without rendering ourselves incapable of understanding how societies work.

Methodological individualist accounts of social processes have to break down because they can't cope with this fact. In one sense, perhaps, all acts and choices are individual. They are, however, only the acts and choices they are against the background of practices and understandings. But this langue can't be reduced to a set of acts, choices, or indeed other predicates of individuals. Its locus is a society. This is the undecomposable kernel against which atomism must break its teeth.

I have been sawing and hacking away at that support of the thesis that goods are decomposable which I have called atomism. I hope that everyone will agree that it is now cut through and collapsing. It is time to connect this to the main issue. Besides taking away one of the strong motives to believe that all goods must be individual, does this understanding of society in terms of the Saussurian circle tell us anything directly about social goods? Perhaps I have removed one of the main reasons for believing a priori that social goods must be decomposable. But have I cast any direct light on what an undecomposable social good might look like?

I think it has. I want in fact to suggest that there are two ways in which one can identify a good as irreducibly social, and an understanding of the langue-parole dimensions of social action helps to clarify them.

The first way emerges directly out of the above discussion. If we refer to the background of practices, institutions, and understandings which form the langue-analogue for our action in a given society as our "culture" (in one possible use of this rather overworked term), then it is clear that the culture can be the locus of goods.

One obvious way in which it might convincingly appear as such to us is this: as individuals we value certain things; we find certain fulfillments good, certain experiences satisfying, certain outcomes positive. But these things can only be good in that certain way, or satisfying or positive after their particular fashion, because of the background understanding developed in our culture. Thus I may value the fulfillment that comes from authentic self-expression, or the experience that arises from certain works of art, or outcomes in which people stand with each other on a footing of frankness and equality. But all this is only possible against the background of a certain culture. Not every human culture has a place for authentic self-expression. Indeed, like "fulfilling" and "sophisticated," the very language of self-expression, including such a term as "authenticity," was not comprehensible in an earlier age. The works of art that give rise to the experience I value may be those of a given age, and hence once again presuppose a certain culture. The relations of frankness and equality I value will seem incomprehensible or even reprehensible to people of a different society—in hierarchical societies, for example, like medieval Japan. Where there are some analogues in that society, they would only hold for relations of close friendship, between very restricted groups, and not for the generally accepted public relations of all citizens at large.

If these things are goods, then other things being equal so is the culture that makes them possible. If I want to maximize these goods, then I must want to preserve and strengthen this culture. But the culture as a good, or more cautiously as the locus of some goods (for there might be much that is reprehensible as well), is not an individual good. Very well, then, one might say, it is a public good in the recognized category, such as national defense or the dam built upstream to protect our houses. Like them it is "public" in that it can't be procured for one person without being secured for a whole group. But the goods it produces are surely those of individuals: X's fulfillment, Y's experience, the relations of the individuals in this group.

But here's where the analogy becomes strained. Even leaving aside the case of frank and equal relations, to which I return later, there is something very different here. The dam and the army stand in a causal relation to the goods they produce. These goods could come about by some other means, even though it may be empirically unlikely. But a culture is related to the acts and experiences it makes intelligible in no such external way. The idea that the culture is only valuable instrumentally in this kind of case rests on a confusion. But this is essential to the ordinary understanding within welfarism of how public goods are decomposable. To the objection one might make to this thesis, that after all the dam is a single entity and helps many people, and therefore it is a social good, the answer is clear: the dam is a single entity, but the goods are all individual—X's house being preserved from flood, Y's house being preserved, and so on. The dam itself is not good, only its effects are. It is merely instrumentally valuable.

This kind of reply is not possible in regard to the culture. It is not a mere instrument of the individual goods. It can't be distinguished from them as their merely contingent condition, something they could in principle exist without. That makes no sense. It is essentially linked to what we have identified as good. Consequently, it is hard to see how we could deny it the title of good, not just in some weakened, instrumental sense, like the dam, but as intrinsically good. To say that a certain kind of self-giving heroism is good, or a certain quality of aesthetic experience, must be to judge the cultures in which this kind of heroism and that kind of experience are conceivable options as good cultures. If such virtue and experience are worth cultivating, then the cultures have to be worth fostering, not as contingent instruments, but for themselves.

But now, second, the valuable culture, unlike the dam, is an irreducible feature of the society as a whole. The dam, just as an instrument, is not a feature of society at all. This opens up another crucial disanalogy. A good is public in a common sense of welfarist theory, we saw, when its provision to one requires its being supplied for all. But this too, in the ordinary case, is a contingent restriction. In fact, with available technology and taking account of cost factors, the only solution to my flooding problem is a dam which also will protect all of you. But with a different gamut of possible technologies, or if I had much larger resources, there might be another solution: I encase my property in some force field that only operates against water pressing from the outside; and then I watch all of you with smug satisfaction, as you rush to evacuate in your boats. But this possibility makes no sense in the cultural case. This good is inherently social.

This is one way in which we can identify irreducibly social goods. But there is another, which picks out a partially overlapping class of such goods. Once again, we can see what it's like if we start from the ordinary welfarist understanding of a public good. This was judged decomposable, as we saw, because we can identify its being good with its being good for A, for B, for C, and so on, severally.

But now let's look more closely at the third example of culturally conditioned goods, the case of frank and equal relations. I entered a caveat at treating this as a good of individuals only, and now I want to explain why. The crucial point is that our relations being of this kind is itself an irreducibly social fact. That our relations are of a certain kind is not just the combination of a fact about me, say my disposition, and a fact about you. What this decomposition leaves out is the crucial factor, that we are not only well or ill disposed to the other, but that we have some common understanding about this. And it is futile and wrong-headed to try to define common or mutual understanding as a compound of individual states. Our having a common understanding about something is distinct from my understanding it, plus your understanding it, plus perhaps my knowing that you understand, and your knowing that I understand; nor does it help to add further levels, say that I know that you know that I understand. This kind of convoluted situation sometimes exists in the more delicate or strained human relations, or on the diplomatic level between states. But it is recognizably distinct from the case where we have something out between us and come to a common understanding.

There is another crucial distinction here, alongside that between meaning events and plain events, which has been totally ignored by the empiricist-utilitarian tradition but which is of the greatest human importance. It is that between what is convergent and what is genuinely common. A convergent matter is one that has the same meaning for many people, but where this is not acknowledged between them or in public space. Something is common when it exists not just for me and for you, but for *us,* acknowledged as such. Much of human life is quite unintelligible if we ignore this distinction. To start with, we could never understand why people strive to maintain the convoluted type of relations mentioned above. Nor could we grasp what friendship and love consist in, because it is essential to them that they repose to a large degree on common understandings.[9]

Common understandings are undecomposable. This is because, as I just put it, it is essential to their being what they are that they be not just for me and for you, but for us. That we have a common understanding presupposes that we have formed a unit, a "we" who understand together, which is by definition analytically undecomposable. If it were, the understanding would not be genuinely common. A relation of friendship is an example of one which reposes on a common understanding and is thus not susceptible of atomist analysis.

But friendship is usually judged a good. And where an undecomposable relation is a good, then some stronger condition generally holds: it is essential to its being a good relation that the common understanding englobe its goodness. Friendship presupposes not just mutual understanding, but understanding around this, that our friendship is valuable. The mutual recognition in love always includes some common sense of what this means to us. When this comes in doubt, when it looks as though we no longer value it in the same way, the love is under threat.

Here is another way, then, that a good can be social in an irreducible fashion: where it is essential to its being a good that its goodness be the object of a common understanding. We don't find such goods only in intimate life, such as love and friendship. My social example of frank and equal relations is also of this type. We don't in fact stand on such a footing with each other unless there is some common understanding of this. And we can't maintain the footing unless the common understanding englobes the rightness of this footing. The footing doesn't exist unless there is some common sense that we *are* equal, that we command equal treatment, that this is the appropriate way to deal with each other. Essential to this set of relations as a good is something that is undecomposable.

So we see two ways of defining irreducibly common goods: (1) the goods of a culture that makes conceivable actions, feelings, valued ways of life, and (2) goods that essentially incorporate common understandings of their value. There is obviously a substantial overlap between the two, in that a cultural good may also exist only to the extent that it is commonly prized. Indeed, the last example seems to have a foot in both categories: that our culture offers the possibility of public relations of frankness and equality shades over into our actually standing in such relations. Neither can perhaps long survive the demise of the other.

So what? Perhaps I'm right here, as a matter of philosophical analysis. But we may want to ask what follows for our social and political life. Is this just an academic dispute?

The answer ought to be already showing through. It can be gleaned from the examples I used that the conception of irreducibly social goods is bound up with some important strands of modern politics. So in articulating this kind of good I am spelling out the philosophical presuppositions of some political positions that are widely held.

Almost the first example that springs to mind is modern linguistic or cultural nationalism. Perhaps this springs first to my mind because I live in Montreal, and have been trying to make sense of what goes on here for the last half-century. It is clear that all stripes of nationalist sentiment in this province concur in seeing the culture of Quebec, and that means in practice the French language, at least as a common good in sense 1, the presupposition of the life they value; and sometimes as a good in sense 2 as well. What has emerged is a politics of defending the language as a common good, considered an important enough goal to take priority in some cases over individual goals that would otherwise have been considered as beyond legitimate constraint. Thus there have been restrictions on where parents could send their children to state-supported schools (totally private schools are unregulated); that is, on the language of schooling they could choose for their children. In response to pleas for freedom of parents' choice as a right, nationalist theorists have developed theories of "collective" rights, which are alleged to take precedence in certain cases over individual rights.

I'm not making a judgment here, just reporting a bit of contemporary politics based on concepts that would have to be philosophically explicated in something like the manner I have just outlined. But let me turn to another, perhaps (to some of you) less morally dubious example.

This is one of the central strands of modern democratic culture. I'm talking about the politics that takes participatory self-rule as a good in itself—not simply as something instrumental to other goals, like justice or peace or stability, but as something valued for its own sake. This has a long history in our culture. It connects to the tradition of thought in the modern West which has been called "civic humanist," and which took the ancient polis or republic as a model. Its major thinkers include Machiavelli (an idiosyncratic case, but he built on an influential strand in the Renaissance), Montesquieu, Rousseau, Tocqueville, and in our day Arendt. Its moments of decisive political impact, after the Italian Renaissance, are the civil-war period in England; the American revolution and constitution building; the French revolution; after which it has become a major strand in the self-understanding of western liberal democracies.

It takes the life of the citizen, of a person who is not simply subjected to power but participates in his/her own rule, as an essential component of human dignity. And it contrasts the life in which the citizen turns toward the great issues, where the fate of peoples and cultures hangs in the balance, to the narrow confines of a life focused only on self-enrichment or private pleasures. Civic humanism coins a special sense of the term "freedom" (or borrows it from the ancients), distinct from the common sense of "negative" freedom, to describe this political condition. Tocqueville eloquently described the attractions of this kind of liberty:

> Ce qui, dans tous les temps lui a attaché si fortement le coeur de certains hommes, ce sont ses attraits mêmes, son charme propre, indépendant de ses bienfaits; c'est le plaisir de pouvoir parler, agir, respirer sans contrainte, sous le seul gouvernement de Dieu et des lois. Qui cherche dans la liberté autre chose qu'elle-même est fait pour servir.

And Tocqueville finishes the passage grandly by saying that you either understand this taste for liberty or you don't: "On doit renoncer à le faire comprendre aux âmes médiocres qui ne l'ont jamais ressenti."[10]

But shorn of Tocqueville's aristocratic sensibility, we recognize a widespread aspiration and political value of our time. Now a regime in which people govern themselves as equal citizens is a common good in sense 2 above. It can't exist without some common understanding that this is the basis on which we stand with each other, and the common understanding must englobe the rightness of this basis. Of course this insight goes far back into the civic-humanist tradition of thought about republican rule, right back to the ancients. This kind of regime absolutely requires that we share a love for the "laws," what Montesquieu defined as "vertu."

But the outlook I'm describing here, following Sen, as "welfarist" can't assimilate this kind of good; it can't allow for an undistorted description of it. The politics of nationalism, or republican rule, emerge in its language as the cherishing of some instrumental public good. Or else their status as goods is understood in a purely subjectivist fashion: they are goods to the extent that people desire them. A certain proportion of Quebeckers have a "taste" for the preservation of the French language, and so this is a good, just like chocolate-chip ice cream and transistor radios.

But both views grievously distort the nature of the good sought, particularly the last. The spokesmen for nationalism, or republican rule, don't see its value as contingent on its popularity. They think that these are goods whether we recognize them or not, goods we ought to recognize. This stance sometimes goes unrecognized because it is somehow morally reprehensible: what right do these people have to tell us that we ought to give our national culture a higher priority in our lives? Or that we ought to participate in our own rule? Are they going to force us to be free? There seems to be something undemocratic in this attitude.

But this is a confusion. Democracy concerns our collective decision-making procedures. A proponent of nationalism or citizen rule can be a democrat as well as anyone else, in the sense of respecting these procedures (and there is a paradox in a proponent of republican rule failing to respect them, as has been tragically enough illustrated over and over again in modern history). But one doesn't have to tailor opinions about the good to the tastes of the majority. What an individual *advocates* must surely be independent of majority taste. The temptation to think otherwise comes from the rampant subjectivism in so much modern philosophy.

Now for the purposes of this discussion, I take no stand in favor of nationalism and citizen rule. Indeed, I could hardly do so because there are many strands of modern nationalism, and some of them are visibly evil. As a matter of fact, I've spent much of my political life combatting certain strands I dislike. I do confess to being a strong partisan of citizen self-rule, but all this is meant to be beside the point. What I want to bring out here is the way in which an important set of issues that figure in modern politics shows up distortively in the perspective of welfarism. Some alternatives can't be

undistortively formulated in this perspective. If these were intellectually incoherent, then it would be entirely to the credit of welfarism to have shown
them up as such. But since I argue that this kind of common good is perfectly coherent, I draw the opposite conclusion. The view that all social
goods are decomposable is a view we have to scrap, and not just for reasons
of intellectual rigor, because it's wrong—but also because it prevents us
from adequately understanding important aspects of modern social and political life.

But I haven't yet finished my attack. The welfarist outlook doesn't only
distort the political aspirations to common goods; it occludes to some extent
the opposition to these aspirations, because this philosophy is not neutral.
The utilitarian view is aligned with one of the contestants in the modern
struggle to define liberal democracy.

In fact, there are several strands of thought and political aspiration which
have gone into making contemporary western societies. The civic-humanist
strand is just one, and perhaps not the most powerful. Also of great importance have been the understanding of society as an association of bearers of
rights; and the picture of society as an association of bearers of interests,
either groups or individuals. The rights perspective goes back to the great
seventeenth-century natural rights theories, and even beyond if we trace it
out properly.[11] The picture of society as set up to serve the interests of its
members also goes back to foundational writers in the seventeenth century.
Locke is an important figure for both strands. But the full development of
the interest strand comes only in the eighteenth century, with the utilitarian
Enlightenment. Today this picture of society as a common instrument for
diverse group interests is visible in, for instance, the theories of interest-
group pluralism or the "economic" or elite theories of democracy.[12]

This interest strand has been in tension with the republican strand almost
since the beginning of the modern representative liberal state. J. G. Pocock
has traced the intellectual conflict in eighteenth-century England.[13] The
tension can be seen in the work of the writers of the American constitution.
And it is evident today.

In our day it turns on our attitude to centralization and bureaucracy.
From one perspective these can be positively valued, since they seem to be
the conditions of more effective production of goods that people (individually) want. Moreover, greater production can be thought to be the condition of fairer distribution, since it's easier to give to those who have less if

you don't have to take away from those who have more. Rapid growth can make social redistribution less of a zero-sum game. And fairness in distribution has always been a central concern of the interest perspective.

On the other side, concentration and bureaucratic organization are seen as the greatest adversaries of self-rule, gradually stifling it or rendering it irrelevant, and producing despair and cynicism in an age of giant, irresponsible agglomerations of power.

Now one of these strands of thought wants to think in terms of individual goods; it wants to see society merely in instrumental terms. It wants to be clear about who is getting what good, because it is concerned about "delivering the goods" maximally and (usually also) equally. The welfarist perspective is a good one to adopt in order to deliberate about alternatives, *granted the goods in which it is interested.* Welfarism is as congenial to this strand of thinking as it is inhospitable to the republican one.

Now if challenged to defend itself as a moral position, this strand would have something to say, because it comes from a moral tradition of some depth. There is an important line of modern moral thinking that I have called elsewhere the "affirmation of ordinary life," which starts with the Reformation and is secularized in the Enlightenment.[14] By "ordinary life" I mean the life of production and reproduction, of work and the family. The central idea is that the good life for human beings is not to be found in some higher activity, beyond ordinary life—be it contemplation or religious asceticism or even citizen rule. It is to be found at the very center of everyday existence, in the acquisition through labor of the means to live and the reproduction of life in the family. This idea perhaps starts with the Puritan stress on the "calling," and then it mutates into the Enlightenment conception of human happiness in a life according to nature. Rousseau too made it central, trying to combine it, paradoxically and perhaps impossibly, with an ethic of citizen rule. And it is visible in the exaltation of man the producer in the work of Marx.

Polemically, thinkers in this strand have directed their attacks on what they saw as the false prestige of the "higher" goods, which often served as a cover to justify the privileged status of a "higher" class properly dedicated to these goods—be it those with leisure to contemplate; or those who have dedicated themselves to religious askesis; or those who seek honor and fame in public life. In this context it is worth remembering that the ethic of republican rule was in a very real sense an aristocratic one for most of human history. Even ancient democracies were far from comprehensive, and they existed on the backs of an underclass of slaves, not to mention the exclusion of metics and the lower status of women. The ethic of ordinary life has always been hostile to that of honor and fame.

So the proponents of welfarism, a politics of instrumental reason aimed at the production of individual happiness, have an answer to the haughty claim of Tocqueville. They can plead that they are not interested in the illusion of supposedly higher concerns; that too much has already been sacrificed of human happiness on such altars; that what they are after is concrete, tangible human welfare; that theirs is the politics of real philanthropy, altruism, and concern for the human good.

A full-scale moral argument is about to break out here, one of some depth and passion, one that could illuminate our current predicament if we carried it forward. And that is what's wrong with welfarism. It prevents this argument from happening. For it not only distorts its opponent's position, but occludes its own. As long as you think that all goods must be individual, and that any other construal is incoherent, you can't see that there is a *moral* argument here. The burden of advocacy of the welfarist stance to policy seems entirely borne by *logical* arguments. The issue seems one of thinking straight, rather than one of acting well. Welfarism, as a doctrine about the nature of the good, has to be dispelled before the really interesting argument, between welfarism as a theory of *what things are good* and its opponents, can swim into focus.

As a philosophical doctrine, welfarism is acting as a screen, which prevents us from seeing our actual moral predicament and from identifying the real alternatives. It pretends to a neutrality it doesn't really enjoy. The result is that it distorts its opponent and, perhaps even more fatefully, hides from itself the rich moral outlook that motivates it. To set it aside is more than a demand of intellectual rigor. It is also a requirement of political and moral lucidity.

And this is why it is worth showing to all sides in the debate that there are, indeed, irreducibly social goods.

— 8 —

Comparison, History, Truth

T here are a number of connected issues which seem to recur in interdisciplinary discussions between philosophers, anthropologists, historians, and students of religion. One might speak of them as "zones of puzzlement," within which we tend to lose our bearings and talk at cross-purposes. Somewhat rashly, I would like to explore four of these areas in this chapter. I start by listing them, not necessarily in logical order.

1. The boundary between myth and science is a troublesome one for anthropologists and students of religion. Is myth only what "they" (the people studied) do, and not what "we" (scholars) engage in? Or is this an outrageously presumptuous and ethnocentric assumption?

2. Another recurring problem concerns whether or how any understanding we propose of a religion or a society at a given moment of time needs to be embedded in a view of history. The extreme case of this kind of embedding, of course, is something we see in Hegel or Marx: the very intelligibility of any society or culture is bound up with the place it occupies in a certain line of development, itself defined by definite "stages." In full flight from this (and with good reason), some of us might want to deny that any embedding in a broader historical picture is necessary for understanding. But the issue is whether something of the kind always and necessarily haunts us, even when we want to repudiate it.

3. There is a set of problems about comparison. These inevitably arise for any group of people engaged in understanding a culture or religion

which is not theirs. How does the home culture obtrude? Can we neutralize it altogether, and ought we to try? Or are we always engaged in some, implicit if not explicit, comparison when we try to understand another culture? If so, where do we get the language in which this can be non-distortively carried out? If it is just our home language, then the enterprise looks vitiated by ethnocentrism from the start. But whose language, if not ours? And isn't the language of science "our language"? We get back here to issue 1: maybe science is our "myth," so that all we're doing is encoding others' myths in ours, and so on.

4. Does understanding necessarily raise issues of truth? To understand another culture, do we (implicitly or explicitly) have to be making or relying on judgments about the truth or validity of the claims made by people in that culture? Or can we duck the issue, as most of us who consider Hegelian syntheses as outrageously presumptuous would dearly like to do?

These "zones" are obviously related. In fact, even I had trouble keeping them apart at times. They have a common origin in a continuing malaise. We are engaged in a family of enterprises (I include philosophers as consumers if not producers of such studies) which originally defined themselves as offering sober, rational discourse about ways of life/discourses that often lacked those qualities. This discourse supposedly had another manner of access to its objects than they had to themselves. It had the benefit of reflective and rational understanding. It was Science (in the broad sense, like German "Wissenschaft"—which has nothing to do with the crazy claims to model human beings on natural science). From this standpoint, all the areas of puzzlement above clear up without remainder. The boundary myth/science expresses this difference of access; the scientific discourse offered the medium of comparison. *Of course* it offered judgments of validity. It was itself a discourse of greater validity. And clearly, all this went along with a certain understanding of growth in history, since the culture in which science flourishes has itself grown out of earlier, less favored cultures. The others are behind us.

We have trouble believing this now, for the well-known reasons. We have big doubts about some of the "scientific" claims (these are quite independent of doubt for positivist and reductivist claims about the language and methods of natural science, but plainly they also have had an influence). And we find the kind of satisfied ethnocentrism that the older view embodies both unbelievable and somewhat discreditable.

But at the same time, the discourse we use is continuous with that of our forebears. We write books and treatises like *The Golden Bough,* with claims supported by not totally dissimilar canons of evidence and argument. We can't just repudiate this rational and sober discourse—not sincerely, at least, because it's what we still speak; and feel we ought to speak, when it comes to that. We argue and trip each other up according to the same canons of argument, even when we're supporting theses like the nondistinction of science and myth which would seem to make nonsense of these canons. It's very painful and confusing.

My whole way of thinking on these issues has been much influenced by Gadamer (with some input, I have to admit, from Hegel as well), and so I'm naturally tempted to start off on this gamut of questions from the bottom, with some mixture of 3 and 4.

I think a crucial insight is the one that animates Gadamer's critique of Dilthey. The aim of understanding should not be to surmount or escape our own point of view, in order to "get inside" another. We do often talk this way, and sometimes harmlessly. But there are some assumptions this language suggests which are very wrong. The reason why it rings all the wrong bells is something to do with our natural-science tradition. Since the seventeenth century, the progress of natural science has been inseparable from our separating ourselves from our own perspective, even from the human perspective as such, in order to come as close as possible to "the view from nowhere."[1] This starts with the sidelining of "secondary" qualities in the seventeenth century, and continues through our detachment from the most fundamental features of the experienced world, with the acceptance of such things as curved space. The aim is to identify and then neutralize those features of the way the world appears which depend on our particular makeup. Science is only concerned with what is beyond this.

But the procedure is impossible in human science. It gets nowhere, and that for a reason of principle. If the aim of human sciences is to make people intelligible, and not just to predict their behavior (we have ample proof that the range of the merely predictive sciences is very narrow in human affairs),[2] we have to rely on a kind of understanding of human affairs which sets the forms and limits of intelligibility. Each one of us has such an understanding from our home culture, and it is woven very deeply into our lives: we don't mainly use it to make people intelligible in theoretical contexts, but to understand and deliberate about our own motives and actions, and those of the people we deal with every day. Indeed, much of our understanding is quite inarticulate; it is in this sense a form of pre-understanding. It shapes our judgments without our being aware of it.

But that's what we have to draw on to make other people intelligible, because this sets the forms and standards of intelligibility for us. The idea that I should pursue human science by attempting to neutralize this understanding in me, as I must pursue physics by neutralizing my Euclidean intuitions about space, is obviously crazy. It wouldn't make a foreign culture any more accessible. On the contrary, it would just dissolve the field of human action into meaningless motion. This would fit a program of strict behaviorism (which no one has ever really practiced), but would be against the very thrust of any more promising science.

This might seem to lock us into ethnocentric prisons. But as Gadamer points out, the fortunate thing about human beings is that understanding can change. And one of the important sources of this learning can be meeting foreign cultures. In terms of the motives I recognize as understandable, the Aztecs act pretty weirdly. Their normal behavior, in any case of priests and rulers, includes things like ripping people's hearts out, which I would expect only from psychopaths. Unless I want to rule out the whole society as pathological, which conflicts with other evidence, I have to face a challenge.

I meet this challenge by altering and enlarging my understanding, remaking its forms and limits. This means that I articulate things that were purely implicit before, in order to put them into question. In particular, I articulate what were formerly limits to intelligibility, in order to see them in a new context, no longer as inescapable structures of human motivation, but as one in a range of possibilities. That is why other-understanding changes self-understanding, and in particular prizes us loose from some of the most fixed contours of our former culture. The very questioning we are engaged in here is an instance of this. The sober and rational discourse which tries to understand other cultures has to become aware of itself as one among many possibilities in order properly to understand the others. But then it no longer goes without saying that we ought to subscribe to its canons.

This offers a model for how in principle ethnocentrism can be overcome, while showing how it will be very difficult in practice. The latter follows immediately from the fact that the exigencies of understanding the other may require us to relativize features of our own self-understanding that we cherish. Some levels of understanding of some others will be resisted fiercely if unconsciously. But the thing can be done. It comes about, however, through a quite different route than that suggested by the natural-science model.

What emerges from this model is that other-understanding is always in a sense comparative. That is because we make the other intelligible through our own human understanding. This is always playing a role, and can't just be put out of action. The more we think we have sidelined it or neutralized it, as in the natural-science model, the more it works unconsciously and hence all the more powerfully to ethnocentric effect. In a sense we only liberate the others and "let them be" when we can identify and articulate a contrast between their understanding and ours, thereby ceasing in that re-spect just to read them through our home understanding, and allowing them to stand apart from it on their own. But the necessary condition here is that the understanding we personally have as students of the other has grown beyond what I've just called the home understanding, because in making this contrast we have identified, articulated, and shown to be one possibility among others, what we previously felt as a limit.

If this account is right, then the great leaps in other-understanding take place through (perhaps implicit) comparisons or contrasts. The hope that we can escape ethnocentrism reposes on the fact that these contrasts tran-scend and often incommode the previous home understanding. But we might object: the new understanding is also "ours" in an important sense. It belongs to the community of scholars who are usually confined to the home culture (and in the case of history, or the study of past religions, this condition is insurmountable). The new understanding will also have limits. These will now define the common background against which the contrast is understood. Maybe this still distorts the other, maybe it still commands an ethnocentric reading.

There is no answer in principle against these charges. They are probably often correct. On my account, there is no way to go except forward; to apply, that is, further doses of the same medicine. We must try to identify and place in contrast the new limit, and hence "let the other be" that much more effectively. This process may go on indefinitely, but that doesn't make the earlier stages without value: severe distortions may be overcome at any of them.

But, in a sense, understanding on this Gadamer view is always, in one way, from a limited perspective. When we struggle to get beyond our lim-ited home understanding, we struggle not toward a liberation from this understanding as such (the error of the natural-science model) but toward a wider understanding which can englobe the other undistortively. Gadamer uses the image of a conversation, where in face of mutually strange reactions the interlocutors strive to come to some common mind (*eine Verständigung*—this expression has the right semantic reach to link understanding and common purpose). Of course, in many cases, the other can't talk back. But the image of the conversation conveys how the goal is to reach a common language, common human understanding, which would allow both us and them undistortively to be. Still this means that our understanding of, say, the Romans could never be considered an objective reading in the sense striven after by natural science. The latter tries for a perspective-free account of subatomic particles, for instance. What we get if successful is an understanding that allows us not to distort the Romans. Some other culture or age would have to develop a rather different language and understanding to achieve their own undistortive account of the Romans. The aim is fusion of horizons, not escaping horizons. The ultimate result is always tied to someone's point of view.

Let's imagine the ideal case, here not of historical but of contemporary intercultural language. Suppose a group of Christian and Muslim scholars with great effort and ecumenical understanding elaborated a language in which their differences could be undistortively expressed, to the satisfaction of both sides. This would still not be an objective, point-of-view-less language of religion. The effort would have to be started all over again if either wanted to reach an understanding with Buddhists, for instance.

Of course, in each case, something is gained; some narrowness is overcome. But this leaves other narrownesses still unovercome. The Gadamer perspective allows us the idea of an omega point, as it were, when all times and cultures of humanity would have been able to exchange and come to an undistortive horizon for all of them. But even this would still be only de facto universal. If it turned out that one culture had been left out by mistake, the process would have to start again. The only possible ideal of objectivity in this domain is that of inclusiveness. The inclusive perspective is never attained de jure. You only get there de facto, when everybody is on board. And even then the perspective is in principle limited in relation to another possible understanding which might have arisen. But all this doesn't mean that there is no gain, no overcoming of ethnocentrism. On the contrary; it is overcome in inclusiveness.

How does this broader understanding arise? It comes, I would claim, in comparisons or contrasts, which let the other be. Contrasts are crucial. But they come out in the broader understanding, which in turn comes from our articulating things formerly taken as given. So the contrast is in a language of our devising. That was the ground of an objection above, that it is always we who are devising the language in which the other is understood. But here I want to come at that objection from another angle.

It seems to me that it is not entirely true that the contrast is made by our (broader) language. In a sense, the contrast can be said to precede the devising of the language. First, I argued, there is a challenge because others don't really make sense against our home understanding. The challenge can just remain at the level of the strange and bewildering. But this is almost impossible to sustain. In fact, we almost always proceed to another stage; we find a way of placing the strange practice as corresponding to one (some) of ours. Even the gut Spanish reaction to the Aztecs, which saw their religion as devilish, is an instance of this. The contrast was simple: we worship God, they worship the devil. Understanding is complete. We pass to action.

In other words, we place the strangeness opposite some piece of our lives, as it were. The challenge has a specific form, and we can go to work on it to make sense of the difference. Sometimes the way we place it impedes understanding. Our location reflects some limit we can't get around, which would have to be overcome to understand it. Thus Frazer categorized magic and religion as modes of attempted control of the world. Magic works by finding impersonal connections; religion by propitiating and inducing the intervention of superhuman personal beings. These are thus lined up with each other, and with our own religion and also, of course, our technology. Seen this way, the contrast would turn just on how much one knew and understood about the workings of the universe. Magic had to be placed quite differently before it could be better understood. (I'm not sure we've yet placed it adequately.)

But what I draw from this is that the intuition of contrast is in a sense primary. It is the challenge given a shape, when it has ceased to be something just bewildering and frightening (though it may still be both). We have a feel for the contrasts long before we think we understand, or have developed a language of contrast. In that sense, too, comparison seems basic to understanding.

I've been discussing issue 3, but now I'd like to turn to number 4. It seems to me that some validity claims are inseparable from understanding.

Gadamer makes this point very forcefully as well. In fact, you understand another against the background of the surrounding reality. You see a man waving his hands wildly. Then you look closer, and you see that some nasty flies are swarming around him. His action becomes intelligible against his background. People can only be understood against the background of their (presumed) world. It may be that closer scrutiny reveals no flies, but he tells you that he is warding off flies. Here too his action becomes (more) intelligible. There is something else here to explain.

This story gives in simplified form the predicament of the explainer. It shows, I think, why there can't be explanation without a judgment of truth or validity. We understand the waving man against his world. Yet we cannot but have our view about the contents of this world. Where his view differs from ours, we start to explain him in terms of illusion; and we identify something else to explain. Where the flies are real, the explanation stops there. Our account is shaped throughout by what we understand to be the reality of the case.

We come across a myth of the origin of the world at the hand of giants. We try to interpret this myth, to explain the power it had in this culture, why it became their origin myth. But we never consider that there might have been giants. I'm not complaining of the narrowness of our perspective, just pointing out that our whole search for an explanation presupposes that there were no giants. If there were, then the myth has a quite different and much simpler explanation. In this way, our sense of reality is decisive for our understanding of these people. We know there aren't any flies, and that structures our entire quest.

This point is obscured because we feel our superiority to, say, Frazer, who seemed to be saying that earlier people were simply mistaken about magic. They made the understandable but erroneous leap from noting similarity between two things to postulating some kind of influence of one on the other. Unfortunately, they just got it wrong. When we begin to place magic differently, and we see it for instance as an interpretation of the moral significance of things, and their relation to human purposes, we see it all in an altered light. These people no longer seem just wrong, inferior to us in knowledge. Now there are things they know how to do, perhaps ways to come to terms with and treat the stresses of their lives, ways we seem to have lost and could benefit by. The balance of superiority is not all on one side.

We feel more satisfied with this interpretation, first because it seems to make the others more intelligible. If they were trying to find the best instruments for their purposes, in the way modern people do with technology, then they look dumb, too dumb to be believable. They didn't need a course in statistics to see that the rate of success with some of these cherished *nostra* was quite low. By imputing to them purposes that are somewhat less intelligible to our contemporary home understanding, which require more work and stretching on our part, we make them, overall, more comprehensible.

But we also feel more satisfied with this account because it is less crassly ethnocentric. This reason isn't entirely detachable from the first, since we also think it implausible that one people should be constitutionally superior to others, but it also has a moral thrust which is independent.

So far so good. But it would be a mistake to think that this means we are no longer making judgments of truth where Frazer was. We are still operating out of our conception of reality just as he was. Ours resembles his in that we don't really think that dances have any effect whatever on rain. But it differs from his in that we recognize other essential human purposes. We see how important it is for human beings to make sense of their world, to find some meaning in the things they experience. Even disease can be more easily repelled by the organism where the person can make sense of it all, and can mobilize his energies against it. High Victorian rationalists had trouble with this kind of thing—as do many people today, of course, including much of the medical profession—and this led to a too-narrow identification of what was going on in these practices. They were wrongly "placed." But this is still an understanding of the actions and beliefs of the people concerned in the light of what we recognize as reality. It has been slightly enlarged, and that's all to the good. But it is still operative.

It is all but unimaginable what it might be to operate without such a conception. True, one can study religions, for instance, and be genuinely agnostic about the existence of God. But some discriminations are still working. Thus the religion in question will have different theological expressions, different canonical statements. The student will inevitably be making some discrimination between them; all can't be taken as equally central and serious. How discriminate? You might just decide to go by the majority, or what the power centers opted for. But even this may be indeterminate, unless you had some sense of what is a more insightful or a less crass statement of the religion. And to the extent that you did discriminate completely on the basis of some such conforming criterion, you would be in effect operating on the assumption that religious formulations are not rankable on any internal criterion, on their richness or depth or inherent plausibility. This is, of course, a view no believer in the religion could share—it would betray a reductive view of religion, which recognizes no good grounds that can be given for belief.

Of course, the student's sense of reality doesn't have to be all that standard in his home culture. Here the discussion about comparison is relevant. I may be jogged out of a high Victorian view about human purposes, come to recognize the importance of finding a meaning in what happens to us, just because I'm bothered and challenged by this phenomenon of magic. In the process, I place this phenomenon differently, come to recognize the ways in which we also find meaning in what happens, and see through the contrast how these aren't the only ways. My language and understanding will have been extended.

But this discussion adds an important nuance to the previous one. There I was saying that making the other intelligible requires a language or mode of human understanding which will allow both us and them to be undistortively described. But from what has just been said, this has to be understood as compatible with our understanding them as, in important respects, wrong about their world. We can't say that understanding them without distortion means showing them to be unmistaken in any important respect. It does mean getting at the meanings things had for them in a language that makes them accessible for us, finding a way of reformulating their human understanding. But this may have to be in an account that also portrays them as being out of touch with important facets of reality.

I have been talking about problem areas 3 and 4. Now I'd like to turn to 1 and 2. And maybe I should start by saying something about the first, the boundary between myth and science, or between myth and rational discourse. It is naturally a place at which we feel strongly the basic dilemma or cross-pressure I described above. This distinction is a way of ranking discourses. We see ourselves as having climbed out of "myth" (let this for the moment stand duty for all the not-yet-rational forms) into science or reason. In the course of this, something was supposedly gained, some clarity, self-conscious control of thinking, greater capacity to grasp truth, or something of the sort.

But ranking discourses seems to entail ranking societies or cultures, according to the discourses they make possible or are hospitable to. So to put reason above myth seems to be putting, say, the modern West above tribal Africa or Tahiti before Captain Cook. But since we are averse to this kind of ethnocentric ranking, we are led to relativize this distinction, or to make it somehow nonhierarchical. For instance, we can say that rationality is *our* myth, thus different from but on the same footing as theirs.

The dilemma or conflict arises because we can't really treat reason in this way. It represents certain *standards;* otherwise it is no concept of reason at all. Rational and sober discourse constitutes a demand on us, which we try to meet. We argue with each other in the light of its canons, and blame each other for not living up to them in our arguments: "you're being illogical," "you're not being consistent," "that's a sloppy argument." In our actual practice we can't treat the distinction rational/less rational as a nonhierarchical one, because it defines how we ought to think.

We find ourselves in a bind. We embark on the comparativist enterprise, or the study of other religions, because of some deep intuition about the equal value of cultures. I think this has been a theme throughout the long history of concern and study of other cultures in the West, even though it was subordinate in the earlier, triumphalist period. But the Jesuits in the sixteenth and seventeenth centuries who tried to assimilate to Indian or Chinese culture in order to convert these peoples, instrumentally as they may have acted, had already separated off the superiority of the Christian faith, about which they had no doubts, from any purported superiority of western culture, which they were putting in question. True, there arose between them and us lots of progress theories that reduced everyone else to stepping stones to ours as the definitive culture. But this other intuition has always been there, and has motivated much of the work in other-cultural studies.

In any case, today this intuition of equal value seems almost an axiom. So we suspect ourselves of still being in an ethnocentric trap when we find ourselves believing a depreciating story. The conflict comes because the intuition of equal value leads us to engage in an enterprise, cultural studies, which is a discourse with rational canons, hence to value this; at the same time, we note that it wasn't in the repertory of many cultures. Indeed, we might state the conflict more sharply: whatever it is that has pushed modern western culture to study others, at least nominally in a spirit of equality (it is because they recognize this spirit as legitimate that orientalists feel calumnied by the attacks of such critics as Edward Said), is missing in many other cultures. Our very valuing of this equality seems to mark a superiority of our culture over some others.

This is one form of the dilemma, frequently noted, of western universalism. There is a paradox in the view that wants to value, say, Khomeinist Iran, which rejects this value root and branch. Can we value them precisely in their rejection of all other-valuing?

What seems to emerge is that the axiom of equality can't be worked out by making the distinction reason/not-yet-reason a simple nonhierarchical difference, at least not if we want to go on reasoning, as we do. I think it's the wrong move.

But moves of this kind, such as "reason is our myth," can seem plausible because we are vague about what we mean by reason. I won't exactly conquer vagueness, but I think one can clarify things a little by extracting a core sense out of the tradition that comes to us from the Greeks. Taking reason back to logos, I think we can find the basic demands it makes on us in a certain notion of articulacy. Socrates always wanted to make his interlocutors say what they thought, bring out the intuitions they were implicitly acting by. But this articulacy sees itself as under certain disciplines: the descriptions given must (a) check out by the best means of validation recognized at the time for descriptions of their type, and (b) they must be consistently applied. If this situation is described as F, then so must other like situations. You can't deny F to them without pointing out a relevant difference. Socrates trips up his unfortunate interlocutors by showing how their first-off articulations of "justice," "piety," and the rest, when applied across the board, generate utterly unacceptable results, like giving a homicidal maniac back his sword.

From this we can generate canons of reasoning, as Aristotle does. But beyond any formal statement of these canons, there are the demands of argumentative rigor. Rationality ought to be considered as applying primarily to discourses, and derivatively to texts or statements. I mean by discourses here the interchanges that generate texts. Whatever failings any particular text exhibits, it is part of rational discourse if it is seen as vulnerable to attack on the basis of the above standards, and if its authors see themselves as having to defend or amend it in the light of this attack.

Now there are two views about the scope of these demands, each of which generates in some form the temptation to take our distance from rationality, or to consider it just one set of possible demands among others. One of these draws its boundaries too broad, the other too narrow.

The first incorporates the changing principles of inference which different cultures and intellectual communities come to accept. Requirement (a) referred to the "best means of validation recognized" in a given society.

These change. The way people argued about issues of natural science before the Galilean revolution was very different from the way they argued after. Roughly speaking, where the whole background to understanding of the natural world was based on the notion that it bodies forth in some way the order of Ideas, certain inferences become obvious and unchallengeable. So some Paduan philosophers refuted Galileo's discovery of the moons of Jupiter by reasoning thus:

> There are seven windows given to animals in the domicile of the head . . . What are these parts of the microcosmos? Two nostrils, two eyes, two ears and a mouth. So in the heavens as in a macrocosmos, there are two favorable stars, two unpropitious, two luminaries, and Mercury undecided and indifferent. From this and from many other similarities in nature, such as the seven metals, etc., which it were tedious to enumerate, we gather that the number of planets is necessarily seven.[3]

This raises a smile today, and it reminds us of the philosophers in Brecht's play about Galileo, but it made a great deal of sense within that whole outlook. If you take off from the basis that a list of things reflects the order of Ideas, then this kind of reasoning is very powerful.

Now if you include these deeper views about the nature of things, which underlie our principles of inference in the category of rationality, then it seems that there are several such and that there is no such thing as a universal standard. But I'm suggesting that we should distinguish these views and principles from the demands I stated above, which while not accepted as important in every culture are nevertheless not themselves differently conceived from culture to culture.

The second wrong view makes reason too narrow. It is a form of articulacy, I argued. This is often forgotten, and we concentrate only on the demands made on articulacy. It seems then that we sufficiently answer these demands by avoiding any *infraction* of them, whether we manage to articulate anything significant in the process or not. Various modern procedural conceptions of rationality have tended in this direction. Reason is a matter of applying some canonical procedure, or avoiding inconsistency, or remaining up to some standard of rigor in our inferences. The issue of how articulate this allows us to be about important matters is left completely aside. In the end, some of the most important things are not talked about at all in the name of reason. Pushed to an extreme we would find our safest refuge against illogic in saying nothing—playing it safe, with a vengeance.

Needless to say, this departs crucially from the original Platonic conception. You really know something when you can *logon didonai,* give its logos. It is important that this meet the constraints of reason, but it is also important that it be articulated. Aristotle speaks for the full demands of reason when, in the famous passage of *Ethics* 1.3, he advises us "to expect that amount of exactness in each kind which the nature of the particular subject admits."

Now the too-narrow definitions of reason have bred a certain dissatisfaction, a sense that the important things have to violate its canons in order to be expressed. And this too has contributed to our frequent downgrading of reason, and seeing it as just one myth among others. But if we set aside both mistaken views, the too broad and the too narrow, we identify something we can't so easily repudiate, which indeed informs what we recognize as our best practice when we try to study culture, ours or others'.

Of course, if we look back at the account of the comparative enterprise, which consists in enlarging our human understanding so that we can make the other undistortively intelligible, we have to admit that this task doesn't necessarily call for rational discourse. Perhaps someone could do this effectively by writing a novel about some strange culture. William Golding's *The Inheritors* does a remarkable job of taking us outside our normal understanding of things in presenting an imaginative reconstruction of what a clan of Neanderthalers might have been like. Suppose they really were like that; then perhaps this novel would be more effective in enlarging our understanding of them than many a scholarly monograph. But we are committed to the specific enterprise of enlarging our understanding by sober and rational discourses. And what we gain by this is the self-consciously critical stance which allows us to learn from our mistakes and to ground our conviction that one account is better than another. Maybe this enterprise is doomed to meager success in comparison to literature. But it is clearly our enterprise, and it amounts to a commitment to rational discourse.

I'd now like, very reluctantly and hesitantly, to tackle issue 2. To what extent, if any, does our understanding of other cultures require that we embed them and us in a view of history? Hegel represents what we are fleeing from. But can we flee from all of it? Let me break down his view into components in order to get at this question.

Hegel's theory of history (a) makes crucial use of Aristotle's concept of potentiality. What is *an sich* unfolds *für sich* in history; we have it in us from the beginning to become what we later become. (b) This unfolding potentiality is the same for all human beings, even though some societies don't seem to get as far along in the process as others—at least at the moment of their historical flourishing they don't (it's not clear that Hegel rules out a second appearance of, say, China as a modern state, under European influence of course). There is, in other words, a single line of unfolding potentiality, and (c) this unfolds in fixed stages, where each is the precondition of what follows.

Now clearly we find (b), and hence (c), difficult to credit, for reasons I mentioned above and will return to later. But can we do without some variant of (a)? Let's take this case of reason, which I have been trying to describe. If we don't take our distance from it, and thus refrain from reducing it to an indifferent distinction (where the difference between rational and not-yet-rational involves no ranking)—and I have tried to argue that we can't authentically do so—then don't we have to read its arising in history as a gain? This, of course, was one of the reasons for the widespread admiration of the Greeks in post-Renaissance culture, that they pioneered the definition of the demands of rationality in our tradition. They brought about an important gain for human beings, brought to light and developed an important capacity. Can we really separate ourselves from this admiration and the judgments it is founded on? I think we can't. And by this I don't mean just psychologically can't, such as I'm unable to experience certain smells without nausea. I mean rather that granted the things we do strive after, the standards we consider binding on us, we couldn't authentically deny this admiration.

But then doesn't that amount to saying that we see rationality as a human potentiality, which the Greeks to their credit developed? We see it as a capacity that needed to be brought to fruition. Moreover, if we consider certain changes in history, of which the development of rational discourse is an example, we see another pattern reminiscent of Hegel: once they come about, they are more or less irreversible. They could be reversed by a massive disruption of human society, by some natural or man-made catastrophe. But, normally speaking, people don't want to go back on them. They become permanent and inescapable aspirations. There are other examples: perhaps the rise of citydwelling is one, the invention of writing, and various kinds of technical advances.

These are often grouped under the title "civilization," and made the object of an ineluctable progress story. The ineluctable part is more dubious, as is Hegel's assumption (b) about the single track of human potentiality, but the important insight here is what I call the ratchet effect. History seems to exhibit some irreversible developments. Some of these may have nothing to do with what we could define as human potentiality: we might so pollute the planet that we would have drastically to alter the way we live, and this might be irreversible. But I'm talking about changes that seem irreversible because those who go through them can't envisage reversing them, because they become standards for those who come after them: the way, for instance, that even for the barbarians who have destroyed them, cities retain their prestige, as the locus of a higher form of life, and come thus to be reconstituted.

I'm arguing that some notion of potentiality is needed to make sense of these changes. At the very least, they are changes such that those who have undergone them tend irresistibly to *define* them as development, or evolution, or advance, or realization of the properly human. So at least local history has a shape; there is a before and after, a watershed. By "local" I mean something broader in scale. The Greeks and we are in one "locality," and we have to read their development of rational discourse as a gain whose standards now define us. History, in this civilization and in this respect, had a direction.

This is true, incidentally, of more than rationality. One of the important features of modern culture is its universalism, the premise that all human beings count and have rights; another is its lower tolerance of avoidable suffering or death, which motivates the vast campaigns for famine or flood or earthquake relief, surely without precedent in history. It is hard not to read these as gains, and to see a Torquemada as existing before a watershed.

This has not prevented the twentieth century from witnessing crimes that would have made Torquemada blanch with horror—the holocaust, the killing fields. This may seem to call into question the rise in humanitarian standards I'm imputing to our age. I haven't the space to go into it here, but I think these two developments, higher standards and unprecedented gruesomeness, are paradoxically and perversely connected. In any case, their coexistence in the same age is reflected in the fact that these great crimes were kept secret.

But if we have to admit advance, at least locally, what does this do to what I have called the axiom of equality? This is badly named, I agree. It seems to imply some kind of likeness, homogeneity of cultures, whereas what is crucial and difficult to recognize is just the opposite, how different they are. But what I was trying to get at with the term is the insight that all cultures allow for human flourishing. So what is ruled out is a reading of another culture strictly in terms of deprivation: they lack what we have.

But isn't this what you have to do when you think in terms of potentialities, and define changes as advances or developments? Weren't the pre-philosophical Greeks deprived of something? Of course. But here's where we have to separate clearly Hegel's assumptions (a) and (b). To speak of potentialities doesn't mean to suppose a unitary set. We can and increasingly do recognize diverse lines of possible development, some of which seem incompatible with each other, at least at first blush. This, of course, has been salient in various post-Romantic traditions, which have regretted the passing of earlier forms of life, relegated by Progress, the Enlightenment, Industrialization, Disenchantment, or whatever. It is wrong to think that we have to choose between two readings of history, as progress or decline, fulfillment or loss. The most plausible view seems to be that it contains elements of both.

In other words, we should be able to think about the conflicts between the requirements of incompatible cultures on analogy to the way we think about conflicts between nonjointly realizable goods in our lives. When we find we can't maximize both freedom and equality, for instance, we don't immediately conclude that one of these isn't a real good. This is precisely the mark of the ideological mind, one convinced a priori that there can be only one system of goods. People with this mindset feel forced to tell us that one or the other goal shouldn't be sought or that, really, getting one will bring you the other (equality is true freedom, or free markets will bring you perfect equality).

But if we keep our heads, we recognize that the world can be nasty enough to put us in a dilemma, give us a tough choice, that genuine goods can conflict. Let's say that reason tends to sap and dissipate other valuable things in human life, such as our attunement to the world or our sense of community. This is not by itself a reason not to consider reason a good—though it may be to make an all-things-considered judgment that it shouldn't be fostered (if such a judgment could really be acted on, which I doubt). Nor is it a good ground, having espoused reason, to consider the things it saps as without value.

Precisely the aim of the comparative exercise is to enable us to understand others undistortively, and hence to be able to see the good in their life, even while we also see that their good conflicts with ours. The point is to get us beyond seeing them simply as the transgressors of our limits, to let them be in the way our original home understanding couldn't let them be, because it couldn't accommodate their meanings; to allow us to see two goods where before we could only see one and its negation.

The idea here is that what is true of a single life—that conflict doesn't invalidate or relativize the goods that clash, but on the contrary presupposes their validity—should hold for the opposition between cultures as well. But there might seem to be an important disanalogy. When we have a conflict in life, we feel justified and called on to make a choice, to sacrifice or trade off one good for another. In the intercultural context, we might feel that this is presumptuous. But this is based on a confusion. There are generally good reasons why we shouldn't *intervene* in the life of another culture or society, even to effect something that would be good if it came about spontaneously. But this doesn't mean that we have no right to make all-things-considered *judgments* about what ought to be sacrificed for what. Have we any doubt that the Jews and Moriscos ought not to have been expelled from Spain, even though it increased the homogeneity of the society, which in that day was considered an unquestioned good? Wouldn't we welcome the discontinuance of suttee or human sacrifice? (I hope these are rhetorical questions.)

Of course, these judgments are *ours,* and the suspicion can arise, even as it did with our contrastive understanding, that it is still too ethnocentric. There is no general-purpose measure to guarantee us against this. We just have to try again, and meet the challenges as they come. But what is important to recognize is that successfully meeting them might reverse some of our present judgments; it wouldn't make judgment itself impossible or inappropriate.

Nor does moral thinking have to confine itself to determining sacrifices or tradeoffs. The conflicts don't all have to be taken as ineluctable or as incapable of mitigation. Just as with the case of freedom and equality, within a general recognition of the difficulty of combining them, we can nevertheless strive to find forms for combining them at higher levels, so we can strive to recover in some form those goods that reason or urbanization or disenchantment, in short "civilization," has relegated.

What seems to be emerging here is a hazy picture of history in which our understanding will be embedded. It rejects altogether the Hegelian single line of development, but it retains something like the notion of potentiality. This structures at least local history into a before and after, and allows us to speak of advance. But because potentialities are diverse and frequently, at least by our present lights and capacities, incompatible, the gains will also involve losses, and the goods of different cultures will clash. But this shouldn't frighten us into a relativization of goods, or into a disclaimer of the universal relevance of our own goods, about which we could never be sincere anyway.

It does point us to a future of humanity in which the kind of undistorted understanding of the other aimed at by "the comparativist enterprise" will be increasingly valuable. Not only to avoid political and military conflict where possible, but also to give people of every culture some sense of the immense gamut of human potentialities. This will serve not only to enlighten our judgments where goods clash, but will help where imagination and insight are capable of mediating the clash, and bring two hitherto warring goods to some degree of common realization. We can hope to advance in this direction, to the extent that the community of comparativists will increasingly include representatives of different cultures, will in effect start from different home languages.

Understanding the other undistortively, without being led to deprecate or relativize the goods one still subscribes to: this can confer another important benefit. Most of the great religions or secular world views are bound up with a depreciatory view of others in contrast to which they define themselves. Christianity relative to Judaism as "merely" a religion of law, or relative to Buddhism and Hinduism as religions unconcerned for the world— depreciatory stories abound. These stories form part of the support system for faith everywhere. The contrasts are real; and so to come to understand the view against which one's own is defined, and hence to see its spiritual force, must bring about a profound change. The depreciatory story is no longer credible; this prop to faith is knocked away. Where the faith was nourished exclusively by the story, it will wither. But where not, it will be free to nourish itself on better food, on something like the intrinsic power of whatever the faith or vision points us toward. In this sense, comparative understanding lets our own faith be too. It liberates our selves along with the other.

── 9 ──

To Follow a Rule

Great puzzlement has arisen about rules and conventions, once we try to understand their place in human life in the light of modern philosophy. One facet of this was pressed more acutely and famously by Wittgenstein in his *Philosophical Investigations,* and further elaborated by Saul Kripke in his book on the subject.[1] It concerns what it means to understand a rule. Understanding seems to imply knowledge or awareness, and yet Wittgenstein shows that the subject not only isn't but *couldn't* be aware of a whole host of issues which nevertheless have a direct bearing on the correct application of a rule.

Wittgenstein shows this by raising the possibilities of misunderstanding. Some outsider, unfamiliar with the way we do things, might misunderstand what are to us perfectly clear and simple directions. You want to get to town? Just follow the arrows. But suppose what seemed the natural way of following the arrow to him was to go in the direction of the feathers and not of the point? (We can image a scenario: there are no arrows in his culture, but a kind of ray gun whose discharge fans out like the feathers on our arrows.)

Now this kind of example triggers a certain reaction in our intellectualist philosophical culture. What the stranger fails to understand (you follow arrows toward the point), we must understand. We *know* how to follow arrows. But what does this mean? From the intellectualist perspective, it must be that somewhere in our mind, consciously or unconsciously, a premise has been laid down about how you follow arrows. From another angle, once we see his mistake, we can explain to the stranger what he ought to do. But if we can give an explanation, we must already *have* an explanation. So the thought must reside somewhere in us that you follow arrows this way.

Or we could come to the same place from another direction. Suppose we didn't have such a thought. Then when the issue arises whether we really ought to follow arrows toward the point, we would be in doubt. How would we know that this is right? And then how would we ourselves follow the directions?

Now this kind of reply runs into insuperable difficulties. That's because the number of potential misunderstandings is endless. Wittgenstein says this over and over again. There are an indefinite number of points at which, for a given explanation of a rule and a given run of cases, someone could nevertheless misunderstand, as our stranger did the injunction to follow the arrows. For instance (87), I might say that by "Moses" I mean the man who led the Israelites out of Egypt, but then my interlocutor might have trouble with the words "Egypt" and "Israelites." "Nor would these questions come to an end when we get down to words like 'red,' 'dark,' 'sweet.'" Nor would even mathematical explanations be proof to this danger. We could imagine someone to whom we teach a series by giving him a sample range, say: 0, 2, 4, 6, 8 . . . He might carry on quite well till 1000, and then write 1004, 1008, 1012. He is indignant when we tell him he's got it wrong. He misunderstood our sample range to be illustrating the rule: "Add 2 up to 1000, 4 up to 2000, 6 up to 3000, and so on" (185).

If in order to understand directions or know how to follow a rule, we have to know that all these deviant readings are deviant, and if this means that we must have already formulated thoughts to this effect, then we need an infinite number of thoughts in our heads even to follow the simplest instructions. Plainly this is crazy. The intellectualist is tempted to treat all these potential issues as though they would already have to be *resolved* by us, if we are to understand the directions. "It may easily look as if every doubt merely *revealed* an existing gap in the foundations; so that secure understanding is only possible if we first doubt everything that *can* be doubted, and then remove all these doubts" (87). But since any explanation leaves some potential issues unresolved, it stands in need of further explanations to back it up. Further explanations would have the same disability, and so the job of explaining to somebody how to do something would be literally endless. "'But then how does an explanation help me to understand, if after all it is not the final one? In that case the explanation is never completed; so I still don't understand what he means, and never shall!'—As though an explanation as it were hung in the air unless supported by another one" (87).

The last remark, not in single quotes, is Wittgenstein's reply to his interlocutor. It hints at the mindset of the intellectualist. This outlook seeks securely founded knowledge. We recognize an obsession of the modern intellectual tradition, from Descartes on. It didn't see this as a problem, because it thought we could find such secure foundations, explanations that were self-explanatory or self-authenticating. That's why the imagined interlocutor placed his hopes in words like "red," "dark," "sweet," referring to basic empirical experiences on which we can ground everything else. The force of Wittgenstein's argument lies in the radical undercutting of any such foundationalism.

Why can someone always misunderstand? And why don't we have to resolve all these potential questions before we can understand ourselves? The answer to these two questions is the same. Understanding is always against a background of what is taken for granted, just relied on. Someone can always come along who lacks this background, and so the plainest things can be misunderstood, particularly if we let our imagination roam, and imagine people who never even heard of arrows. But at the same time, the background, as what is just relied on, isn't the locus of resolved questions. When the misunderstanding comes from a difference of background, what needs to be said to clear it up articulates a bit of the explainer's background which may never have been articulated before.

Wittgenstein stresses the unarticulated—at some points even unarticulable—nature of this understanding: "'obeying a rule' is a practice" (202). Giving reasons for one's practice in following a rule has come to an end. "My reasons will soon give out. And then I shall act, without reasons" (211). Or later: "If I have exhausted my justifications I have reached bedrock, and my spade is turned. Then I am inclined to say: 'This is simply what I do'" (217). More laconically: "When I obey a rule, I do not choose. I obey the rule *blindly*" (219).

There are two broad schools of interpretation of what Wittgenstein is saying here, which correspond to two ways of understanding the phenomenon of the unarticulated background. The first would interpret the claim that I act without reasons as involving the view that no reasons can be given here; no demand for reasons can arise. That's because the connections that form our background are just de facto links, not susceptible of any justification. For instance, they are simply imposed by our society; we are conditioned to make them. They become "automatic," and so the question never arises. The view that society imposes these limits is the heart of Kripke's interpretation of Wittgenstein. Or else they can perhaps be considered as "wired in." It's just a fact about us that we react this way, as it is that we blink when something approaches our eyes, and no justification is in order.

The second interpretation takes the background as really incorporating understanding; that is, as a grasp on things which although quite unarticulated may allow us to formulate reasons and explanations when challenged. In this case, the links would not simply be de facto, but would make a kind of sense, which is precisely what we would try to spell out in the articulation.

On the first view, then, the "bedrock" our explicit explanations rest on is made up of brute connections; on the second, it is a mode of understanding and thus makes a kind of unarticulated sense of things.

What suggests the first interpretation is a phrase like "I obey the rule blindly," and perhaps even the image of bedrock itself, whose unyielding nature may imply that nothing further *can* be said. What tells against it is other passages where Wittgenstein says, for instance, that following a rule is not like the operations of a machine (193–194), or when he says: "To use a word without justification does not mean to use it without right" (289—although I can imagine an interpretation of this compatible with the first view). Above all, I want to say that it is his insistence that following rules is a *social* practice. Granted, this may also fit with Kripke's version of the first view. But I think this connection of background with society reflects in reality an alternative vision which has jumped altogether outside the old monological outlook that dominates the epistemological tradition.

Whatever Wittgenstein thought, this second view seems to me right. What the first can't account for is the fact that we do give explanations, that we can often articulate reasons when challenged. Following arrows toward the point is not just an arbitrarily imposed connection; it makes sense, granted the way arrows move. What we need to do is follow a hint from Wittgenstein and attempt to give an account of the background as understanding, which also places it in social space. This is what I would now like to explore.

My exploration runs against the grain of much modern thought and culture, in particular our scientific culture and its associated epistemology. This in turn has molded our contemporary sense of self.

Among the practices that have helped to create this modern sense are those that discipline our thought to disengagement from embodied agency and social embedding. Each of us is called upon to become a responsible, thinking mind, self-reliant in our judgments (this, at least, is the standard). But this ideal, however admirable in some respects, has tended to blind us to important facets of the human condition. There is a tendency in our intellectual tradition to read it less as an ideal than as something already established in the human constitution. This reification of the disengaged first-person-singular self is already evident in the founding figures of the modern epistemological tradition, for instance in Descartes and Locke.

It means that we easily tend to see the human agent as primarily a subject of representations: representations, first, about the world outside; second, depictions of ends desired or feared. This subject is a monological one. We are in contact with an "outside" world, including other agents, the objects we and they deal with, our own and others' bodies, but this contact is through the representations we have "within." The subject is first of all an inner space, a "mind" to use the old terminology, or a mechanism capable of processing representations, if we follow the more fashionable computer-inspired models of today. The body and other people may form the content of my representations; they may also be causally responsible for some of them. But what "I" am, as a being capable of having such representations, the inner space itself, is definable independently of body or other. It is a center of monological consciousness.

It is this stripped-down view of the subject which has made deep inroads into social science, breeding the various forms of methodological individu-alism, including the most recent and virulent variant, rational-choice theory. It stands in the way of a richer and more adequate understanding of what the human sense of self is like, and hence of a proper understanding of the real variety of human culture, and hence of a knowledge of human beings.

What this kind of consciousness leaves out is: the body and the other. Both have to be brought back in, if we are to grasp the kind of background understanding that Wittgenstein seems to be adverting to. In fact, restoring the first involves retrieving the second. I want to sketch briefly what is involved in this connection.

A number of philosophical currents in the last two centuries have tried to get out of the cul-de-sac of monological consciousness. Prominent in this century is the work of Heidegger, Merleau-Ponty, and of course Witt-genstein himself. What these men have in common is that they see the agent not primarily as the locus of representations, but as engaged in practices, as a being who acts in and on a world.

Of course no one has failed to notice that human beings act. The crucial difference is that these philosophers set the primary locus of the agent's understanding in practice. On the mainline epistemological view, what distinguishes the agent from inanimate entities that can also affect their surroundings is the human's capacity for inner representations, whether these are placed in the mind or in the brain understood as a computer. What we have that animate beings don't—understanding—was identified with representations and the operations we effect on them.

To situate our understanding in practices is to see it as implicit in our activity, and hence as going well beyond what we manage to frame representations of. We do frame representations: we explicitly formulate what our world is like, what we aim at, what we are doing. But much of our intelligent action in the world, sensitive as it usually is to our situation and goals, is carried on unformulated. It flows from an understanding that is largely inarticulate.

This understanding is more fundamental in two ways: (1) it is always there, whereas we sometimes frame representations and sometimes do not, and (2) the representations we do make are only comprehensible against the background provided by this inarticulate understanding. It provides the context within which alone they make the sense they do. Rather than representations being the primary locus of understanding, they are only islands in the sea of our unformulated practical grasp on the world.

Seeing that our understanding resides first of all in our practices involves attributing an inescapable role to the background. The connection figures, in different ways, in virtually all the philosophies of the contemporary counter-current to epistemology, and famously in Heidegger and Wittgenstein.

But this puts the role of the body in a new light. Our body is not just the executant of the goals we frame, nor just the locus of causal factors shaping our representations. Our understanding itself is embodied. That is, our bodily know-how, and the way we act and move, can encode components of our understanding of self and world. I know my way around a familiar environment in being able to get from any place to any place with ease and assurance. I may be at a loss when asked to draw a map, or even give explicit directions to a stranger. I know how to manipulate and use the familiar instruments in my world, usually in the same inarticulate fashion.

But it is not only my grasp of the inanimate environment which is thus embodied. My sense of myself, of the footing I am on with others, is in large part also embodied. The deference I owe you is carried in the distance I stand from you, in the way I fall silent when you start to speak, in the way I hold myself in your presence. Alternatively, the sense I have of my own importance is carried in the way I swagger. Indeed, some of the most pervasive features of my attitude to the world and to others is encoded in the way I project myself in public space; whether I am macho, or timid, or eager to please, or calm and unflappable.

In all these cases, the person concerned may not even possess the appropriate descriptive term. For instance, when I stand respectfully and defer to you, I may not have the word "deference" in my vocabulary. Very often, words are coined by more sophisticated others to describe important features of people's stance in the world. (Needless to say, these others are often social scientists.) This understanding is not, or only imperfectly, captured in our representations. It is carried in patterns of appropriate action, which conform to a sense of what is fitting and right. Agents with this kind of understanding recognize when they or others have put a foot wrong. Their actions are responsive throughout to this sense of rightness, but the "norms" may be quite unformulated, or only in fragmentary fashion.

In recent years Pierre Bourdieu has coined a term to capture this level of social understanding, the "habitus."[2] This is one of the key terms we need to give an account of the background understanding invoked above. I will return to this in a minute, but first I want to make the connection between the retrieval of the body and that of the other.

We can see right away how the other also figures. Some of these practices that encode understanding are not carried out in the acts of a single agent. The example of my deference can be a case in point. Deferent and deferred-to play out their social distance in a conversation, often with heavily ritualized elements. And indeed conversations in general rely on small, usually focally unnoticed rituals.

But perhaps I should say a word about this distinction I'm drawing between acts of a single agent (let's call them "monological" acts) and those of more than one ("dialogical"). From the standpoint of the old epistemology, all acts were monological, although often the agent coordinates her actions with those of others. But this notion of coordination fails to capture the way in which some actions require and sustain an integrated agent. Think of two people sawing a log with a two-handed saw or a couple dancing. A very important feature of human action is rhythming, cadence. Every apt, coordinated gesture has a certain flow. When you lose this, as occasionally happens, you fall into confusion, your actions become inept and uncoordinated. Similarly, the mastery of a new kind of skilled action goes along with the ability to give your gestures the appropriate rhythm.

Now in cases like log sawing and ballroom dancing, it is crucial to their rhythming that they be shared. They come off only when we can place ourselves in a common rhythm, in which our component action is taken up. This is a different experience from coordinating my action with yours, as for instance when I run to the spot on the field where I know you're going to pass the ball.

Sawing and dancing are paradigms of dialogical actions. But there is frequently a dialogical level to actions that are otherwise merely coordinated. A conversation is a good example. Conversations with some degree of ease and intimacy move beyond mere coordination, and have a common rhythm. The interlocutor not only listens, but participates with head nodding, "unh-hunh," and the like, and at a certain point the "semantic turn" passes over to the other by a common movement. The appropriate moment is felt by both partners together in virtue of the common rhythm. The bore and the compulsive talker thin the atmosphere of conviviality because they are impervious to this. There is a continuity between ordinary, convivial conversation and more ritualized exchanges: the litanies, or alternate chanting, that one sees in many earlier societies.[3]

I have taken actions with a common rhythming as paradigms of the dialogical, but they are in fact only one form. An action is dialogical, in the sense I'm using it here, when it is effected by an integrated, nonindividual agent. This means that for those involved in it, its identity as this kind of action essentially depends on the agency being shared. These actions are constituted as such by a shared understanding among those who make up the common agent. Integration into a common rhythm can be one form this shared understanding takes. But it can also come to be outside the situation of face-to-face encounter. In a different form it can also constitute a political or religious movement, whose members may be widely scattered, but who are animated together by a sense of common purpose—such as linked the students in Tienanmen Square and their colleagues back on the campuses and, indeed, a great part of the population of Beijing. This kind of action exists in a host of other forms, and on a great many other levels as well.

The importance of dialogical action in human life shows the utter inadequacy of the monological subject of representations which emerges from the epistemological tradition. We can't understand human life merely in terms of individual subjects, who frame representations about and respond to others, because a great deal of human action only happens insofar as the agent understands and constitutes himself as integrally part of a "we."

Much of our understanding of self, society, and world is carried through dialogical action. I would like to argue, in fact, that language itself serves to set up spaces of common action, on a number of levels, intimate and public. This means that our identity is never simply defined in terms of our individual properties. It also places us in some social space. We define ourselves partly in terms of what we come to accept as our appropriate place within dialogical actions. If I really identify myself with my deferential attitude toward wiser people like you, then this conversational stance becomes a constituent of my identity. Social reference figures even more clearly in the identity of the dedicated revolutionary.

Background understanding, which underlies our ability to grasp directions and follow rules, is to a large degree embodied. This helps to explain the combination of features it exhibits: it is a form of understanding, a making sense of things and actions; at the same time, it is entirely unarticulated; and third, it can be the basis of fresh articulation. As long as we think of understanding in the old intellectualist fashion, as residing in thoughts or representations, it is hard to explain how we can know how to follow a rule, or in any way behave rightly, without having the thoughts to justify this behavior as right. We are driven to a foundationalist construal, which would allow us to attribute only a finite list of such thoughts justifying an action from scratch, as it were. Or else, abandoning this, we are forced to conceive of a supporting background in the form of brute, de facto connections. This is because intellectualism leaves us only with the choice between an understanding that consists of representations and no understanding at all. Embodied understanding provides us with the third alternative we need to make sense of ourselves.

At the same time, it allows us to show the connections of this understanding to social practice. My embodied understanding doesn't only exist in me as an individual agent, but also as the coagent of common actions. This is the sense we can give to Wittgenstein's claim that obeying a rule is a practice. He means by this a social practice. Earlier (198) he asks: "What has the expression of a rule—say a sign-post—got to do with my actions? What sort of connection is there here?" His answer is: "Well, perhaps this one: I have been trained to react to this sign in a particular way, and now I do so react to it." This may sound like the first interpretation I mentioned above; the training would set up a brute tendency to react, and the connection would be merely causal. But Wittgenstein moves right away to set aside this reading. His imaginary interlocutor says, "But that is only to give a causal connection," and the Wittgenstein voice in the text answers: "On the contrary; I have further indicated that a person goes by a sign-post only in so far as there exists a regular use of sign-posts, a custom *(einen ständigen Gebrauch, eine Gepflogenheit)."*

This standing social use makes the connection, and it is not to be understood as a merely causal one. The standing use gives my response its *sense*. It doesn't merely bring it on through a brute causal link. But the sense is embodied and not represented. That's why Wittgenstein can ask in the immediately following passage (199): "Is what is called 'obeying a rule' something it would be possible for only *one* man to do only *once* in his life?" This rhetorical question demanding a negative answer is understood by Wittgenstein to point not just to a factual impossibility, but to something that doesn't make sense. "This is a note," he adds, "on the grammar of the expression 'to obey a rule.'" But if the role of society were just to set up the causal connections underlying my reactions, it couldn't be senseless to suppose that those connections held only for one person at one time, however bizarrely unlikely. In fact, the social practice is there to give my actions the meaning they have, and that's why there couldn't just be one action with this meaning.

Just as intellectualist epistemology made deep inroads into social science to ill effect, so it is important that the scientific consequences of embodied understanding be developed. This is what makes Bourdieu's notion of habitus so important and potentially fruitful.

Anthropology, like any other social science, can't do without some notion of rule. Too much of human social behavior is "regular," in the sense not just of exhibiting repeated patterns, but also of responding to demands or norms that have some generalizable form. In certain societies, women defer to men, young to old. There are certain forms of address and marks of respect which are repeatedly required. Not conforming is seen as wrong, as a "breach." So we quite naturally say that women use these forms of address not just haphazardly, and not (in the ordinary sense) as a reflex, but to follow a rule.

Suppose we are trying to understand this society. We are anthropologists who have come here precisely to get a picture of what their life is like. Then we have to discover and formulate some definition of this rule; we identify certain kinds of predicament, say, a woman meeting her husband, or meeting a man not her husband in the village, or meeting this man in the fields, and define what is required in each situation. Perhaps we can even rise to some more general rule from which these different situational requirements can be deduced. But in one form or another, we are defining a rule through a *representation* of it. Formulating in this case is creating a representation.

So far so necessary. But then intellectualism enters the picture, and we slide easily into seeing the rule-as-represented as somehow causally operative. We may attribute formulations of the rule-as-thought to the agents. But more likely, since this is very implausible in some cases, we see the rule-as-represented as defining an underlying "structure." We conceive this as what is really causally operative, behind the backs of the unsophisticated agents, as it were.

So argues Bourdieu. "L'intellectualisme est inscrit dans le fait d'introduire dans l'objet le rapport à l'objet, de substituer au rapport pratique à la pratique le rapport à l'objet qui est celui de l'observateur."[4] Of course, writing on the French scene, Bourdieu naturally gives an important place to structuralism, which is his main target in *Le Sens pratique*. It bulks less large in the English-speaking world. But the reified understanding of rule-as-representation doesn't only haunt the school of Lévi-Strauss. It obtrudes in a confused and uncertain form wherever the issue Bourdieu wants to pose has not been faced: just how do the rules *we* formulate operate in *their* lives? What is their "Sitz im Leben"? So long as this issue is not resolved, we are in danger of sliding into the reification that intellectualist epistemology invites, in one or the other of the two ways mentioned. "Passer de la *régularité*, c'est-à-dire de ce qui se produit avec une certaine fréquence statistiquement mesurable et de la formule qui permet d'en rendre raison, au *règlement* consciemment édité et consciemment respecté ou à la *régulation inconsciente* d'une mystérieuse mécanique cérébrale ou sociale, telles sont les deux manières les plus communes de glisser du modèle de la réalité à la réalité du modèle" (67).

There's a mistake here, but is it important? If we have to represent the rules to grasp them, and if we define them right, what does it matter how exactly they operate in the lives of the agents? Bourdieu argues that an important distortion occurs when we see the rule-as-represented as the effective factor. The distortion arises from the fact that we are taking a situated, embodied sense and providing an express depiction of it. We can illustrate the difference in the gap that separates our inarticulate familiarity with a certain environment, enabling us to get around in it without hesitation, on one hand, and a map of this terrain, on the other. The practical ability exists only in its exercise, which unfolds in time and space. As you get around a familiar environment, the different locations in their interrelation don't all impinge at once. Your sense of them is different, depending on where you are and where you're going. And some relations never impinge at all. The route and the relation of the landmarks look different on the way out and the way back; the way stations on the high road bear no relation to those on the low road. A way is essentially something you go through in time. The map, on the other hand, lays out everything simultaneously, and relates every point to every point without discrimination (58–59).

Maps or representations, by their nature, abstract from lived time and space. To make something like this the ultimate causal factor is to make the actual practice in time and space derivative, a mere application of a disengaged scheme. It is the ultimate end in Platonism. But it is still a temptation, not only because of the intellectualist focus on the representation, but also because of the prestige of the notion of law as it figures in natural science. The inverse-square law is a timeless, aspatial formula that "dictates" the behavior of all bodies everywhere. Shouldn't we be seeking something similar in human affairs? This invitation to imitate the successful modern sciences also encourages reification of the rule.

But this reification crucially distorts. And this in three related ways: (1) it blocks out certain features that are essential to action; (2) it doesn't allow for the difference between a formula and its enactment; and (3) it doesn't take account of the reciprocal relation between rule and action, that the second doesn't just flow from the first but also transforms it.

Abstracting from lived time and space means abstracting from action, because the time of action is asymmetrical. It projects a future always under some degree of uncertainty. A map or a diagram of the process imposes symmetry. Take a society, such as those described by Marcel Mauss, or the Kabyle communities studied by Bourdieu, where a reciprocal exchange of gifts plays an important role in defining and confirming relationships. One can make an atemporal schema of these exchanges and of the "rules" they obey. One may then be tempted to claim, as Lévi-Strauss does, that this formula of exchange "constitue le phénomène primitif, et non les opérations discrètes en lesquelles la vie sociale les décompose" (167).[5]

But this leaves out of account the crucial dimension of action in time. Bourdieu points out several ways in which this might matter. Not all of them directly back up his main point. For instance, he says that there is a proper time *(kairos)* for reciprocating a favor. If you give something back right away, it stands as a rebuff, as if you don't want to be beholden to the giver. If you delay too long, it's a sign of neglect. But this is an aspect of time which could itself be expressed in some abstract formula. Where the time of action becomes crucial is where we have to act in uncertainty and our action will irreversibly affect the situation. In the rule book of exchanges (which would be an anthropologist's artifact), the relations look perfectly reversible. But on the ground there is always uncertainty, because there are difficult judgment calls. In Kabylia, the gift relation is a recognition of rough equality of honor between the participants. So you can make a claim on a higher-ranked person by giving him a gift, and expose yourself to the danger of a brutal refusal if you've presumed too much (or have your prestige raised if your gamble pays off). At the same time, you dishonor yourself if you initiate a gift to someone too far below you.

What on paper is a set of dictated exchanges under certainty, on the ground is lived in suspense and uncertainty. This is partly because of the asymmetrical time of action (1), but also because of (2) what is involved in actually acting on a rule. This doesn't apply itself; it has to be applied, which may involve difficult and finely tuned judgments. This was the point made by Aristotle, as basic to his understanding of the virtue of phronesis. Human situations arise in infinite varieties. Determining what a norm amounts to in any given situation can take a high degree of insightful understanding. Just being able to formulate rules will not be enough. The person of real practical wisdom is less marked by the ability to formulate rules than by knowing how to act in each particular situation. There is a crucial "phronetic gap" between the formula and its enactment, and this too is neglected by explanations that give primacy to the rule-as-represented.

These two points together yield the uncertainty, the suspense, the possibility of irreversible change, which surrounds all significant action, however "rule-guided." I give you a gift, in order to raise myself to your level. You pointedly ignore it, and I'm crushed. I have irremediably humiliated myself, and my status has declined. But this gains added importance, once we take account of (3) the way in which the rules are transformed through practice. This is not the simple putting into effect of unchangeable formulas. The formula as such only exists in the treatise of the anthropologist. In its operation, the rule exists in the practice it guides. But we have seen that the practice not only fulfills the rule, but also gives it concrete shape in particular situations. Practice is, as it were, a continual interpretation and reinterpretation of what the rule really means. If enough of us give a little "above" ourselves and our gesture is reciprocated, we will have altered the generally understood margins of tolerance for this kind of exchange between equals. The relation between rule and practice is like that between Saussure's *langue* and *parole:* the latter is only possible because of the pre-existence of the former, but at the same time the acts of parole are what keep the langue in being. They renew it and at the same time alter it. Their relation is thus reciprocal.

This reciprocity is what the intellectualist theory leaves out. In fact, what it shows is that the "rule" lies essentially *in* the practice. The rule is what is animating the practice at any given time, and not some formulation behind it, inscribed in our thoughts or our brains or our genes, or whatever. That's why the rule is, at any given time, what the practice has made it. But then this shows how conceiving the rule as an underlying formula can be scientifically disastrous. We miss the entire interplay between action under uncertainty and varying degrees of phronetic insight, on one hand, and the norms and rules that animate this action, on the other. The map gives only half the story; to make it decisive is to distort the whole process.

A rule that exists only in the practices it animates, and does not require and may not have any express formulation. How can this be? Only through our embodied understanding. This is what Bourdieu is trying to get at with the habitus. It is a "system of durable and transposable dispositions" (88), dispositions to bodily comportment, say, to act, to hold oneself, or to gesture in a certain way. A bodily disposition is a habitus when it encodes a certain cultural understanding. The habitus in this sense always has an expressive dimension. It gives expression to certain meanings that things and people have for us, and it is precisely by giving such expression that it makes these meanings exist.

Children are inducted into a culture, are taught the meanings which constitute it, partly through inculcating the appropriate habitus. We learn how to hold ourselves, how to defer to others, how to be a presence for others, all largely through taking on different styles of bodily comportment.

Through these modes of deference and presentation, the subtlest nuances of social position, of the sources of prestige, and hence of what is valuable and good, are encoded.

> On pourrait, déformant le mot de Proust, dire que les jambes, les bras sont pleins d'impératifs engourdis. Et l'on n'en finirait pas d'énumérer les valeurs faites corps, par la transsubstantiation qu'opère la persuasion clandestine d'une pédagogie implicite, capable d'inculquer toute une cosmologie, une éthique, une métaphysique, une politique, à travers des injonctions aussi insignifiantes que "tiens-toi droit" ou "ne tiens pas ton couteau de la main gauche" et d'inscrire dans les détails en apparence les plus insignifiants de la *tenue,* du *maintien* ou des *manières* corporelles et verbales les principes fondamentaux de l'arbitraire culturel, ainsi placés hors des prises de la conscience et de l'explicitation. (117)

This is one way in which rules can exist in our lives, as "values made flesh." Of course it is not the only way. Some rules *are* formulated. But these are in close interrelation to our habitus. The two normally dovetail and complement each other. Bourdieu speaks of habitus and institutions as two ways of objectifying past history (95–96). Institutions are generally the locus of express rules or norms. But rules aren't self-interpreting; without a sense of what they're about, and an affinity to their spirit, they remain dead letters or become a travesty in practice. This sense and this affinity can only exist where they do in our unformulated, embodied understanding. They are in the domain of the habitus, which "comme sens pratique opère la *réactivation* du sens objectivé dans les institutions."

We return here to the question we started with, the place of rules in human life. We started with the puzzle of how an agent can understand a rule, be guided by it, without having an inkling of a whole host of issues that must (it would appear) be resolved, before the rule can guide us properly. The intellectualist bent of our philosophical culture made this seem paradoxical. But the answer is to be found in a background understanding, which makes these issues irrelevant, keeps them off our agenda. Rules operate in our lives, as patterns of reasons for action, as against merely constituting causal regularities. But reason giving has a limit, and in the end must repose in another kind of understanding.

What is this understanding? I've been arguing that we should see it as embodied. Bourdieu has explored how this kind of understanding can arise and how it can function in our lives, along with the institutions that define our social existence. So he too recurs to a picture very much like the one I would attribute to Wittgenstein. Express rules can only function in our lives along with an inarticulate sense encoded in the body. It is this habitus that "activates" the rules. If Wittgenstein has helped us to break the philosophical thrall of intellectualism, Bourdieu has begun to explore how social science could be remade, once freed from its distorting grip.

— 10 —

Cross-Purposes: The Liberal-Communitarian Debate

$$W$$
e often hear talk of the difference between liberals and communitarians in social theory, and in particular in the theory of justice.[1] Certainly a debate seems to have been engaged between two "teams," with people like John Rawls, Ronald Dworkin, Thomas Nagel, and T. M. Scanlon on one side (team L) and Michael Sandel, Alasdair MacIntyre, and Michael Walzer on the other (team C). There are genuine differences, but I think there are also a lot of cross-purposes and just plain confusion in this debate. That is because two quite different issues tend to get run together. We can call them, respectively, ontological issues and advocacy issues.

The ontological questions concern what you recognize as the factors you will invoke to account for social life. Or, put in the formal mode, they concern the terms you accept as ultimate in the order of explanation. The big debate in this area, which has been raging now for more than three centuries, divides "atomists" from "holists." The atomists are often referred to as methodological individualists. They believe that in (a), the order of explanation, you can and ought to account for social actions, structures, and conditions in terms of properties of the constituent individuals; and in (b), the order of deliberation, you can and ought to account for social goods in terms of concatenations of individual goods. In recent decades, Karl Popper has declared himself a militant advocate of (a), while (b) is a key component of what Amartya Sen has defined as "welfarism," a central if often inarticulate belief of most writers in the field of welfare economics.[2]

Advocacy issues concern the moral stand or policy one adopts. Here there is a gamut of positions, which at one end give primacy to individual rights and freedom and, at the other, give higher priority to community life or the good of collectivities. We could describe the positions on this scale as more or less individualist and collectivist. At one extreme we would find people like Robert Nozick and Milton Friedman and other libertarians; at the other, Enver Hodja's Albania or the Red Guards of China's cultural revolution define the ultimate benchmarks. Of course most sane people, when not in the grip of some relentless ideology, find themselves much closer to the middle; but there are still significant differences between, say, liberals like Dworkin who believe that the state should be neutral between the different conceptions of the good life espoused by individuals, on one hand,[3] and those who believe that a democratic society needs some commonly recognized definition of the good life, on the other—a view I will defend later.

The relation between these two congeries of issues is complex. They are distinct, in the sense that taking a position on one doesn't force your hand on the other. Yet they are not completely independent, in that the stand you take on the ontological level can be part of the essential background of the view you advocate. Both these relations, the distinctness and the connection, are inadequately appreciated, and this confuses the debate.

Now when people refer to "liberals" and "communitarians," they often talk as though each of these terms describes a package of views, linking the two issues. The underlying assumption seems to be that they are not distinct, that a given position on one commits you to a corresponding view on the other. Thus, while the principal point of Michael Sandel's important book *Liberalism and the Limits of Justice* is ontological in my terms, the liberal response to it has generally been as a work of advocacy.[4] Sandel tries to show how the different models of the way we live together in society—atomist and holist—are linked with different understandings of self and identity: "unencumbered" versus situated selves. This is a contribution to social ontology, which can be developed in a number of directions. It could be used to argue that because a totally unencumbered self is a human impossibility, the extreme atomist model of society is a chimera. Or one could argue that both (relatively) unencumbered and situated selves are possibilities, as would be also (relatively) atomist and holist societies, but that the viable combinations between these two levels are restricted: a highly collectivist society would be hard to combine with an unencumbered identity, or a highly individualist life form would be impossible where selves are thickly situated.

Taken in either direction, the tenor of these theses about identity would still be purely ontological. They don't amount to an advocacy of anything. What they purport to do, like any good ontological thesis, is to structure the field of possibilities in a more perspicuous way. But this does leave us with choices, which we need some normative, deliberative arguments to resolve. Even taken in the first direction, which purports to show the impossibility of atomist society, it leaves us with important choices between more or less liberal societies; the second direction is concerned precisely to define options of this kind.

Both relations are illustrated here. Taking an ontological position doesn't amount to advocating something; but at the same time, the ontological does help to define the options it is meaningful to support by advocacy. The latter connection explains how ontological theses can be far from innocent. Your ontological proposition, if true, can show that your neighbor's favorite social order is an impossibility or carries a price he or she did not count with. But this should not induce us to think that the proposition *amounts to* the advocacy of some alternative.

Both this impact of the ontological and the misperception of it can be seen in the debate around Sandel's book. Sandel made a point about Rawls's invocation of the Humean "conditions of justice." According to Hume, justice is a relevant virtue when there are scarcities, and people are not spontaneously moved by ties of affection to mutual benevolence. Where the former does not hold, there is no point in dividing up shares; where the latter does not hold, there is no call to hold people to some rule of distribution. What is more, in this second case, trying to enforce a rule will quite possibly disrupt the existing ties: to insist punctiliously on sharing expenses with a friend is to imply that the links of mutual benevolence are somehow lacking or inadequate. There is no faster way of losing friends.[5] Similarly, insistence on clearly defined rights can create distance in a close family.

Sandel has sometimes been read as if his point was to advocate a society that would have close relations analogous to a family, and thus would have no need to concern itself with justice. This proposal has been, rightly, ridiculed. But this seems to me to miss the relevance of his argument. First we have to see that the choice is not simply between a close, familylike community and a modern, impersonal society. Even within the latter, there are important choices about how zealously we entrench in legislation, or enforce through judicial action, various facets of equality that justice might dictate. What do we entrust to the spirit of social solidarity and the social mores that emerge from it? In certain societies the answer may be: very little. But there this spirit is weak or lacking. Where it is strong, there may be problems with overenforcement of our intuitions about fair dealing. Trying to define and enforce in detail some of our common feelings about equality may weaken the common sense of moral commitment and mutual solidarity from which these feelings grow. Sometimes, of course, legislation can help to crystallize a growing consensus: the civil-rights laws in the United States in the 1960s are a good example. But sometimes overenforcement can work the other way. Sandel's point about the conditions of justice should serve to open up this whole issue, which gets left in the shade if we ask only what the principles of justice ought to be between mutually indifferent contracting individuals.

I'll come back to this point from another angle later, when I consider the relative advantages of two models of citizen dignity, one based on political participation, the other on judicial retrieval.

The same point about the impact of the ontological emerges even more clearly from one of Sandel's central criticisms of Rawls. He argues that Rawls's egalitarian difference principle, which involves treating the endowment of each as part of the jointly held resources for the benefit of society as a whole,[6] presupposes a high degree of solidarity among the participants. This sense of mutual commitment could be sustained only by encumbered selves who share a strong sense of community. And yet the contractors are defined very much as mutually indifferent. Here again it is clear that the point of the argument, whether right or wrong, is to define the alternatives in an important choice. Sandel's point pushes us toward the issue of whether the kind of egalitarian redistribution Rawls recommends can be sustained in a society that is not bound in solidarity through a strong sense of community; and whether, in turn, a strong community can be forged around a common understanding that makes justice the principal virtue of social life, or whether some other good should have to figure as well in the definition of community life. My point is just that this kind of defined choice is the central function of what I have been calling ontological propositions. This is how Sandel's critique of Rawls has to be read here, not as a counter-advocacy.

This is not to say that Sandel does not also want to make an important normative statement about the future course of American society. This has become more and more evident with what he has written since 1982.[7] It is simply that his contribution to the ontological debate should not be lost from view behind them. This would be a loss, not just because the contribution is important in its own right, but also because it is part of the background to what he advocates; grasping this relation helps us to understand exactly what his position is. But when these normative points are misconstrued as recommendations, the most bizarre interpretations emerge, and the debate is beclouded beyond hope of recovery.

I think the misconstruals occur because there has been widespread insensitivity to the difference between the two kinds of issue. The portmanteau terms "liberal" and "communitarian" will probably have to be scrapped before we can get over this, because they carry the implication that there is only one issue here, or that your position on one determines what you hold on the other. But a cursory look at the gamut of actual philosophical positions shows exactly the contrary. Either stand on the atomism-holism debate can be combined with either stand on the individualist-collectivist question. There are not only atomist individualists (Nozick) and holist collectivists (Marx), but also holist individualists (Humboldt)—and even atomist collectivists, as in the nightmarish programmed utopia of B. F. Skinner, "beyond freedom and dignity." This last category may be of interest only for the student of the bizarre or the monstrous, but I would argue that Humboldt and his ilk occupy an extremely important place in the development of modern liberalism. They represent a trend of thought that is fully aware of the (ontological) social embedding of human agents but, at the same time, prizes liberty and individual differences very highly. Humboldt was one of the important sources for Mill's doctrine of liberty. In the face of this, it is astonishing that anyone should read a defense of holism as entailing an advocacy of collectivism. But the rich tradition that Humboldt represents seems to have been forgotten by Mill's heirs in the English-speaking world.

Recovering the distinction I'm making here is therefore worth the trouble, if it can allow this tradition to return to its rightful place in the debate. This is a big part of my (not so hidden) agenda, because it is the line of thought I identify with. But I also believe that the confusion of issues has contributed to a kind of eclipse of ontological thinking in social theory. Since this is the level at which we face important questions about the real choices open to us, the eclipse is a real misfortune. Sandel's first book was important because he brought out some issues that a properly aware liberalism ought to face. The reaction of the "liberal" consensus (to use one of the portmanteau terms I've just impugned) was that to obtrude issues about identity and community into the debate on justice was an irrelevancy. My thesis is that, quite the contrary, these matters are highly relevant, and the only alternative to discussing them is relying on an implicit and unexamined view of them. Moreover, since unexamined views on these matters in Anglo-Saxon philosophical culture tend to be heavily infected with atomist prejudices, the implicit understanding tends to be—according to my holistic outlook—wrong. The result is that an ontologically disinterested liberalism tends to be blind to certain important questions. Why is this so?

There is a family of liberal theories that is now very popular, not to say dominant, in the English-speaking world, which I will call "procedural." It sees society as an association of individuals, each of whom has a conception of a good or worthwhile life and, correspondingly, a life plan. The function of society ought to be to facilitate these life plans, as much as possible and following some principle of equality. That is, the facilitation ought not to be discriminatory, although there is obviously some room for serious question as to exactly what this means: whether the facilitation ought to aim at equality of results, resources, opportunities, capacities, or whatever.[8] But many writers seem to agree on the proposition that the principle of equality or nondiscrimination would be breached if society itself espoused one or another conception of the good life. This would amount to discrimination, because we assume that in a modern pluralist society, there is a wide gamut of views about what makes a good life. Any view endorsed by society as a whole would be that of some citizens and not others. Those who see their views denied official favor would not be treated with equal respect in relation to their compatriots espousing the established view.

Thus, it is argued, a liberal society should not be founded on any particular notion of the good life. The ethic central to a liberal society is an ethic of the right rather than the good. That is, its basic principles concern how society should respond to and arbitrate the competing demands of individuals. These principles would obviously include the respect of individual rights and freedoms, but central to any set that could be called liberal would be the principle of maximal and equal facilitation. This does not in the first instance define what goods the society will further, but rather how it will determine the goods to be advanced, given the aspirations and demands of its component individuals. What is crucial here are the procedures of decision, which is why I want to call this brand of liberal theory "procedural."[9]

There are grave problems with this model of liberalism, which can be properly articulated only when we open up ontological issues of identity and community. There are questions about the viability of a society that would really meet these specifications, and an issue about the applicability of this formula in societies other than the United States (and perhaps Britain) where it has been mainly developed, which also have a prima facie right to be called liberal. In other words, the theory can be taxed with being unrealistic and ethnocentric. Both objections are directed against procedural liberalism's exclusion of a socially endorsed conception of the good.

The viability issue has been raised by thinkers in the civic-humanist tradition. One of the central themes of this line of thought concerns the conditions for a free society. "Free" is understood here not in the modern sense of negative liberty, but more as the antonym to "despotic." Ancient writers, followed by such moderns as Machiavelli, Montesquieu, and Tocqueville, have all tried to define the conditions in terms of political culture where a participatory regime can flourish. The underlying reasoning, in its different forms, has been of the following sort. Every political society requires some sacrifices and demands some disciplines from its members: they have to pay taxes, or serve in the armed forces, and in general observe certain restraints. In a despotism, a regime where the mass of citizens are subject to the rule of a single master or a clique, the requisite disciplines are maintained by coercion. In order to have a free society, one has to replace this coercion with something else. This can only be a willing identification with the polis on the part of the citizens, a sense that the political institutions in which they live are an expression of themselves. The "laws" have to be seen as reflecting and entrenching their dignity as citizens, and hence to be in a sense extensions of themselves. This understanding that the political institutions are a common bulwark of citizen dignity is the basis of what Montesquieu called "vertu," the patriotism that is "une préférence continuelle de l'intérêt public au sien propre,"[10] an impulse that can't be placed neatly in the very modern classification of egoistic-altruistic. It transcends egoism in the sense that people are really attached to the common good, to general liberty. But it is quite unlike the apolitical attachment to universal principle that the stoics advocated or that is central to modern ethics of rule by law.

The difference is that patriotism is based on an identification with others in a particular common enterprise. I'm not dedicated to defending the liberty of just anyone, but I feel the bond of solidarity with my compatriots in our common enterprise, the common expression of our respective dignity. Patriotism is somewhere between friendship or family feeling, on one side, and altruistic dedication on the other. The latter has no concern for the particular: I'm inclined to act for the good of anyone anywhere. The former attaches me to particular people. My patriotic allegiance doesn't bind me to individual people in this familial way; I may not know most of my compatriots, and may not particularly want them as friends when I do meet them. But particularity enters in because my bond to these people passes through our participation in a common political entity. Functioning republics are like families in this crucial respect, that part of what binds people together is their common history. Family ties or old friendships are deep because of what we have lived through together, and republics are bonded by time and climactic transitions.

Here is where we find ourselves pushed back into the ontological issues of community and identity. Of course there was a (premodern) time in the history of our civilization when patriotism was intellectually unproblematic. But the last three centuries have seen the growing power of atomist modes of thought, particularly in the English-speaking world, and more, these have fostered the constitution of an unreflecting common sense shot through with atomist prejudices. According to this outlook, there are individuals, with inclinations and goals and life plans. These inclinations include affection for others, which may be mutual and hence bring about bonding. Families and friendships find a place. Beyond these, however, common institutional structures have to be understood as in the nature of collective instruments. Political societies in the understanding of Hobbes, Locke, Bentham, or the twentieth-century common sense they have helped to shape are established by collections of individuals to obtain benefits through common action they could not secure individually. The action is collective, but the point of it remains individual. The common good is constituted out of individual goods, without remainder. This construal of society incorporates the atomist component of Sen's welfarism.

This implicit ontology has no place for functioning republics, societies bonded by patriotism. For these are grounded on a common good of a stronger kind than atomism allows. To see this we have to dive deeper into the ontological waters. I want to take a plunge now for a few paragraphs and raise an issue wider than the political, before returning to this question of the nature of republics.

There is a distinction largely ignored, or mischaracterized, in post-Cartesian thought: that between matters which are for me and for you, on one hand, and those which are for us, on the other. This distinction plays a tremendously important and pervasive role in human affairs, in ways both banal and fateful. In a banal context, we transfer matters from one category to the other when we open an ordinary conversation over the back fence. "Fine weather we're having," I say to my neighbor. Prior to this, he was aware of the weather, may have been attending to it; obviously I was as well. It was a matter for him and also for me. What the conversation opener does is to make it a matter for *us:* we are now attending to it together. It is important to see that this attending-together is not reducible to an aggregation of attendings-separately. Obviously it involves something more than each of us enjoying the weather on our own. But our atomist prejudices may tempt us to account for this more in terms of aggregations of monological mind states: for example, now I know that you are attending, and you know that I am attending, and you know that I know that you know, and so on.[11] But just adding these monological states does not get us the dialogical condition where things are for us. In certain circumstances, I can know just by seeing you that you are enjoying the weather, and you know the same of me, and since we're both in plain view of each other, each will know that the other knows, and so on. Nevertheless, it is very different when we actually start conversing.

A conversation is not the coordination of actions of different individuals, but a common action in this strong, irreducible sense; it is *our* action. It is of a kind with—to take a more obvious example—the dance of a group or a couple, or the action of two men sawing a log. Opening a conversation is inaugurating a common action. This common action is sustained by little rituals we barely notice, such as the interjections of accord ("unh-hunh") with which the nonspeaking partner punctuates the discourse of the speaker, and with rituals that surround and mediate the switch of the "semantic turn" from one to the other.[12]

This threshold, which conversation takes us over, is one that matters in all sorts of ways and on all sorts of levels in human life. In human terms, we stand on a different footing when we start talking about the weather. That is the main point of conversation, where frequently the actual new information imparted may be sparse or nonexistent. Certainly I don't tell you anything new with my opener. On a deeper level, those I talk to about the things that matter to me are my intimates. Intimacy is an essentially dialogical phenomenon: it is a matter of what we share, of what's for us. We could never describe what it is to be on an intimate footing with someone in terms of monological states. On a transpersonal, institutional level, the same difference can play an important role. The steamy personal life of a political candidate may be an open secret, known to all insiders, journalists, politicians, even cab drivers in the capital. But a significant line is crossed when it breaks into the media and becomes public knowledge. This has to do with the number and kind of people (unsophisticated country folks, for example) who know about it, of course, but not only. It is also a matter of the way in which even those who "always" knew now know: it is now for us, out there in public space. Analogous thresholds exist in the diplomatic world between states. Some things unsaid, or kept discreet, can be tolerated, which you have to react to once they are public. The move from the for-me-and-you to the for-us, the move into public space, is one of the most important things we bring about in language, and any theory of language has to take account of it.[13]

We have been looking at an example of a common focus of attention. But the monological-dialogical distinction is just as evident in relation to goods. Some things have value to me and to you, and some things essentially have value to us. That is, their being for us enters into and constitutes their value for us. On a banal level, jokes are much funnier when they're told in company. The really funny joke is an integral part of a conversation, using that word in a broad sense. What raises a smile when I read it alone can put me in stitches mediated in the ritual of telling, which puts it in common space. Or again, if we are lovers or close friends, Mozart-with-you is a quite different experience from Mozart-alone. I will call goods of this kind "mediately" common goods. But there are other things we value even more, such as friendship itself, where what centrally matters to us is just that there are common actions and meanings. The good is that we share. This I will call "immediately" common goods.

These contrast with other goods that we enjoy collectively but that I want to call "convergent," to mark the difference. To take the classic examples of welfare economics, we enjoy security from various dangers through our system of national defense, our police forces, our fire departments, and the like. This is collectively provided and could not be obtained otherwise. No individual could afford it alone. These are classic cases of collective instrumental action as understood in the Hobbes-Locke tradition. We might normally speak of these goods as "common" or "public," to mark that they not only in fact are secured collectively but that we could not get them any other way. In my language they are convergent, because all this concerns only how we have to go about providing them. It has nothing to do with what makes them goods. Security as a valued end is always security for A, and for B, and for C. It is in no wise a different good, let alone a more valued one, because it is in fact ensured collectively. In the unlikely event that an individual could secure it for himself, he would be getting the same valued condition that we all get now from social provision.

A little story may illustrate the difference. Jacques lived in Saint Jérôme, and his greatest desire was to hear the Montreal Symphony Orchestra under Charles Dutoît playing in a live concert. He had heard them on records and radio, but he was convinced that these media could never give total fidelity, and he wanted to hear the real thing. The obvious solution was to travel to Montreal, but his aged mother would fall into a state of acute anxiety whenever he went farther than the next town. So Jacques got the idea of recruiting other music lovers in the town to raise the required fee to bring the orchestra to Saint Jérôme. Finally the great moment came. As Jacques walked into the concert hall that night, he looked on the Montreal symphony visit as a convergent good between him and his fellow subscribers. But then, when he actually experienced his first live concert, he was enraptured not only by the quality of the sound, which was as he had expected quite different from what you get on records, but also by the dialogue between orchestra and audience. His own love of the music fused with that of the crowd in the darkened hall, resonated with theirs, and found expression in an enthusiastic common act of applause at the end. Jacques also enjoyed the concert in a way he had not expected, as a mediately common good.

What has all this to do with republics? That it is essential to them, that they are animated by a sense of a shared immediate common good. To that degree, the bond resembles that of friendship, as Aristotle saw.[14] The citizen is attached to the laws as the repository of his and others' dignity. That might sound like the way I'm indebted to the Montreal Urban Community for its police service. But the crucial difference is that the police relationship secures what we all understand as a merely convergent good, whereas the identification of the citizen with the republic as a common enterprise is essentially the recognition of a common good. My attachment to the MUC for its police service is based on enlightened self-interest. My (frequently inoperative) moral commitment to the welfare of all humans is altruistic. But the bond of solidarity with my compatriots in a functioning republic is based on a sense of shared fate, where the sharing itself is of value. This is what gives this bond its special importance, what makes my ties with these people and to this enterprise peculiarly binding, what animates my "vertu" or patriotism.

In other words, the very definition of a republican regime as classically understood requires an ontology different from atomism, falling outside atomism-infected common sense. It requires that we probe the relations of identity and community, and distinguish the different possibilities, in particular the possible place of we-identities as against merely convergent I-identities, and the consequent role of common as against convergent goods. If we abstract from all this, then we are in danger of losing the distinction between collective instrumentality and common action, of misconstruing the republic as a hyped-up version of the Montreal Urban Community, delivering a product of much greater importance and about which the beneficiaries feel (on grounds that are hard to fathom but that have possibly irrational roots) particularly strongly.[15]

Perhaps it doesn't matter too much practically, if this kind of regime has no relevance to the modern world. And such is the view of many students of modern politics. But if we are going even to consider the basic thesis of the civic-humanist tradition, we can't simply assume it from the outset. This thesis, to repeat, is that the essential condition of a free (nondespotic) regime is that the citizens have a deeper patriotic identification. This may have seemed self-evident to them because of their concept of freedom. It was not defined mainly in terms of so-called negative liberty. Freedom was thought of as citizen liberty, that of the active participant in public affairs. This citizen was "free" in the sense of having a say in decisions in the political domain, which would shape everyone's lives. Since participatory self-government is itself usually carried out in common actions, it is perhaps normal to see it as properly animated by common identifications. Since we exercise freedom in common actions, it may seem natural that we value it as a common good.

The underlying reasoning of the thesis, as I said, is that the disciplines which would be externally imposed by fear under a despotism have to be self-imposed in its absence, and only patriotic identification can provide the motivation. But the case could also be argued in slightly different terms. We could say that a free, that is, participatory, regime calls on citizens to provide for themselves things that a despotism may provide for them. The foremost example of this is national defense. A despotic regime may raise money and hire mercenaries to fight for it; a republican regime will generally call on its citizens to fight for their own freedom. The causal links run in both directions. Citizen armies guarantee freedom because they are an obstacle to despotic takeover, just as large armies at the disposal of powerful generals invite a coup, as the agony of the Roman republic illustrates. But at the same time, only people who live in and cherish a free regime will be motivated to fight for themselves. This relation between citizen armies and freedom was one of the main themes of Machiavelli's work.

So we could say that republican solidarity underpins freedom, because it provides the motivation for self-imposed discipline; or else that it is essential for a free regime, because its members are asked to do things that mere subjects can avoid. In one case, we think of the demands on members as the same, and the difference concerns the motivation to meet them: fear of punishment versus an inwardly generated sense of honor and obligation. In the other case, the demands of freedom are defined as more onerous, and the issue concerns what can motivate this extra effort.

The second formulation very much depends on seeing freedom in participatory terms. Free regimes are more onerous because they require service in public life, both military and political, that the unfree do not. The importance of service in the civic-humanist tradition shows the degree to which freedom was understood in terms of participation. But one can extract a broader thesis from this tradition about the essential bases of nondespotic society. This would define nondespotism not just in terms of participation, but by a broader gamut of freedoms, including negative ones. It would draw on the first formulation to argue a link between the solidarity of patriotism and free institutions, on the grounds that a free society needs this kind of motivation to provide what despotisms get through fear; to engender the disciplines, the sacrifices, the essential contributions it needs to keep going, as well as to mobilize support in its defense when threatened.

If we call this basic proposition connecting patriotism and freedom the "republican thesis," then we can speak of narrower and broader forms of this, with the former focused purely on participatory freedom and the latter taking in the broader gamut of liberties. With all these preliminaries behind us, we can finally address the first criticism of procedural liberalism, that it offers a nonviable formula for a free regime.

We can see right off how this kind of liberalism seems to run athwart the republican thesis. It conceives of society as made up of individuals with life plans, based on their conceptions of the good, but without a commonly held conception espoused by the society itself. But that seems to be the formula for an instrumental society, designed to seek merely convergent goods; it seems to exclude the republican form altogether.

This is the usual reaction of people steeped in the civic-humanist tradition when they first confront the definitions of procedural liberalism. I confess that I find myself reacting this way. But the criticism as it stands is not quite right. There are confusions here, and what's interesting is that they are not all on one side, not only in the mind of the critic.

What's wrong with the criticism? The liberal can respond to the republican that he is not at all committed to a merely instrumental society. His formula does indeed exclude a societally endorsed common *good,* but not at all a common understanding of the *right;* actually it calls for this. The misunderstanding turns on two senses of "good." In the broad sense, it means anything valuable we seek; in the narrower sense, it refers to life plans or ways of living so valued. Procedural liberalism can't have a common good in the narrow sense, because society must be neutral on the question of the good life. But in the broader sense, where a rule of right can also count as "good," there can be an extremely important shared good.

So procedural liberalism can parry the objection of nonviability. This objection, to recall, came out of the republican thesis and, reading this type of liberal society as necessarily instrumental, saw it as lacking citizen identification with a common good. But since this is a condition of a nondespotic regime, it judged this form of liberalism to be by its nature self-undermining. A free society, which thus needs to rely on a strong spontaneous allegiance from its members, is eschewing the indispensable basis of this: strong citizen identification around a sense of common good—what I have been calling patriotism.

One reply to this attack would remain entirely within the assumptions of modern atomism. It would simply reject the republican thesis, and suppose that viable liberal societies can rely on quite different bases: either the eighteenth-century view that the citizens' allegiance could be grounded on enlightened self-interest; or the idea that modern civilization has educated people to higher moral standards, so that citizens are sufficiently imbued with the liberal ethos to support and defend their society; or the idea current in modern "revisionist" democratic theory, that a mature liberal society doesn't demand very much of its members, as long as it delivers the goods and makes their lives prosperous and secure. As a matter of fact, on this view it is better if the citizens don't participate too actively, but instead elect governments every few years and then let them get on with it.[16]

But procedural liberalism need not reply in this way. It can accept the republican thesis, and plead that it *does* have a place for a common good, hence patriotism, and that it can be viable as a free society.

Which reply ought liberalism to make? Those of an atomist outlook will opt for the first. They will think that the republican thesis, whatever its validity in ancient times, is irrelevant in modern mass bureaucratic society. People in the modern age have become individualist, and societies can only be held together in one or another of the ways I just described. To hanker after the unity of earlier republics is to indulge in bootless nostalgia. If this is right, then all the ontological discussion of the previous pages, designed to make sense of republican societies, is of purely antiquarian interest, and the civic-humanist critique of liberalism can be shrugged off.

But plausible as this atomist view might seem, it is wide of the mark. We can see this if we look at the recent history of the United States, which is after all the main society of reference for procedural liberals. Think of the reaction to Watergate and, to a lesser degree, to the Iran-Contra misdemeanors. In the first case, citizen outrage actually drove a president from power. Now I want to make two, admittedly contestable, points about these reactions, which together amount to an important confirmation of the continuing relevance of the republican thesis.

The first is that the capacity of the citizenry to respond with outrage to this kind of abuse is an important bulwark of freedom in modern society. It is true that Americans are perhaps especially sensitive to acts of executive abuse, in comparison to other contemporary democracies—think, for instance, of the absence of French reaction to the bombing of the Greenpeace ship, *Rainbow Warrior*. But the general point would be that, although the targets might vary from society to society, most democratic electorates are disposed to react to violations of the norms of liberal self-rule, and this is a crucial support for these regimes. Where this disposition has been relatively lacking—for example in a number of Latin American countries, where many people are ready to tolerate "disappearances" perpetrated by semi-clandestine arms of the military, or to welcome army putsches—then one is in danger of ending up with an Argentine junta or a murderous Pinochet regime.

The second point is that this capacity for outrage is not fueled by any of the sources recognized by atomism. Most people do not respond this way because they calculate that it is in their long-term interest. Nor do most people respond just because of their general commitment to the principles of liberal democracy. This too plays a role, but by itself it would not lead to, say, an American reacting more vigorously to Nixon's violations than to Pinochet's or Enver Hodja's. Now there are certainly some people who feel very strongly about the fate of democracy everywhere, but they too are, alas, a relatively small minority of most electorates. Third, people would barely respond at all if they thought of their society purely instrumentally, as the dispenser of security and prosperity.

What generates the outrage is something in none of the above categories, neither egoism nor altruism, but a species of patriotic identification. In the case of the United States, there is widespread identification with "the American way of life," a sense of Americans sharing a common identity and history, defined by a commitment to certain ideals, articulated famously in the Declaration of Independence, Lincoln's Gettysburg Address, and such documents, which in turn derive their importance from their connection to certain climactic transitions of a shared history. It is this sense of identity, and the pride accompanying it, that is outraged by the shady doings of a Watergate, and this is what provokes the irresistible reaction.

My second point is that republican patriotism remains a force in modern society, one that was palpably operative during the days of Watergate. It goes unnoticed, partly because of the hold of atomist prejudices on modern theoretical thinking, and partly because its forms and focus are somewhat different from those of classical times. But it is still very much with us and plays an essential role in maintaining our contemporary liberal democratic regimes. Of course patriotism is also responsible for a lot of evil, today as at any time. It can take the form of virulent nationalism and, in its darker forms, encourage someone like Oliver North to violate the norms of a free society, even as it is generating a healthy defense against the danger so created. But whatever menace the malign effects have spawned, the benign effects have been essential to the maintenance of liberal democracy.[17]

This point is of course controversial. It involves a certain reading of recent history, and of its causes, which is far from being universally accepted. But I will make the point even stronger. Not only has patriotism been an important bulwark of freedom in the past, but it will remain unsubstitutably so for the future. The various atomist sources of allegiance have not only been insufficient to generate the vigorous defensive reaction to crimes like Watergate; they will never be able to do so, in the nature of things. Pure enlightened self-interest will never move enough people strongly enough to constitute a real threat to potential despots and putschists. Nor will there be enough people who are moved by universal principle, unalloyed with particular identifications, moral citizens of the cosmopolis, Stoic or Kantian, to stop these miscreants in their tracks. As for those who support a society because of the prosperity and security it generates, they are only fair-weather friends and are bound to let you down when you need them. In other words, I want to claim that the republican thesis is as relevant and true today as it was in ancient or early modern times, when the paradigms of civic humanism were articulated.

If I am right about this, then liberalism can't answer the charge of non-viability just by assuming atomism and dismissing the republican thesis. To do so would be to be blind to the crucial dynamics of modern society. But that leaves the other answer: a procedural liberal society can be republican in a crucial respect. And indeed that is one way of reading the Watergate reaction. What the outraged citizens saw as violated was precisely a rule of right, a liberal conception of rule by law. That is what they identified with, and what they rose to defend as their common good. We no longer need to argue that, in theory, procedural liberalism allows for patriotism; we have a living case, or at least a close approximation, of such a patriotism of the right. The confusion in the mind of the critic would be to have thought that procedural liberalism entails an atomist ontology, on the grounds that it speaks of individual life plans, and that hence it can draw allegiance only from atomist sources. But in fact a procedural liberal can be a holist; what is more, holism captures much better the actual practice of societies that approximate this model. Thus runs a convincing answer to the critic— which incidentally illustrates again how essential it is not to confuse the ontological issue of atomism-holism with questions of advocacy opposing individualism and collectivism.

Now here it is the critics who seem to have fallen prey to this confusion. But they may not be the only victims. For once we understand procedural liberalism holistically, certain questions arise which its protagonists rarely raise.

We can question whether a patriotic liberal regime really meets the proceduralist demands. The common good is, indeed, a rule of right. But we have to remember that patriotism involves more than converging moral principles; it is a common allegiance to a particular historical community. Cherishing and sustaining this has to be a common goal, and it is more than just consensus on the rule of right. Put differently, patriotism involves, beyond convergent values, a love of the particular. Sustaining this specific historical set of institutions and forms is and must be a socially endorsed common end.

In other words, while the procedural liberal state can indeed be neutral between (a) believers and nonbelievers in God, or between (b) people with homo- and heterosexual orientations, it cannot be between (c) patriots and antipatriots. We can imagine its courts hearing and giving satisfaction to those who, under (a), object to school prayers, or those who, under (b), petition to ban a manual of sex education that treats homosexuality as a perversion. But supposing someone, under (c), objected to the pious tone with which American history and its major figures are presented to the young. The parents might declare themselves ready to abide by the rules of the procedural republic and to educate their children to do so, but they will do it for their own hyper-Augustinian reasons, that in this fallen world of depraved wills, such a modus vivendi is the least dangerous arrangement. But they'll be damned (no mere figure of speech, this) if they'll let their children be brainwashed into taking as their heroes the infidel Jefferson or the crypto-freethinker Washington, with all their shallow and impious cant about human perfectibility. Or we might imagine a less ideological objection, where parents who espouse an apolitical lifestyle object to the implicit endorsement of active citizenship that flows from the patriot's view of American history.

These examples sound fanciful, and they are indeed unlikely to happen. But why? Surely because, while fighting about religion in schools has become a very American thing to do and the battle continues well beyond the point where a less litigious people might have settled on a workable compromise, just because Americans on both sides feel that what they advocate is dictated by the constitution, so a questioning of the value of patriotism is profoundly un-American and close to unthinkable as a public act.[18] Logically such a challenge is possible, and it would be no more illegitimate on the terms of procedural liberalism than those under (a) and (b). But any court that gave satisfaction to such a suit would be undermining the very regime it was established to interpret. A line has to be drawn here before the demands of proceduralism.

This may not be a major problem. No political theory can be implemented in all the purity of its original model. There have to be some compromises with reality, and a viable procedural republic would have to favor patriotism. But another issue, touched on earlier, must be explored.

This patriotic liberal regime differs from the traditional republican model. We have imagined that the values enshrined in the historically endorsed institutions are purely those of the rule of right, incorporating something like the rule of law, individual rights, and principles of fairness and equal treatment. What this leaves out is the central good of the civic-humanist tradition: participatory self-rule. In fact, one could say that the center of gravity of the classical theory was at the opposite end of the spectrum. Ancient theories were not concerned with individual rights, and they allowed some pretty hairy procedures judged by our modern standards of personal immunity—such as ostracism. Moreover, their notions of equal treatment were applied selectively from our point of view. But they did think citizen rule was of the very essence of the republic.

Now the question arises of what we make of this good in our modern liberal society. Procedural liberals tend to neglect it, treating self-rule as purely instrumental to the rule of law and equality. Indeed, to treat it as the republic tradition does, which sees self-rule as essential to a life of dignity, as itself the highest political good, would take us beyond the bounds of procedural liberalism. A society organized around this proposition would share and endorse, qua society, at least that notion of the good life. This is a clear, unconfused point of conflict between procedural liberals and republicans. Thinkers like Hannah Arendt and Robert Bellah clearly have an incompatible political ideal, which this liberalism cannot incorporate.[19] Well, so what? Why is that a problem for procedural liberalism?

Perhaps it isn't, but important questions arise before we can be sure. The issue is, can our patriotism survive the marginalization of participatory self-rule? Patriotism is a common identification with a historical community founded on certain values. These can vary widely, and there can of course be patriotisms in unfree societies, for example, founded on race or blood ties and finding expression in despotic forms, as in fascism; or the patriotism of Russians, under tsars and Bolsheviks, which was/is linked to authoritarian forms of rule. A free society requires a patriotism, according to the republican thesis. But it must be one whose core values incorporate freedom. Historically, republican patriotism has incorporated self-rule in its very definition of freedom.

Does this have to be so? The point is that the patriotism of a free society has to celebrate its institutions as realizing a meaningful freedom, one that safeguards the dignity of citizens. Can we define a meaningful freedom in this sense, which can capture people's allegiance without including self-rule as a central element?

We could argue this point in general terms: what will moderns recognize as genuine citizen dignity? This has to be defined not only in terms of what is to be *secured* for a citizen; the modern notion of the dignity of the person is essentially that of an agent, who can affect his or her own condition. Citizen dignity involves a notion of citizen capacity. Two major models are implicit in much of my discussion.

Model A focuses on individual rights and equal treatment, as well as a government performance that takes account of the citizens' preferences. This is what has to be secured. Citizen capacity consists mainly in the power to retrieve these rights and ensure equal treatment, as well as to influence the effective decisionmakers. This retrieval may take place largely through the courts, in systems with a body of entrenched rights, such as we find in the United States (and recently in Canada). But it will also be effected through representative institutions, and in the spirit of this model, these institutions have an entirely instrumental significance. They tend to be viewed as they were on the "revisionist" model mentioned earlier. Thus no value is put on participation in rule for its own sake. The ideal is not "ruling and being ruled in turn,"[20] but having clout. This is compatible with not engaging in the participatory system at all, provided one can wield a credible threat to those who are so engaged, to make them take notice; or one can engage in the system in an adversarial way, where the governors are defined as "them" to our "us," and pressured through single-issue campaigns, or petitions or lobbies, to take us into account.

Model B, by contrast, defines participation in self-rule as the essence of freedom, as part of what must be secured. It is also seen as an essential component of citizen capacity. In consequence, a society in which the citizens' relation to government is normally adversarial, even where they manage to bend it to their purposes, has not secured citizen dignity and allows only a low degree of citizen capacity. Full participation in self-rule means, at least part of the time, to have some part in forming a ruling consensus, with which one can identify along with others. To rule and be ruled in turn means that at least some of the time the governors can be "us," not always "them." The sense of citizen capacity is seen as incompatible with our being part of an alien political universe, which we can perhaps manipulate but never identify with.

These two kinds of capacity are incommensurable. We can't say simply which is greater. For people of an atomist bent, there is no doubt that model A will seem preferable, and for republicans model B will seem the only genuine one. But ranking them in the abstract is not the issue. The point is to see which can figure in the definition of citizen dignity in a viable patriotism. This requires us to share an allegiance to and cherish in common a historical set of institutions as the common bulwark of our freedom and dignity. Can model A be the focus of some such common sentiment?

The reasons for being skeptical are that this model of citizen capacity is so adversarial that it would seem impossible to combine it with the sense that our institutions are a shared bulwark of dignity. If I win my way by manipulating the common institutions, how can I see them as reflecting a purpose common to me and those who participate in these institutions? But there are also reasons to be skeptical of a too-simple logic. Once again the reality of United States experience gives us pause. We could argue that America has moved in the last century more and more toward a definition of its public life based on model A. It has become a less participatory and more procedural republic.[21] Judicial retrieval has become more important; at the same time, participation in elections seems to be declining. Meanwhile, political-action committees and lobbyists threaten to increase the leverage of single-issue politics.

These are exactly the developments that republicans deplore, seeing in them a decline in civic spirit and ultimately a danger for free society. But liberals could counter that the continuing vigor of American political life shows that a patriotism of model A is viable; that underlying the adversarial relation to the representative institutions is a continuing sense that the political structure of which they are a part remains a common bulwark of freedom. The law invites us to litigate as adversaries to get our way; but it entrenches and enshrines for both sides their freedom and capacity as citizens. After all, they may add, the agon of citizens struggling for office and honor was central to the classical polis. That regime also united adversaries in solidarity.

I don't know who will turn out to be right. Republicans argue that the continued growth of bureaucratic, centralized society and the consequent exacerbation of participant alienation can only undermine patriotism in the long run. Liberals will reply that the resources of rights retrieval will increase to empower people *pari passu* with the spread of bureaucratic power. Such measures as the freedom-of-information acts already show that countervailing power can be brought to bear.

But the question can't be settled in purely general terms. It is not just a matter of whether in the abstract people can accommodate to one or other model of citizen dignity. The question must be particularized to each society's tradition and culture. Procedural liberals seem to assume that something like model A is consonant with the American tradition, but this is vigorously contested by others, who argue that participation was an important part of early American patriotism and remains integral to the ideal by which American citizens will ultimately judge their republic.[22]

My aim is not to settle this issue. I raise it only to show how placing procedural liberalism against the background of a holist ontology, while answering the oversimple charge of nonviability in principle, opens a wide range of concrete questions about its viability in practice. These questions can be properly addressed only after we have settled issues on the ontological level, in fact in favor of holism. Both my main theses about the relation of the two levels are illustrated here: once you opt for holism, extremely important questions remain open on the level of advocacy; at the same time, your ontology structures the debate between the alternatives, and forces you to face certain questions. Clarifying the ontological question restructures the debate about advocacy.

When I said that procedural liberals might be confused about these levels, and not only those who proffer the simple republican criticism, I was referring to this. Certainly this liberalism has an answer to the nonviability objection, and perhaps it will prove viable in practice. But procedural liberals seem quite unaware that the issue has to be addressed. Could it be that they are still too much in the thrall of atomist notions, of the instrumental model of society, or of the various atomist sources of allegiance, to see that there are questions here? Are they too insensitive to the ontological issues to see the point of the republican critique? I suspect this is so. And thus they fail to articulate the distinction between ontological and advocacy questions, and take their communitarian critics to be simply advancing a different *policy*, which they vaguely apprehend as more collectivist; instead of seeing how the challenge is based on a redrawn map of political possibilities.

Having gone on at some length about the viability objection, I have little space left to address the charge of ethnocentricity. Fortunately I can make the point tersely, having laid some of the groundwork. Whether or not model A is the one entrenched in the American tradition and can ensure a free society in the United States, it is clearly not the only possible model. Other societies are more oriented to model B, Canada for one. Indeed, this is a principal difference between the political cultures of the two countries, which expresses itself in all sorts of ways, such as the relatively higher voting participation and the greater emphasis on collective provision in Canada, reflected, for instance, in the Canadian public-health service.

There are other societies where the fusion between patriotism and free institutions is not so total as in the United States, whose defining political culture has always been centered on free institutions. There are also modern democratic societies where patriotism centers on a national culture, which in many cases has come to incorporate free institutions, but which is also defined in terms of some language or history. Quebec is the prominent example in my experience, but there are many others.

The procedural model will not fit these societies because they can't declare neutrality between all possible definitions of the good life. A society like Quebec can't but be dedicated to the defense and promotion of French culture and language, even if this involves some restriction on individual freedoms. It can't make cultural-linguistic orientation a matter of indifference. A government that could ignore this requirement would either not be responding to the majority will or would reflect a society so deeply demoralized as to be close to dissolution. In either case, the prospects for liberal democracy would not be rosy.

But then one is entitled to raise questions about the procedural model as a proper definition of *liberal* society. Are these other types of society, organized around model B or a national culture, not properly liberal? This could of course be made true by definitional fiat, in which case the claim is uninteresting. But if proceduralism is an attempt to define the essence of modern liberalism, it has to find a place for these alternatives. The discussion up to now has suffered from a certain parochialism. It has to come to terms with the real world of liberal democracy, to echo one of my compatriots, most of which lies outside the borders of the United States.

But these vistas can only be opened if we can clarify the ontological issues, and allow the debate between liberals and communitarians to be the complex, many-leveled affair that it really is.

— 11 —

Invoking Civil Society

In recent years the notion of civil society has come back into circulation. The intention is to invoke something like the concept that developed at the turn of the nineteenth century, which stands in contrast to "the state." But in fact those who introduced it were trying to articulate features of the development of western civilization which go back much farther.

One of the first fields of application of the revived term was to the polities of Eastern Europe. "Civil society" defined what they had been deprived of and were struggling to recreate: a web of autonomous associations, independent of the state, which bound citizens together in matters of common concern, and by their mere existence or action could have an effect on public policy. In this sense, western liberal democracies were thought to have functioning civil societies.

"Civil society" in this sense refers to what the Leninist model of rule had essentially negated. That model arose first in the Soviet Union, then was reproduced in other "Marxist-Leninist" regimes, finally was imitated more or less completely, and sometimes caricaturally, by a number of newly independent third-world countries. The essential virtue of the model for its protagonists was that it offered a kind of total mobilization of society toward what were seen as revolutionary goals. The central instrument was a vanguard party dominated by a revolutionary elite. And a crucial feature of this system was the satellitization of all aspects of social life to this party. Trade unions, leisure clubs, even churches, all had to be permeated and made into "transmission belts" of the party's purposes. Leninism in its heyday was one of the principal sources of modern totalitarianism.

This system has been in decay for a number of decades—since the death of Stalin in its original homeland, and somewhat later in countries that followed the Russian example with an indigenous revolutionary elite, such as China and Cuba. In fact there was a long period of retreat, where the drive to total mobilization flagged more and more visibly, but without any of the fundamental principles of the system being renounced. Future generations will probably describe this period of slow inner decay as the Age of Brezhnev. With Gorbachev, we entered a new phase, in which some of the tenets of total mobilization were themselves challenged. Unanimity was no longer an unambiguously good thing. They began to have real, if restricted, elections in Moscow. But under Brezhnev the goal was to keep the facade of unanimity unbroken. In principle no dissident opinions should be expressed, everyone should turn out for Leninist holidays, people should pass spontaneous resolutions on critical occasions denouncing U.S. imperialism; at the same time, the demands of the regime on private life were lessening. Governments like Czechoslovakia's even encouraged a kind of privatization of life. Let everyone cultivate their gardens, provided they turned out for May Day parades and otherwise kept their mouths shut. It was a Leninism of fatigue.

In these circumstances, as the furious terror of Stalinism receded, the pressure rose in certain East European societies for reform. A total change of regime seemed, for obvious geopolitical reasons, utopian. The goal was rather to undo Leninism partially from below, to open a margin of free association out of party control but enjoying legal recognition. It is understandable that an aspiration of this kind should find expression in a distinction between civil society and the state. For on this model, the state—understood in flatly Weberian terms as the agency with the monopoly of physical force—would have an entirely different basis than society would. Its ultimate foundation would be external, in the threat of Soviet intervention, whereas the different components of the newly freed "civil society" would express indigenous social forces.

But in using this term, thinkers in both East and West wanted to express something more than the mutual independence of state and society. They wanted also to invoke something of the history and practice of the western democracies as a model. The notion was, first, that in the West there already is a civil society and, second, that this contemporary reality is heir to a centuries-long development of the distinction between society and state. There is truth in both claims, but to get at it we have to modulate the meaning of "civil society." This turns out to be a more complex and many-faceted idea than one might have thought at first. The nuances are worth exploring because they color the models of the political process we want to steer our lives by in coming decades.

To take the first claim: civil society already exists in the West. Yes, there is in western societies a web of autonomous associations, independent of the state, and these have an effect on public policy. But there has also been a tendency for these to become integrated into the state, the tendency toward what has been called (often in a slightly sneering tone, because of the origins of the term in fascist Italy) "corporatism." States like Sweden, Holland, and Germany, but also many others, have gone some way to integrating trade unions, employers' associations, and the like into government planning. To speak of integration "into the state" may be tendentious here; some people see it as a loss of government independence to special interests. But in fact what occurs is an interweaving of society and government to the point where the distinction no longer expresses an important difference in the basis of power or the dynamics of policymaking. Both government and associations draw on and are responsive to the same public. For instance, issues of national income policy, debated between management and labor unions in tripartite negotiations with the government as third party, can also be debated in parliament, where the same social forces are represented in the form of the social-democratic and conservative parties. In fact, these two loci of negotiation and debate are generally complementary; the issue about corporatism could be phrased as a question—how much of the crucial negotiation takes place outside parliament?

Of course, there are many associations in western societies which are not involved in corporatist negotiations. Some of these are capable of having an impact on policy through lobbying or public campaigns, while others are marginal and easy to ignore. But the drift toward corporatism in modern industrial democracies consists in the first category, with strong associations being more and more integrated into the process of decisionmaking. It makes sense for a democratic government to consult before deciding, not only to determine the most popular policy, but also to soften the edges of confrontation with the losers, who will at least have the sense that they have been listened to and will be listened to again.

This style of government is roundly condemned, on the right and the left. But it is not clear that either has come up with a viable alternative. The attack from the right is mainly in evidence in the English-speaking countries. Margaret Thatcher was its best-known protagonist. She certainly upset the rules of the game as they were understood under her predecessors of both parties. She introduced a politics of conflict into what formerly had been negotiation. It has been argued by her supporters that this was necessary in order to challenge the position that the labor unions had won in British society. She had to fight a war, ending in the bruising battle of a miners' strike. But the outcome of war is generally peace restored on a new basis. Confrontation as a style of government is not sustainable in the long run in democratic countries.

Of course, right-wing politicians like Thatcher don't subscribe theoretically to endless conflict. They envisage a new dispensation after the special interests have been dealt with, and various enterprises and functions privatized. Many things that the government now orchestrates will run themselves without state interference. State and society will do their own thing without getting in each other's way. This is especially espoused by the right because of their belief in the efficacy of unadulterated market forces.

Now I believe that this hope is utopian—or dystopian, if you don't share the moral outlook of the right. Too much is at stake to allow government and society to coexist without coordination. The really successful economies in the late twentieth century are resolutely corporatist, for instance, Germany and Japan. The idea that there is another path to competitive success on world markets seems to be a nostalgic illusion of the English-speaking countries, remembering an earlier, braver era of economic purity. But those days are gone forever. The obvious failure of the Marxist policy of suppressing the market altogether can be taken only by the simple-minded as proof that total reliance on the market is the best policy. Obviously we are all going to have to live with some mix of market and state orchestration. The difficult question is what mix suits each society. In fact, right-wing governments go on orchestrating for more than they admit. And to the extent that they refrain from doing so—that, say, Britain and the United States turn their backs on industrial policy—they will probably live to rue the day.

What is the relevance of all this to the idea of civil society? It is that the anti-corporatist aspiration can very well be, and often is, expressed in this society/state distinction. So the idea that civil society is something we *have* in the West needs to be nuanced. In one sense we do; in another sense it is a goal that has to be striven for against the grain of modern democratic government.

Let's look more closely at these different senses. (1) In a minimal sense, civil society exists where there are free associations that are not under tutelage of state power. (2) In a stronger sense, civil society exists where society as a whole can structure itself and coordinate its actions through such free associations. (3) As an alternative or supplement to the second sense, we can speak of civil society wherever the ensemble of associations can significantly determine or inflect the course of state policy.

No one can deny that civil society exists in sense (1) in the West; or that it was lacking under Leninism and was a crucial aspiration of those living under Leninist regimes. But civil society as contrasted with the state in western political theory incorporated more than this; it involved (2) and sometimes (3). It was in virtue of this that it could be referred to in the singular as civil *society*. We might say that (2) and (3) introduce a public dimension that has been crucial to the concept in the western tradition.

One aspect of the right-wing indictment of corporatism could be formulated in the charge that it has suppressed civil society in sense (2). Sense (3) might be thought to be integrally fulfilled by corporatist mechanisms of negotiation. But this will not be easily accepted by one who suspects that the associations are in fact being integrated into the state apparatus, rather than bringing to bear their independent weight on it.

This brings us to the left-wing criticism of corporatism, which also can be and sometimes is expressed in terms of civil society. Here too it is the enriched concept involving senses (2) and (3) which is in play. I'm thinking of the criticism that comes from what are sometimes called the "new social movements," and which has found expression, for instance, in Germany's green party.

On this outlook, the state and the large powerful associations it consults form a unity. They tend equally toward elite control and growing distance from the constituencies they claim to speak for. In addition, they are equally committed to increasing bureaucratic control in the name of technological efficacy over more and more aspects of human life. Even such seemingly benign features of modern society as the welfare state, originally introduced on the initiative of the left, become suspect as mechanisms of control and "normalization." To be a beneficiary of the welfare state is to submit to bureaucratic regulation, to have your life shaped by categories that may cut across those in which you want to live your life.

One response to this has been to try to open a sphere of independent self-regulation by spontaneously associating groups. Another has been to try to win for the new social movements themselves greater impact on the formation of policy. These correspond to senses (2) and (3) respectively, and so it is not surprising that this New Left has also been tempted to bring the term "civil society" into play. The sense, justified or not, of an analogy between their situation and that of dissidents in the eastern European bloc has strengthened this temptation.[1]

So the first claim mentioned above, that civil society already exists in the West, is more problematic than it appeared. But the second claim is also not simply true, and it would be worth exploring at even greater length.

The relative freedom we enjoy is seen as having sources deep in the history of the West, and in particular in conceptions of society going back to medieval Christendom. These sources can be articulated with something like the conception of civil society. In the context of contemporary Eastern Europe, the obvious pole of comparison is Russia. At successive stages, Russia took a different political path from western polities. The development of an independent noble class, of free cities, and hence of a regime of "estates" was cut short at crucial moments by the state building of Ivan the Terrible and later by Peter the Great. Subsequent initiatives aimed at joining the West were repressed by Nicholas I and then by Lenin. A mainstay of western development, that is, a church independent of political authority, never existed in the Russian Orthodox tradition.

So runs the story, and it obviously has a great deal of truth to it, and particular relevance to the situation of Eastern Europe; at least to Hungary, Poland, Czechoslovakia, East Germany. These societies developed in close cultural contact and symbiosis with western Europe. They share analogous institutional developments and some of the same ideals. For instance, republican ideals of self-rule were present in Poland and enshrined even in the name of the pre-partition state, Rzeczpospolita Polska (the Commonwealth of Poland). The poignant fate of these societies was to have been forced to accept an alien political system, in fact of Russian origin, which ran against the grain of those societies and was the cause of endless conflict. The aspiration to greater freedom is in effect synonymous with an aspiration to rejoin Europe. That is why it finds natural expression in a view of the European political tradition and in the notion of civil society.[2]

Perhaps this contrast between Russia and the West has been overdrawn.

Sometimes it is put in such a way as to imply that the tragic political plight of Russia has been virtually inevitable from the Mongol conquest on. And western freedom is described in a symmetrically self-congratulatory way as flowing inevitably out of a more remote past. In fact, there were moments when things could have been reversed. Arguably, the Bolshevik takeover was a contingent political disaster for Russia, which interrupted the slow development of civil society that had been gathering pace in the last decades of tsarism. Arguably, Peter's was not the only road to modernization open to Russia. At the same time, when Peter did try to imitate Europe, he took what was seen as the latest, most effective model, the so-called absolute monarchies. Those were in fact constrained by a context of law and independent associations. But no one would then have predicted confidently that they wouldn't grow stronger, that they would give way before a totally different governing formula, then effective only in England and Holland. Western democracy was never written in the genes. At the same time, the chauvinistic idea that representative institutions can't take root outside their home culture is refuted by the existence of such societies as India and Japan (and, dare we hope, post-Gorbachev Russia and post-Deng China).

But when all this is said, it remains true that western liberal democracy has deep roots in its past, that certain socially entrenched self-conceptions greatly facilitated its rise, and that many of these were absent in Russia or were ruthlessly rooted out by earlier rulers. What were these roots, and how do they relate to the term "civil society"?

There are a number of factors worth talking about in this connection; some of them are ideas, some are institutions, but most often they are both at once: institutions and practices that incorporate their own self-interpretation. In one form or another, they seem to be part of the background of western democratic society. But the relation is sometimes more complex and ambiguous than at first appears, mainly because modern democracy itself is a more complex and tension-ridden reality than is generally acknowledged. Some of these tensions will emerge from looking at how the society/state distinction arose.

(A) The medieval notion of society is one of those which has turned out to be important in the development of the West. What is important is in a sense a negative fact: that society is not defined in terms of its political organization. The underlying issue is this: what gives a society its identity? What are the features without which it would cease to be a society, or would become a wholly different one? In many civilizations and eras, these questions are answered in terms of political structure. For both the Greeks and the Romans, the identity of society was defined by its *politeia,* its political constitution. Under the Empire unity came from a common subjection to authority, although a fiction was maintained that this authority came from an act of the people. Now to the extent that a society is defined by its political organization, to that degree it is permeable by political power. It lacks a principle of resistance to the invasive force of sovereign political authority. Just being politically defined is hardly a sufficient condition for this kind of takeover by despotic power, as the Greek polis attests. It is rather that the basis for a certain kind of limitation on this power is lacking, whenever the conditions ripen for its advance.

Now unlike the ancient conceptions, the notion that developed in the early Middle Ages was of a society where political authority was one organ among others. Royal authority, for instance, was *singulis major* but *universis minor.* This idea, that society is not identical with its political organization, can be seen as a crucial differentiation, one of the origins of the later notion of civil society and one of the roots of western liberalism.

(B) This differentiation was carried further by one of the most important features of Latin Christendom: the development of an idea of the church as an independent society. In principle, the inhabitants of Christendom were Christian. But these same people were organized in two societies, one temporal and one spiritual, of which neither could be simply subordinated to the other. This was, of course, a formula for perpetual struggle, and extravagant claims were made for one side or the other, including an arrogation of *plenitudo potestatis* by Pope Innocent III. But the underlying common understanding remained within the Gelasian definition of "two swords." There were two sources of authority, both granted for different purposes by God. Each was subordinate to the other for some purposes and supreme for others. Western Christendom was in its essence bifocal.

Alongside these two pervasive features, there were particular facets of medieval political arrangements which with hindsight appear important. (C) One is the development of a legal notion of subjective rights. This was linked to the peculiar nature of feudal relations of authority. The relations of vassalage were seen in a quasi-contractual light. The superior had obligations as well as the inferior. To repudiate these obligations was a felony, as much as for the vassal. So inferiors were seen as the beneficiaries of obligations, privileges enjoyed as a kind of property. This is the origin of the western notion of subjective rights. It starts off as a notion of purely positive law, before being transposed by the natural-rights doctrines of the seventeenth and eighteenth centuries. But it meant that medieval sovereigns faced a society that was partly defined as a skein of rights and duties, which imposed on them the necessity of winning consent for important changes. This, along with the existence of relatively independent, self-governing cities (D), brought about the standard political structures of medieval polities (E), in which a monarch ruled with the intermittent and uncertain support of a body of estates, which had to be called together from time to time to raise the resources he needed to govern and wage war. This dyarchy constituted another, purely secular dualism, linking the political structure to society at large.

We can recognize our roots in all of this. But it didn't ensure trouble-free progress for modern liberal democracy. Between us and that time lies the great early-modern attempt over most of Europe to set up absolute monarchies. Kings won the power to raise taxes without calling the estates, built standing armies on these resources, which in turn made their power harder to challenge. Around 1680 this looked like the wave of the future; it must have seemed to many that only this kind of state could be militarily effective. Moreover, influential theories justified the new model of political society. On one hand, the concepts of Roman law, favoring monarchical power, become dominant. On the other hand, Bodin and later Hobbes develop a notion of sovereignty which quite undermines or supersedes the medieval understanding of society. The notion comes to be accredited that a society, in order to exist at all, must be held together by sovereign power, that is, by a power unlimited by any other. In other words, the identification of society with its political organization returns, and in a form that is unambiguously favorable to despotism. Important vestiges of feature A emerge in social-contract doctrines, where society is accorded existence prior to government, as it is with the jurists Grotius and Pufendorf. This is the feature of contract theory that Hobbes wanted to suppress. But even with Grotius and Pufendorf in the seventeenth century, the "contract of subjection" is seen as setting up absolute power, against which society henceforth has no legal recourse.

Meanwhile, throughout this period, a satellitization of the church is taking place in a number of Protestant countries, and the very division of Christendom undermines the idea at the heart of B, that everyone belongs to a single alternative society.

As I said above, absolute monarchies were really rather limited exercises in despotism, seen in the light of twentieth-century dictatorships. They did away with D and E, but remained limited by C, the entrenched traditions of rights. Of course, nothing assured that C in turn would not be eroded if absolutism pursued its course. The important stream of reform thinking in the eighteenth century that looked to "enlightened despotism" to reorder society on rational lines was hostile to traditional rights, wanted them swept aside in the name of reason. But absolutism couldn't run its course. What undermined it was the military, and behind that the economic success of the at-first relatively minor powers who operated on another, more consensual model, especially England and the Low Countries. In that sense, the end of the eighteenth century may have parallels with the end of the twentieth.

Around this alternative model, there crystallized a number of anti-absolutist doctrines. The most celebrated and influential was that of Locke. In a sense he transposed and renewed both A and B and brought them back into political theory. Feature A returns in the unprecedentedly strong form that defines government as a trust.[3] Society exists before government; it issues from a first contract that takes individuals out of the state of nature. The newly formed body then sets up government. This may be defined as supreme, but it is in fact in a fiduciary relation to society. Should it violate its trust, society recovers its freedom of action.

But Locke also reintroduces a version of B. Prior to all political society, mankind forms a kind of community. We are constituted as such by being under natural law, which is enjoined on us by God.[4] We are made a community, in other words, by our enjoyment of natural rights. This community is in fact defined as a transform of C, now written into the order of things rather than simply inscribed in positive law. Any particular political society has to respect this higher law, since those who set it up were bound by it, and they couldn't pass on powers they didn't have.

Locke is, of course, still using the term "civil society" in its traditional sense, where it is synonymous with "political society." But he is preparing the ground for the emergence of the new, contrastive sense a century later. This contrast arises out of the anti-absolutist doctrines of the eighteenth century, but in two rather different ways. One develops out of Locke's embryonic notion of mankind as a prepolitical community. Locke's state of nature is not the scene of devastation portrayed by Hobbes. It lacks security, which is why humans are driven to set up governments. But otherwise it is the possible scene of great progress in what was later called civilization, of economic development, the division of labor, the development of money, and the accumulation of property. This idea was developed in the eighteenth century into a picture of human social life in which much that is valuable is seen as coming about in a pre- or nonpolitical realm, at best under the protection of political authority, but by no means under its direction.

There was another source of the contrast, which we can perhaps most handily identify with Montesquieu. His portrait of monarchy in *De l'esprit des lois* offers an alternative anti-absolutist doctrine to Locke's. Unlike Locke, he assumes a strong monarchical government that is unremovable. The important issue turns on whether this government is unchecked, and veering toward despotism, or whether it is limited by law. But limitation by law is ineffective unless independent bodies exist which have a standing in this law and are there to defend it. The rule of law and the *corps intermédiares* stand and fall together. Without law, bodies like parliament and estates like the nobility have no standing; without such bodies and estates, the law has no effective defenders. The free monarchy (a pleonasm for Montesquieu, since the unfree one is despotism) is in equilibrium between a powerful central authority and an interlocking mass of agencies and associations it has to work with.

Montesquieu's theory draws on different elements of the tradition from Locke's. It is based on elements C, D, and E of the medieval constitution. Indeed, the long debate in France over the rise of absolutism was seen as one that pitted the ancient constitution, inherited originally from the Frankish conquerors, against models drawn from Roman law. Montesquieu saw himself as reformulating the "German" case. Speaking of the English constitution, which he admired, Montesquieu says that it was derived from the ancient Germans. "Ce beau système a été trouvé dans les bois."[5] What he doesn't need to draw on at all is A and B. Society is not defined independently of its political constitution. On the contrary, the free society is identified with a certain such constitution.

For all the importance of the medieval constitution to him, in this respect Montesquieu thinks more like an ancient. The polis too was defined politically. The very terms we use show this to be a tautology. This vision of things allowed no place for a distinction between civil society and the state. This would have been incomprehensible to a Greek or Roman. Montesquieu, along with many anti-absolutists of his era, was an admirer of ancient freedom. But he didn't make it an alternative model to absolute rule. His genius was rather to articulate a third standard, in some ways antithetical to the polis, which was nevertheless one of freedom and dignity for the participant. Monarchy was antithetical to the republic because the latter supposed "vertu," a dedication to the public good as well as austere mores and equality; but monarchy required a lively sense of one's own rights and privileges, and thrived on differences of status and displays of wealth and power, which were bound up with honor. Patriotic virtue was what kept society free in the ancient republic, because it led people to defend laws to the death against internal and external threats. The lively sense of one's own rights and status protected freedom in the modern monarchy, because it made the privileged resist royal encroachment and feel shame in obeying any order that derogated their code.

So while retaining a thoroughly political definition of society, like the ancients, Montesquieu laid the ground for a society/state distinction that was alien to the ancients. He did this with a view of society as poised between central power and a skein of entrenched rights.

Both anti-absolutist doctrines are reflected in the distinction eventually drawn around the turn of the century, which found its most celebrated statement in Hegel's *Philosophy of Right*. But in fact they sit uneasily together in this new concept of civil society. There is a tension between them, and between the different models for a free society which can be articulated with this new concept.

Thus two streams come together into "civil society." Let's call them the L-stream and the M-stream, after the figures I have somewhat arbitrarily chosen to represent them. What I want to do here is map the convergence and highlight some of the tensions.

The central feature of the L-stream is the elaboration of a richer view of society as an extrapolitical reality. One facet of this elaboration has dominated the discussion of civil society until quite recently: the development of a picture of society as an "economy," that is, as an entity of interrelated acts of production, exchange, and consumption which has its own internal dynamic, its own autonomous laws. This crystallizes in the eighteenth century with the work of the physiocrats and, more definitively, with Adam Smith. Just how great an intellectual revolution is involved here can be measured in the transformation of the word's meaning. "Economics" is etymologically the art of household management; it designated a particular field of prudent administration. The *nomos* was that imposed by the manager, the head of household or *oikos*. It already involved one revolution in thinking to begin to consider whole kingdoms as like households, needing to have their production and consumption "managed" in this way. This gives us the jump to "political economy." But the important change is to a view of this domain as in a sense organizing itself, following its own laws of equilibrium and change. The *nomos* in the word now comes to resemble its use in a term like "astronomy," referring us to an "autonomous" domain of causal laws. The modern "economy" is born, as a domain with its own organization.

This gives a new twist and a new force to the idea of society as enjoying an extrapolitical identity. The "economy" now defines a dimension of social life in which we function as a society potentially outside the ambit of politics. Of course, there are differences among the practitioners of the new science as to how autonomous it should be. Even Adam Smith was in favor of much more state regulation than his popular reputation allows. But this intellectual revolution allows us to raise the issue of economic autonomy; without the notion of the economic as governed by its own laws, the issue couldn't even be framed. Now everyone thinks in these terms, interventionist and free-enterpriser alike. They differ only in their assessment of the likely outcome of unregulated flow, and hence of the need or lack of it for remedial action of a more or less radical kind. Even Marx, especially Marx, has a theory of unimpeded flow. It is the disaster scenario laid out in *Capital*.

This provided an important part of the content of the new concept of civil society, at least of its L-facet. It figures in Hegel's formulation, where the self-regulating, entrepreneurial economy is given a central place on this level of society. Marx took over Hegel's concept and reduced it almost exclusively to this, and it is partly due to Marx's influence that "civil society" was for so long defined in economic terms. But this represents an impoverishment of Hegel's concept. It also owed something to the M-stream, so that his civil society incorporated bodies engaged in conscious self-management—the corporations—which were also integrated in their own way into the state.

But I want to return to this later, when we look at the tension between the two streams. Right now it is important to see that, even in what I call the L-stream, the economy is not the only component. What is also of great importance is the development in the eighteenth century of an autonomous public with its own "opinion."

This involves a quite new use of the notion of "public." The term designates what is of common concern, and not just objectively or from an outsider's perspective, but what is commonly recognized as of common concern. So public is what matters to the whole society, or belongs to this whole society, or pertains to the instruments, institutions, or loci by which the society comes together as a body and acts. So plainly the political structure of a society is public—its executive organs, the loci of its legislative power, and whatever spaces of assembly these require—from the agora in which the citizen assembly meets to the court where a king exercises his rule. These are loci of what one might call public space.

The new notion of opinion in the eighteenth century defines a quite different model of public space. Through the circulation of newspapers, reviews, and books among the educated classes, and scattered, small-scale personal exchanges in salons, coffeehouses, and (in some cases) political assemblies, there emerges a sense of nation, or its literate segment, an opinion that deserves to be called "public." Public opinion, as originally conceived, is not just the sum of our private individual opinions, even where we spontaneously agree. It is something that has been elaborated in debate and discussion, and is recognized by everyone as something held in common. This element of common recognition is what makes it public, in the strong sense.

This is also what gives it its force, a new force in history. The novel aspect is that public opinion is elaborated entirely outside the channels and public spaces of the political structure. More radically, it is developed outside the channels and public spaces of any authority whatever, since it is also independent of that second focus of European societies, the church. Governments were used to facing the independent power of religious opinion, articulated by churches. What was new was opinion, presented as that of society, which was elaborated through no official, established, hierarchical organs of definition.[6]

Like the economy, public opinion was here to stay. And though some thinkers envisaged a kind of absolute rule which would align itself on enlightened opinion, in fact free opinion and absolute power don't consort too well. But it can't be simply forgotten, and so contemporary despotisms are forced not only to suppress public opinion, but also to counterfeit it. Official newspapers write editorials and report meetings and resolutions, all of which purportedly come spontaneously from individual authors and initiators. The orchestrated character of all this has to be hidden from view. Such is the prestige of public opinion.

The self-regulating economy and public opinion—these are two ways in which society can come to some unity or coordination outside the political structures. They give body to the Lockean idea, which in turn has medieval roots, that society has its own identity beyond the political dimension. It seems to follow from this that political authority ought to respect the autonomy of society in the spheres where it is manifest. This involves a new kind of limitation of authority. It was always understood as limited in Christendom by the church, to some degree or other; and also by rights ascribed to individuals or corporations. But the political used to be the only domain in which secular social purpose could be articulated and carried out. To the extent that these new spheres of nonpolitical social identity become recognized, this is no longer the case.

Indeed, the new space of public opinion, mediated by printed materials, can be the source of a more radical challenge, questioning the primacy of political structures on their own ground. Previously it was axiomatic that societies found their political identities and defined their political direction through the traditionally established political structures, and only there—whether these were royal courts or parliaments or some combination of the two. Unofficial pressure might be exercised through agitation and pamphleteering, but this didn't challenge the principle that the authoritative locus for defining political ends lay in the established bodies. With the development of the new space of public opinion, more far-reaching claims had to be made. It has been argued, for instance, that in early eighteenth-century America a new form of discourse emerges in newspapers and pamphlets.[7] It is a discourse that implicitly arrogates to this print-sustained space the power and duty to define the goals of the people and to call the established bodies to book for their deviations from these goals. The discourse is cast in the traditional rhetoric of republicanism, but under this familiar cover a radically new formula is being advanced. In republican societies, the people did indeed criticize and control their officers, but assembled in the *ekklesia* or general meeting. This was itself a governing body, the foundational one. Now the powers of the assembled people are being arrogated to a new print-mediated public space, unembodied in any traditional structure or, indeed, in face-to-face meetings of any kind. The political identity of society shifts to an unprecedented locus. Whether or not this analysis holds for the eighteenth-century British colonies, something like this shift plainly became central to modern democratic self-understanding.

This congeries of ideas about the economy and public space constituted one of the strands in the new notion of "civil society" as distinguished from the state. It comprised a public, but not a politically structured domain. The first feature was essential: civil society was not the private sphere. Where Aristotle distinguishes *polis* from *oikos,* and only the first is a public domain, Hegel distinguishes three terms in *Sittlichkeit:* family, civil society, and the state. Civil society is not identical with the third term, the polis, and not with the first term either. That is why I argue that any definition of civil society in sense (1), which identifies it simply with the existence of autonomous associations free from state tutelage, fails to do justice to the historical concept. This defines a pattern of public social life, and not just a collection of private enclaves.

This notion of civil society, the L-variant, can inspire radical political hopes, sometimes of an anti-political kind. Even Locke saw the political structure as an emanation of a society that in one sense was already political, because people had put in common their power to enforce the Law of Nature, but had as yet no political structure. With the enriching of the concept, we can formulate the idea that society has its own prepolitical life and unity which the political structure must serve. Society has the right and power to make and unmake political authority, according as it does so serve or fail to serve.

This is the radical doctrine of Thomas Paine. In a somewhat less radical variant, something like this was acted on by the American colonists in their war of independence. It was less radical because the decision to rebel was taken by political authorities in the thirteen colonies. The early-modern idea, that a rebellion against a supreme authority in violation of its trust could be carried out by duly constituted subordinate authority (the central notion of *vindiciae contra tyrannos*), would also have served to justify the rebellion. Americans saw themselves as fighting for established right as against usurpation. But in fact the language they adopted, that of "We, the People," had a more radical impact. It seemed to draw the revolutionary conclusion from the L-variant: the people have an identity, they have purposes, even a will, outside any political structure. In the name of this identity, following this will, they have the right to make and unmake these structures. The duality of focus in the western concept of society, which goes back in different forms to the Middle Ages, finally takes on its most revolutionary formulation.

This has become a commonplace of modern thought. Between 1776 and now, the notion of a people's prepolitical identity has taken a new and much more powerful form, that of the nation. We now speak of this right to make and unmake structures as the right of self-determination. No one today dares deny this in principle, however suppressed it may be in practice.

But radical hopes can also take an antipolitical form. One could dream of the nonpolitical spheres of society becoming more and more autonomous, more and more self-sufficient. Taken to the extreme, this offers a vision of a society without politics, where the government of men gives way to the administration of things, as Saint-Simon articulated it, followed by Engels. In less extreme fashion, one could hope for a society in which the development of industry and commerce would serve to tie people together in peace, and thus drastically reduce the role of government, lessening its policing function and doing away with war altogether.

The eighteenth-century developments described above, which gave us the notions of economy and public opinion, also provided a notion of "civilization." A civilized society was partly so in virtue of its political constitution—indeed, the term in some respects replaces the earlier French expression *état policé*. But "civilization" included a lot more—pacification, enlightenment, technical development, arts and sciences, polished mores. Within the self-definition of modern Europe as civilized, in contrast to other societies and to its own past, the virtues of peaceful production bulked large, and the older warrior virtues were seen in an unfavorable light. European society gained in polish as it turned its back on these and on the honor ethic behind them. But it was also the honor ethic that gave the political life intrinsic value. For the new social ethic of peaceful productivity, as we see for instance with the utilitarians, political structures had purely instrumental significance. The less we needed them, the better.

So two rather different kinds of political hopes arise from this notion of society as having a pre- or nonpolitical identity. The one moves toward the norm of self-determination; the other toward the goal of marginalizing the political. So we can see why the L-stream was not the only one to feed the new concept of civil society. It was not just that these hopes each in their own way undermine the very distinction between society and state. This they did, of course. Radical self-determination swallows up the state in society, in a supposed common will; while the goal of marginalization tries to approach as closely as possible to anarchy.

But also, much more importantly, both hopes pose a threat to freedom, and the distinction was introduced in the first place in the context of counter-absolutist thought. One recurring threat to freedom has come from the politics of what would later be called the general will. This *idée force,* as elaborated by Rousseau, fuses the idea of a people's will independent of all political structure with the ethic of ancient republicanism, drawing its power from both. Rousseau invokes the prepolitical in the very unancient idea of a social contract, of society as constituted by will, as well as in his understanding of nature as inner voice. He invokes the ancient ethic of virtue in the ideal of a transparent face-to-face political society. The latter, of course, drops out of the picture as unrealizable in the modern world. What remains is the notion of popular will as the ultimate justification for all political structures and authority.

The most thoroughgoing destruction of civil society has been carried out in the name of some variants and successors of this idea in the twentieth century, notably the nation and the proletariat. A strange and horrifying reversal has taken place, whereby an idea whose roots lie in a prepolitical concept of society can now justify the total subjection of life to an enterprise of political transformation. And in less spectacular form, the power of the state has often been enhanced by its self-definition as an instrument of the national will.

But in a more subtle way, the politics of marginalizing politics has also been seen as posing a threat to freedom. This is particularly so when the sphere of society in the name of which the political is being marginalized is that of the self-regulating economy. For in this domain the disposition of things in society as a whole is seen as arising not out of any collective will or common decision, but by way of an "invisible hand." To leave our collective fate to blind economic forces can be portrayed as a kind of alienation. On top of this, all those whose allegiance is to an ideal of the political life as good in itself will see the marginalization of politics as an abandonment of what is most valuable in life, a flight from the public into the narrower and less significant sphere of private satisfactions, the "petty and paltry pleasures" of which Tocqueville speaks in *Democracy in America.*

Marx, who developed a theory of alienation, himself subscribed to his own version of a world without politics. But Tocqueville spelled out the dangers implicit in the kinds of hopes generated by the L-theory. The modern democracy of the general will can degenerate, he argues, into a kind of mild despotism *(despotisme doux)* in which citizens fall prey to a tutelary power that dwarfs them; and this is both cause and effect of a turn away from the public to the private which, although tempting, represents a diminution of their human stature.

Those who are thus dissatisfied with the L-variant of the notion of civil society are induced to turn to Montesquieu. Tocqueville can be seen as the greatest disciple of Montesquieu in the nineteenth century. But Hegel, in his dissatisfaction with the L-variant, had already drawn on Montesquieu. Like Marx after him, Hegel couldn't believe in the benign effects of an autonomous, unregulated economic sphere. And he produced his own variant of the civic-humanist doctrine that the life of the citizen had value in itself. At the same time, his theory of modern life, in distinction from the ancients, turned on the differentiated development of this nonpolitical public sphere, which related individuals in their separate identities. The result was the Hegelian concept of civil society—a separate sphere, but not self-sufficient. Not only did its constituent economic processes need regulation, which was undertaken partly within civil society, but this society could only escape destruction by being incorporated in the higher unity of the state, that is, society as politically organized.

Hegel combines both the L- and the M-streams in his concept of civil society. If the L-concept, to repeat, turns on the idea of a nonpolitical dimension to society, Montesquieu's contribution is the picture of a society defined by its political organization, but where this is constitutionally diverse, distributing power among many independent agencies. It is important here too that there be independent associations for nonpolitical purposes. But their significance is not that they form a nonpolitical social sphere, but rather that they form the basis for the fragmentation and diversity of power *within* the political system. What is relevant is not their life outside, but the way they are integrated into the political system and the weight they have in it.

Thus the different elements of Hegel's political society take up their role in the state, make up the different estates, and form the basis for a differentiated constitution, whose formula was partly inspired by Montesquieu. In this way, we avoid both the undifferentiated homogeneity of the general-will state, which Hegel thought must lead inevitably to tyranny and terror, and also the unregulated and ultimately self-destructive play of blind economic forces, which then seemed to be menacing England.

With Tocqueville, the heritage of Montesquieu is even clearer. The only bulwark against mild despotism is free associations. Voluntary associations for all purposes are valuable. But their significance is that they give us the taste and habit of self-rule, and so they are essential for political purposes. But if they are to be real loci of self-rule, they have to be nongigantic and numerous, and exist at many levels of the polity. This itself should be decentralized, so that self-government can be practiced also at the local and not just the national level. If it dies out at the former, it is in danger at the latter. "In democratic countries the science of association is the mother of science," according to Tocqueville.

So our notion of civil society is complex. It is an amalgam of two rather different influences, which I have called the L-stream and the M-stream. It clearly goes beyond the minimal definition (1) above. But it hovers between the other two because of its dual origin. For the purposes of deconstructing a Leninist dictatorship, any one of these definitions will do. But when we come to ask how the concept of civil society relates to the freedom of western liberal democracies, we find a more complex story.

We can see now why the question discussed at the outset, whether we in fact have a functioning independent civil society in the West, was not so easy to answer. Among the other reasons is the fact that there are different definitions of what this independence involves, which have equally strong warrant in our two-streamed tradition. No easier to answer is the question of what role a concept of civil society has to play in the future defense of freedom.

It is tempting to think that it is almost guaranteed a role, just because of its place in the complex intellectual and institutional background of western liberty. The distinction between civil society and the state is indeed important to the western tradition, not just because of all the roots of the idea in earlier epochs, but more especially because it has been central to the different forms of counter-absolutist thinking. Indeed, it owes its existence and relevance to the development in the West of reforming absolutism, of "the well-ordered police state" in the seventeenth and eighteenth centuries.[8] It made no sense in the context of the polis, or in the medieval polity, no more than it did in a host of traditional nonwestern polities. It arose, one might say, as a necessary instrument of defense in face of the specific *threats* to freedom implicit in the western tradition. But precisely to the extent that the modern state is still drawn to a vocation of mobilizing and reorganizing its subjects' lives, the distinction would seem to be guaranteed a continuing relevance.

So one can argue that the distinction is essential to our conception of what it is to preserve freedom. But it has also been shouldered aside by supposedly simpler and more arresting definitions of a free society, which turn on the idea of a general will or a politics-free sphere. To make the notion of civil society central to our political discourse ought to involve a rejection of these seductively limpid formulas.

But those who find these simpler definitions unsatisfactory (as I do), and want to recur to "civil society," will find that it is not a unified idea. Both its sources are deeply woven into our political traditions and way of life. Which definition we accept of civil society will have important consequences for our picture of the free society and hence our political practice.

In fact, our choice today lies not simply between the two variants. The force of the L-idea is too great and too obtrusive to be altogether denied. The choice seems to lie between a view of civil society almost exclusively concerned with the L-stream and one that tries to balance both. In the first category fall those critics of corporatist politics on the right who aim to roll back the power of the state. In the second are found the contemporary followers of Tocqueville, some of whom along with a bewilderingly diverse variety of utopians end up on the ecological left, but who are also found near the center of many western societies. I hope an impression has emerged that the second view, which balances both streams, is greatly superior to the first; more, that the first is in constant danger of falling victim to the simpler formulas of a prepolitical freedom that end up subverting the distinction or neutralizing its force as a counter-thrust to bureaucratic power. In any case, this is what I propose.

— 12 —

The Politics of Recognition

A number of strands in contemporary politics turn on the need, sometimes the demand, for recognition. The need, it can be argued, is one of the driving forces behind nationalist movements in politics. And the demand comes to the fore in a number of ways in today's politics, on behalf of minority or "subaltern" groups, in some forms of feminism, and in what is called the politics of multiculturalism.

The demand for recognition in these cases is given urgency by the supposed links between recognition and identity, where "identity" designates something like an understanding of who we are, of our fundamental defining characteristics as human beings. The thesis is that our identity is partly shaped by recognition or its absence, often by the *mis*recognition of others, and so a person or group of people can suffer real damage, real distortion, if the people or society around them mirror back a confining or demeaning or contemptible picture of themselves. Nonrecognition or misrecognition can inflict harm, can be a form of oppression, imprisoning someone in a false, distorted, and reduced mode of being.

Thus some feminists have argued that women in patriarchal societies have been induced to adopt a depreciatory image of themselves. They have internalized a picture of their own inferiority, so that even when some of the objective obstacles to their advancement fall away, they may be incapable of taking advantage of the new opportunities. And beyond this, they are condemned to suffer the pain of low self-esteem. An analogous point has been made in relation to blacks: that white society has for generations projected a demeaning image which some blacks have been unable to resist adopting. Their own self-depreciation, on this view, becomes one of the most potent instruments of their oppression. Their first task ought to be to purge themselves of this imposed and destructive identity. A similar point has been made in relation to indigenous and colonized people in general. It is held that since 1492 Europeans have projected an image of such people as somehow inferior, "uncivilized," and through the force of conquest have often been able to impose this image on the conquered. The figure of Caliban has been held to epitomize this crushing portrait of contempt for New World aboriginals.

Within these perspectives, misrecognition shows not just a lack of due respect. It can inflict a grievous wound, saddling its victims with a crippling self-hatred. Due recognition is not just a courtesy we owe people. It is a vital human need.

In order to examine some of these issues, I'd like to take a step back, achieve a little distance, and look first at how this discourse of recognition and identity came to seem familiar, or at least readily understandable, to us. For it was not always so, and our ancestors of more than a few centuries ago would have stared at us uncomprehendingly if we had used these terms in their current sense. How did we get started on this?

Hegel comes to mind right off, with his famous dialectic of master and slave. This is an important stage, but we need to go a little farther back to see how this passage came to have the sense it did. What changed to make this kind of talk have sense for us?

We can distinguish two changes that together have made the modern preoccupation with identity and recognition inevitable. The first is the collapse of social hierarchies, which used to be the basis for honor. I'm using *honor* in the ancien régime sense in which it is intrinsically linked to inequalities. For some to have honor in this sense, it is essential that not everyone have it. This is how Montesquieu uses it in his description of monarchy. Honor is intrinsically a matter of preferences.[1] It is also the sense in which we use the term when we speak of honoring someone by giving her a public award, for instance, the Order of Canada. Clearly, this award would be without worth if tomorrow we decided to give it to every adult Canadian.

As against this notion of honor, we have the modern notion of dignity, now used in a universalist and egalitarian sense, where we talk of the inherent "dignity of human beings" or of citizen dignity. The underlying premise here is that everyone shares in it.[2] It is obvious that this concept of dignity is the only one compatible with a democratic society, and that it was inevitable that the old concept of honor was superseded. But it has also meant that the forms of equal recognition have been essential to democratic culture. For instance, calling everyone "Mr.," "Mrs.," or "Miss," rather than calling some people "Lord" or "Lady" and others simply by their surnames—or, even more demeaning, by their first names—has been thought essential in some democratic societies, such as the United States. More recently, for similar reasons, "Mrs." and "Miss" have been collapsed into "Ms." Democracy has ushered in a politics of equal recognition, which has taken various forms over the years, and has now returned in the form of demands for the equal status of cultures and of genders.

But the importance of recognition has been modified and intensified by the new understanding of individual identity that emerged at the end of the eighteenth century. We might speak of an *individualized* identity, one that is particular to me and that I discover in myself. This notion arises along with an ideal, that of being true to myself and my own particular way of being. Following Lionel Trilling's usage in his brilliant study, I will speak of this as the ideal of "authenticity."[3] It will help to describe in what it consists and how it came about.

One way of describing its development is to see its starting point in the eighteenth-century notion that human beings are endowed with a moral sense, an intuitive feeling for what is right and wrong. The original point of this doctrine was to combat a rival view, that knowing right and wrong was a matter of calculating consequences, in particular, those concerned with divine reward and punishment. The idea was that understanding right and wrong was not a matter of dry calculation, but was anchored in our feelings.[4] Morality has, in a sense, a voice within.

The notion of authenticity develops out of a displacement of the moral accent in this idea. On the original view, the inner voice was important because it tells us the right thing to do. Being in touch with our moral feelings matters here, as a means to the end of acting rightly. What I'm calling the displacement of the moral accent comes about when being in touch with our feelings takes on independent and crucial moral significance. It comes to be something we have to attain if we are to be true and full human beings.

To see what is new here, we have to see the analogy to earlier moral views, where being in touch with some source—for example, God or the

Idea of the Good—was considered essential to full being. But now the source we have to connect with is deep within us. This is part of the massive subjective turn of modern culture, a new form of inwardness, in which we come to think of ourselves as beings with inner depths. At first, this idea that the source is within may not exclude our being related to God or the Ideas; it can be considered our proper way of relating to them. In a sense, it can be seen as just a continuation and intensification of the development inaugurated by Augustine, who saw the road to God as passing through our own self-awareness. The first variants of this new view were theistic, or at least pantheistic.

The most important philosophical writer who helped to bring about this change was Jean-Jacques Rousseau. Rousseau is important not because he inaugurated the change; rather, I would argue that his great popularity comes in part from his articulating something that was in a sense already occurring in the culture. Rousseau frequently presents the issue of morality as that of our following the voice of nature within us. This voice is often drowned out by the passions that are induced by our dependence on others, the main one being *amour propre,* or pride. Our moral salvation comes from recovering authentic moral contact with ourselves. Rousseau even gives a name to the intimate contact with oneself, more fundamental than any moral view, that is a source of such joy and contentment: "le sentiment de l'existence."[5]

The ideal of authenticity becomes crucial owing to a development that occurs after Rousseau, which I associate with the name of Herder—once again, as its major early articulator rather than its originator. Herder put forward the idea that each of us has an original way of being human: each person has his or her own "measure."[6] This idea has burrowed very deep into modern consciousness. It is a new idea. Before the late eighteenth century, no one thought that the differences between human beings carried this kind of moral significance. There is a certain way of being human that is *my* way. I am called upon to live my life in this way, and not in imitation of anyone else's life. But this notion gives a new importance to being true to myself. If I am not, I miss the point of my life; I miss what being human is for *me.*

This is the powerful moral ideal that has come down to us. It accords moral importance to a kind of contact with myself, with my own inner nature, which it sees as in danger of being lost, partly through the pressures toward outward conformity, but also because in taking an instrumental stance toward myself, I may have lost the capacity to listen to this inner voice. It greatly increases the importance of this self-contact by introducing the principle of originality: each of our voices has something unique to say. Not only should I not mold my life to the demands of external conformity; I can't even find the model by which to live outside myself. I can only find it within.[7]

Being true to myself means being true to my own originality, which is something only I can articulate and discover. In articulating it, I'm also defining myself. I'm realizing a potentiality that is properly my own. This is the background understanding to the modern ideal of authenticity, and to the goals of self-fulfillment and self-realization in which the ideal is usually couched. I should note here that Herder applied his concept of originality at two levels, not only to the individual person among other persons, but also to the culture-bearing people among other peoples. Just like individuals, a *Volk* should be true to itself, that is, to its own culture. Germans shouldn't try to be derivative and (inevitably) second-rate Frenchmen, as Frederick the Great's patronage seemed to be encouraging them to do. The Slavic peoples had to find their own path. And European colonialism ought to be rolled back to give the peoples of what we now call the third world their chance to be themselves unimpeded. We can recognize here the seminal idea of modern nationalism, in both benign and malignant forms.

This new ideal of authenticity was, like the idea of dignity, also in part an offshoot of the decline of hierarchical society. In those earlier societies, what we would now call identity was largely fixed by one's social position. The background that explained what people recognized as important to themselves was to a great extent determined by their place in society, and whatever roles or activities attached to this position. The birth of a democratic society doesn't by itself do away with this phenomenon, because people can still define themselves by their social roles. What does decisively undermine this socially derived identification, however, is the ideal of authenticity itself. As this emerges, for instance with Herder, it calls on me to discover my own original way of being. By definition, this way of being cannot be socially derived, but must be inwardly generated.

But in the nature of the case, there is no such thing as inward generation, monologically understood. In order to understand the close connection between identity and recognition, we have to take into account a crucial feature of the human condition that has been rendered almost invisible by the overwhelmingly monological bent of mainstream modern philosophy.

This crucial feature of human life is its fundamentally dialogical character. We become full human agents, capable of understanding ourselves, and hence of defining our identity, through our acquisition of rich human languages of expression. For my purposes here, I want to take language in a broad sense, covering not only the words we speak, but also other modes of expression whereby we define ourselves, including the "languages" of art, of gesture, of love, and the like. But we learn these modes of expression through exchanges with others. People do not acquire the languages needed for self-definition on their own. Rather, we are introduced to them through interaction with others who matter to us—what G. H. Mead called "significant others."[8] The genesis of the human mind is in this sense not monological, not something each person accomplishes on his or her own, but dialogical.

Moreover, this is not just a fact about *genesis,* which can be ignored later on. We don't just learn the languages in dialogue and then go on to use them for our own purposes. We are of course expected to develop our own opinions, outlook, stances toward things, and to a considerable degree through solitary reflection. But this isn't how things work with such important issues as the definition of our identity. We define our identity always in dialogue with, sometimes in struggle against, the things our significant others want to see in us. Even after we outgrow some of these others—our parents, for instance—and they disappear from our lives, the conversation with them continues within us as long as we live.[9]

Thus the contribution of significant others, even when it is provided at the beginning of our lives, continues indefinitely. Some people may still want to hold on to some form of the monological ideal. It is true that we can never liberate ourselves completely from those whose love and care shaped us early in life, but we should strive to define ourselves on our own to the fullest extent possible, coming as best we can to understand and thus get some control over the influence of our parents, and not fall into any more such dependent relationships. We need relationships to fulfill, but not to define, ourselves.

The monological ideal seriously underestimates the place of the dialogical in human life. It wants to confine it as much as possible to genesis. It forgets how our understanding of the good things in life can be transformed by our enjoying them in common with people we love; how some goods become accessible to us only through such common enjoyment. Because of this, it would take a great deal of effort, and probably many wrenching breakups, to *prevent* our identity's being formed by the people we love. Consider what we mean by identity. It is who we are, "where we're coming from." As such it is the background against which our tastes and desires and opinions and aspirations make sense. If some of the things I value most are accessible to me only in relation to the person I love, then she becomes part of my identity.

To some people this might seem a limitation, from which they might aspire to free themselves. This is one way of understanding the impulse behind the life of the hermit or, to take a case more familiar to our culture, the solitary artist. But from another perspective, we might see even these lives as aspiring to a certain kind of dialogicality. In the case of the hermit, the interlocutor is God. In the case of the solitary artist, the work itself is addressed to a future audience, perhaps still to be created by the work. The very form of a work of art shows its character as *addressed*.[10] But however one feels about it, the making and sustaining of our identity, in the absence of a heroic effort to break out of ordinary existence, remains dialogical throughout our lives.

Thus my discovering my own identity doesn't mean that I work it out in isolation, but that I negotiate it through dialogue, partly overt, partly internal, with others. That is why the development of an ideal of inwardly generated identity gives a new importance to recognition. My own identity crucially depends on my dialogical relations with others.

Of course, the point is not that this dependence on others arose with the age of authenticity. A form of dependence was always there. The socially derived identity was by its very nature dependent on society. But in the earlier age recognition never arose as a problem. General recognition was built into the socially derived identity by virtue of the very fact that it was based on social categories that everyone took for granted. Yet inwardly derived, personal, original identity doesn't enjoy this recognition a priori. It has to win it through exchange, and the attempt can fail. What has come about with the modern age is not the need for recognition but the conditions in which the attempt to be recognized can fail. That is why the need is now acknowledged for the first time. In premodern times, people didn't speak of "identity" and "recognition"—not because people didn't have what we call identities, or because these didn't depend on recognition, but rather because these were then too unproblematic to be thematized as such.

It is not surprising that we can find some of the seminal ideas about citizen dignity and universal recognition, even if not in these specific terms, in Rousseau, who is one of the points of origin of the modern discourse of authenticity. Rousseau is a sharp critic of hierarchical honor, of *preferences*. In a significant passage of the *Discourse on Inequality*, he pinpoints a fateful moment when society takes a turn toward corruption and injustice, when people begin to desire preferential esteem.[11] By contrast, in republican society, where all can share equally in the light of public attention, he sees the source of health.[12] But the topic of recognition is given its most influential early treatment in Hegel.[13]

The importance of recognition is now universally acknowledged in one form or another; on an intimate plane, we are all aware of how identity can be formed or malformed through the course of our contact with significant others. On the social plane, we have a continuing politics of equal recognition. Both planes have been shaped by the growing ideal of authenticity, and recognition plays an essential role in the culture that has arisen around this ideal.

On the intimate level, we can see how much an original identity needs and is vulnerable to the recognition given or withheld by significant others. It is not surprising that in the culture of authenticity, relationships are seen as the key loci of self-discovery and self-affirmation. Love relationships are not just important because of the general emphasis in modern culture on the fulfillments of ordinary needs. They are also crucial because they are the crucibles of inwardly generated identity.

On the social plane, the understanding that identities are formed in open dialogue, unshaped by a predefined social script, has made the politics of equal recognition more central and stressful. It has, in fact, considerably raised the stakes. Equal recognition is not just the appropriate mode for a healthy democratic society. Its refusal can inflict damage on those who are denied it, according to a widespread modern view, as I indicated at the outset. The projection of an inferior or demeaning image on another can actually distort and oppress, to the extent that the image is internalized. Not only contemporary feminism but also race relations and discussions of multiculturalism are undergirded by the premise that the withholding of recognition can be a form of oppression. We may debate whether this factor has been exaggerated, but it is clear that the understanding of identity and authenticity has introduced a new dimension into the politics of equal recognition, which now operates with something like its own notion of authenticity, at least so far as the denunciation of other-induced distortions is concerned.

And so the discourse of recognition has become familiar to us, on two levels. First, in the intimate sphere, where we understand the formation of identity and the self as taking place in a continuing dialogue and struggle with significant others. And then in the public sphere, where a politics of equal recognition has come to play a bigger and bigger role. Certain feminist theories have tried to show the links between the two spheres.[14] I want to concentrate here on the public sphere, and try to work out what a politics of equal recognition has meant and could mean.

In fact, it has come to mean two rather different things, connected, respectively, with the two major changes I've been describing. With the move from honor to dignity has come a politics of universalism, emphasizing the equal dignity of all citizens, and the content of this politics has been the equalization of rights and entitlements. What is to be avoided at all costs is the existence of first-class and second-class citizens. Naturally, the actual detailed measures justified by this principle have varied greatly, and have often been controversial. For some, equalization has affected only civil rights and voting rights; for others, it has extended into the socioeconomic sphere. People who are systematically handicapped by poverty from making the most of their citizenship rights are deemed on this view to have been relegated to second-class status, necessitating remedial action through equalization. But through all the differences of interpretation, the principle of equal citizenship has come to be universally accepted. Every position, no matter how reactionary, is now defended under the colors of this principle. Its greatest, most recent victory was won by the U.S. civil-rights movement of the 1960s. It is worth noting that even the adversaries of extending voting rights to blacks in the southern states found some pretext consistent with universalism, such as tests to be administered to would-be voters at the time of registration.

By contrast, the second change, the development of the modern notion of identity, has given rise to a politics of difference. There is, of course, a universalist basis to this as well, making for the overlap and confusion between the two. *Everyone* should be recognized for his or her unique identity. But recognition here means something else. With the politics of equal dignity, what is established is meant to be universally the same, an identical basket of rights and immunities; with the politics of difference, what we are asked to recognize is the unique identity of this individual or group, its distinctness from everyone else. The idea is that it is precisely this distinctness that has been ignored, glossed over, assimilated to a dominant or majority identity. And this assimilation is the cardinal sin against the ideal of authenticity.[15]

Now underlying the demand is a principle of universal equality. The politics of difference is full of denunciations of discrimination and refusals of second-class citizenship. This gives the principle of universal equality a point of entry within the politics of dignity. But once inside, as it were, its demands are hard to assimilate to that politics. For it asks that we give acknowledgment and status to something that is not universally shared. Or, otherwise put, we give due acknowledgment only to what is universally present—everyone has an identity—through recognizing what is peculiar to each. The universal demand powers an acknowledgment of specificity.

The politics of difference grows organically out of the politics of universal dignity through one of those shifts with which we are long familiar, where a new understanding of the human social condition imparts a radically new meaning to an old principle. Just as a view of human beings as conditioned by their socioeconomic plight changed the understanding of second-class citizenship, so that this category came to include, for example, people in inherited poverty traps, so here the understanding of identity as formed in interchange, and as possibly so malformed, introduces a new form of second-class status into our purview. As in the present case, the socioeconomic redefinition justified social programs that were highly controversial. For those who had not gone along with this changed definition of equal status, the various redistributive programs and special opportunities offered to certain populations seemed a form of undue favoritism.

Similar conflicts arise today around the politics of difference. Where the politics of universal dignity fought for forms of nondiscrimination that were quite "blind" to the ways in which citizens differ, the politics of difference often redefines nondiscrimination as requiring that we make these distinctions the basis of differential treatment. So members of aboriginal bands will get certain rights and powers not enjoyed by other Canadians, if the demands for native self-government are finally agreed on, and certain minorities will get the right to exclude others in order to preserve their cultural integrity, and so on.

To proponents of the original politics of dignity, this can seem like a reversal, a betrayal, a simple negation of their cherished principle. Attempts are therefore made to mediate, to show how some of these measures meant to accommodate minorities can after all be justified on the original basis of dignity. These arguments can be successful up to a point. For instance, some of the (apparently) most flagrant departures from "difference-blindness" are reverse discrimination measures, affording people from previously un-favored groups a competitive advantage for jobs or places in universities. This practice has been justified on the grounds that historical discrimination has created a pattern within which the unfavored struggle at a disadvantage. Reverse discrimination is defended as a temporary measure that will eventu-ally level the playing field and allow the old "blind" rules to come back into force in a way that doesn't disadvantage anyone. This argument seems co-gent enough—wherever its factual basis is sound. But it won't justify some of the measures now urged on the grounds of difference, the goal of which is not to bring us back to an eventual "difference-blind" social space but, on the contrary, to maintain and cherish distinctness, not just now but for-ever. After all, if we're concerned with identity, then what's more legitimate than our aspiration that it never be lost?[16]

So even though one politics springs from the other, by one of those shifts in the definition of key terms with which we're familiar, the two diverge quite seriously from each other. One basis for the divergence comes out even more clearly when we go beyond what each requires that we acknowl-edge—certain universal rights in one case, a particular identity on the other—and look at the underlying intuitions of value.

The politics of equal dignity is based on the idea that all humans are equally worthy of respect. It is underpinned by a notion of what in human beings commands respect, however we may try to shy away from this "metaphysical" background. For Kant, whose use of the term *dignity* was one of the earliest influential evocations of this idea, what commanded re-spect in us was our status as rational agents, capable of directing our lives through principles.[17] Something like this has been the basis for our intuitions of equal dignity ever since, though the detailed definition of it may have changed.

Thus what is picked out as of worth here is a *universal human potential,* a capacity that all humans share. This potential, rather than anything a person may have made of it, is what ensures that each person deserves respect. Indeed, our sense of the importance of potentiality reaches so far that we extend this protection even to people who through some circumstance that has befallen them are incapable of realizing their potential in the normal way—handicapped people or those in a coma, for instance.

In the case of the politics of difference, we might also say that a universal potential is at its basis, namely, the potential for forming and defining one's own identity, as an individual and also as a culture. This potentiality must be respected equally in everyone. But at least in the intercultural context, a stronger demand has recently arisen: that we accord equal respect to actually evolved cultures. Critiques of European or white domination, to the effect that they have not only suppressed but failed to appreciate other cultures, consider these depreciatory judgments not only factually mistaken but somehow morally wrong. When the novelist Saul Bellow is quoted as saying something like, "When the Zulus produce a Tolstoy we will read him,"[18] this is taken as a quintessential statement of European arrogance, not just because Bellow is allegedly being insensitive to the value of Zulu culture, but frequently also because it is seen to reflect a denial in principle of human equality. The possibility that the Zulus, while having the same potential for culture formation as anyone else, might nevertheless have come up with a culture that is less valuable than others is ruled out from the start. Even to entertain this possibility is to deny human equality. Bellow's error here, then, would not be a (possibly insensitive) particular mistake in evaluation, but a denial of a fundamental principle.

To the extent that this stronger reproach is in play, the demand for equal recognition extends beyond an acknowledgment of the equal value of all humans potentially, and comes to include the equal value of what they have made of this potential in fact. This creates a serious problem, as we shall see below.

These two modes of politics, then, both based on the notion of equal respect, come into conflict. For one, the principle of equal respect requires that we treat people in a difference-blind fashion. The fundamental intuition that humans command this respect focuses on what is the same in all. For the other, we have to recognize and even foster particularity. The reproach the first makes to the second is just that it violates the principle of nondiscrimination. The reproach the second makes to the first is that it negates identity by forcing people into a homogeneous mold that is untrue to them. This would be bad enough if the mold were itself neutral—nobody's mold in particular. But the complaint generally goes further. The claim is that the supposedly neutral set of difference-blind principles is in fact a reflection of one hegemonic culture. As it turns out, then, only the minority or suppressed cultures are being forced to take alien form. So the supposedly fair and difference-blind society is not only inhuman (because suppressing identities) but also, in a subtle and unconscious way, itself highly discriminatory.[19]

This last attack is the cruelest and most upsetting of all. The liberalism of equal dignity seems to have to assume that there are some universal, difference-blind principles. Even though we may not have defined them yet, the project of defining them remains alive and essential. Different theories may be put forward and contested—and a number have been proposed in our day[20]—but the shared assumption of all of them is that one is right.

The charge leveled by the most radical forms of the politics of difference is that blind liberalisms are themselves the reflection of particular cultures. And the worrying thought is that this bias might not just be a contingent weakness of all hitherto proposed theories, that the very idea of such a liberalism may be a kind of pragmatic contradiction, a particularism masquerading as the universal.

I want now to move, gently and gingerly, into this nest of issues, glancing at some of the important stages in the emergence of these two kinds of politics in western societies. First let's look at the politics of equal dignity.

The politics of equal dignity has emerged in western civilization in two ways, which we could associate with the names of two standard bearers, Rousseau and Kant. This doesn't mean that all instances of each have been influenced by those masters (though that is arguably true for the Rousseauean branch), just that Rousseau and Kant are prominent early exponents of the two models. Looking at the models should enable us to gauge to what extent they are guilty of the charge of imposing a false homogeneity.

I stated earlier that Rousseau can be seen as one of the originators of the discourse of recognition. I say this not because he uses the term, but because he begins to think out the importance of equal respect and, indeed, deems it indispensable for freedom. Rousseau, as is well known, tends to oppose a condition of freedom-in-equality to one characterized by hierarchy and other-dependence. In this state, you are dependent on others not just because they wield political power, or because you need them for survival or success in your cherished projects, but above all because you crave their esteem. The other-dependent person is a slave to "opinion."

This idea is one of the keys to the connection that Rousseau assumes between other-dependence and hierarchy. Logically, these two things are separable. Why can't there be other-dependence in conditions of equality? It seems that for Rousseau this can't be, because he associates other-dependence with the need for others' good opinion, which in turn is understood in the framework of the traditional conception of honor, that is, as intrinsically bound up with preferences. The esteem we seek in this condition is intrinsically differential. It is a positional good.

It is because of this crucial place of honor that the depraved condition of mankind has a paradoxical combination of properties such that we are unequal in power, and yet *all* dependent on others—not just the slave on the master, but also the master on the slave. This point is frequently made. The second sentence of *The Social Contract,* after the famous first line about men born free and yet everywhere in chains, runs: "Tel se croit le maître des autres, qui ne laisse pas d'être plus esclave qu'eux" (One thinks himself the master of others, and still remains a greater slave than they).[21] And in *Emile* Rousseau tells us that in this condition of dependence, "maître et esclave se dépravent mutuellement" (master and slave corrupt each other).[22] If it were simply a question of brute power, one might think the master free at the expense of the slave. But in a system of hierarchical honor, the deference of the lower orders is essential.

Rousseau often sounds like the stoics, who undoubtedly influenced him. He identifies pride as one of the great sources of evil. But he doesn't end up where the stoics do. There is a long-standing discourse on pride, both stoic and Christian, which recommends that we completely overcome our concern for the good opinion of others. We are asked to step outside this dimension of human life, in which reputations are sought, gained, and unmade. How you appear in public space should be of no concern to you. Rousseau sometimes sounds as if he endorses this line. In particular, it is part of his own self-dramatization that he could maintain his integrity in the face of undeserved hostility and calumny from the world. But when we look at his accounts of a potentially good society, we can see that esteem does still play a role in them, that people live very much in the public gaze. In a functioning republic, the citizens do care very much what others think. In a passage of "Considerations on the Government of Poland," Rousseau describes how ancient legislators took care to attach citizens to their fatherland. One of the means used to achieve this connection was public games. Rousseau speaks of the prizes with which, aux acclamation de toute la Grèce, on couronnoit les vainqueurs dans leurs jeux qui, les embrasant continuellement d'émulation et de gloire, portèrent peur courage et leurs vertus à ce degré d'énergie dont rien aujourd'hui ne nous donne l'idée, et qu'il n'appartient pas même aux modernes de croire.

successful contestants in Greek games were crowned amidst applause from all their fellow-citizens—these are the things that, by constantly re-kindling the spirit of emulation and the love of glory, raised Greek courage and Greek virtues to a level of strenuousness of which nothing existing today can give us even a remote idea—which, indeed, strikes modern men as beyond belief.[23]

Glory, public recognition, mattered very much here. Moreover, the effect of their mattering was highly beneficent. Why is this so, if modern honor is such a negative force?

The answer seems to be equality or, more exactly, the balanced reciprocity that underpins equality. One might say (Rousseau didn't) that in these ideal republican contexts, though everyone did depend on everyone else, all did so equally. Rousseau is arguing that the key feature of these events, games, festivals, and recitations, which made them sources of patriotism and virtue, was the total lack of differentiation or distinction between different classes of citizen. They took place in the open air, and they involved everyone. People were both spectator and show. The contrast drawn in this passage is with modern religious services in enclosed churches, and above all with modern theater, which operates in closed halls, which you have to pay to get into, and consists of a special class of professionals making presentations to others.

This theme is central to the "Letter to D'Alembert," where again Rousseau contrasts modern theater and the public festivals of a true republic, which take place in the open air. Here he makes it clear that the identity of spectator and performer is the key to these virtuous assemblies.

Mais quels seront les objets de ces spectacles? Qu'y montrerat-on? Rien, si l'on veut. Avec la liberté, partout où règne l'affluence, le bien-être y régne aussi. Plantez au milieu d'une place un piquet couronné de fleurs, rassemblez-y le peuple, et vous aurez une fête. Faîtes mieux encore: donnez les spectateurs en spectacle; rendez-les acteurs eux-mêmes; faîtes que chacun se voie et s'aime dans les autres, afin que tous en soient mieux unis.

But what then will be the objects of these entertainments? What will be shown in them? Nothing, if you please. With liberty, wherever abundance reigns, well-being also reigns. Plant a stake crowned with flowers in the middle of a square; gather the people together there, and you will have a festival. Do better yet; let the spectators become an entertainment to themselves; make them actors themselves; do it so that each sees and loves himself in the others so that all will be better united.[24]

Rousseau's unstated argument would seem to be this: a perfectly balanced reciprocity takes the sting out of our dependence on opinion, and makes it compatible with liberty. Complete reciprocity, along with the unity of purpose that it makes possible, ensures that in following opinion I am not in any way pulled outside myself. I am still "obeying myself" as a member of this common project or general will. Caring about esteem in this context is compatible with freedom and social unity, because the society is one in which all the virtuous will be esteemed equally and for the same (right) reasons. In contrast, in a system of hierarchical honor, we are in competition; one person's glory must be another's shame, or at least obscurity. Our unity of purpose is shattered, and in this context attempting to win the favor of another, who by hypothesis has goals distinct from mine, must be alienating. Paradoxically, the bad other-dependence goes along with separation and isolation;[25] the good kind, which Rousseau doesn't call other-dependence at all, involves the unity of a common project, even a "common self."[26]

Thus Rousseau is at the origin of a new discourse about honor and dignity. To the two traditional ways of thinking about honor and pride he adds a third, which is quite different. There was a discourse denouncing pride, as I mentioned above, which called on us to remove ourselves from this whole dimension of human life and to be utterly unconcerned with esteem. And then there was an ethic of honor, frankly nonuniversalist and inegalitarian, which saw the concern with honor as the first mark of the honorable man. Someone unconcerned with reputation, unwilling to defend it, had to be a coward, and therefore contemptible.

Rousseau borrows the denunciatory language of the first discourse, but he doesn't end up calling for a renunciation of all concern with esteem. On the contrary, in his portrait of the republican model, caring about esteem is central. What is wrong with pride or honor is its striving after preferences, hence division, hence real other-dependence, and therefore loss of the voice of nature; consequently corruption, the forgetting of boundaries, and effeminacy. The remedy is not rejecting the importance of esteem, but entering into a quite different system, characterized by equality, reciprocity, and unity of purpose. This unity makes possible the equality of esteem, but the fact that esteem is in principle equal in this system is essential to the unity of purpose itself. Under the aegis of the general will, all virtuous citizens are to be equally honored. The age of dignity is born.

This new critique of pride, leading not to solitary mortification but to a politics of equal dignity, is what Hegel took up and made famous in his dialectic of master and slave. Against the old discourse on the evil of pride, he takes it as fundamental that we can flourish only to the extent that we are recognized. Each consciousness seeks recognition in another, and this is not a sign of a lack of virtue. But the ordinary conception of honor as hierarchical is crucially flawed, because it doesn't answer the need that sends people after recognition in the first place. Those who fail to win out in the honor stakes remain unrecognized. But even those who do win are more subtly frustrated, because they win recognition from the losers, whose acknowledgment is by hypothesis not really valuable, since they are no longer free, self-supporting subjects on the same level with the winners. The struggle for recognition can find only one satisfactory solution, and that is a regime of reciprocal recognition among equals. Hegel follows Rousseau in finding this regime in a society with a common purpose, one in which there is a "'we' that is an 'I', and an 'I' that is a 'we.'"[27]

But if we think of Rousseau as inaugurating the new politics of equal dignity, we can argue that his solution is crucially flawed. In terms of the question posed at the beginning of this section, equality of esteem requires a tight unity of purpose that seems to be incompatible with any differentiation. The key to a free polity for Rousseau seems to be a rigorous exclusion of any differentiation of roles. Rousseau's principle seems to be that for any two-place relation R involving power, the condition of a free society is that the two terms joined by the relation be identical: xRy is compatible with a free society only when x equals y. This is true when the relation involves the x's presenting themselves in public space to the y's, and it is of course famously true when the relation is "exercises sovereignty over." In the social-contract state, the people must be both sovereign and subject.

In Rousseau three things seem to be inseparable: freedom (nondomination), the absence of differentiated roles, and a very tight common purpose. We must all be dependent on the general will, lest there arise bilateral forms of dependence.[28] This has been the formula for the most terrible forms of homogenizing tyranny, starting with the Jacobins and extending to the totalitarian regimes of our century. But even where the third element of the trinity is set aside, the aligning of equal freedom with the absence of differentiation has remained a tempting mode of thought. Wherever it reigns, be it in modes of feminist thought or liberal politics, the margin to recognize difference is very small.

We might well agree with this analysis, and want to gain some distance from the Rousseauean model of citizen dignity. Yet still we might want to know whether any politics of equal dignity, based on the recognition of universal capacities, is bound to be equally homogenizing. Is this true of those models—which I inscribed above, perhaps arbitrarily, under the banner of Kant—that separate equal freedom from the two other elements of the Rousseauean trinity? These models not only have nothing to do with a general will, but abstract from any issue of the differentiation of roles. They simply look to an equality of rights accorded to citizens. Yet this form of liberalism has come under attack by radical proponents of the politics of difference as in some way unable to give due acknowledgment to distinctness. Are the critics correct?

The fact is that there are forms of this liberalism that in the minds of their own proponents can give only a very restricted acknowledgment of distinct cultural identities. The notion that any of the standard schedules of rights might apply differently in one cultural context than they do in another, that their application might have to take account of different collective goals, is considered quite unacceptable. The issue, then, is whether this restrictive view of equal rights is the only possible interpretation. If it is, then it would seem that the accusation of homogenization is well founded. But perhaps it isn't. I think it isn't, and perhaps the best way to lay out the issue is to see it in the context of the Canadian case, where this question has played a role in the impending breakup of the country. In fact, two conceptions of rights liberalism have confronted each other, albeit in confused fashion, throughout the long and inconclusive constitutional debates of recent years.

The issue came to the fore because of the adoption in 1982 of the Canadian Charter of Rights, which aligned Canada's political system in this regard with the American system in having a schedule of rights to serve as a basis for the judicial review of legislation at all levels of government. The question had to arise how to relate this schedule to the claims for distinctness put forward by French Canadians, particularly Quebeckers, on the one hand, and aboriginal peoples on the other. Here what was at stake was the desire of these peoples for survival, and their consequent demand for certain forms of autonomy in their self-government, as well as the ability to adopt certain kinds of legislation deemed necessary for survival.

For instance, Quebec has passed a number of laws in the area of language. One regulates who can send their children to English-language schools (not francophones or immigrants); another requires that businesses with more than fifty employees be run in French; a third outlaws commercial signs in any language other than French. In other words, restrictions have been placed on Quebeckers by their government, in the name of their collective goal of survival, which in other Canadian communities might easily be disallowed by virtue of the Charter.[29] The fundamental question was: is this variation acceptable or not?

The issue was addressed by a proposed constitutional amendment, named after the site of the conference where it was first drafted, Meech Lake. The Meech amendment proposed to recognize Quebec as a "distinct society," and wanted to make this recognition one of the bases for judicial interpretation of the rest of the constitution, including the Charter. This seemed to open up the possibility for variation in its interpretation in different parts of the country. For many, such variation was fundamentally unacceptable. Examining why brings us to the heart of the question of how rights liberalism is related to diversity.

The Canadian Charter follows the trend of the last half of the twentieth century, and gives a basis for judicial review on two scores. First, it defines a set of individual rights that are similar to those protected in other charters and bills of rights in western democracies. Second, it guarantees equal treatment of citizens in a variety of respects, or, alternatively put, it protects against discriminatory treatment on a number of irrelevant grounds, such as race or sex. There is a lot more in the Charter, including provisions for linguistic rights and aboriginal rights, which could be understood as according powers to collectivities, but the two themes I singled out dominate in the public consciousness.

This is no accident. The two kinds of provisions are now quite common in entrenched schedules of rights that provide the basis for judicial review. In this sense, the western world, perhaps the world as a whole, is following U.S. precedent. The Americans were the first to write out and entrench a bill of rights, which they did during the ratification of their constitution and as a condition of its successful outcome. One might argue that they weren't entirely clear on judicial review as a method of securing those rights, but this rapidly became the practice. The early amendments protected individuals, and sometimes state governments,[30] against encroachment by the new federal government. It was after the Civil War, in the period of triumphant reconstruction, and particularly with the Fourteenth Amendment, which called for "equal protection" for all citizens under the law, that the theme of nondiscrimination became central to judicial review. But this theme is now on a par with the older norm of the defense of individual rights, and in public consciousness perhaps even ahead.

For a number of people in "English Canada," a political society's espousing certain collective goals threatens to run against both of these basic provisions of the Charter, or indeed any acceptable bill of rights. First, the collective goals may require restrictions on the behavior of individuals that violate their rights. For many nonfrancophone Canadians, both inside and outside Quebec, this feared outcome had already materialized with Quebec's language legislation. Quebec legislation prescribes, as already mentioned, the type of school to which parents can send their children; and in the most famous instance, it forbids certain kinds of commercial signage. The latter provision was struck down by the Supreme Court as contrary to Quebec's bill of rights, as well as the Charter, and only reenacted through the invocation of a clause in the Charter that permits legislatures in certain cases to override decisions of the courts relative to the Charter for a limited period of time (the so-called notwithstanding clause).

But second, even if overriding individual rights were not possible, espousing collective goals on behalf of a national group can be thought to be inherently discriminatory. In the modern world it will always be the case that not all those living as citizens under a certain jurisdiction will belong to the national group thus favored. This in itself could be thought to provoke discrimination. But beyond this, the pursuit of the collective end will probably involve treating insiders and outsiders differently. Thus the schooling provisions of Law 101 forbid (roughly speaking) francophones and immigrants to send their children to English-language schools, but allow Canadian anglophones to do so.

This sense that the Charter clashes with basic Quebec policy was one of the grounds of opposition in the rest of Canada to the Meech Lake accord. The cause for concern was the distinct-society clause, and the common demand for amendment was that the Charter be "protected" against this clause, or take precedence over it. There was undoubtedly in this opposition a certain amount of old-style anti-Quebec prejudice, but there was also a serious philosophical point.

Those who take the view that individual rights must always come first, and, along with nondiscrimination provisions, must take precedence over collective goals, are often speaking from a liberal perspective that has become more and more widespread in the Anglo-American world. Its source is of course the United States, and it has recently been elaborated and defended by some of the nation's best philosophical and legal minds, including John Rawls, Ronald Dworkin, and Bruce Ackerman.[31] There are various formulations of the main idea, but perhaps the one that encapsulates most clearly the relevant point is expressed by Dworkin in his short paper on "Liberalism."

Dworkin makes a distinction between two kinds of moral commitment. We all have views about the ends of life, about what constitutes a good life, which we and others ought to strive for. But we also acknowledge a commitment to deal fairly and equally with each other, regardless of how we conceive our ends. We might call this latter commitment "procedural," while commitments concerning the ends of life are "substantive." Dworkin claims that a liberal society is one that adopts no particular substantive view about the ends of life. The society is, rather, united around a strong procedural commitment to treat people with equal respect. The reason that the polity as such can espouse no substantive view—say that one of the goals of legislation should be to make people virtuous—is that this would involve a violation of its procedural norm. For, given the diversity of modern societies, it would unfailingly be the case that some people and not others would be committed to the favored conception of virtue. They might be in a majority; indeed, it's likely that they would be, for otherwise a democratic society probably wouldn't espouse their view. Yet this view would not be everyone's view, and in espousing this substantive outlook the society would not be treating the dissident minority with equal respect. It would be saying to them, in effect, "your view is not as valuable, in the eyes of this polity, as that of your more numerous compatriots."

There are profound philosophical assumptions underlying this view of liberalism, which is rooted in the thought of Kant. Among other features, this view understands human dignity to consist largely in autonomy, that is, in the ability of each person to determine for himself or herself a view of the good life. Dignity is associated less with any particular understanding of the good life, such that one's departure from this would detract from one's own dignity, than with the power to consider and espouse for oneself some view or other. We don't respect this power equally in all subjects, it is claimed, if we raise the outcome of some people's deliberations officially over that of others. A liberal society must remain neutral on the good life and restrict itself to ensuring that, however they see things, citizens deal fairly with one another and the state deals equally with all.

The popularity of this view of the human agent as primarily a subject of self-determining or self-expressive choice helps to explain why this model of liberalism is so strong. But we must also consider that it has been urged with great force and intelligence by liberal thinkers in the United States, and precisely in the context of constitutional doctrines of judicial review.[32] Thus it is not surprising that the idea has become widespread, well beyond those who might subscribe to a Kantian philosophy, that a liberal society can't accommodate publicly espoused notions of the good. This is the conception, as Michael Sandel has noted, of the procedural republic, which has a strong hold on the political agenda in the United States, and which has helped to place increasing emphasis on judicial review at the expense of the ordinary political process of building majorities with a view to legislative action.[33]

But a society with collective goals like Quebec's violates this model. It is axiomatic for Quebec governments that the survival and flourishing of French culture in Quebec is a good. Political society is not neutral between those who value remaining true to the culture of our ancestors and those who might want to cut loose in the name of some individual goal of self-development. It might be argued that you could after all capture a goal like *survivance* for a proceduralist liberal society. You could consider the French language, for instance, as a collective resource that individuals might want to make use of, and act for its preservation just as you do for clean air or green spaces. But this can't capture the full thrust of policies designed for cultural survival. It is not just a matter of having the French language available for those who might choose it. This might be seen to be the goal of some of the measures of federal bilingualism over the last twenty years. But it also involves making sure that there is a community of people in the future that will want to avail itself of the opportunity to use the French language. Policies aimed at survival actively seek to *create* members of the community, for instance, in their assuring that future generations continue to identify as French speakers. There is no way that these policies could be seen as just providing a facility to already existing people.

So Quebeckers, and those who give similar importance to this kind of collective goal, tend to opt for a rather different model of liberal society. On their view, a society can be organized around a definition of the good life, without this being seen as a depreciation of those who do not personally share this definition. Where the nature of the good requires that it be sought in common, this is the reason for its being a matter of public policy. According to this conception, a liberal society singles itself out as such by the way in which it treats minorities, including those who do not share public definitions of the good, and above all by the rights it accords to its members. But now the rights in question are conceived to be the fundamental and crucial ones that have been recognized as such from the very beginning of the liberal tradition: rights to life, liberty, due process, free speech, free practice of religion, and so on. On this model, there is a dangerous overlooking of an essential boundary in speaking of fundamental rights to things like commercial signs in the language of one's choice. One has to distinguish the fundamental liberties, those that should never be infringed and therefore ought to be unassailably entrenched, from privileges and immunities that are important but can be revoked or restricted for reasons of public policy—although one would need a strong reason to do this.

A society with strong collective goals can be liberal, on this view, provided it is also capable of respecting diversity, especially when dealing with those who don't share its common goals; and provided it can offer adequate safeguards for fundamental rights. There will undoubtedly be tensions and difficulties in pursuing these objectives together, but such a pursuit is not impossible, and the problems are not in principle greater than those encountered by any liberal society that has to combine, for example, liberty and equality, or prosperity and justice.

Here are two incompatible views of liberal society. One of the great sources of our current disharmony is that the sides have squared off against each other over the last decade. The resistance to the "distinct society" that called for precedence to be given to the Charter came in part from a spreading procedural outlook in English Canada. From this point of view, attributing the goal of promoting Quebec's distinct society to a government is to acknowledge a collective goal, and this move had to be neutralized by being subordinated to the existing Charter. From the standpoint of Quebec, this attempt to impose a procedural model of liberalism not only would deprive the distinct-society clause of some of its force as a rule of interpretation, but would bespeak a rejection of the model of liberalism on which this society was founded. Each society misperceived the other throughout the Meech Lake debate. But here both perceived each other accurately—and didn't like what they saw. The rest of Canada saw that the distinct-society clause legitimated collective goals. And Quebec saw that the move to give the Charter precedence imposed a form of liberal society that was alien, and to which Quebec could never accommodate itself without surrendering its identity.[34]

I have delved into this case because it seems to illustrate the fundamental questions. There is a form of the politics of equal respect, as enshrined in a liberalism of rights, that is inhospitable to difference, because (a) it insists on uniform application of the rules defining these rights, without exception, and (b) it is suspicious of collective goals. Of course, this doesn't mean that the model seeks to abolish cultural differences. That would be an absurd accusation. But I call it inhospitable to difference because it can't accommodate what the members of distinct societies really aspire to, which is survival. This is (b) a collective goal, which (a) almost inevitably will call for some variations in the kinds of law we deem permissible from one cultural context to another, as the Quebec case clearly shows.

I think this form of liberalism is guilty as charged by the proponents of a politics of difference. Fortunately, however, there are other models of liberal society that take a different line on (a) and (b). These forms do call for the invariant defense of certain rights, of course. There would be no question of cultural differences determining the application of *habeas corpus,* for example. But they distinguish these fundamental rights from the broad range of immunities and presumptions of uniform treatment that have sprung up in modern cultures of judicial review. They are willing to weigh the importance of certain forms of uniform treatment against the importance of cultural survival, and opt sometimes in favor of the latter. They are thus in the end not procedural models of liberalism, but are grounded very much on judgments about what makes a good life—judgments in which the integrity of cultures has an important place.

Although I can't argue it here, obviously I would endorse this kind of model. Indisputably, though, more and more societies today are turning out to be multicultural, in the sense of including more than one cultural community that wants to survive. The rigidities of procedural liberalism may rapidly become impractical in tomorrow's world.

The politics of equal respect, then, at least in this more hospitable variant, can be cleared of the charge of homogenizing difference. But there is another way of formulating the charge that is harder to rebut. In this form, however, it perhaps ought not to be rebutted, or so I want to argue.

The charge I'm thinking of is provoked by the claim sometimes made on behalf of difference-blind liberalism that it can offer a neutral ground on which people of all cultures can meet and coexist. On this view, it is necessary to make a certain number of distinctions—between what is public and what is private, for instance, or between politics and religion—and only then can one relegate the contentious differences to a sphere that doesn't impinge on the political.

But a controversy like that over Salman Rushdie's *Satanic Verses* shows how wrong this view is. For mainstream Islam, there is no question of separating politics and religion as we have come to expect in western liberal society. Liberalism is not a possible meeting ground for all cultures; it is the political expression of one range of cultures, and quite incompatible with other ranges. Moreover, as many Muslims are well aware, western liberalism is not so much an expression of the secular, postreligious outlook that happens to be popular among liberal *intellectuals* as it is a more organic outgrowth of Christianity—at least as seen from the alternative vantage of Islam. The division of church and state goes back to the earliest days of Christian civilization. The early forms of the separation were very different from ours, but the basis was laid for modern developments. The very term *secular* was originally part of the Christian vocabulary.[35]

All this is to say that liberalism can't and shouldn't claim complete cultural neutrality. Liberalism is also a fighting creed. The hospitable variant I espouse, as well as the most rigid forms, has to draw the line. There will be variations when it comes to applying the schedule of rights, but not where incitement to assassination is concerned. This shouldn't be seen as a contradiction. Substantive distinctions of this kind are inescapable in politics, and at least the nonprocedural liberalism I was describing is fully ready to accept this.

But the controversy is still disturbing, for the reason mentioned above: all societies are becoming increasingly multicultural while, at the same time, becoming more porous. The two developments go together. Their porousness means that they are more open to multinational migration; more of their members live the life of diaspora, whose center is elsewhere. In these circumstances there is something awkward about replying simply, "This is how we do things here." This reply must be made in cases like the Rushdie controversy, where "how we do things" covers issues such as the right to life and freedom of speech. The awkwardness arises from the fact that there are substantial numbers of citizens who also belong to the culture that calls into question our philosophical boundaries. The challenge is to deal with their sense of marginalization without compromising our basic political principles.

This brings us to the issue of multiculturalism as it is often debated today, which has a lot to do with the imposition of some cultures on others, and with the assumed superiority that powers this imposition. Western liberal societies are thought to be supremely guilty in this regard, partly because of their colonial past, and partly because of their marginalization of segments of their populations that stem from other cultures. It is in this context that "This is how we do things here" can seem crude and insensitive. Even if, in the nature of things, compromise is close to impossible—one either forbids murder or allows it—the attitude presumed by the reply is seen as one of contempt. Often, in fact, this presumption is correct. So we arrive again at the issue of recognition.

Recognition of equal value was not what was at stake—at least in a strong sense—in my earlier discussion. There it was a question of whether cultural survival will be acknowledged as a legitimate goal, whether collective ends will be allowed as legitimate considerations in judicial review, or for other purposes of major social policy. The demand there was that we let cultures defend themselves, within reasonable bounds. But the further demand we're looking at here is that we all recognize the equal value of different cultures; that we not only let them survive, but acknowledge their *worth.*

What sense can be made of this demand? In a way it has been operative in an unformulated state for some time. The politics of nationalism has been powered for well over a century partly by the sense that people have had of being despised or respected by others around them. Multinational societies can break up because of a lack of perceived recognition of the equal worth of one group by another. This is, I believe, the case in Canada—though my diagnosis will certainly be challenged by some. On the international scene, the tremendous sensitivity of certain supposedly closed societies to world opinion—as shown in their reactions to findings of, say, Amnesty International, or in their attempts through UNESCO to build a new world information order—attests to the importance of external recognition.

But all this is still *an sich,* not *für sich,* in the Hegelian jargon. The actors themselves are often the first to deny that they are moved by such considerations, and plead other factors, say inequality, exploitation, and injustice, as their motives. Very few Quebec independentists, for instance, can accept that what's winning them their fight is the lack of recognition from English Canada.

What is new, therefore, is that the demand for recognition is now explicit. And it has been made explicit, in the way I indicated above, by the spread of the idea that we are formed by recognition. We could say that, thanks to this idea, misrecognition has now graduated to the rank of a harm that can be hardheadedly enumerated along with those mentioned in the previous paragraph.

One of the key authors in this transition is undoubtedly Frantz Fanon, who in his influential *Les Dammés de la terre* (1961) argued that the major weapon of the colonizers was the imposition of their image of the colonized on the subjugated people. The colonized, in order to be free, must first of all purge themselves of these demeaning self-images. Fanon recommended violence as the way to this freedom, matching the original violence of the alien imposition. Not all those who have drawn from Fanon have followed him in this, but the notion that there is a struggle for a changed self-image, which takes place both within the subjugated and against the dominator, has been very widely applied. The idea has become crucial to certain strands of feminism, and is also an important element in the contemporary debate on multiculturalism.

The main locus of this debate is the world of education (in a broad sense). One focus is on university humanities departments, where demands are made to alter, enlarge, or scrap the canon of accredited authors on the grounds that the one currently favored consists almost entirely of "dead white males." A greater place ought to be made for women and for people of non-European races and cultures. A second focus is on the secondary schools, where an attempt is being made, for instance, to develop Afrocentric curricula for pupils in mainly black schools.

The reason for these proposed changes is not, or not mainly, that all students may be missing something important through the exclusion of a certain gender or certain races or cultures, but rather that women and students from the excluded groups are given, either directly or by omission, a demeaning picture of themselves, as though all creativity and worth inhered in men of European provenance. Enlarging and changing the curriculum is essential not so much in the name of a broader culture for everyone as in order to give due recognition to the hitherto excluded. The background premise of these demands is that recognition forges identity, particularly in its Fanonist application: dominant groups tend to entrench their hegemony by inculcating an image of inferiority in the subjugated. The struggle for freedom and equality must therefore pass through a revision of these images. Multicultural curricula are meant to help in this process of revision.

Although it is not often stated clearly, the logic behind some of these demands seems to depend on a premise that we owe equal respect to all cultures. This emerges from the nature of the reproach made to the designers of traditional curricula. The claim is that the judgments of worth on which these curricula were based were in fact corrupt, marred by narrowness or insensitivity or, even worse, a desire to downgrade the excluded. The implication seems to be that, without these distorting factors, true judgments of value of different works would place all cultures more or less on the same footing. Of course the attack could come from a more radical, neo-Nietzschean standpoint, which questions the very status of judgments of worth as such, but short of this extreme step (whose coherence I doubt), the presumption seems to be one of equal worth.

I'd like to maintain that there is something valid in this presumption, but that it is by no means unproblematic and involves something like an act of faith. As a presumption, the claim is that all human cultures that have animated whole societies over some considerable stretch of time have something important to say to all human beings. I word it this way to exclude partial cultural milieux within a society, as well as short phases in a major culture. There is no reason to believe that, for instance, the different art forms of a given culture should all be of equal, or even of considerable, value; and every culture can go through phases of decadence.

But when I call this claim a presumption, I mean that it is a starting hypothesis with which we ought to approach the study of any other culture. The validity of the claim has to be demonstrated concretely in the actual study of the culture. Indeed, for a culture sufficiently different from our own, we may have only the foggiest idea *ex ante* of what its valuable contribution might be. Because, for a sufficiently different culture, the very understanding of what it means to be of worth will be strange and unfamiliar to us. To approach, say, a raga with the presumptions of value implicit in the well-tempered clavier would be forever to miss the point. What has to happen is what Gadamer calls a "fusion of horizons."[36] We learn to move in a broader horizon, where what we once took for granted as the background to valuation can be situated as one possibility alongside the different background of the unfamiliar culture. The fusion of horizons operates through our developing new vocabularies of comparison, for articulating these new contrasts.[37] So that if and when we ultimately find substantive support for our initial presumption, it is on the basis of an assessment of worth that we couldn't possibly have had at the beginning. We have reached the judgment partly through transforming our standards.

We might want to argue that we owe all cultures a presumption of this kind. From this point of view, withholding the presumption might be seen as the fruit of prejudice or ill will. It might even be tantamount to a denial of equal status. Something like this might lie behind the accusation leveled by supporters of multiculturalism against defenders of the traditional canon. Supposing that the reluctance to enlarge the canon comes from a mixture of prejudice and ill will, the multiculturalists charge them with the arrogance of assuming their superiority over formerly subjugated peoples.

This presumption would help to explain why the demands of multiculturalism build on established principles of equal respect. If withholding the presumption is tantamount to a denial of equality, and if important consequences flow for people's identity from the absence of recognition, then a case can be made for insisting on the universalization of the presumption as a logical extension of the politics of dignity. Just as all must have equal civil rights, and equal voting rights, regardless of race or culture, so all should enjoy the presumption that their traditional culture has value. This extension, however logically it may seem to flow from the accepted norms of equal dignity, fits uneasily within them because it challenges the difference-blindness that was central to them. Yet it does indeed seem to flow from them, albeit uneasily.

I'm not sure about the validity of demanding this presumption as a right. But we can leave this issue aside, because the demand being made seems much stronger. The claim is that a proper respect for equality requires more than a presumption that further study will make us see things this way; there have to be actual judgments of equal worth applied to the customs and creations of these different cultures. Such judgments seem to be implicit in the demand that certain works be included in the canon, and in the implication that these works were not included earlier only because of prejudice or ill will or the desire to dominate. (Of course the demand for inclusion is *logically* separable from a claim of equal worth. The demand could be: "Include these because they're ours, even though they may be inferior." But this isn't how the people making the demand talk.)

Still there's something very wrong with the demand in this form. It makes sense to insist as a matter of right that we approach the study of certain cultures with a presumption of their value. But it can't make sense to insist as a matter of right that we come up with a final concluding judgment that their value is great, or equal to others'. That is, if the judgment of value is to register something independent of our own wills and desires, it can't be dictated by a principle of ethics. On examination, either we'll find something of great value in culture C, or we won't. But it makes no more sense to demand that we do so than it does to demand that we find the earth round or flat, the temperature of the air hot or cold.

I have stated this rather flatly when, as everyone knows, there is a vigorous controversy over the "objectivity" of judgments in this field, and whether there is a "truth of the matter" here, as there seems to be in natural science or, indeed, whether even in natural science objectivity is a mirage.[38] I don't have much sympathy for these forms of subjectivism, which I find shot through with confusion. But there seems to be some special confusion in invoking them in this context. The moral and political thrust of the complaint concerns unjustified judgments of inferior status allegedly made of nonhegemonic cultures. But if those judgments are ultimately a question of the human will, then the issue of justification falls away. One doesn't, properly speaking, make judgments that can be right or wrong; one expresses liking or dislike, one endorses or rejects another culture. But then the complaint must shift to address the refusal to endorse, and the validity or invalidity of judgments has nothing to do with it.

Then, however, the act of declaring another culture's creations to be of worth and the act of declaring yourself on their side, even if their creations aren't all that impressive, become indistinguishable. The difference is only in the packaging. Yet the first is normally understood as a genuine expression of respect, the second as insufferable patronizing. The supposed beneficiaries of the politics of recognition, the people who might actually benefit from acknowledgment, make a crucial distinction between the two acts. They know they want respect, not condescension. Any theory that wipes out the distinction seems at least prima facie to be distorting crucial facets of the reality it purports to deal with.

In fact, subjectivist, half-baked, neo-Nietzschean theories are quite often invoked in this debate. Deriving frequently from Foucault or Derrida, they claim that all judgments of worth are based on standards that are ultimately imposed by and further entrench structures of power. It should be clear why these theories proliferate. A favorable judgment on demand is nonsense, unless some such theories are valid. Moreover, the giving of a judgment on demand is an act of breathtaking condescension. No one can really mean it as a genuine act of respect. It is more in the nature of a pretended act of respect given at the insistence of its supposed beneficiary. Objectively, such an act involves contempt for the latter's intelligence; to be an object of such an act demeans. The proponents of neo-Nietzschean theories hope to escape this nexus of hypocrisy by turning the entire issue into one of power and counterpower. Then the question is no longer one of respect, but of taking sides, of solidarity. This is hardly a satisfactory solution, because in taking sides they miss the driving force of this kind of politics, which is precisely the search for recognition and respect.

Moreover, even if we could demand it of them, the last thing we want at this stage from Eurocentered intellectuals is positive judgments of the worth of cultures they have not studied intensively. For real judgments of worth suppose a fused horizon of standards, where we have been transformed by the study of the other, so that we are not simply judging by our old familiar standards. A favorable judgment made prematurely would be not only condescending but ethnocentric. It would praise the other for being like us.

Here is another severe problem with much of the politics of multiculturalism. The peremptory demand for favorable judgments of worth is paradoxically—perhaps tragically—homogenizing. For it implies that we already have the standards to make such judgments. The standards we have, however, are those of North Atlantic civilization. And so the judgments implicitly and unconsciously will cram the others into our categories. We will think of their "artists" as creating "works," which we then can include in our canon. By implicitly invoking our standards to judge all civilizations and cultures, the politics of difference can end up making everyone the same.[39]

In this form, the demand for equal recognition is unacceptable. But the story doesn't simply end there. The enemies of multiculturalism in the American academy have perceived this weakness, and have used it as an excuse to turn their backs on the problem. This won't do. A response like that attributed to Saul Bellow, to the effect that we will be glad to read the Zulu Tolstoy when he comes along, shows the depths of ethnocentricity. First, there is the implicit assumption that excellence has to take forms familiar to us: the Zulus should produce a *Tolstoy*. Second, we are assuming that their contribution is yet to be made (*when* the Zulus produce a Tolstoy). These two assumptions obviously go hand in hand. If the Zulus have to produce our kind of excellence, then obviously their only hope lies in the future. Roger Kimball puts it more crudely: "The multiculturalists notwithstanding, the choice facing us today is not between a 'repressive' Western culture and a multicultural paradise, but between culture and barbarism. Civilization is not a gift, it is an achievement—a fragile achievement that needs constantly to be shored up and defended from besiegers inside and out."[40]

There must be something midway between the inauthentic and homogenizing demand for recognition of equal worth, on the one hand, and the self-immurement within ethnocentric standards, on the other. There are other cultures, and we have to live together more and more, both on a world scale and commingled in each individual society.

What we have is the presumption of equal worth: a stance we take in embarking on the study of the other. Perhaps we don't need to ask whether it's something that others can demand from us as a right. We might simply ask whether this is the way we ought to approach others.

Well, is it? How can this presumption be grounded? One ground that has been proposed is religious. Herder, for instance, had a view of divine providence, according to which all this variety of culture was no mere accident but meant to bring about a greater harmony. I can't rule out such a view. But merely on the human level, one could argue that it's reasonable to suppose that cultures that have provided the horizon of meaning for large numbers of human beings, of diverse characters and temperaments, over a long period of time—that have, in other words, articulated their sense of the good, the holy, and the admirable—are almost certain to have something that deserves our admiration and respect, even if it goes along with much that we have to abhor and reject. Put another way: it would take supreme arrogance to discount this possibility a priori.

Perhaps there is a moral issue here after all. We only need a sense of our own limited part in the whole human story to accept the presumption. It is only arrogance, or some analogous moral failing, that can deprive us of this. But what the presumption requires is not peremptory and inauthentic judgments of equal value, but a willingness to be open to comparative cultural study of the kind that must displace our horizons in the resulting fusions. What it requires above all is an admission that we are very far away from that ultimate horizon where the relative worth of different cultures might be evident. This would mean breaking with an illusion that still holds many multiculturalists—as well as their most bitter opponents—in its grip.

— 13 —

Liberal Politics and the Public Sphere

What exactly is a liberal society? What makes it possible? And what are the dangers it faces? These are the questions I'd like to explore, but the problem is that they all permit of answers of indefinite length. The dangers to liberal society, for instance, are not denumerable. Threats can come from an uncountable number of directions. So I have to be selective. There are certain difficulties that seem to me widespread in our age, and I'll put them in the foreground. In doing so, I'm aware that I speak out of a parochial experience. Societies of a liberal type are now aspired to almost everywhere on the globe, in radically different conditions. No finite discussion can do justice to all these situations.

But surely, if the dangers are infinite, the first question, which calls for a definition of liberal society, can have a clear and finite answer. So one might think, and a number of thinkers have tried to proffer definitions. But I think that here too the complexity of the reality and the multiplicity of its facets defeat us. Indeed, I think there is a danger in trying to make clear definitions, because it may narrow the scope of our attention in damaging or even fatal ways.

But don't we have to know what we're talking about? I will grudgingly admit this, and even offer a rough delineation of what I mean by liberal society. But as the discussion proceeds, the slippery and multifaceted nature of this description will, I hope, become evident.

We can delineate liberal society in terms of its characteristic forms, for instance, representative government, the rule of law, a regime of entrenched rights, the guarantor of certain freedoms. But I'd prefer to start off on another footing, and think of a liberal society as one that is trying to realize in the highest possible degree certain goods or principles of right. We might think of it as trying to maximize the goods of freedom and collective self-rule, in conformity with rights founded on equality. The unsatisfactory nature of this as a definition springs to our attention as soon as we ponder what freedom means here. Clearly this is much contested. For some, it might only mean negative freedom, being able to do what you want without interference from others, particularly from authority. But for others the meaningful freedom involves real self-determination, an excellence of moral development. Someone who is merely negatively free, doing what he or she wants, might be largely governed by unreflective convention, or timidly conforming to norms that were not at all inwardly accepted and that he or she might even chafe at. This wouldn't be the more robust freedom of self-responsible life choice, which Mill makes his standard in *On Liberty,* as when he praises "a person whose desires and impulses are his own—are the expression of his own nature, as it has been developed and modified by his own culture."[1]

But with all its fuzziness and uncertainties, this description will be good enough to be getting along with. It will enable us to begin examining some of the bases and dangers of a society dedicated to these ends.

I want to start by looking at western liberal societies, the original models. Among the bulwarks of freedom have been, for instance, an emphasis on the rule of law, on entrenched rights recoverable by judicial action, and various modes of dividing power. I mean not only the "division of powers" as it exists in the U.S. constitution, but other ways of distributing power in different hands, for instance through federal structures, autonomous local governments, and the like.

But in part freedom in the western liberal tradition has been based on the development of social forms in which society as a whole can function outside the ambit of the state. These forms have often been referred to under the general description "civil society," taking the term in its post-Hegelian meaning as designating something distinct from the state.[2] The notion of civil society comprises the host of free associations existing outside official sponsorship, and often dedicated to ends we generally consider nonpolitical. No society can be called free in which these voluntary associations are not able to function, and the pulse of freedom will beat very slowly where they are not being spontaneously formed.

But civil society in a strong sense exists when, beyond the free multiple associations, society can operate as a whole outside the ambit of the state. I mean by this ways in which society can be said to act, or to generate or sustain a certain condition, without the agency of government. The very idea that there can be modes of extrapolitical action or pattern maintenance by the whole society is foreign to a great many historical civilizations; for instance, traditional Chinese society, or—to take an example very far removed from this—the ancient polis. And if we take other civilizations, like the Indian or the medieval European, where the society also has extrapolitical authorities, the striking difference from the modern West lies in the fact that the forms of civil society are purely secular.

Two major forms of civil society which have played a big role in western freedom (or at any rate have been thought to play such a role) are the public sphere and the market economy. To put some flesh on this rather abstract discussion of extrapolitical and secular action, I will talk in a little more detail about the rise of the public sphere.

What is a public sphere? I want to describe it as a common space in which the members of society meet, through a variety of media (print, electronic) and also in face-to-face encounters, to discuss matters of common interest; and thus to be able to form a common mind about those matters. I say "a common space" because, although the media are multiple, as well as the exchanges taking place in them, they are deemed to be in principle intercommunicating. The discussion we may be having on television right now takes account of what was said in the newspaper this morning, which in turn reports on the radio debate of yesterday, and so on. That's why we usually speak of the public sphere, in the singular.

The public sphere is a central feature of modern society. So much so that, even where it is in fact suppressed or manipulated, it has to be faked. Modern despotic societies have generally felt compelled to go through the motions. Editorials appear in the party newspapers, purporting to express the opinions of the writers, offered for the consideration of their fellow citizens; mass demonstrations are organized, purporting to give vent to the felt indignation of large numbers of people. All this takes place as if a genuine process were in train of forming a common mind through exchange, even though the result is carefully controlled from the beginning.

Why this semblance? Because the public sphere is not only a ubiquitous feature of any modern society; it also plays a crucial role in its self-justification as a free self-governing society, that is, as a society in which (a) people form their opinions freely, both as individuals and in coming to a common mind, and (b) these common opinions matter—they in some way take effect on or control government. Just because it has this central role, the public sphere is the object of concern and criticism in liberal societies as well. One question is whether the debate is not being controlled and manipulated there too, in a fashion less obvious than within despotic regimes but all the more insidiously, by money, or government, or some collusive combination of the two. Another is whether the nature of certain modern media can permit the truly open, multilateral exchange which is supposed to issue in a truly common opinion on public matters.

There is a tendency to consider something so important and central to our lives almost as a fact of nature, as if something of the sort had always been there. Modern liberal society would then have innovated in allowing the public sphere its freedom, making government responsible to it instead of the other way around. But something like public opinion has always existed. To think this, however, would be an anachronistic error, which obscures what is new, and not yet fully understood, in this kind of common space. I'd like to cast a little more light on this, and in the process get clearer on the transformations in background understanding and social imaginary which produced modern civilization.

In particular, I want to draw on two interesting books, one published over thirty years ago in Germany and now available in English, Jürgen Habermas' *Structural Transformation,* which deals with the development of public opinion in eighteenth-century western Europe; the other is a 1990 publication of Michael Warner's, *The Letters of the Republic,* which describes the analogous phenomenon in Britain's American colonies.[3]

A central theme of Habermas' book is the emergence in the eighteenth century of a new concept of public opinion. Getting clear what was new in this will help to define what is special about the modern public sphere. People had, of course, always recognized something like a general opinion, which held in a particular society or perhaps among mankind as a whole. This might be looked down on, as a source of error, following Plato's low estimation of *doxa.* Or it might be seen in other contexts as setting standards for right conduct.[4] But in either case it is different from the new form in three important respects: "the opinion of mankind" is seen as (1) unreflected, (2) unmediated by discussion and critique, and (3) passively inculcated in each successive generation. Public opinion, by contrast, is meant

(1) to be the product of reflection, (2) to emerge from discussion, and (3) to reflect an actively produced consensus.

The difference lies in more than the evaluation of passive acceptance there, critical thinking here. It is not just that the eighteenth century decided to pin Cartesian medals on the opinion of mankind. The crucial change is that the underlying process is different. Where the opinion of mankind was supposed to have passed down in each case from parents and elders, in a myriad of unlinked, local acts of transmission, public opinion was deemed to have been elaborated by a discussion among those who held it, wherein their different views were somehow confronted and they were able to come to a common mind. The opinion of mankind is probably held in identical form by you and me, since we are formed by the same socializing process. We share in a common public opinion, if we do, because we have worked it out together. We don't just happen to have identical views; we have elaborated our convictions in a common act of definition.

But now in each case, whether as opinion of mankind or public opinion, the same views can be held by people who have never met. That's why the two can be confused. But in the later case, something else is supposed: that the two widely separated people sharing the same view have been linked in a kind of space of discussion, wherein they have been able to exchange ideas and reach a common end.

What is this common space? It's a rather strange thing, when you come to think about it. The two people I'm invoking here have never met. But they are seen as linked in a common space of discussion through media—in the eighteenth-century print media. Books, pamphlets, and newspapers circulated among the educated public, carrying theses, analyses, arguments, counterarguments, referring to and refuting one another. These were widely read and often discussed in face-to-face gatherings, in drawing rooms, coffeehouses, salons, or in more (authoritatively) "public" places, such as parliament. The sensed general view resulting from all this counted as "public opinion" in the new sense.

I say "counted as" public opinion. And here we get to the heart of the strangeness: an essential part of the difference is made by what the process is deemed to amount to. The opinion of mankind spreads through myriad unlinked acts of transmission, as I said, while public opinion is formed by the participants together. But if one made an exhaustive list of all the face-to-face encounters that occur in each case, the two processes wouldn't look all that different. In both cases, masses of people sharing the same views never meet, but everyone is linked to everyone through some chain of personal or written transmission. Crucial to the difference is that in the formation of public opinion each of these linked physical or print-mediated encounters is understood by the participants as forming part of a single discussion proceeding toward a common resolution. This can't be all, of course; the encounters couldn't be the same in all other respects, and only differ in how they were understood by the participants. For instance, it is crucial to these linked encounters that they are constantly inter-referring: I attempt to refute in my conversation with you today the *Times* editorial of last week, which took some public figure to task for a speech she made the week before. It is also crucial that they be carried on as arguments. If in each case, someone just passively accepts what another tells him—as in the ideal-typical case, of authoritative transmission of tradition from parents to children—these events couldn't be plausibly construed as forming part of a society-wide discussion. But without this common understanding of their linkage on the part of the participants, no one even from the outside could take them as constituting a common discussion with a potentially single outcome. A general understanding of what things count as is constitutive of the reality we call the public sphere.

In a similar fashion, there are clearly infrastructural conditions to the rise of the public sphere. There had to be printed materials, circulating from a plurality of independent sources, for there to be the bases of what could be seen as a common discussion. As is often said, the modern public sphere relied on "print capitalism" to get going. But as Warner shows, printing itself, and even print capitalism, didn't provide a sufficient condition. The printed words had to be taken up in the right cultural context, where the essential common understandings could arise.

We are now in a slightly better position to understand what kind of thing a public sphere is, and why it was new in the eighteenth century. It's a kind of common space, I said, in which people who never meet understand themselves to be engaged in discussion, and capable of reaching a common mind. Let me introduce some new terminology. We can speak of "common space" when people come together in one act of focus for whatever purpose, be it ritual, the enjoyment of a play, conversation, the celebration of a major event. Their focus is common, as against merely convergent, because it is part of what is commonly understood that they are attending to the common object, or purpose, together, as against each person just happening, on his or her own, to be concerned with the same thing. In this sense, the opinion of mankind offers a merely convergent unity, while public opinion is supposedly generated out of a series of common actions.

Now an intuitively understandable kind of common space is set up when people are assembled for some purpose, be it on an intimate level for conversation, or on a larger, more "public" scale for a deliberative assembly, a ritual, a celebration, the enjoyment of a football match or an opera, and the like. Common space arising from assembly in some locale I want to call "topical common space."

But the public sphere is something different. It transcends topical spaces. We might say that it knits together a plurality of such spaces into one larger space of nonassembly. The same public discussion is deemed to pass through our debate today, and someone else's earnest conversation tomorrow, and the newspaper interview on Thursday, and so on. I want to call this larger kind of nonlocal common space "metatopical." The public sphere that emerges in the eighteenth century is a metatopical common space. What we have been discovering about such spaces is that they are partly constituted by common understandings; that is, they are not reducible to, but cannot exist without, such understandings. New, unprecedented kinds of spaces require new understandings. Such is the case for the public sphere.

What is new is not metatopicality. The church and the state were extant metatopical spaces. But getting clear about the novelty brings us to the essential features of modernity. We can articulate the new on two levels: what the public sphere does, and what it is.

First, what it does—or what is done in it. The public sphere is the locus of a discussion potentially engaging everyone (although in the eighteenth century the claim was only to involve the educated or "enlightened" minority) so that the society can come to a common mind about important matters. This common mind is a reflective view, emerging from critical debate, and not just a summation of whatever views happen to be held in the population.[5] So it has a normative status: government ought to listen to it. There were two reasons for this, and one tended to gain ground and ultimately swallow up the other. The first is that this opinion is likely to be enlightened, and hence government would be well advised to follow it. This statement by the dramatist Louis-Sébastien Mercier in 1778 gives clear expression to the idea:

> Les bons livres dépendent des lumiéres dans toutes les classes du peuple; ils ornent la vérité. Ce sont eux qui déjá gouvernent l'Europe; ils éclairent

le gouvernement sur ses devoirs, sur sa faute, sur son véritable intérêt, sur l'opinion publique qu'il doit écouter et suivre: ces bons livres sont des maîtres patients qui attendent le réveil des administrateurs des états et le calme de leurs passions.[6]

Kant famously had a similar view.

The second reason emerges with the view that the people is sovereign. Government is then not only wise to follow opinion; it is morally bound to do so. Governments ought to legislate and rule in the midst of a reasoning public. Parliament, or the court, in taking its decisions ought to be concentrating and enacting what has already been emerging out of enlightened debate among the people. From this arises what Warner, following Habermas, calls the "principle of supervision," which insists that the proceedings of governing bodies be public, open to the scrutiny of the discerning public.[7] In this way legislative deliberation informs public opinion and allows it to be maximally rational, while at the same time exposing itself to its pressure, and thus acknowledging that legislation should ultimately bow to the clear mandates of this opinion.[8]

The public sphere is, then, a locus in which rational views are elaborated which should guide government. This comes to be seen as an essential feature of a free society. As Burke put it, "in a free country, every man thinks he has a concern in all public matters."[9] There is, of course, something very new about this in the eighteenth century, compared to the immediate past of Europe. But one might ask, is it new in history? Isn't it a feature of all free societies?

No—there is a subtle but important difference. Let's compare modern society with an ancient republic. In the polis, we can imagine that debate on public affairs carried on in a host of settings: among friends at a symposium, between those meeting in the agora, and then in the ekklesia where the matter is finally decided. The debate swirls around and ultimately reaches its conclusion in the competent decisionmaking body. Now the difference is that the discussions outside this body prepare for the action ultimately taken by the same people within it. The "unofficial" discussions are not separated off, not given a status of their own, not seen to constitute a kind of metatopical space.

But that is what happens with the modern public sphere. It is a space of discussion which is self-consciously seen as being outside power. It is supposed to be listened to by those in power, but it is not itself an exercise of power. Here this extrapolitical status is crucial. As we shall see, it links the public sphere with other facets of modern society which also are seen as essentially extrapolitical. The extrapolitical status is not just defined negatively, as a lack of power. It is also seen positively: just because public opinion is not an exercise of power, it can be ideally disengaged from partisan spirit.

In other words, with the modern public sphere comes the idea that political power must be supervised and checked by something outside. What was new was the nature of this outside check. It was not defined as the will of God or the law of Nature (although it could be thought to articulate such), but as a kind of discourse, emanating from reason and not from power or traditional authority. As Habermas puts it, power was to be tamed by reason. The notion was that "veritas non auctoritas facit legem" (truth, not authority, makes the law).[10]

In this way, the public sphere was different from everything preceding it. An unofficial discussion, which nevertheless can come to a verdict of great importance, it is defined outside the sphere of power. It borrows some of the images from ancient assemblies, as we saw from the American case, to project the whole public as one space of discussion. But as Warner shows, it innovates in relation to this model. Those who intervene are, as it were, like speakers before an assembly. But unlike their models in actual ancient assemblies, they strive for a certain impersonality, a certain impartiality, an eschewing of party spirit. They strive to negate their own particularity, and thus to rise above "any private or partial view." This is what Warner calls "the principle of negativity." And we can see it not only as suiting the print, as against spoken, medium, but also as giving expression to this crucial feature of the new public sphere as a discourse of reason on and to power, rather than by power.[11]

As Warner points out, the rise of the public sphere involves a breach in the old ideal of a social order undivided by conflict and difference. On the contrary, it means that debate breaks out and continues, involving in principle everybody, and this is perfectly legitimate. The old unity will be gone forever. But a new unity is to be substituted. For the ever-continuing controversy is not meant to be an exercise in power, a quasi-civil war carried on by dialectical means. Its potentially divisive and destructive consequences are offset by the fact that it is a debate outside power, a rational debate, striving without *parti pris* to define the common good. "The language of

resistance to controversy articulates a norm for controversy. It silently transforms the ideal of a social order free from conflictual debate into an ideal of
debate free from social conflict."[12]

So what the public sphere does is to enable the society to reach a common mind, without the mediation of the political sphere, in a discourse of
reason outside power, which nevertheless is normative for power. Now let's
try to see what, in order to do this, it has to be.

We can perhaps best do this by trying to define what is new and unprecedented in it. First, there is the aspect of its novelty already touched on: its
extrapolitical locus. "Republic of letters" was a common term that the
members of the international society of savants gave themselves toward the
end of the seventeenth century. This was a precursor of the public sphere;
indeed, it contributed to shaping it. Here was a "republic" constituted beyond the political. Both the analogy and the difference gave force and point
to this image: it was a republic as a unified association, grouping all enlightened participants, across political boundaries; but it was also a republic in
being free from subjection; its "citizens" owed no allegiance but to it, as
long as they went about the business of letters.

Something of this goes into the eighteenth-century public sphere. Here
the members of society come together and pursue a common end; they
form and understand themselves to form an association, which is nevertheless not constituted by a political structure. This was not true of the ancient
polis. Athens was a society, a *koinonia,* only as constituted politically. The
same was true of Rome. The ancient society was given its identity by its
laws. On the banners of the legions, SPQR stood for *Senatus populusque
romanus,* but the "populus" here was the assemblage of Roman citizens, that
is, those defined as such by the laws. The people didn't have an identity,
didn't constitute a unity prior to and outside these laws.

By contrast, in projecting a public sphere, our eighteenth century forbears were placing themselves in an association, this common space of discussion, which owed nothing to political structures, but was seen as forming
a society outside the state. Indeed, this society was wider than any one state;
it extended for some purposes to all of civilized Europe. This is an extremely
important aspect and corresponds to a crucial feature of contemporary civilization, which emerges at this time, and is visible in more than the public
sphere.

Now, it is obvious that an extrapolitical, international society is in itself
not new. It is preceded by the stoic cosmopolis and, more immediately, by

the Christian church. Europeans were used to living in a dual society, one organized by two mutually irreducible principles. So a second facet of the newness of the public sphere has to be defined as its *radical secularity*.

This is not easy to define, and I take a risk in using a term already thrown about so loosely in attempts to describe modern civilization. But I adopt it because I think an awareness of its etymology may help us to understand what is at stake here—which has something to do with the way human society inhabits time. But this way of describing the difference can only be brought in later, after some preliminary exploration.

The notation of secularity I'm using here is radical because it stands not only in contrast with a divine foundation for society, but with any idea of society as constituted in something that transcends contemporary common action. For instance, some hierarchical societies conceive themselves as bodying forth some part of the great chain of being. Behind the empirical fillers of the slots of kingship, aristocracy, and so on, lie the Ideas, or the persisting metaphysical realities that these people are momentarily embodying. The king has two bodies, only one being the particular, perishable one, which is now being fed and clothed and will later be buried.[13] Within this outlook, what constitutes a society as such is the metaphysical order it embodies.[14] People act within a framework that is already there.

But secularity contrasts not only with divinely established churches or great chains of being. It is also different from an understanding of our society as constituted by a law that has been ours for time out of mind. This too places our action within a framework that binds us together and makes us a society, and transcends our common action.

In contradistinction to all this, the public sphere is an association constituted by nothing outside the common action we carry out in it: coming to a common mind, where possible, through the exchange of ideas. Its existence as an association is just our acting together in this way. Common action is not made possible by a framework that needs to be established in some action-transcendent dimension: either by an act of God, or in a great chain, or by a law coming down to us since time out of mind. This is what makes it radically secular. And this, I want to claim, gets to the heart of what is new in it.

This is baldly stated. Obviously the notion of secularity must still be made clearer. Perhaps the contrast is obvious enough with mystical bodies and great chains. But I'm claiming a difference from traditional tribal society as well, the kind of thing the German peoples had who founded the modern

North Atlantic polities, or in another form what constituted the ancient republics. And this might be challenged.

These societies were defined by a law. But is that so different from the public sphere? After all, whenever we want to act publicly, we meet a number of structures already in place: there are newspapers, television networks, publishing houses, and the rest. We act within the channels that these provide. Isn't this analogous to any member of a tribe, who also has to act within established structures, of chieftainships, councils, annual meetings, and the rest? Of course the institutions of the public sphere change; newspapers go broke, networks merge, and the like. But no tribe remains absolutely fixed in its forms either. If we wanted to claim that this preexisting structure is valid for ongoing action, but not for the founding acts that set up the public sphere, the answer might be that these are impossible to identify in the stream of time, any more than they are for the tribe. And if we want to insist that there must be such a moment, then we should remark that many tribes as well hand down legends of a founding act, when Lycurgus, for instance, laid down laws for Sparta. Surely he acted outside existing structures.

Talking of actions within structures brings out the similarities. But there is an important difference, which resides in the respective common understandings. It is true that in a functioning public sphere, action at any time is carried out within structures laid down earlier. There is a de facto arrangement of things. But this arrangement doesn't enjoy any privilege over the action carried out within it. The structures were set up during previous acts of communication in common space, on all fours with those we are carrying out now. Our present action may modify these structures, and that is legitimate because they are seen as nothing more than precipitates and facilitators of communicative action.

But the traditional law of a tribe usually enjoys a different status. We may, of course, alter it over time, following the prescription it itself provides. But it is not seen just as precipitate and facilitator of action. The abolition of the law would mean the abolition of the subject of common action, since the law defines the tribe as an entity. Whereas a public sphere could start up again, even where all media had been abolished, simply by founding new ones, a tribe can only resume its life on the understanding that the law, although perhaps interrupted in its efficacy by foreign conquest, is still in force.

That's what I mean when I say that what constitutes the society, what makes the common agency possible, transcends the common actions carried out within it. It is not just that the structures we need for today's action arose as a consequence of yesterday's. Rather the traditional law is a precondition of any common action, at whatever time, because this common agency couldn't exist without it. It is in this sense transcendent. By contrast, in a purely secular association (in my sense), common agency arises simply in and as a precipitate of common action.

The crucial distinction underlying the concept of secularity can thus be related to this issue: what constitutes the association? Or otherwise put, what makes this group of people as they continue over time a common agent? Where this is something that transcends the realm of those common actions this agency engages in, the association is nonsecular. Where the constituting factor is nothing other than common action—whether the founding acts have already occurred, or are now coming about, is immaterial—we have secularity.

Now my claim is that this kind of secularity is modern, that it comes about very recently in the history of mankind. Of course there have been all sorts of momentary and topical common agents which have arisen just from common action. A crowd gathers, people shout protests, and then the governor's house is stoned or the chateau is burned down. But prior to the modern day, enduring, metatopical common agency was inconceivable on a purely secular basis. People could only see themselves as constituted into such by something action-transcendent, be it God or a chain of being or some traditional law. So the eighteenth-century public sphere represents an instance of a new kind: a metatopical common space and common agency without an action-transcendent constitution, an agency grounded purely in its own common actions.

But how about the founding moments that traditional societies often "remembered"? What about Lycurgus' action in giving Sparta its laws? Surely these show us examples of the constituting factor (here law) issuing from common action: Lycurgus proposes, the Spartans accept. But it is in the nature of such founding moments that they are not put on the same plane as contemporary common action. They are displaced onto a higher plane, into a heroic time, an *illud tempus* that is not seen as qualitatively on a level with what we do today. The founding action is not just like our action, not just an earlier similar act whose precipitate structures ours. It is not just earlier but in another kind of time, an exemplary time.

And this is why I am tempted to use the term "secular," in spite of all the misunderstandings that may arise. Clearly I don't just mean, "not tied to religion."[15] The exclusion is much broader. But the original sense of "secular" was "of the age," that is, pertaining to profane time. It was close to the sense of "temporal" in the opposition temporal/spiritual. The understanding was that this profane time existed in relation to (surrounded by, penetrated by: it's hard to find the right words here) another time, God's time. This could also be conceived as eternity, which was not only endless profane time, but a kind of gathering of time into a unity; hence the expression *hoi aiones ton aionon,* or *saecula saeculorum.*

The crucial point is that things and events had to be situated in relation to more than one kind of time. This is why events far apart in profane time could still be closely linked. Benedict Anderson, in a penetrating discussion of the same transition, quotes Eric Auerbach on the relation of prefiguring-fulfilling in which events of the Old Testament were held to stand to those in the New, for instance the sacrifice of Isaac and the crucifixion of Christ.[16] These two events were linked through their immediate contiguous places in the divine plan. They are drawn close to identity in eternity, even though they are centuries (that is, "eons" or "saecula") apart. In God's time there is a sort of simultaneity of sacrifice and crucifixion.

Modern secularization can be seen from one angle as the rejection of divine time, and the positing of time as purely profane. Events now exist only in this one dimension, in which they stand at greater and lesser temporal distance, and in relations of causality with other events of the same kind. The modern notion of simultaneity comes to be, in which events utterly unrelated in cause or meaning are held together simply by their occurrence at the same point in this single profane time line. Modern literature, as well as news media, seconded by social science, has accustomed us to think of society in terms of vertical time slices, holding together myriad happenings, related and unrelated. I think Anderson is right that this is a typically modern mode of social imagination, which our medieval forbears would have found hard to understand; where events in profane time are very differently related to higher time, it seems unnatural simply to group them side by side in the modern relation of simultaneity. This carries a presumption of homogeneity which is essentially negated by our dominant time consciousness.[17]

Now the move to what I call secularity is obviously related to this radically purged time consciousness. Premodern understandings of time seem to have always been multidimensional. The Christian relating of time and eternity was not the only game in town, even in Christendom. There was also the much more widespread sense of a founding act, a "time of origins" as Mircea Eliade called it,[18] which was complexly related to the present moment in ordinary time, in that it could often be ritually approached and its force partly reappropriated at certain privileged moments. That's why it couldn't simply be unambiguously placed in the past (in ordinary time). The Christian liturgical year draws on this kind of time consciousness, widely shared by other religious outlooks, in reenacting the founding events of Jesus' life.

It also seems to have been the universal norm to see the important meta-topical spaces and agencies as constituted in some mode of higher time. States and churches were seen to exist almost necessarily in more than one time dimension, as if it were inconceivable that they have their being purely in profane or ordinary time. A state that bodied forth the great chain of being was connected to the eternal realm of Ideas; a people defined by its law communicated with the founding time where this was laid down.

The move to modern secularity comes when associations are placed firmly and wholly in homogeneous, profane time, whether or not the higher time is negated altogether, or other associations are still admitted to exist in it. Such is the case with the public sphere, and therein lies its unprecedented nature.

I can now perhaps draw this discussion together. The public sphere was a new metatopical space, in which members of society could exchange ideas and come to a common mind. As such it constituted a metatopical agency, but one that was understood to exist outside the political constitution of society and completely in profane time.

An extrapolitical, secular, metatopical space—this is what the public sphere was and is. And the importance of understanding this lies partly in the fact that it was not the only such, that it was part of a development which transformed our whole understanding of time and society, so that we have trouble recalling what it was like before.

I've already mentioned the market economy, as another supposed extra-political bulwark of freedom. This is indeed not a common space, that is, it is not considered the locus of a common action. Rather the notion descending from Adam Smith is that it is a field of interaction, in which a myriad of small-scale, bilateral common actions generate an overall pattern, behind the backs of the agents, by an invisible hand. But the economy is similar to the public sphere in that it is an extrapolitical field of purely secular action, in which society is thought to be capable of generating an overall pattern outside the political domain. I haven't got the space to go into it here, but it seems evident that the two have common origins in the cultural changes of early modern Europe. Habermas makes a similar point.

I have described both public sphere and market economy in their ideal-typical forms, as existing outside the political domain. Neither was ever integrally realized in this form, although in the age of absolutism, the new public sphere was in a sense excluded from power in a way that it most emphatically is not and cannot be in a modern democratic society. Of course, the market is always to some extent steered, controlled, limited by state action. In fact, a totally uncontrolled market economy would rapidly self-destruct. The public sphere is inhabited by all sorts of agents, including those with large political axes to grind, and not least those who are linked to established government. But although encroached on to some degree, the fact that these domains operate and are seen to operate by their own dynamic has been of crucial importance to the limitation of power and hence to the maintenance of freedom in the modern West. This seems to me beyond contest.

The differences arise when we try to define just what this importance is. And here two camps form within western democracies. There are those who hold that their main significance is as limits on potentially all-invasive state power; and that consequently they operate best the more they approach their ideal type of total independence. Let the market economy be as free of state interference as it is possible to make it. Let the public sphere be as clearly demarcated from the political as can be, constituted at the limit exclusively by media that claim total political neutrality. The camp is deeply imbued with the idea that the extrapolitical is the main bulwark of freedom.

Against them is ranged the camp that holds that the attempt to limit power is not our exclusive concern. Liberalism must also be concerned with self-rule, that is, it must strive to make power and in general whatever shapes the conditions of our lives responsive to collective decisions. The exclusive focus on limiting power can hamper this goal. In one obvious way, the concern above all to free the market can foster conditions that adversely affect a great many people, but they can't change them if the limits of interference are narrowly drawn.

The concern of this second tendency is also with the health of democracy as a system of collective self-government. From this standpoint, the public sphere plays not only a limiting, whistle-blowing role. It also can serve or disserve, raise or lower, facilitate or hamper the common debate and exchange which is an intrinsic part of conscious, informed collective decision.

What divides these two views is partly the different priority they place on the two main goods sought by liberal society, individual freedom and self-rule. Plainly those who strive above all to limit power place a greater importance on the first goal relative to the second. The two camps are also frequently divided in their understandings of the requirements of equality. But there also are important differences in their assessment of the conditions of stability and legitimacy in liberal societies.

Citing Tocqueville, many would want to argue that self-rule has become one of the dominant ideals of modern liberal society. Indeed, it could hardly be otherwise. The same cultural and political changes that brought about the public sphere as a space of extrapolitical common action, to which power was obligated to listen, needed only to be carried a little farther to the proposition that the people should rule, that sovereignty belongs to the people. If this ideal really is widely and deeply felt in modern society, then an atrophy of self-rule poses a danger to the stability of liberal society, and hence also to the freedoms it protects. The fate of negative liberty would thus be connected to that of Tocqueville's "political liberty." This far-sighted thinker constantly argued that self-rule was vital to freedom. If you hold this view, then you have an additional reason to adhere to the second camp, and to be concerned with the quality of collective decisions.

But this is a source of great puzzlement in modern democratic society. What exactly are we assessing when we concern ourselves with the quality of our collective decisions? It's easy to express the democratic aspirations: rules and decisions ought to be determined by the people. This means that (1) the mass of the people should have some say in what they are going to be, and not just told what they are; that (2) this say should be genuinely theirs, and not manipulated by propaganda, misinformation, irrational fears; and that (3) it should to some extent reflect their considered opinions and aspirations, as against ill-informed and knee-jerk prejudices.

Once spelled out like this, truly democratic decisionmaking has seemed utopian to many observers. It has been argued that the third condition is virtually never met in mass democracies, that the average voter is too poorly informed, and too marginally interested, to cast an enlightened ballot. Such reflections led to the school of democratic "revisionists" after World War II, who argued that democracy was sufficiently served if the masses could decide the competition between potential governing elites. However irrational the choice, their dependence on the people would force the elites to pay attention to their interests.[19]

Criticism of decisionmaking in mass democracies also comes from another direction, from those who wonder whether the second condition is ever met. The suspicion is that powerful interests are manipulating the public, through their control of the media, major political parties, and the means of propaganda, and in fact steering the public debate into narrow channels that serve their goals.[20]

Trying to assess these claims can be difficult. Just what standard of rationality should we adopt in assessing whether the third condition is met? When are the media leading or controlling the public, and when are they responding to mass prejudice? But underlying all this is a major difficulty, which arises from the very nature of mass decisions as well as from deeply embedded philosophical prejudices.

I'm referring here to a feature mentioned above in connection with the public sphere, that decisions are partly constituted by the common understanding of the participants. The public sphere generated a "public opinion" that was held to arise out of common discussion, even though the participants never met in a single place and moment. The dispersed exchanges of small groups, among whom printed materials circulated, were held to amount to a discussion from which a common sense emerged. An essential condition for this phenomenon of dispersed public opinion is that the participants understand what they are doing.

A similar point holds for democratic decisionmaking in modern polities. There isn't and can't be a meeting of the whole population in council—outside the celebrated cases of some Swiss cantons. What in fact happens is a dispersed process of public discussion through media, the casting of ballots to elect representative assemblies and executive officeholders, and decisions rendered by the latter which then have the value of common decisions. It is crucial to this political reality that the outcome of a dispersed process is understood to count as a decision of the nation or society. A common understanding of a certain kind is a necessary condition.

Necessary, but not sufficient. Things can go wrong. The debate can be manipulated; alternatives can be artificially narrowed through misinformation or control of the channels of decision. But we have difficulty grasping exactly how things can go wrong, because we haven't got too firm a grip on what it is for them to go right. A claim is being made: something is supposed to be a genuine, unforced common decision. The claim can be bogus. We normally understand what is involved in adjudicating this kind of thing: we compare the claim with an independent reality, and see if the two match. But here the reality is not entirely independent. Part of the successful reality consists of people understanding it to be so; and yet this understanding is exactly what we would like to challenge when we fear manipulation, or sense that the process has been vitiated by a lack of real information or comprehension.

The temptation arises to refashion our model of democratic decision in order to avoid these perplexities. We simplify the phenomenon, thus altering the criteria of success. One way, common on the left, is to follow Rousseau and see genuine democratic decision as the effect of a general will, that is, some unanimous purpose. There are moments, and issues, where a whole population feels strongly and at one on some question, often matters of foreign policy: Great Britain in 1940, the United States at the height of the Gulf War. We know what such moments are like, and we know that they seem to admit of little doubt. So we make this the benchmark of democratic decision, and devalue all our ambivalent majority decisions as the result of manipulation and false consciousness.

Of course, philosophical doubt arising from the paradoxes of a social reality partly constituted by self-understanding is not the only motive here. There is the independent force of the Jacobin-Bolshevik tradition, which holds that the true people's will must be unanimous, that division is the result of distortion of some kind: class rule or the work of factions. But the drive for unanimity is partly a drive for transparency, and this is given additional force by the philosophical doubts that center on collective decisionmaking in a diverse society.

Another way of refashioning the model to make the issue more tractable starts from the fact of diversity, and purports to assess democratic decision objectively. People have interests that can be identified prior to decisions; and the decisions favor some interests and frustrate others. Is the majority favored? Then democracy is served. If not, then there has been illegitimate elitist control.

But each of these views offers criteria for valid democratic decision suitable for a social reality that is not the one we live. The Jacobin view can't accommodate real diversity of opinion, aspirations, or agenda. The objective-interest view can't accommodate all those decisions, often reflecting our moral views, where there are no clearly identifiable interests.

More seriously, it can't take account of the fact that people's views can be altered by the interchange, that consensus sometimes emerges, that citizens frequently understand themselves as part of a community and don't vote out of individual interest alone. We might say that, while the Jacobin view can't accommodate diversity, the interest view can't accommodate anything else; in particular, it can't account for the degree to which a political society functions as a community.

The conditions for a genuine democratic decision can't be defined in abstraction from self-understanding. They include (a) that the people concerned understand themselves as belonging to a community that shares some common purposes and recognizes its members as sharing in these purposes; (b) that the various groups, types, and classes of citizens have been given a genuine hearing and were able to have an impact on the debate; and (c) that the decision emerging from this is really the majority preference.

In a society of mutually disinterested agents, intent only on their own individual life plans, (b) and (c)—perhaps even (c) alone—would be all that one could ask. In such a society, the objective-interest criterion would indeed be adequate. But this is not what modern democracies are like. The idea underlying popular sovereignty is that the people who are sovereign form some kind of unit. They are not a scratch team picked by history, with nothing more in common than the passenger list of some international flight. And this is no accident. How could there be a widespread acceptance to abide by the rules and outcomes of democratic decision among people who have no bond whatever? Only those with a super-muscular Kantian conscience would be willing to knuckle under to a majority with which they felt no links.

Dimension (a) of modern democratic society makes self-understanding relevant because there can't be a community in any meaningful sense that doesn't understand itself to be such. But this fact also impacts on what we will want to count as fulfilling condition (b). In our imagined aggregation of mutually disinterested agents, (b) could be measured in purely objective terms, such as the number of column inches devoted to a given position in the newspapers or the number of minutes of television exposure. But if we want to go beyond this, and ask whether a given point of view was really heard, or whether it was screened out and discounted in advance through prejudice or the nonrecognition of its protagonists, it's not clear how this might be assessed. Indeed, we might doubt whether agents who were truly disinterested, and each into their own life plan, could give much sense to the idea of hearing another's point of view. In such a world, there would be nothing between having your point of view ignored by your compatriots and having it endorsed. Agreement would be the only available criterion of genuine hearing.

Things can be very different in a community. Here the sense that you have been given a hearing depends not just on the particular interchange, but on the state of the whole relationship. People can have a sense that they are heard because they know themselves to be valued in a certain way, even when some particular demands are not met. Their sense of being heard will also depend on the relation of their goal to common purposes, and to the goals of other groups with whom they feel some solidarity in the light of these purposes. So a refusal of one of their proposals may be consistent with their having been heard. For instance, in the light of common understanding, certain demands may represent a tall order for some groups, whereas others are relatively easy to grant. Blocking the second may indeed appear indistinguishable from a rejection of those who make the demands, whereas a demurral on the first may be easy to accept.

I've just slipped into putting this in terms of the sense of being heard. But the point is that we can't drive a sharp wedge between perception and reality. It isn't that perceptions can't be mistaken, but that the reality, because it is connected with the whole state of the relationship, can't be entirely divorced from participants' understanding. It is not just a perception-transcendent state of affairs which can be independently assessed. Whether some group is heard on some matter involves a number of things, including the bonds of common understanding and respect which link it with the majority or fail to do so, as well as common understanding of how hard or easy the demands are to accommodate.

Democratic decisionmaking in mass societies is then something like the public sphere; whether and how it comes off has something to do with the self-understandings involved. But democracy is not just like the public sphere. It is plain that the operation of a public sphere is involved centrally in the process. Once we leave behind the Jacobin and objective-interest criteria of democracy, which allow us simply to compare the outcome with some preexisting standard—the general will or individuals' interests—we have to take account of not just the outcome but the process. That is the significance of requirement (b) above, that various types, groups, and classes of citizens have been given a genuine hearing in the debate. But then it becomes clear that, in a modern society, the political system narrowly defined (say, parties, legislatures, and governments) can't carry out adequate debate on its own. A debate within these channels alone would leave out a large number of citizens and groups. The issues also have to be thrashed out in the public sphere, the public space of dispersed discussion circulating through neutral media outside the political system.

A flourishing public sphere is essential to democracy. This is universally felt, which is why contemporary despotisms feel impelled to fake it. But now we can see that this is not just because free media can play a watchdog role, carefully surveying power and sounding the alarm when it oversteps its limits. This function is important, but it doesn't exhaust their relevance. The quality and functioning of media in the public sphere can also do a lot to determine the quality and outreach of the public debate. The dramatic significance of whistle-blowing gives it an aura hard to match in any other function. The saga of Watergate has entered into the imagination of generations of young American reporters. But the tireless attempt to empty the last skeleton from the closet may actually impede the opening of a healthy debate on crucial issues, as the course of recent American presidential campaigning illustrates.

These remarks about genuine democratic decision suggest the different ways in which it can fail. Condition (b) can fail to be met; various groups or classes may be excluded, or their voices very feebly heard, their concerns barely impinging on the national agenda. Or else condition (a) may be in danger, because various groups or classes or subcommunities feel excluded, or perhaps on other grounds no longer understand themselves as linked with their compatriots in a single unit of decision. A democratic society— a "sovereign people"—may find that its capacity to render genuine democratic decisions is enfeebled either through a narrowing of participation or through a rift in the political community. These two modes of failure can obviously be closely interwoven, in that one helps to exacerbate the other. But they are notionally distinct, and in some cases one or the other may be dominant.

I would now like to look by way of illustration at some familiar types of failure of the democratic process, and at possible remedies.

The first is the familiar sense of citizen alienation in large, centralized, bureaucratic societies. The average citizen feels power to be at a great distance, and frequently unresponsive. There is a sense of powerlessness in face of a governing machine that continues on its way without regard for the ordinary people, who seem to have little recourse in making their needs felt. There seems no way that the ordinary citizen can have an impact on this process, either to determine its general direction or to fine-tune its application to the individual case. This effect is the greater the more matters are concentrated in the hands of a remote central government, and the more bureaucratized the procedures of government are. Centralized bureaucratic power does not mean, of course, that the government has everything its own way. Powerful lobbies intervene to affect its course. But these too are remote from ordinary citizens and generally equally impervious to their input.

This is the situation Tocqueville warned of, and one remedy was discussed at length. It consists of decentralizing power, of having certain functions of government exercised on a more local level, where citizen mobilization to make an impact is a less daunting task. But hypercentralization is not only a danger of the political system. It also affects the public sphere. Just as in politics, local concerns may impinge only with difficulty on the center; so the national debate may become concentrated in a small number of mass media that are impervious to local input. The sense becomes widespread that the debate on the major television networks, for instance, is shaped by relatively narrow groups or interests, and its animators operate within a charmed circle that can't be penetrated. Other views, other ways of posing the questions, other agendas cannot get a hearing.

Tocquevillian decentralization is necessary in the public sphere as well. Indeed, one can support the other. The fact that important issues are decided locally enhances the importance of local media, which in turn focus the debate on these issues by those affected. But it is not only a matter of bringing certain issues down to the local level. The national debate can be changed as well by effective local public spheres. The model that seems to work here is one in which smaller public spheres are nested within larger ones, so that what goes on in the smaller ones feeds into the agenda of the national sphere. The public sphere of a regional society can have that kind of impact, provided the political life of this society itself has some significance for the whole—a good example of how political decentralization also facilitates the enlarging of the public sphere.

There are other kinds of smaller sphere as well. An example of a type that has been significant for some western societies is provided by certain political parties and social movements. These can function as nested public spheres to the extent that their internal debate is open to the public. Then, depending on the significance of the party or movement politically, the inner debate can spill over and help to determine the national agenda. Some parties have had this function. But the most striking examples in recent decades are found in some of the "new social movements": for instance, the feminist movement (if we can speak of it in the singular) and ecological campaigns. These movements have not acted on the political process the way lobbies usually do, mobilizing their efforts behind some agreed public stance and keeping their internal discussion to themselves. On the contrary, their internal debates have been out there for all to see, and it is as much through these as through any global impact that they have helped to reshape the public agenda. That is why I speak of them as nested public spheres.

To some extent, the drift toward centralization and bureaucratization is unavoidable in contemporary society. This is bad for democracy. The nightmare scenario is a hypercentralized government, existing in a space of powerful elitist lobbies and national television networks, each impervious to input from local sources. But this drift can be offset by a double decentralization, toward regional societies and nested public spheres, which can mediate the input from masses of ordinary citizens, who otherwise feel excluded from everything but the periodic national elections.

The model of public sphere emerging in this discussion is clearly different from the original eighteenth-century paradigm, and that in at least two respects. The original model seemed to posit a unitary space, and I'm suggesting here a multiplicity of public spheres nested within each other. There is a central arena of debate on national policy, but it is not the public-sphere analogue of a unitary state, but rather of a central government in a federation. Second, the boundary between the political system and the public sphere has to be relaxed. Some of the most effective nested public spheres are in fact political parties and advocacy movements, which operate in the gray zone between the two. In a modern democratic polity, the boundary between political system and public sphere has to be maximally porous.

That is, if we want this sphere to play its role in widening the public debate. If we think of it as a watchdog, limiting power, then the old model seems right. It is obviously easier for national networks, or prestigious newspapers with a national reputation, to take on the power holders. For these purposes, a sphere dominated by large and powerful units, maintaining political neutrality, can seem ideal. But it can be disastrous for a genuine national debate.

Democratic decisionmaking can also be impeded, even stymied altogether, by rifts within the political community. These can arise in a number of ways. One is a modality of class war, in which the least favored citizens sense that their interests are systematically neglected or denied. The kind of solidarity expressed in most western democracies in the various measures of the welfare state, apart from their intrinsic justification, may also be crucial to the maintenance of a functioning democratic society.

Another kind of rift may arise when a group or cultural community feels unrecognized by the larger society, and so becomes less willing to function on a basis of common understanding with the majority. This may give rise to a demand for secession, but short of that it creates a sense of injury and exclusion, in which requirement (b), that all groups be adequately heard, seems impossible. In the climate of presumed exclusion, nothing can count as being heard in the eyes of the group in question short of total compliance with its demands. There is no simple way to deal with this kind of rift once it arises, but one of the major objectives of democratic politics should be to prevent them from arising. This is another reason why ensuring that all groups have a hearing is of the utmost importance. It is not easy to achieve in our present era of multiculturalism.[21]

The effects of centralization and divisions can be exacerbated if they produce what I call political fragmentation—that is, if they affect the political process and change its form. People can respond to a sense of exclusion by practicing a mode of politics which seems predicated on the belief that society is at best composed of mutually disinterested citizens, and perhaps for the most part even malevolent in relation to the group in question. To the extent that the people concerned have already come to accept an atomistic outlook, which sees society as an aggregation of individuals with life plans and denies the reality of political community, this reaction is all the more readily available. Or the response may be powered by a philosophical vision of exclusion, say, a Marxist view of bourgeois society as irretrievably divided by class war, or certain feminist views of liberal society as irremediably vitiated by patriarchy, so that an invocation of political community is made to appear a sham and a delusion.

The kind of politics that tends to emerge out of this sense of exclusion, whether grounded in reality or philosophically projected (and it is often a mixture of both), is one that eschews the building of coalitions around some conception of the general good. Its attempt is rather to mobilize behind the group's demands on a narrow agenda, regardless of the overall picture and the impact on the community at large. Any invocation of the community good as grounds for restraint tends to be viewed with suspicion.

This is political fragmentation, the breaking up of the potential constituencies for majority coalitions behind multifaceted programs, designed to address the major problems of the society as a whole, into a congeries of campaigns for narrow objectives, each mobilizing a constituency determined to defend its turf at all costs.

The picture I offer here is somewhat Tocquevillian, and yet it is significantly different from Tocqueville's. He apprehended a kind of vicious circle, in which citizen apathy would facilitate the growth of irresponsible government power, which would increase the sense of helplessness, which would in turn entrench apathy. But at the end of the spiral would lie what he called *despotisme douce,* in which the people would be governed by an "immense tutelary power."

Now Tocqueville's portrait of mild despotism, much as he means to distinguish it from traditional tyranny, still sounds too despotic in the traditional sense. Modern democratic societies seem far from it because they are full of protest, free initiatives, and irreverent challenges to authority, and governments do in fact tremble before the anger and contempt of the governed, as revealed in the polls that rulers never stop taking.

But if we conceive Tocqueville's fear somewhat differently, then it does seem real enough. The danger is not actual despotic control, but fragmentation, that is, a people less and less capable of forming a common purpose and carrying it out. Fragmentation arises when people come to see themselves more and more atomistically, as less and less bound to their fellow citizens in common projects and allegiances. They may indeed feel linked in some projects with others, but these come to be partial groupings rather than the whole society: a local community, an ethnic minority, the adherents of some religion or ideology, the promoters of some special interest.

Fragmentation comes about partly through a weakening of the bonds of sympathy, through a rift of one of the kinds described above and partly also in a self-feeding way, through the failure of democratic initiative itself. The more fragmented a democratic electorate in this sense, the more will their political energies be transferred to the promotion of partial groupings, and the less possible it will be to mobilize democratic majorities around commonly understood programs. A sense grows that the electorate as a whole is defenseless against the leviathan state; a well-organized and integrated partial grouping may indeed be able to make a dent; but the idea that a majority of the people might frame and carry through a common project comes to seem utopian and naive. And so people give up. This already failing sympathy with others is further weakened by the lack of a common experience of action, and a sense of hopelessness makes it seem a waste of time to try. But that, of course, does make it hopeless, and the vicious circle is joined.

Now a society that goes this route can still be in one sense democratic, egalitarian and full of activity and challenge to authority, as is evident if we look at the United States. Politics begins to take on a different form, in the way I indicated above. One common purpose that remains strongly shared, even as the others atrophy, is that society is organized in the defense of rights. The rule of law and the upholding of rights are seen as very much the "American way," as the objects of a strong common allegiance. The extraordinary reaction to the Watergate scandals, which ended up unseating a president, is testimony to this.

In keeping with this, two facets of political life take on greater and greater saliency. First, more turns on judicial battles. The Americans were the first to have an entrenched bill of rights, augmented since by provisions against discrimination, and important changes have been made in American society through court challenges to legislation or private arrangements allegedly in breach of these entrenched provisions. The famous *Brown v. Board of Education,* which desegregated the public schools in 1954, is a case in point. In recent decades, more and more energy in the American political process is turning toward this process of judicial review. Matters that in other societies are determined by legislation, after debate and sometimes compromise between different opinions, are seen as proper subjects for judicial decision in light of the constitution. Abortion is a case in point. Since *Roe v. Wade* in 1973 liberalized the abortion law in the country, Republican presidents have sought to put conservatives on the Supreme Court in order to get a reversal. The result has been an astonishing intellectual effort, channeled into politics-as-judicial-review, which has made law schools the dynamic centers of social and political thought on American campuses; and a series of titanic battles over what used to be the relatively routine—or at least nonpartisan—matter of senatorial confirmation of presidential appointments to the Supreme Court.

Alongside judicial review and woven into it, American energy is channeled into interest-group or advocacy politics. People throw themselves into single-issue campaigns and work fiercely for their favored cause, as in the abortion battle. Part of the battle is judicial, but it also involves lobbying, mobilizing public opinion, and selective intervention in election campaigns for or against targeted candidates.

All this makes for a lot of activity. A society in which this goes on is hardly a despotism. But the growth of these two facets is connected, part effect and part cause, with the atrophy of a third, which is the formation of democratic majorities around meaningful programs that can then be carried to completion. In this regard, the American political scene is abysmal. The debate between the major candidates becomes ever more disjointed, their statements ever more blatantly self-serving, their communication consisting more and more of "sound bites," their promises risibly unbelievable ("read my lips") and cynically unkept, while their attacks on opponents sink to ever more dishonorable levels, seemingly with impunity. At the same time, voter participation in national elections declines, and has recently hit 50 percent of the eligible population, far below that of other democratic societies.

Something can be said for, and perhaps much can be said against, this lopsided system. We might worry about its long-term stability, worry, that is, whether the citizen alienation caused by its less and less functional representative system can be compensated for by the greater energy of its special-interest politics. The point has also been made that this style of politics makes issues harder to resolve. Judicial decisions are usually winner-take-all; you either win or you lose. In particular, judicial decisions about rights tend to be conceived as all-or-nothing matters. The very concept of a right seems to call for integral satisfaction, if it's a right at all; and if not, then nothing. Abortion once more can serve as an example. Once you see it as the right of the fetus versus the right of the mother, there are few stopping places between the unlimited immunity of the one and the untrammeled freedom of the other. The penchant to settle things judicially, further polarized by rival special-interest campaigns, effectively cuts down the possibilities of compromise.[22]

We might also argue that it makes certain issues harder to address, those requiring a democratic consensus around measures that will also involve some sacrifice and difficulty. Perhaps this is part of the continuing American problem in coming to terms with a declining economic situation through some form of intelligent industrial policy. And perhaps it has something to do with the underdeveloped nature of the welfare state in the United States, particularly the lack of a universal health scheme.[23] These common projects become more difficult to enact where this style of politics is dominant. For they can't be carried through by mobilizing a clearly defined constituency around a single, narrowly focused front. They require instead the building of an alliance that can sustain a broader range of interlinked policies over time—the kind of politics practiced by social-democratic parties in a number of western democracies. (Or, for that matter, by their opponents: the Thatcher counterrevolution is an example.)

This unbalanced system both reflects and entrenches fragmentation. Its spirit is an adversarial one in which citizen efficacy consists in being able to get your rights, whatever the consequences for the whole society. Both judicial review and single-issue politics operate from this stance. A fragmented society is one whose members find it harder and harder to identify with their political society as a community. And this is where a vicious circle can engage. The lack of identification may reflect an atomistic outlook, in which people come to see society purely instrumentally. But it also helps to entrench atomism, because the absence of effective common action on a more broadly based agenda through majority coalitions throws people back on themselves. Fragmentation is certainly intensified by the sense that government is impervious and the citizen powerless, acting through the normal electoral channels, to affect things significantly. But the politics of fragmentation further contributes to the inefficacy of these electoral channels, and a self-feeding spiral is joined. (This is perhaps why one of the most widely held social philosophies in the contemporary United States is the procedural liberalism of neutrality, which combines quite smoothly with an atomist outlook.)

How do you fight fragmentation? It's not easy, and there are no universal prescriptions. It depends very much on the particular situation. But we have seen that fragmentation grows when people no longer identify with their political community, when their sense of corporate belonging is transferred elsewhere or atrophies altogether. And it is fed, too, by the experience of political powerlessness. A fading political identity makes it harder to mobilize effectively, and a sense of helplessness breeds alienation. Now we can see how in principle the vicious circle might be turned into a virtuous circle. Successful common action can bring a sense of empowerment, and strengthen identification with the political community. Indeed, the debate on certain kinds of issue, which foregrounds common goals, even with radical disagreements about the means, can help to make the sense of political community more vivid, and thus offset the tendency of deep political divisions to paint the adversary as devoted to utterly alien values. The contrast is striking with, say, the abortion debate, where both sides readily come to believe that their opponents are enemies of morality and civilization.

This sounds like saying that the way to succeed here is to succeed, which is true if perhaps unhelpful. But there is a little more to say. One of the important sources of the sense of powerlessness is that we are governed by large-scale, centralized, bureaucratic states. What can mitigate this sense is a decentralization of power, as Tocqueville saw. And so devolution, or a division of power as in a federal system, particularly one based on the principle of subsidarity, can be good for democratic empowerment. And this is the more so, if the units to which power is devolved already figure as communities in the lives of their members.

We are back to the theme of Tocquevillian decentralization, which I have said should englobe not only the political system but the public sphere as well. What this points to is a kind of equilibrium that a liberal political system should seek. It is a balance between the party-electoral system, on one hand, and the proliferation of advocacy movements, on the other, unrelated to the partisan struggle. The first is the channel through which broad coalitions on connected issues can be built to effect their purposes. When this atrophies or functions badly, effective citizen action on a large number of issues becomes difficult if not impossible. But if the party system were to exist alone, if the wide range of movements engaged in extra-parliamentary politics were to disappear, then the society would be blocked in another way. It would lack that network of nested public spheres which alone keeps its agenda open, and provides a way into political efficacy for large numbers of people who would never have the same impact through the established parties.

In a sense, there needs to be not only a balance between the two, but a kind of symbiosis—or at least open frontiers through which persons and ideas can pass from social movements to parties and back again. This is the kind of politics that liberal societies need.

I started with a discussion of liberal society and ended up talking about the nature of liberal politics. I'm aware that I have only tabled some of the more important issues; that much more needs to be said; and that there are many other ways in which the political system of a liberal society can go awry.

All this underlines the lesson of how difficult and potentially unfruitful it can be to try to define the nature of liberalism in a few sentences. The temptation is understandable, since the rise of liberal society in the West has been inseparable from the promulgation of striking and unprecedented ideas and social forms. One of these is the public sphere, which gives concrete shape to one of the foundations of western liberalism, captured in the expression "civil society": the understanding that society can also function as a whole outside the political realm, that society is not constituted by the state but limits it. Another such foundational idea has consisted in making the rule of right a central principle of political society.

The temptation consists in taking one of these ideas or forms and making it the exclusive defining feature of liberalism. It is, I think, an intellectual mistake, with possibly damaging practical consequences. The goals of liberalism have been generally plural, including at least the three factors I mentioned at the outset: freedom, self-government, and a rule of right founded on equality. A viable liberal society has to take account of all of them, or risk the disaffection of significant numbers of its citizens. This means that liberal politics has to be concerned with the conditions of genuinely democratic decisionmaking, and that the public sphere must not be seen only as a social form limiting the political, but as itself a medium of democratic politics.

When we try to understand and assess the development of liberal regimes outside the western heartland, we have even more reason not to be too centered on its specifically western foundations. Our central concern should be to see how a political life fostering freedom and self-government under conditions of equality can be developed and promoted. This will certainly require some species of public sphere. But these spheres, existing in different cultural contexts, will in all likelihood be even more distant from our paradigmatic eighteenth-century model than the contemporary western forms are. Some will no doubt surprise us. We will have to be alert to potential new forms that can open channels for democratic decision. And "we" here includes not only westerners but political actors in the new societies who might be tempted to imitate the supposedly successful models of the North Atlantic world.

It will help in discerning these new forms if we have some better idea of what genuine democratic decision amounts to. And that is the issue I have been struggling with in the preceding pages, I hope not entirely in vain.

Notes

1. Overcoming Epistemology

1. Karl Popper, *Logik der Forschung* (Vienna, 1935); *The Open Society and Its Enemies* (Princeton, 1950).

2. Richard Rorty, *Philosophy and the Mirror of Nature* (Princeton, 1979), p. 132.

3. W. V. Quine, "Epistemology Naturalized," *Ontological Relativity and Other Essays* (New York, 1969), pp. 69–90.

4. Rorty, *Philosophy,* pp. 173ff.

5. See Descartes's statement in his letter to Gibieuf of January 19, 1642, where he declares himself "assuré que je puis avoir aucune connaissance de ce qui est hors de moi, que par l'entremise des idées que j'ai eu en moi." The notion that the modern epistemological tradition is dominated by this understanding of representation was pioneered by Martin Heidegger in his "Die Zeit des Weltbildes" (The Age of the World Picture; 1938), in *Holzwege* (Frankfurt, 1952, 1972), pp. 69–104; and the transition from the earlier view is brilliantly described by Michel Foucault in the opening chapters of his *Les Mots et les choses* (Paris, 1966); translated as *The Order of Things* (New York, 1970).

6. See e.g. Aristotle, *De anima* 3.430a20, also 431a1, 431b20–23.

7. Ibid., 3.430a9, 431b32.

8. Daniel Dennett coined the term "semantic engine" to describe the computer, in "Three Kinds of Intentional Psychology," in R. A. Healey, ed., *Reduction, Time and Reality* (Cambridge, Eng., 1981). But it can of course deserve this description only because its functioning first of all matches certain formal operations, which are then understood as *interpreted* in some way. See the discussion in John Haugeland's "Semantic Engines," the introduction to a volume he edited, *Mind Design* (Cambridge, Mass., 1981).

9. H. L. Dreyfus, *What Computers Can't Do,* 2nd ed. (New York, 1979).

10. Edmund Husserl, *Cartesianische Meditationen* (The Hague, 1950), p. 47.

11. See the penetrating analysis by James Tully, "Governing Conduct," in

Edmund Leites, ed., *Conscience and Casuistry in Early Modern Europe* (Cambridge, Eng., 1988).

12. G. W. F. Hegel, *The Phenomenology of Spirit,* trans. A. V. Miller (Oxford, 1977), p. 47.

13. Maurice Merleau-Ponty, *La Phénoménologie de la perception* (Paris, 1945), part 3, chap. 3.

14. It is in terms of this notion of the clearing, I believe, that one has to interpret Heidegger's famous invocation of the Leibnizian question: "Warum ist überhaupt Seiendes und nicht vielmehr Nichts?" (Why is there anything at all rather than Nothing?). *Einführung in die Metaphysik* (Tübingen, 1966), p. 1; *An Introduction to Metaphysics* (New Haven, 1959).

15. In a sense, this question becomes an inevitable one in the modern age. As long as the Platonic or Aristotelian construals were dominant, the question couldn't arise. The universe itself was shaped by Ideas, which were in a sense self-revealing. The "clearing," to use Heidegger's word, was grounded in the nature of the beings known. Once this answer no longer becomes available, the question "What are the bases of intentionality?" is ready to be asked. It takes an insensitivity, which is largely generated and legitimated by the epistemological tradition, to avoid raising it.

16. Immanuel Kant, *Critique of Pure Reason,* A111, A112.

17. I discuss this argument form at greater length in Chapter 2.

18. Heidegger, *Sein und Zeit,* part 1, chaps. 2 and 3A.

19. Of course, a proponent of a computer-based model of human performance would contest this claim and try to explain our skilled performance on the football field in terms of some computation on bits of informational input, which have the same role as the representations in classical theory. But this would be in fact to challenge the grounding of our understanding in our dealings with things. It is to say rather that this order of grounding is merely apparent, merely how things look in experience, whereas the real order is the reverse: skilled performance is based on computation over explicit representations— albeit on an unconscious level. This can't be ruled out by an a priori argument, of course; but its implausibility has been well shown in Dreyfus, *What Computers Can't Do.*

20. I discuss this at greater length in "Language and Human Nature" and "Theories of Meaning," both to be found in my *Human Agency and Language: Philosophical Papers,* vol. 1 (Cambridge, Eng., 1985).

21. See my discussion in "The Opening Arguments of the *Phenomenology,*" in Alasdair MacIntyre, ed., *Hegel: A Collection of Critical Essays* (Notre Dame, 1976); Ludwig Wittgenstein, *Philosophical Investigations* (Oxford, 1953), paras. 28ff, 258ff.

22. See Quine, *From a Logical Point of View* (New York, 1955), p. 4; *Word and Object* (Cambridge, Mass., 1960).

23. Husserl, *Die Krisis der europäischen Wissenschaften und die transzendentalen Phänomenologie* (Hamburg, 1977), sec. 15, pp. 78, 80.

24. I characterize this more fully in Chapter 3.

25. Sandel, *Liberalism and the Limits of Justice* (Cambridge, Eng., 1982).

26. See my "Interpretation and the Sciences of Man," *Philosophy and the Human Sciences: Philosophical Papers,* vol. 2 (Cambridge, Eng., 1985).

27. See my *Hegel and Modern Society* (Cambridge, Eng., 1979), chap. 3.

28. Hannah Arendt, *The Human Condition* (Chicago, 1958). I deal with some of the issues connected with this understanding of politics and modern society in "Legitimation Crisis?" in my *Philosophy and the Human Sciences.*

29. See the interview published as an appendix in the second edition of H. L. Dreyfus and Paul Rabinow, *Michel Foucault: Beyond Structuralism and Hermeneutics* (Chicago, 1983).

30. I discuss the motives and limitations of this kind of procedural ethic in my "Language and Society," in A. Honneth and H. Joas, eds., *Communicative Action* (Cambridge, Eng., 1991); and in "Justice after Virtue," in M. Benedikt and R. Berger, eds., *Kritische Methode und Zukunft der Anthropologie* (Vienna, 1985), pp. 23–48.

31. These points were well made by William Connolly in a debate with me on Foucault. See his "Taylor, Foucault and Otherness," *Political Theory* 13 (August 1985), 365–376.

32. Dreyfus and Rabinow, *Foucault,* chap. 2.

33. Jean-François Lyotard, *La Condition postmoderne* (Paris, 1979), p. 7. The postmodern, according to Lyotard, is characterized by "l'incrédulité à l'égard des métarécits."

2. The Validity of Transcendental Arguments

1. Barry Stroud, "Transcendental Arguments," *Journal of Philosophy* 65 (1968), 241–256.

3. Explanation and Practical Reason

1. Alasdair MacIntyre, *After Virtue* (Notre Dame, 1981), chap. 2.

2. John Stuart Mill, *Utilitarianism,* Hackett ed. (Indianapolis, 1979), pp. 4–5, also p. 34.

3. Ibid., p. 34.

4. See my "What Is Human Agency?" in *Human Agency and Language* (Cambridge, Eng., 1985).

5. Mill, *Utilitarianism,* pp. 8–11.

6. See J. L. Mackie, *Ethics* (Harmondsworth, 1977), for an excellent example of the consequences of uncompromisingly naturalist thinking.

7. See e.g. John McDowell, "Virtue and Reason," *The Monist* 62 (1979), 331–350; also MacIntyre, *After Virtue*. Bernard Williams makes the case very persuasively in his *Ethics and the Limits of Philosophy* (Cambridge, Mass., 1985), chap. 8. See also my "Neutrality in Political Science," *Philosophy and the Human Sciences* (Cambridge, Eng., 1985).

8. I borrow the term from the interesting discussion in Bernard Williams, *Descartes* (Harmondsworth, 1978), pp. 66–67. See also Thomas Nagel, *The View from Nowhere* (New York, 1986). I discuss this issue in my "Self-Interpreting Animals," in *Human Agency and Language*.

9. Mill, *Utilitarianism,* p. 24.

10. MacIntyre, "Epistemological Crises, Dramatic Narrative, and the Philosophy of Science," *The Monist* 60 (1977), 453–472.

11. There is a parallel notion of the asymmetrical possibilities of transition, this time applied to practical reason, in Ernst Tugendhat's "Erfahrungsweg" from one position to another, in *Selbstbewusstsein und Selbstbestimmung* (Frankfurt, 1979), p. 275.

12. Arthur O. Lovejoy, *The Great Chain of Being* (Cambridge, Mass., 1936; Harper/Torchbook, 1960).

13. I am borrowing here from Max Scheler's analysis in his essays "Soziologie des Wissens" and "Erkenntnis und Arbeit," *Schriften zur Soziologie und Weltanschauungslehre* (Bern, 1963).

14. This seems to be implicit in Mary Hesse's view: see her "Theory and Value in the Social Sciences," in C. Hookway and P. Pettit, eds., *Action and Interpretation* (Cambridge, Eng., 1979). She speaks of prediction and control as "pragmatic" criteria of scientific success (p. 2).

15. I discuss this point at somewhat greater length in my "Rationality," *Philosophy and the Human Sciences* (Cambridge, Eng., 1985).

16. See "Foucault on Freedom and Truth," ibid.

17. MacIntyre, "Epistemological Crises," p. 455.

18. I discuss this new affirmation of ordinary life as one of the important constituents of western modernity in *Sources of the Self* (Cambridge, Mass., 1989).

4. Lichtung or Lebensform

1. See Thomas Nagel, *The View from Nowhere* (New York, 1983).

2. Maurice Merleau-Ponty, whom I consider another of these great de-

constructors, focused more than anyone else on this issue of embodied agency. See especially *La Phénoménologie de la perception* (Paris, 1945); *The Phenomenology of Perception* (New York, 1962).

3. These two senses in which experience is shaped by embodiment help to explain the dialogue of the deaf between critics and exponents of computer-inspired theories of the mind. The critics, such as Hubert Dreyfus and John Searle, have often insisted that the computer offers a model of "disembodied" consciousness. See Dreyfus, *What Computers Can't Do* (New York, 1979); Searle, "Minds, Brains and Programmes," *Behavioural and Brain Sciences* 3 (1980), 417–457. Proponents of the computer model, insulted in the very heart of their materialist commitment, generally find this accusation unintelligible. But it is easy to see why the criticism is not understood. Proponents of strong artificial intelligence are thinking of the first kind of relation. The second kind hasn't yet moved into their conceptual ken, and so they have great trouble understanding what they're being accused of.

4. Thomas Nagel, *Mortal Questions* (Cambridge, Eng., 1979), p. 208.

5. The soul "ne s'est pas contentée de juger qu'il y avoit quelque chose hors d'elle qui étoit cause qu'elle avoit ses sentiments, en quoi elle ne se seroit pas trompée; mais elle a passé plus outre." "Et comme ces idées ne sont point naturelles, mais arbitraires, on y a agi avec une grande bizarrerie." Antoine Arnauld and Pierre Nicole, *La Logique ou l'art de penser* (1661), part 1, chap. 9 (Paris, 1970), p. 103.

6. This is of course what underlies the misunderstanding mentioned above in note 3 about the issue of embodiment. Mechanists can't formulate the issue without transcending their favorite explanatory language. Oddly, they have great trouble seeing that this language is so framed as to exclude engaged thinking, but with another part of their minds they are aware of it, and often say so. Thus one of the original motivations for constructing computer realizations of reasoning was that realization on a program was thought to be a good criterion of formal rigor. A formally rigorous proof is one where the transitions depend purely on the shape of the expressions, regardless of their semantic "meaning." But a proof can sometimes seem rigorous in this sense, and fail really to be so, because we can unawares be supplying some of the missing steps through the intuitive leaps we make as we check it. Subjective intelligibility is filling the gaps in formal argument. But if such a proof can be automated, run on a machine, then we *know* that there can be no such surreptitious input from subjective intelligibility, and the proof must be valid. In John Haugeland's words, "automation principle: wherever the legal moves of a formal system are fully determined by algorithms, then that system can be automated." *Artificial Intelligence: The Very Idea* (Cambridge, Mass., 1985), p. 82. Also Marvin Minsky: "If the procedure can be carried out by some very simple machine, so that there

can be no question of or need for 'innovation' or 'intelligence,' then we can be sure that the specification is complete, and that we have an 'effective procedure.'" *Computation: Finite and Infinite Machines* (Englewood Cliffs, 1967), p. 105.

7. See Michael Polanyi, *Personal Knowledge* (New York, 1964) and *The Tacit Dimension* (New York, 1966).

8. See Daniel Dennett, *The Intentional Stance* (Cambridge, Mass., 1988), chaps. 2, 7.

9. David Hume, *An Enquiry concerning Human Understanding,* chap. 7.

10. John Locke, *An Essay concerning Human Understanding,* 2.2.2.

11. "Die Seinsart dieses Seienden ist die Zuhandenheit. Sie darf jedoch nicht als blosser Auffassungscharakter verstanden werden, als würden dem zunächst begegnenden 'Seienden' solche 'Aspekte' aufgeredet, als würde ein zunächst an sich vorhandener Weltstoff in dieser Weise 'subjektiv gefärbt.'" Heidegger, *Sein und Zeit* (Tübingen, 1927), p. 71.

12. Locke, *An Essay concerning Human Understanding,* 3.2.2.

13. Ludwig Wittgenstein, *Philosophical Investigations,* trans. G. E. M. Anscombe, Ger. text of *Philosophische Untersuchungen* and Eng. trans. (Oxford, 1953), para. 257.

14. See e.g. Sabina Lovibond, *Realism and Imagination in Ethics* (Oxford, 1983).

5. The Importance of Herder

1. Isaiah Berlin, "Herder and the Enlightenment," in his *Vico and Herder* (New York, 1976).

2. See my *Hegel* (Cambridge, Eng., 1975). Later I use the fuller term "expressive-constitutive"—see Chapter 6.

3. Ludwig Wittgenstein, *Philosophical Investigations* (Oxford, 1953), para. 1.

4. This is the term I use in "Language and Human Nature," *Human Agency and Language* (Cambridge, Eng., 1985).

5. Etienne Condillac, *Essai sur l'origine des connoissances humaines,* 2.1.1.

6. *Abhandlung über den Ursprung der Sprache,* in *Johann Gottfried von Herder's Sprachphilosophie* (Hamburg, 1960), pp. 12–13. An English translation, *On the Origin of Language,* was published by University of Chicago Press in 1986.

7. Condillac, *Essai,* 2.1.1., para. 3.

8. See Donald Davidson, *Inquiries into Truth and Interpretation* (Oxford, 1985), chaps. 1–5, 9, 13.

9. See Davidson, "The Very Idea of a Conceptual Scheme," ibid., chap. 13. This question is bedeviled by the confusion of two issues. One concerns the claim that arises out of the Cartesian-empiricist tradition, that I grasp my

own thoughts directly, including my understanding of language, in a way my interlocutor can never match. The other is the issue about subjective understanding I've been discussing here. The two are quite distinct. Subjective understanding is usually elaborated between people, members of the same culture. Indeed, that's what makes them members of the same culture. The phenomenon of incommensurable conceptual schemes arises between cultures and is more than a mere logical possibility; rather, it is a continuing source of historical tragedy. But if we run the two issues together, then the discredit under which Cartesian-empiricist privileged access justly labors blinds us to the real differences of subjective understanding. I try to show why meaning can't be understood exclusively in terms of truth conditions in "Theories of Meaning," *Human Agency and Language*.

10. See Hans Aarsleff, *From Locke to Saussure* (Minneapolis, 1982). Aarsleff's dismissal of Herder as an innovator is a good illustration of how easily the two sides in the debate can talk past each other. If we take no account of Herder's shift in perspective, then he can indeed seem to be recapitulating a number of themes from Condillac, while at the same time confusedly protesting his disagreement with him.

11. See Vicki Hearne, *Adam's Task* (London, 1987).

12. See W. V. Quine, *Word and Object* (New York, 1960), chap. 2.

13. George Herbert Mead, *Mind, Self and Society* (Chicago, 1934), pp. 46–47.

14. J. L. Austin, *How To Do Things with Words* (Cambridge, Mass., 1962, 1975); see also J. R. Searle, *Speech Acts* (Cambridge, Eng., 1969).

15. Herder, *Ursprung*, p. 23.

16. Ibid., pp. 24–25.

17. Condillac, *Essai*, 1.1.4, para. 45.

18. John Locke is the great source of this reifying language. He often uses images of construction out of materials when speaking of the mind. See *An Essay concerning Human Understanding*, 2.2.2.

19. The reference, in the by now canonical form, is to page 104 of the first edition of Kant's *Critique: Kritik der reinen Vernunft*, Prussian Academy ed., in *Kants Werke*, vol. 4 (Berlin, 1968).

20. For the suspicion of unthinking custom, see Locke, *Essay*, 1.2.22–26. For further discussion of this connection between disengagement and modern epistemology, see Chapters 1 and 4.

21. Herder, *Ursprung*, p. 21.

22. See also Maurice Merleau-Ponty, *La Phénoménologie de la perception* (Paris, 1945), part 1, chap. 6.

23. See e.g. Jacques Derrida, *De la grammatologie* (Paris, 1967). Derrida's almost obsessive attempt to deny any special status whatever to speech in the

human language capacity raises the question whether he doesn't have more in common with the Cartesian tradition than he'd like to admit. "L'écriture" and "la différence," while embedded in culture (or constitutive of it), are peculiarly disembodied functions. See *L'Ecriture et la différence* (Paris, 1967).

24. See e.g. Merleau-Ponty, *Phénoménologie.*

25. Herder, *Ursprung,* pp. 24–25.

26. See e.g. Herder in *Ideen zur Philosophie der Geschichte der Menschheit,* book 9, chap. 2: "Wie sonderbar, dass ein bewegter Lufthauch das einzige, wenigstens das beste Mittel unsrer Gedanken und Empfindungen sein sollte! Ohne sein unbegreifliches Band mit allem ihm so ungleichen Handlungen unsrer Seele wären diese Handlungen ungeschehen." And a little later: "Ein Volk hat keine Idee, zu der es kein Wort hat: die lebhafteste Anschauung bleibt dunkles Gefühl, bis die Seele ein Merkmal findet und es durchs Wort dem Gedächtnis, der Rückerinnerung, dem Verstande, ja endlich dem Verstande der Menschen, der Tradition einverleibt; eine reine Vernunft ohne Sprache ist auf Erden ein utopisches Land."

27. Herder, *Ursprung,* p. 25.

28. Ferdinand de Saussure, *Cours de linguistique générale* [1916] (Paris, 1978), p. 166.

29. See e.g. Wittgenstein, *Philosophical Investigations,* para. 257.

30. Thomas Hobbes, *Leviathan* (Oakeshott ed.), chap. 4, p. 21.

31. Wilhelm von Humboldt, *On Language,* trans. Peter Heath (Cambridge, Eng., 1988), p. 49.

32. These terms were made famous by C. K. Ogden and I. A. Richards in their *The Meaning of Meaning* (New York, 1923). This is a magnificent example of a holdout, well into the twentieth century, of the old designative theory, in all its crudity and naiveté, quite oblivious of any of the insights generated in the aftermath of Herder.

6. Heidegger, Language, and Ecology

1. "Denn eigentlich spricht die Sprache" (For strictly, it is language that speaks). From "Dichterisch wohnet der Mensch" (Poetically Man Dwells), *Vorträge und Aufsätze,* vol. 2 (Pfulligen, 1954), p. 64; hereafter abbreviated *VA.*

2. "Enframing" is not used here in the sense of efficient ordering, which is the meaning of Heidegger's term *Gestell,* although there is obviously an affinity between the two.

3. For further discussion see my "Language and Human Nature," *Human Agency and Language* (Cambridge, Eng., 1985).

4. See Hobbes, *Leviathan* (Oakeshott ed.), chap. 4, p. 20; Locke, *Essay con-*

cerning Human Understanding, 3.3.2; Condillac, *Essai sur l'origine des connoissances humaines,* 1.2.4, paras. 45–46.

5. Herder, *Abhandlung über den Ursprung der Sprache,* in *Johann Gottfried von Herders Sprachphilosophie* (Hamburg, 1960), pp. 12–14.

6. Ibid., p. 12.

7. I argue for this reconstruction of Herder in terms of irreducible rightness at greater length in Chapter 5.

8. Locke, *Essay,* 3.2.2.

9. Charles Guignon has used the term "expressive" for this view of language, in specific application to Heidegger. See his "Truth as Disclosure: Art, Language, History" in *Heidegger and Praxis,* ed. Thomas Nenon, supplement to *Southern Journal of Philosophy* 28 (1989), 105–120. It follows that this is just as legitimate a term as "constitutive" or my double-barreled combination.

10. Wilhelm von Humboldt, *On Language,* trans. Peter Heath (Cambridge, Eng., 1988), p. 49.

11. I discuss this phenomenon of common space in "Theories of Meaning," *Human Agency and Language.*

12. Ernst Cassirer, *The Philosophy of Symbolic Forms* (New Haven, 1953).

13. "Symbol" is being used here as it was used in the tradition started by Goethe. When, in "The Origin of the Work of Art," Heidegger says the artwork is *not* a symbol, he is accepting a use of the term that treats it as synonymous with "allegory," which means pointing beyond itself. Goethe, on the contrary, was contrasting allegory and symbol.

14. Page numbers in text are cited from Heidegger's *Holzwege* (Frankfurt, 1950, 1972). This essay is available in English in Heidegger, *Poetry, Language, Thought,* trans. Albert Hofstadter (New York, 1971).

15. This claim seems to me indisputable as far as the later Heidegger is concerned. A question might arise about the author of *Sein und Zeit* (1927) on the extent to which he was a constitutive theorist. I would argue that the Herder tradition was very much present in the earlier phase as well, although Heidegger had not yet drawn all the conclusions from it that shape his later philosophy. In particular, the discussions in *Sein und Zeit* about the "apophantic as" have, I think, to be understood in the light of some doctrine of the semantic or linguistic dimension (secs. 32–33).

16. At least this seems to be Heidegger's view. "Self-revealing and self-concealing in the animal are one in such a way that human speculation practically runs out of alternatives ... Because the animal does not speak, self-revealing and self-concealing, together with their unity, possess a wholly different life-essence with animals." *VA,* vol. 3, p. 70.

17. Aristotle, *Ethics* 1.7.

18. In his essay on Heraclitus, "Logos," Heidegger explains that a human reading *(legein)* cannot define the logos, but neither does it simply copy *(nachbilden)* it. We have to find a third way between these two extremes: "Is there a path for mortal thinking to that place?" *VA*, vol. 3, p. 21.

19. "Die Frage nach der Technik" (The Question concerning Technology), *VA*, vol. 1.

20. *Unterwegs zur Sprache;* (On the Way to Speech; Pfulligen, 1959), p. 27.

21. "Bauen Wohnen Denken" (Building Dwelling Thinking), *VA*, vol. 2.

22. "Brief über den Humanismus" (Letter on Humanism), *Wegmarken* (Frankfurt, 1949, 1967), pp. 328, 338. "Der Mensch ist nicht Herr des Seienden. Der Mensch ist Hirt des Seins."

23. "Das Ding" (The Thing), *VA*, vol. 2, pp. 27, 50.

24. "Building Dwelling Thinking," pp. 25–26.

25. "The Thing," p. 55.

26. "Building Dwelling Thinking," p. 25.

27. "Origin of the Work of Art," p. 23.

28. "The Thing," p. 42.

29. *Unterwegs zur Sprache,* pp. 27–29.

30. Heidegger's placing of "Dichten" (poetry) alongside "Denken" (thinking) reflects the fact that his view is substantially anticipated not only in the practice but also in the self-understanding of some twentieth-century poets, notably Rainer Maria Rilke. In the ninth *Duino Elegy*, he offers his understanding of the word of power, as a word of praise: "Preise dem Engel die Welt . . . Sag ihm die Dinge . . . Zeig ihm, wie glücklich ein Ding sein kann, wie schuldlos und unser" (Praise the world to the angel . . . Tell him about the things . . . Show him how happy a thing can be, how blameless and ours). The word "thing" here is taking on a special force, closely related to Heidegger's. Our task is to *say* things. And Rilke's list of examples is very reminiscent of Heidegger's: "Sind wir vielleicht *hier*, um zu sagen: Haus, Brücke, Brunnen, Tor, Krug, Obstbaum, Fenster—höchstens, Säule, Turm" (Are we *here* perhaps just to say: house, bridge, well, gate, jug, fruit tree, window—at most, column, tower). This saying is a kind of rescue: "Und diese, von hingang tebenden Dinge verstehn, dass die sie ruhmst: vergänglich, traun sie ein Rettendes uns, den Vergänglichsten, zu" (And these things that live, slipping away, understand that you praise them; transitory themselves, they trust us for rescue, us, the most transient of all). The rescue is all the more necessary because of the rush of technological society to turn everything into a storehouse of power deprived of all form, as the seventh *Elegy* says. "Weite Speicher der Kraft schafft sich der Zeitgeist, gestaltlos wie der Spannende Drang, den er aus allem gewinnt. Tempel kennt er nicht mehr" (The spirit of the times makes vast storehouses of power, formless as the stretched tension it gathers from everything. Temples it

knows no longer). The concept of "standing reserve" was originally a poetic image of Rilke's.

31. "Eigentliche Dichtung ist niemals nur eine höhere Weise ... der Alltagssprache. Vielmehr ist umgekehrt das alltägliche Reden ein vergessenes und darum vermutztes Gedicht, aus dem kaum noch ein Ruren erklingt" (Poetry proper is never merely a higher mode of everyday language. It is rather the reverse: everyday language is a forgotten and therefore used-up poem, from which there no longer resounds a call). *Unterwegs zur Sprache,* p. 28.

32. The different uses of words of power are discussed with characteristic insight by Vaclav Havel in his "Words on Words," the speech (he would have) delivered on receiving a German book prize. It is printed in *New York Review of Books,* January 18, 1990, pp. 5–8. The Heideggerian provenance of some of his thinking on this score (partly via Patocka) is evident in the text.

7. Irreducibly Social Goods

1. Amartya Sen, "Utilitarianism and Welfarism," *Journal of Philosophy* 76.9 (1979), 468.

2. Ludwig Wittgenstein, *Philosophical Investigations* (Oxford, 1953), paras. 258ff.

3. See Hobbes, *Leviathan,* chaps. 4 and 5; Locke, *An Essay concerning Human Understanding,* bk. 3; Condillac, *Essai sur l'origine des connoissances humaines,* part 2.

4. Of course Wittgenstein was not the first to make this point. It was central to the theories of language in the Romantic age. Herder had already attacked Condillac in his *Ursprung der Sprache* (1772). See Chapter 5.

5. Locke, *Essay,* 3.2.8.

6. Ferdinand de Saussure, *Cours de linguistique générale* (Paris, 1978), chap. 4.

7. This is also why it is no accident that the later Wittgenstein's thesis about language as the meaning background of individual terms serves as part of a proof of the impossibility of private language. Where for the classical theories public language was only a convergence of private lexica, Wittgenstein shows the status of privately invented meanings as parasitic on public language.

8. On one reading, of course, being a father is simply a biological fact. But I'm talking here about the social role, recognized in different societies with different meanings and obligations, and with varying emotional significance. In our society it is embedded in a certain understanding of the nuclear family. This is in fact an excellent example of the way in which langue changes over time through acts of parole. Our understanding of what a family is and how it should function is being stretched and changed by the variety of unions in which people now live. But all these newer syntagms draw on our existing "vocabu-

lary" of family love and responsibility, sometimes in a bewildering way. Recently in Vancouver one member of a lesbian menage sued the other for child support, having had a child (by artificial insemination) while living with her partner, who later abandoned her for another woman. The bemused judge threw out the case. But such may be the wave of the future.

9. I discuss this distinction extensively in my "Theories of Meaning," *Human Agency and Language* (Cambridge, Eng., 1985), pp. 248–292.

10. Alexis de Tocqueville, *L'Ancien Régime et la révolution* (1856; reprint Paris, 1967), pp. 267–268.

11. See the interesting works by Richard Tuck, *Natural Rights Theories* (Cambridge, Eng., 1979), and James Tully, *A Discourse on Property* (Cambridge, Eng., 1980).

12. On interest groups, see e.g. David B. Truman, *The Governmental Process* (New York, 1951), and David Easton, *A Systems Analysis of Political Life* (New York, 1965). On economic theories, see e.g. Joseph Schumpeter, *Capitalism, Socialism and Democracy* (New York, 1950), and Robert Dahl, *Who Governs?* (New Haven, 1961).

13. J. G. Pocock, *The Machiavellian Moment* (Princeton, 1975), part 3.

14. See my "Humanismus und moderne Identität," in Krzysztof Michalski, ed., *Der Mensch in den modernen Wissenschaften* (Stuttgart, 1985).

8. Comparison, History, Truth

1. Thomas Nagel, *The View from Nowhere* (New York, 1985).

2. I try to draw the boundaries between these two kinds of science in my "Peaceful Coexistence in Psychology," *Human Agency and Language* (Cambridge, Eng., 1985).

3. Quoted from S. Warhaft, ed., *Francis Bacon: A Selection of His Works* (Toronto, 1965), p. 17.

9. To Follow a Rule

1. Ludwig Wittgenstein, *Philosophical Investigations* (Oxford, 1953); references to this book in the text will cite paragraph number (from part 1). Saul A. Kripke, *Wittgenstein on Rules and Private Language* (Cambridge, Mass., 1982).

2. Pierre Bourdieu, *Outline of a Theory of Practice* (Cambridge, Eng., 1977), and *Le Sens pratique* (Paris, 1980).

3. See the work of Greg Urban, from which I have drawn much of this analysis; e.g., "Ceremonial Dialogues in South America," *American Anthropologist* 88 (1986), 371–386.

4. Bourdieu, *Le Sens pratique,* p. 58. Unaccompanied page references in the text are to this work.

5. Bourdieu quotes here from Claude Lévi-Strauss, "Introduction à l'oeuvre de Marcel Mauss," in *Sociologie et anthropologie* (Paris, 1950), p. xxxviii.

10. Cross-Purposes

1. This chapter applies a distinction that has been defined and explored in depth by Mimi Bick in her dissertation for Oxford, "The Liberal-Communitarian Debate: A Defense of Holistic Individualism" (Trinity College, 1987). My discussion owes a great deal to her work.

2. Amartya Sen, "Utilitarianism and Welfarism," *Journal of Philosophy* 76 (1979), 463–489. I discuss the atomist component of welfarism in Chapter 7.

3. See Ronald Dworkin, "Liberalism," in Stuart Hampshire, ed., *Public and Private Morality* (Cambridge, Eng., 1978); and "What Liberalism Isn't," *New York Review of Books* 20 (January 1983), 47–50.

4. Michael Sandel, *Liberalism and the Limits of Justice* (Cambridge, Eng., 1982). Instances of liberal criticism: Amy Gutmann, "Communitarian Critics of Liberalism," *Philosophy and Public Affairs* 14 (Summer 1985), 308–322. Brian Barry offers a particularly crass example of the confusion. See his review of Sandel's book in *Ethics* 94 (April 1984), 523–525.

5. Sandel, *Liberalism,* p. 35.

6. John Rawls, *A Theory of Justice* (Cambridge, Mass., 1971), p. 101.

7. See e.g. Michael Sandel, "Democrats and Community," *New Republic,* February 22, 1988, pp. 20–23.

8. See the debate between Amartya Sen, "Equality of What?" in *Choice, Welfare and Measurement* (Oxford, 1982), and "Capability and Well-Being," Wider Research Paper (forthcoming); G. A. Cohen, "Equality of What? On Welfare, Resources and Capabilities," Wider Research Paper (forthcoming); Ronald Dworkin, "What is Equality? Part 2. Equality of Resources," *Philosophy and Public Affairs* 10 (1981), 283.

9. I have tried to sketch some common features that unite the theories of Dworkin, Rawls, and Scanlon in *Utilitarianism and Beyond,* Amartya Sen and Bernard Williams, eds. (Cambridge, Eng., 1982).

10. Montesquieu, *De l'esprit des lois,* 4.5.

11. See Stephen Schiffer's account of "mutual knowledge" in *Meaning* (Oxford, 1972), pp. 30ff.

12. See Greg Urban, "Ceremonial Dialogues in South America," *American Anthropologist* 88 (1986), 371–386.

13. I argue this in my "Theories of Meaning," *Human Agency and Language* (Cambridge, Eng., 1985).

14. Aristotle, *Nicomachean Ethics* 1167b3.

15. There is another version of the civic-humanist tradition, and of what I later refer to as its republican thesis, which has been articulated by Quentin Skinner and attributed by him to Machiavelli. See Skinner, "The Idea of Negative Liberty: Philosophical and Historical Perspectives," in Richard Rorty, J. B. Schneewind, and Quentin Skinner, eds., *Philosophy in History* (Cambridge, Eng., 1984). According to this, the appeal of the theory is purely instrumental. The only way to defend any of my freedoms is to sustain a regime of activity participation, because otherwise I am at the mercy of others who are far from having my interests at heart. On this version, we do without common goods altogether, and freedom is redefined as a convergent value. Skinner may be right about Machiavelli, but this interpretation could not capture, for example, Montesquieu, Rousseau, Tocqueville, Mill (in *On Representative Government*), or Arendt. (Skinner doesn't claim that it does.) In that sense my description remains historically relevant. The issue concerns which of these variants is relevant to today's politics. I'm convinced that mine is.

16. For this revisionist theory of democracy, see Joseph Schumpeter, *Capitalism, Socialism and Democracy* (New York, 1950).

17. The United States is peculiarly fortunate in that, from the very beginning, its patriotism welded together the sense of nationality and a liberal representative regime. For other western nations these have been distinct, even in tension. Think of France, where until recent decades a strong sense of national identity went along with a deep rift in the society, where an important segment rejected liberal democracy, even saw the greatness of France as entailing its rejection. The stability of contemporary western democracies results from the ultimate fusion between national identity and free regimes, so that now English-speaking countries are proud to share a democratic civilization. But what happened at the beginning in the United States was achieved late and sometimes painfully in other countries, as in Germany or Spain. I discuss this issue in "Alternative Futures," in Alan Cairns and Cynthia Williams, eds., *Constitutionalism, Citizenship and Society in Canada* (Toronto, 1985).

18. Of course there have been challenges to the pledge of allegiance, and the issue of whether it should be imposed was the occasion of some fairly base demagoguery in the 1988 presidential election. But this punctual challenge to a particular ritual on, say, religious grounds, although it poses a dilemma for a republican regime, does not frontally attack the central beliefs and attitudes that patriotism lives by, as my constructed examples were meant to do.

19. See Hannah Arendt, *The Human Condition* (Chicago, 1958); Robert Bellah et al., *Habits of the Heart* (Berkeley, 1985); and William Sullivan, *Reconstructing Public Philosophy* (Berkeley, 1982).

20. Aristotle, *Politics* 1259b5.

21. See Michael Sandel, "The Procedural Republic and the Unencumbered Self," *Political Theory* 12 (February 1984), 81–96.

22. Rawls seems to define the American liberal tradition pretty well exclusively in terms of the procedural ideal. See "Justice as Fairness: Political not Metaphysical," *Philosophy and Public Affairs* 14 (Summer 1985), 223–251. Sandel takes issue with this view of American history, arguing for the recent hegemony of the procedural republic; see his "Procedural Republic" and a forthcoming book. The issue is also hotly debated among American historians.

11. Invoking Civil Society

1. For a work in which both predicaments are discussed together in a very illuminating way, see John Keane, ed., *Civil Society and the State* (London, 1988). The civil-society tradition has been mediated to thinkers on the left partly through the work of Antonio Gramsci, who had a much richer concept than Marx, one more indebted to Hegel. It should also be said that the concern on the left with the "colonization of the life-world" by bureaucracies dedicated to technological efficacy is not confined to ecological green parties. A well-known theorist who has addressed this issue, and who is in no sense a "green," is Jürgen Habermas. See his *Theorie des kommunikativen Handelns* (Frankfurt, 1981); *The Theory of Communicative Action*, 2 vols. (Boston, 1985, 1989).

2. For a discussion of Eastern Europe in this context, see Jenö Szücs, "Three Historical Regions of Europe," and Mihaly Vajda, "East-Central European Perspectives," in Keane, *Civil Society*.

3. See *Second Treatise of Civil Government*, paras. 221–222, in Peter Laslett, ed., *Locke's Two Treatises of Government*, 2nd ed. (Cambridge, Eng., 1967), p. 430.

4. Ibid., para. 172. Locke speaks of "the common bond whereby humane kind is united into one fellowship and societie" (Laslett, p. 401).

5. Montesquieu, *De l'esprit des lois*, 11.6, in *Oeuvres complètes* (Paris, 1964), p. 590.

6. This whole development has been interestingly discussed by Jürgen Habermas in his *Strukturwandel der Öffentlichkeit* (Berlin, 1962); *Structural Transformation* (Cambridge, Mass., 1989).

7. I have drawn here on the interesting discussion in Michael Warner, *The Letters of the Republic* (Cambridge, Mass., 1989).

8. See Marc Raeff, *The Well-Ordered Police State* (New Haven, 1983). Of course the term is used not in its twentieth-century sense. "Police" translates the eighteenth-century German "Polizei," which covered the state's action in ordering the lives of its subjects rather than in suppressing violence.

12. The Politics of Recognition

1. "La Nature de l'honneur est de demander des préférences et des distinctions." Montesquieu, *De l'esprit des lois,* 3.7.

2. The significance of this move from "honor" to "dignity" is interestingly discussed by Peter Berger in his "On the Obsolescence of the Concept of Honour," *Revisions: Changing Perspectives in Moral Philosophy,* ed. Stanley Hauerwas and Alasdair MacIntyre (Notre Dame, 1983), pp. 172–181.

3. Lionel Trilling, *Sincerity and Authenticity* (New York, 1969).

4. I discuss the development of this doctrine at greater length, at first in the work of Francis Hutcheson, drawing on the writings of the Earl of Shaftesbury, and its adversarial relation to Locke's theory in my *Sources of the Self* (Cambridge, Mass., 1989), chap. 15.

5. "Le sentiment de l'existence dépouillé de toute autre affection est par lui-même un sentiment précieux de contentement et de paix qui suffiroit seul pour rendre cette existence chère et douce à qui sauroit écarter de soi toutes les impressions sensuelles et terrestres qui viennent sans cesse nous en distraire et en troubler ici bas la douceur. Mais la pluspart des hommes agités de passions continuelles connoissent peu cet état et ne l'ayant gouté qu'imparfaitement durant peu d'instans n'en conservent qu'une idée obscure et confuse qui ne leur en fait pas sentir le charme." Jean-Jacques Rousseau, *Les Rêveries du promeneur solitaire,* "Cinquième promenade," in *Oeuvres complètes* (Paris, 1959), 1.1047.

6. "Jeder Mensch hat ein eigenes Maass, gleichsam eine eigne Stimmung aller seiner sinnlichen Gefühle zu einander." J. G. Herder, *Ideen,* chap. 7, sec. 1, in *Herders Sämtliche Werke,* ed. Bernard Suphan (Berlin, 1877–1913), 13.291.

7. John Stuart Mill was influenced by this Romantic current of thought when he made something like the ideal of authenticity the basis for one of his most powerful arguments in *On Liberty.* See especially chap. 3, where he argues that we need something more than a capacity for "ape-like imitation": "A person whose desires and impulses are his own—are the expression of his own nature, as it has been developed and modified by his own culture—is said to have a character." "If a person possesses any tolerable amount of common sense and experience, his own mode of laying out his existence is the best, not because it is the best in itself, but because it is his own mode." *Three Essays* (Oxford, 1975), pp. 73, 74, 83.

8. George Herbert Mead, *Mind, Self, and Society* (Chicago, 1934).

9. This inner dialogicality was explored by Mikhail Bakhtin and those who have drawn on his work. See especially Bakhtin's *Problems of Dostoyevsky's Poetics,* trans. Caryl Emerson (Minneapolis, 1984). Also Michael Holquist and Katerina Clark, *Mikhail Bakhtin* (Cambridge, Mass., 1984); and James Wertsch, *Voices of the Mind* (Cambridge, Mass., 1991).

10. See Bakhtin, "The Problem of the Text in Linguistics, Philology and the Human Sciences," in *Speech Genres and Other Late Essays,* ed. Caryl Emerson and Michael Holquist (Austin, 1986), p. 126, for this notion of a "super-addressee" beyond our existing interlocutors.

11. Rousseau is describing the first assemblies: "Chacun commença à regarder les autres et à vouloir être regardé soi-même, et l'estime publique eut un prix. Celui qui chantait ou dansait le mieux; le plus beau, le plus fort, le plus adroit ou le plus éloquent devint le plus considéré, et ce fut là le premier pas vers l'inégalité, et vers le vice en même temps." *Discours sur l'origine et les fondements de l'inégalité parmi les hommes* (Paris, 1971), p. 210.

12. See e.g. the passage in "Considerations sur le gouvernement de Pologne" where he describes the ancient public festival in which all the people took part, in *Du contrat social* (Paris, 1962), pp. 345–346; and the parallel passage in "Lettre à D'Alembert sur les spectacles," in *Du contrat social,* pp. 224–225. The crucial principle was that there should be no division between performers and spectators, but that all should be seen by all. "Mais quels seront enfin les objets de ces spectacles? Qu'y montrera-t-on? Rien, si l'on veut . . . Donnez les spectateurs en spectacles; rendez-les acteurs eux-mêmes; faites que chacun se voie et s'aime dans les autres, que tous en soient mieux unis."

13. G. W. F. Hegel, *The Phenomenology of Spirit,* trans. A. V. Miller (Oxford, 1977), chap. 4.

14. There are a number of strands that have linked these two levels, but special prominence in recent years has been given to a psychoanalytically oriented feminism, which roots social inequalities in the early upbringing of men and women. See e.g. Nancy Chodorow, *Feminism and Psychoanalytic Theory* (New Haven, 1989); Jessica Benjamin, *Bonds of Love: Psychoanalysis, Feminism and the Problem of Domination* (New York, 1988).

15. A prime example of this charge from a feminist perspective is Carol Gilligan's critique of Lawrence Kohlberg's theory of moral development, for presenting a view of human development that privileges only one facet of moral reasoning, precisely the one that tends to predominate in boys rather than girls. See her *In a Different Voice* (Cambridge, Mass., 1982).

16. Will Kymlicka, in his very interesting and tightly argued book *Liberalism, Community and Culture* (Oxford, 1989), argues for a kind of politics of difference, notably in relation to aboriginal rights in Canada, but from a basis that is firmly within a theory of liberal neutrality. He wants to argue on the basis of certain cultural needs—minimally, the need for an integral and undamaged cultural language with which one can define and pursue his or her own conception of the good life. In certain circumstances, with disadvantaged populations, the integrity of the culture may require that we accord them more resources or rights than others. The argument is parallel to that made in relation

to socioeconomic inequalities. But where Kymlicka's argument fails to recapture the actual demands made by the groups concerned—say Indian bands in Canada or French-speaking Canadians—is with respect to their goal of survival. Kymlicka's reasoning is valid (perhaps) for *existing* people who find themselves trapped within a culture under pressure, and can flourish either within it or not at all. But it doesn't justify measures designed to ensure survival in indefinite future generations. For the populations concerned, however, that's what is at stake. We need only think of the historical resonance of "la survivance" among French Canadians.

17. See Immanuel Kant, *Grundlegung der Metaphysik der Sitten* (Berlin, 1968), p. 434; *Groundwork of the Metaphysics of Morals,* trans. H. J. Paton (New York, 1964).

18. I have no idea whether such a statement was actually made by Saul Bellow, or by anyone else. I report it only because it captures a widespread attitude, which is of course why the story had currency in the first place.

19. One hears both kinds of reproach today. In the context of some modes of feminism and multiculturalism, the claim is the strong one, that the hegemonic culture discriminates. In the former Soviet Union, however, alongside a similar reproach leveled at the hegemonic Great Russian culture, one also hears the complaint that Marxist-Leninist communism was an alien imposition on all equally, even on Russia itself. The communist mold, on this view, is truly nobody's. Solzhenitsyn made this claim, but it is voiced by Russians of a great many different persuasions today, and has something to do with the extraordinary phenomenon of an empire that has broken apart through the quasi-secession of its metropolitan society.

20. See John Rawls, *A Theory of Justice* (Cambridge, Mass., 1971); Ronald Dworkin, *Taking Rights Seriously* (London, 1977), and *A Matter of Principle* (Cambridge, Mass., 1985); Jürgen Habermas, *The Theory of Communicative Action* (Boston, 1985, 1989).

21. Rousseau, *The Social Contract and Discourses,* trans. G.D.H. Cole (New York, 1950), pp. 3–4.

22. *Emile* (Paris, 1964), bk. 2, p. 70.

23. "Considerations sur le gouvernement de Pologne," p. 345; *Considerations on the Government of Poland,* trans. Wilmoore Kendall (Indianapolis, 1972), p. 8.

24. "Lettre à D'Alembert," p. 225; "Letter to M. D'Alembert on the Theatre," in Jean-Jacques Rousseau, *Politics and the Arts,* trans. Allan Bloom (Ithaca, 1968), p. 126.

25. A little later in the passage I quoted above from the essay on Poland, Rousseau describes gatherings in our depraved modern society as "des cohues

licencieuses," where people go "pour s'y faire des liaisons secrètes, pour y chercher les plaisirs qui séparent, isolent le plus les hommes, et qui relâchent le plus les coeurs."

26. *Du contrat social,* p. 244. I have benefited in this area from discussions with Natalie Oman. See her "Forms of Common Space in the Work of Jean-Jacques Rousseau" (Master's research paper, McGill University, July 1991).

27. Hegel, *Phenomenology of Spirit,* p. 110.

28. In justifying his famous (or infamous) slogan about the person coerced to obey the law as "forced to be free," Rousseau goes on: "car telle est la condition qui donnant chaque citoyen à la Patrie le garantit de toute dépendance personnelle." *Du contrat social,* p. 246.

29. The Supreme Court of Canada did strike down one of these provisions, the one forbidding commercial signs in languages other than French. But in their judgment the justices agreed that it would have been quite reasonable to demand that all signs be in French, even though accompanied by another language. In other words, it was permissible in their view for Quebec to outlaw unilingual English signs. The need to protect and promote the French language in the Quebec context would have justified it. Presumably this would mean that legislative restrictions on the language of signs in another province might well be struck down for quite another reason. (Incidentally, the signage provisions are still in force in Quebec, because of a provision of the Charter that in certain cases allows legislatures to override judgments of the courts for a restricted period.)

30. The First Amendment, e.g., which forbids Congress to establish any religion, was not originally meant to separate church and state as such. It was enacted at a time when many states had established churches, and it was plainly meant to prevent the new federal government from interfering with or overruling these local arrangements. It was only later, after the Fourteenth Amendment, following the so-called incorporation doctrine, that these restrictions on the federal government were held to apply to all governments, at any level.

31. Rawls, *Theory of Justice,* and "Justice as Fairness: Political Not Metaphysical," *Philosophy and Public Affairs* 14 (1985), 223–251; Dworkin, *Taking Rights Seriously,* and "Liberalism," in *Public and Private Morality,* ed. Stuart Hampshire (Cambridge, Eng., 1978); Bruce Ackerman, *Social Justice in the Liberal State* (New Haven, 1980).

32. See e.g. the arguments deployed by Lawrence Tribe in *Abortion: The Clash of Absolutes* (New York, 1990).

33. Michael Sandel, "The Procedural Republic and the Unencumbered Self," *Political Theory* 12 (1984), 81–96.

34. See Guy Laforest, "L'Esprit de 1982," in *Le Québec et la restructuration du Canada, 1980–1992,* ed. Louis Balthasar, Guy Laforest, and Vincent Lemieux (Quebec, 1991).

35. The point is well argued in Larry Siedentop, "Liberalism: The Christian Connection," *Times Literary Supplement,* March 24–30, 1989, p. 308. See also my "The Rushdie Controversy," *Public Culture* 2 (Fall 1989), 118–122.

36. Hans-Georg Gadamer, *Wahrheit und Methode* (Tübingen, 1975), pp. 289–290; *Truth and Method,* rev. ed. (New York, 1988).

37. For fuller discussion of comparison, see Chapter 8; and my "Understanding and Ethnocentricity," *Philosophy and the Human Sciences* (Cambridge, Eng., 1985).

38. I discuss objectivity at somewhat greater length in part 1 of *Sources of the Self* (Cambridge, Mass., 1989).

39. The same homogenizing assumptions underlie the negative reaction that many people have to claims of superiority on behalf of western civilization, say in regard to natural science. But it is absurd to cavil at such claims in principle. If all cultures have made a contribution of worth, they can't be identical or even embody the same kind of worth. To expect this would be to vastly underestimate the differences. In the end, the presumption of worth imagines a universe in which different cultures complement one another with different kinds of contribution. This picture not only is compatible with but demands judgments of superiority-in-a-certain-respect.

40. Roger Kimball, "Tenured Radicals," *New Criterion,* January 1991, p. 13.

13. Liberal Politics and the Public Sphere

1. From John Stuart Mill, "On Liberty," in *Three Essays* (Oxford, 1975), p. 74.

2. I discuss this in Chapter 11.

3. Jürgen Habermas, *Structural Transformation,* trans. Thomas Burger (Cambridge, Mass., 1989); *Strukturwandel der Öffentlichkeit* (Berlin, 1962). Michael Warner, *The Letters of the Republic* (Cambridge, Mass., 1990).

4. Habermas, *Structural Transformation,* p. 91, refers to Locke in this connection.

5. This indicates how far the late eighteenth-century notion of public opinion is from the object of poll research today. The phenomenon that "public opinion research" aims to measure is, in terms of my distinction, a convergent unity, and doesn't need to emerge from discussion. It is analogous to the general opinion of mankind. The ideal underlying the eighteenth-century version emerges in this passage from Edmund Burke, quoted in Habermas, *Structural Transformation,* pp. 117–118: "In a free country, every man thinks he has a con-

cern in all public matters; that he has a right to form and deliver an opinion on them. They sift, examine and discuss them. They are curious, eager, attentive and jealous; and by making such matters the daily subjects of their thoughts and discoveries, vast numbers contract a very tolerable knowledge of them, and some a very considerable one . . . Whereas in other countries none but men whose office calls them to it having much care or thought about public affairs, and not daring to try the force of their opinions with one another, ability of this sort is extremely rare in any station of life. In free countries, there is often found more real public wisdom and sagacity in shops and manufactories than in cabinets of princes in countries where none dares to have an opinion until he comes to them."

6. Quoted in Habermas, *Structural Transformation,* p. 119.

7. Warner, *Letters,* p. 41.

8. See Charles Fox's speech, quoted in Habermas, *Structural Transformation,* pp. 65–66: "It is certainly right and prudent to consult the public opinion . . . If the public opinion did not happen to square with mine; if, after pointing out to them the danger, they did not see it in the same light with me, or if they conceived that another remedy was preferable to mine, I should consider it as my due to my king, due to my Country, due to my honour to retire, that they might pursue the plan which they thought better, by a fit instrument, that is by a man who thought with them . . . but one thing is most clear, that I ought to give the public the means of forming an opinion."

9. Cited in Habermas, *Structural Transformation,* p. 117.

10. Ibid., p. 82.

11. See *Letters,* pp. 40–42. Warner also points to the relationship of this overdetermined mode to the impersonal agency of modern capitalism (pp. 62–63), as well as the close fit between the impersonal stance and the battle against imperial corruption which was so central a theme in the British colonies (pp. 65–66).

12. Ibid., p. 46.

13. See Ernst Kantorowicz, *The King's Two Bodies* (Princeton, 1957).

14. For a non-European example, see Clifford Geertz, *Negara* (Princeton, 1980), where the pre-Conquest Balinese state is described.

15. As a matter of fact, excluding the religious dimension is not even necessary to my concept of secular. A secular association is one grounded purely on common action, and this excludes any divine grounding for the association, but nothing prevents the people so associated from continuing a religious form of life; indeed, this form may even require that political associations be purely secular. There are also religious motives for espousing a separation of church and state.

16. Benedict Anderson, *Imagined Communities* (London, 1983), pp. 28–31.

17. Anderson borrows a term from Walter Benjamin to describe modern profane time: he sees it as "homogeneous, empty time." Homogeneity captures the aspect I'm describing here, that all events now fall into the same kind of time. But the emptiness of time takes us into another issue: the way in which both space and time come to be seen as "containers" that things and events contingently fill, rather than as constituted by what fills them. This step is part of the metaphysical imagination of modern physics, as we can see with Newton. But it is the step to homogeneity which is crucial for secularization, as I conceive it. The step to emptiness is part of the objectification of time which has been so important a part of the modern outlook of instrumental reason. Time has been in a sense "spatialized." In *Being and Time* Heidegger mounted a strong attack on this whole conception in his understanding of temporality. But distinguishing secularity from the objectification of time allows us to situate him on the modern side of the divide. Heideggerian temporality is also a mode of secular time.

18. Mircea Eliade, *The Sacred and the Profane* (New York, 1959), pp. 80ff.

19. See Joseph Schumpeter, *Capitalism, Socialism and Democracy* (New York, 1950), for an eloquent statement of this view.

20. See Noam Chomsky, *Deterring Democracy* (London, 1991), for one of the most hard-hitting criticisms of this manipulation.

21. I discuss the background of the "politics of recognition" in Chapter 12.

22. Mary Ann Glendon, *Abortion and Divorce in Western Law* (Cambridge, Mass., 1987), has shown how this has made a difference to American decisions on this issue, as compared with those in other western societies.

23. For more on democratic stability, see Chapter 10. There is a good discussion of the slide toward this lopsided package in American politics in Michael Sandel, "The Procedural Republic and the Unencumbered Self," *Political Theory* 12 (February 1984). I compare the American and Canadian systems in "Alternative Futures," in Alan Cairns and Cynthia Williams, eds., *Constitutionalism, Citizenship and Society in Canada* (Toronto, 1985). There is a good critique of the American political culture in Robert Bellah et al., *Habits of the Heart* (Berkeley, 1985), and *The Good Society* (Berkeley, 1991).

Credits

The author would like to thank the following publishers and institutions for permission to reuse material that originally appeared in their publications.

1. "Overcoming Epistemology." In Kenneth Baynes, James Bohman, and Thomas McCarthy, eds., *After Philosophy,* MIT Press. Cambridge, 1987.

2. "The Validity of Transcendental Arguments." *Proceedings of the Aristotelian Society.* London, 1978–79.

3. "Explanation and Practical Reason." *Wider Working Papers,* World Institute for Development Economics Research of the United Nations University. Helsinki, August 1989.

4. "Lichtung or Lebensform." In *The Lion Speaks . . . and We Cannot Understand Him,* Suhrkamp Verlag. Frankfurt, 1991.

5. "The Importance of Herder." In Edna and Avishai Margalit, eds., *Isaiah Berlin: A Celebration,* University of Chicago Press and Hogarth Press. Chicago and London, 1991.

6. "Heidegger, Language, and Ecology." In Hubert Dreyfus and Harrison Hall, eds., *Heidegger: A Critical Reader,* Basil Blackwell. Oxford, 1992.

7. "Irreducibly Social Goods." In Geoffrey Brennan and Cliff Walsh, eds., *Rationality, Individualism and Public Policy,* Centre for Research on Federal Financial Relations, Australian National University. Canberra, 1990.

8. "Comparison, History, Truth." In Frank E. Reynolds and David Tracey, eds., *Myth and Philosophy,* State University of New York Press. Albany, 1990.

9. "To Follow a Rule." In Mette Hjort, ed., *Rules and Conventions,* Johns Hopkins University Press. Baltimore, 1992.

10. "Cross-Purposes." In Nancy L. Rosenblum, ed., *Liberalism and the Moral Life,* Harvard University Press. Cambridge, 1989.

11. "Invoking Civil Society." Working paper, Center for Psychological Studies. Chicago, 1990.

12. "The Politics of Recognition." In Amy Gutmann, ed., *Multiculturalism and "The Politics of Recognition,"* Princeton University Press. Princeton, 1992.

13. "Liberal Politics and the Public Sphere." Previously unpublished in English.

Index

Absolutism, 212–215, 220, 223
Ackerman, Bruce, 245
Agency. *See* Disengaged agency; Engaged
 agency
Anderson, Benedict, 270
Arendt, Hannah, 15, 141, 199
Aristotle, 113, 114, 120, 121, 127, 159,
 160, 177, 219; theory of knowledge, 3,
 5, 65; physics and nature, 42–44; the
 good life, 128, 191. *See also* Platonic-
 Aristotelian tradition
Atomism, 72, 76, 91, 128–130, 134, 188,
 192, 196, 197, 281; criticism of, 8, 11,
 15; construal of society, 7, 13, 183,
 194–195, 285; theory of knowledge
 and, 10, 71, 189; individualism and,
 14, 130–131, 133, 134, 135–136, 181;
 of input, 63–65, 71, 73, 74, 90; of
 meaning, 74, 93, 135; vs. holism, 181,
 182, 185–186, 197
Auerbach, Eric, 270
Augustine, 74, 75, 80, 89, 96, 198, 228
Austin, J. L., 87
Authenticity, 227–234
Autonomy, 7–8, 215–216, 218, 220, 222,
 245–246, 258

Background/background understanding,
 12, 68, 76–77, 89, 90–91, 92, 136,
 150, 153, 185, 229, 260; for experience, 15, 23, 73, 74; intelligibility and,
 69–71; disengaged view and, 71, 72,
 73–74; for language, 83, 89–90, 93,
 95, 96, 97, 110, 132–133; of meanings,

131, 132, 133–134; rules and conven-
 tions, 167, 168–169, 170, 171, 173
Bakhtin, Mikhail, 99
Being (*Dasein*), Heidegger's concept, 11–
 13, 25, 31, 76, 77, 107, 115–116
Bellah, Robert, 199
Bellow, Saul, 236, 255
Bentham, Jeremy, 38, 129, 188
Berlin, Isaiah, 79
Bodin, Jean, 212
Bourdieu, Pierre, 171, 174–180
Brecht, Bertolt, 158
Brentano-Husserl tradition, 10
Brezhnev, Leonid, 205
Burke, Edmund, 264

Cartesianism, 63, 67, 91, 261
Cassirer, Ernst, 98, 110
Chomsky, Noam, 85
Christianity, 156, 164, 238, 249, 267,
 270–271
Civic-humanist tradition, 15, 141–142,
 143, 187, 192–195, 197, 199, 222
Civil society, 204, 209, 211–212, 213,
 216, 221–222, 223–224; vs. state, 205–
 208, 210, 215, 218–219, 220, 223
Clearing (*Lichtung*). *See* Heidegger
Common action/purpose, 151, 172, 188,
 189, 192, 241–242
Common sense, 63, 64, 65, 66, 68, 127,
 141, 184, 188, 192
Common space. *See* Public sphere
Communitarianism, 181–186, 188, 197,
 202

313

Goethe, Johann Wolfgang von, 110, 113
Golding, William, 159
Good, 36, 113, 162, 164, 179, 238;
 concept/Idea of, 44, 45, 114, 129,
 164, 228, 246–247; irreducible social,
 127, 130, 136–138, 139–140, 143,
 145, 187; individual, 128, 129, 136,
 137, 138, 144, 145, 181; life, 128, 144,
 163, 182, 186, 199, 203, 245–246,
 247, 248; public/common, 129, 137,
 138, 140, 142, 143, 187–188, 190–
 192, 194, 195, 197–198, 247, 265–
 266, 281–282
Gorbachev, Mikhail, 205
Greenpeace, 195
Grotius, Hugo, 212

Habermas, Jürgen, 17, 99, 260, 264, 265,
 272
Hearne, Vicki, 86
Hegel, Georg Wilhelm Friedrich, 13, 18,
 115, 118, 130, 146, 147, 226, 232,
 241, 250; critique of epistemology, 8,
 9, 16; Herder and, 79; theory of spirit,
 117, 119–120; theory of history, 159–
 161, 162, 163–164; concept of civil society, 215, 216, 219, 222
Heidegger, Martin, 76, 90, 91, 99, 117,
 119, 120, 124; critique of epistemology, 1, 8, 9, 11, 12, 13, 16, 18; clearing (*Lichtung*) concept of experience
 (disclosure), 9, 11, 12, 13, 15, 17, 77,
 112, 113, 119, 120–122; theory of
 embodied/engaged agency, 21, 61–62,
 63, 68, 73–74, 75, 77, 78, 169–170;
 concept of pre-understanding, 48, 69,
 70; ecology, 100–101, 123, 125–126;
 view of language, 101, 107, 111–116,
 120–121, 124–125
Helvétius, 90
Herder, Johann Gottfried, 79, 228, 229,
 256; theory of language, 13, 80–81,
 82–83, 89, 90–93, 97–99, 102, 103;
 theory of reflection, 87, 88, 92, 103,
 105, 112; on linguistic understanding,
 95, 110; constitutive theory and, 106–
 109, 111–112

Hitler, Adolf, 125
Hobbes, Thomas, 67, 80, 96, 101, 102,
 129, 191; political theory, 188, 212,
 213
Hobbes-Locke-Condillac (HLC) theory
 of language, 102, 106, 108, 109, 133
Hodja, Enver, 182, 196
Holism. *See* Atomism, vs. holism
Honor, 50, 58, 144, 145, 193, 215, 220,
 226, 227, 233; hierarchical, 232, 238,
 240. *See also* Dignity
Humboldt, Wilhelm von, 15, 118, 185;
 theory of language, 13, 85, 95–96, 97,
 99, 109, 110, 119
Hume, David, 5, 10, 11, 71, 72, 90, 183
Husserl, Edmund, 6–7, 10, 14, 16

Identity, 13, 182–183, 187, 188, 192,
 196, 210–211, 218; prepolitical, 219–
 220, 221
Individualism, methodological, 130–131,
 133–136, 181, 182, 185, 188, 195,
 197
Intelligibility, 63, 67–72, 74–75, 146,
 148, 149; through understanding, 150,
 153, 154, 155
Intentionality, 10–18, 72, 91
Irreducible rightness, 84, 85, 88, 89, 93,
 94, 103–105, 106, 108, 110
Irreducible social good, 127, 130, 136–
 138, 139–140, 143, 145, 187
Ivan the Terrible, 209

Jacobinism, 242, 275, 276, 277
Jefferson, Thomas, 198

Kabyle communities, 176, 177
Kant, Immanuel, 2, 11, 15, 18, 22, 58,
 73, 93, 111, 115, 197, 246, 264, 276;
 transcendental arguments, 9, 10, 20–
 21, 26–27, 33, 71, 72, 90; theory of
 knowledge, 72, 74, 90–91; on dignity,
 235, 237, 242, 245
Kimball, Roger, 256
Kripke, Saul, 165, 168
Kuhn, Thomas, 42, 44, 46

The essays in this collection reflect most of the concerns with which Charles Taylor has been involved throughout his career—language, ideas of the self, political participation, the nature of modernity. His intellectual range is extraordinary, as is his ability to clarify what is at stake in difficult philosophical disputes. Taylor's analyses of liberal democracy, welfare economics, and multiculturalism have real political significance.

"Among the leading philosophers of our time, Charles Taylor stands out for the sheer breadth of his interests and influence... Illuminating and rewarding."

—David Miller, *Times Literary Supplement*

"A deeply engaging collection... [Taylor] combines a practical interest in current political topics... with a continuing quest for the deepest meanings of language, knowledge, and human beings."

—Stan Persky, *Toronto Globe and Mail*

"Taylor is a highly distinctive thinker... a figure of very broad intellectual (and indeed emotional and political) sympathies and interests."

—John Dunn, *Times Higher Education Supplement*

CHARLES TAYLOR is Professor of Philosophy at McGill University and the author of many books, including *Sources of the Self* and *The Ethics of Authenticity* (both from Harvard).

Harvard University Press

Cambridge, Massachusetts
London, England

Cover design by Lisa Clark

ISBN 0-674-66477-9

90000

9 780674 664777